Health Geographies

Critical Introductions to Geography

Critical Introductions to Geography is a series of textbooks for undergraduate courses covering the key geographical sub disciplines and providing broad and introductory treatment with a critical edge. They are designed for the North American and international market and take a lively and engaging approach with a distinct geographical voice that distinguishes them from more traditional and out-dated texts.

Prospective authors interested in the series should contact the series editor:
John Paul Jones III
School of Geography and Development
University of Arizona
jpjones@email.arizona.edu

Published

Cultural Geography
Don Mitchell

Geographies of Globalization
Andrew Herod

Geographies of Media and Communication
Paul C. Adams

Social Geography
Vincent J. Del Casino Jr

Mapping
Jeremy W. Crampton

Research Methods in Geography
Basil Gomez and John Paul Jones III

Political Ecology, Second Edition
Paul Robbins

Geographic Thought
Tim Cresswell

Environment and Society, Second Edition
Paul Robbins, Sarah Moore and John Hintz

Urban Geography
Andrew E.G. Jonas, Eugene McCann, and Mary Thomas

Health Geographies: A Critical Introduction
By The right of Tim Brown, Gavin J. Andrews, Steven Cummins, Beth Greenhough, Daniel Lewis, and Andrew Power

Health Geographies

A Critical Introduction

Tim Brown

Gavin J. Andrews

Steven Cummins

Beth Greenhough

Daniel Lewis

Andrew Power

WILEY Blackwell

This edition first published 2018
© 2018 John Wiley & Sons Ltd

The right of Tim Brown, Gavin J. Andrews, Steven Cummins, Beth Greenhough, Daniel Lewis, and Andrew Power to be identified as the authors of this work has been asserted in accordance with law.

Registered Offices
John Wiley & Sons, Inc., 111 River Street, Hoboken, NJ 07030, USA
John Wiley & Sons Ltd, The Atrium, Southern Gate, Chichester, West Sussex, PO19 8SQ, UK

Editorial Office
9600 Garsington Road, Oxford, OX4 2DQ, UK

For details of our global editorial offices, customer services, and more information about Wiley products visit us at www.wiley.com.

Wiley also publishes its books in a variety of electronic formats and by print-on-demand. Some content that appears in standard print versions of this book may not be available in other formats.

Library of Congress Cataloging-in-Publication Data

Names: Brown, Tim, 1968– author. | Andrews, Gavin J., 1970– author. | Cummins, Steven, (Geographer), author. | Greenhough, Beth, author. | Lewis, Daniel (Geographer), author. | Power, Andrew, 1979– author.
Title: Health geographies : a critical introduction / Tim Brown, Gavin J. Andrews, Steven Cummins, Beth Greenhough, Daniel Lewis, Andrew Power.
Description: Chichester, UK ; Hoboken, NJ : John Wiley & Sons, 2018. | Includes bibliographical references and index.
Identifiers: LCCN 2016057491 (print) | LCCN 2017009192 (ebook) | ISBN 9781118739037 (cloth) | ISBN 9781118739020 (pbk.) | ISBN 9781118738993 (Adobe PDF) | ISBN 9781118739013 (ePub)
Subjects: LCSH: Medical geography.
Classification: LCC RA792 .A53 2017 (print) | LCC RA792 (ebook) | DDC 614.4/2–dc23
LC record available at https://lccn.loc.gov/2016057491

Cover Image: © JOEL SAGET/Gettyimages
Cover Design: Wiley

Set in 10/12pt Minion by SPi Global, Pondicherry, India
Printed and bound in Malaysia by Vivar Printing Sdn Bhd

10   9   8   7   6   5   4   3   2   1

Contents

List of Figures

List of Tables

List of Boxes

Notes on Contributors

Tim Brown is Senior Lecturer in Human Geography at Queen Mary University of London. His research explores the critical geographies of public health and more recently global health. He is widely published in these areas in leading geographical and interdisciplinary health journals and is the author/editor of several books, including *A Companion to Health and Medical Geography* (Wiley-Blackwell 2010) and *Bodies Across Borders* (Ashgate 2015).

Gavin J. Andrews is a full Professor and a health geographer based at McMaster University in Canada. His wide-ranging empirical interests include ageing, holistic medicine, health care work, sports and fitness cultures, health histories of places and popular music. Much of his work is positional and considers the development, state-of-the-art and future of health geography. In terms of theoretical approaches, in recent years he has developed an interest in non-representational theory and its potential to animate the energies and movements in the 'taking place' of health and health care.

Steven Cummins is Professor of Population Health and Director of the Healthy Environments Research Programme at the London School of Hygiene & Tropical Medicine, UK. He is a geographer with training in epidemiology and public health and earned his PhD from the MRC Social & Public Health Sciences Unit, University of Glasgow. He has published extensively on how the urban environment affects health in a range of disciplines including geography, epidemiology, urban studies and health policy.

Beth Greenhough is Associate Professor of Human Geography and Fellow of Keble College, University of Oxford. Her research explores the social and cultural dimensions of health and biomedical research, and has been funded by the AHRC, ESRC, Brocher Foundation and the Wellcome Trust. She has published widely in leading geography and interdisciplinary journals and is co-editor of *Bodies Across Borders* (Ashgate 2015).

Daniel Lewis is a Research Fellow at the London School of Hygiene & Tropical Medicine, UK. He has a BA in Geography from LSE, and an MSc in Geographic Information Science and PhD in Geography from UCL. Daniel is a health geographer who is interested in deepening our understanding of the social and spatial determinants of health and health inequalities, and the complex relationships linking individuals and their environments.

Andrew Power is Associate Professor in Geography at University of Southampton. His research examines issues relating to disability, welfare, care and community voluntarism, and has been funded by the AHRC, ESRC and British Society of Gerontology. He has published extensively in leading geographical and disability studies' journals and is the author/contributor of several books, including *Landscapes of Care* (Ashgate 2010) and *Active Citizenship and Disability* (Cambridge University Press 2013).

Foreword

New texts in any area sometimes struggle. We might expect this to be the case in health geography which is well served by two introductory texts and a comprehensive edited handbook summarising recent research. A unique selling point is necessary. It is gratifying therefore to welcome and endorse the publication of *Health Geographies: A Critical Introduction*. It is an important and necessary addition to the literature that takes us to the current frontiers of inquiry in health geography, engaging the reader with the social, the cultural, the political and the epidemiological, and doing so in a way that highlights the importance of geography. The text offers a critical perspective and brings us a health geography that is mature, confident and theorised, able to build on secure foundations and move forward. Interdisciplinary in reach but firmly anchored in geography, the authors have drawn deeply on their research and teaching expertise to assemble a systematic overview of the topics that have emerged at the cutting edge of the health geography in the past few years. Ideas about place, wellbeing, care, identity, relationality, complexity, biopolitics and global health are now increasingly commonplace in health geography but, to date, we have lacked a critical assessment. In addressing this need, the authors have ably navigated the challenges of summarising complex ideas, working with theory, and setting out a critically-engaged analysis. The results of their labours should provide undergraduates and commencing graduate students with the necessary background to understand and contribute to the further development of a critical health geography.

Graham Moon
Southampton, 2016

Acknowledgements

This book project was first initiated in 2009, and Tim would like to thank Susan Craddock for allowing him to take their original proposal forward. As with any such project, the book has undergone a number of subsequent iterations and we would like to thank anonymous reviewers for their comments on the proposal and draft manuscript. We would also like to thank everyone at Wiley-Blackwell for all their hard work and also for their patience. It is also important that we acknowledge and thank colleagues and students (past and present) whose conversations and exchanges have helped us to hone our critical edge. Finally, we would like to pay special thanks to Graham Moon who read and commented on the draft manuscript, and who ultimately helped us to recognise the importance of what we were collectively trying to achieve.

Chapter 1

Introduction

Introduction

The task of introducing a book such as this is not inconsiderable, especially as it has been co-authored by scholars who place themselves very differently within, and in some cases without, the field of health geography. We should be clear about this latter point right from the outset. This text is a critical introduction to health geograph*ies* – deliberately presented in the plural rather than the singular form – and it is written by scholars with different and sometimes quite jarring epistemological perspectives and ontological positions. Like many of our contemporaries, we do not see health geography as a single field of study and how we each approach the question of health differs considerably. Moreover, some of us are less concerned with health as an object of investigation than we are with subjects that appear to fit a little more comfortably under the rubric of medical, or perhaps more appropriately biomedical, geography. For example, there is as much focus on disease and biomedicine in this textbook as there is on questions of health and health care. In practice, then, this book works across disciplinary and sub-disciplinary boundaries that have been established by those writing within the field (e.g. Kearns 1993; Mayer and Meade 1994; Kearns and Moon 2002; Rosenberg 2016) but perhaps tend to overlook what is going on outside of it (e.g. Parr 2004; Philo 2000, 2007; Dorn et al. 2010).

As a second point of introduction we should also say a little about why we targeted our ideas for this book at the Wiley-Blackwell *Critical Introductions to Geography* series. You will be aware that there are numerous textbooks covering the field of health geography, from Kelvyn Jones' and Graham Moon's (1987) classic *Health, Disease and Society: An Introduction to Medical Geography* to more recent, and sometimes a little more specialist, texts such as Robin Kearns' and Wilbert Gesler's (2002) *Culture, Place and Health*, Sarah Curtis' (2004) *Health and Inequality*, Anthony Gatrell's and Susan Elliott's (2009) *Geographies of Health: An Introduction* and Peter Anthamatten's and Helen Hazen's (2011) *An Introduction*

Health Geographies: A Critical Introduction, First Edition. Tim Brown, Gavin J. Andrews, Steven Cummins, Beth Greenhough, Daniel Lewis, and Andrew Power.
© 2018 John Wiley & Sons Ltd. Published 2018 by John Wiley & Sons Ltd.

to the Geography of Health. To these texts on health geography, we might also add Melinda Meade's various editions of *Medical Geography* (e.g. Meade and Emch 2010). Each of these books offers their readership invaluable insights into the field, however we were struck by the idea that the Wiley-Blackwell series is committed to providing 'broad and introductory' textbooks with a 'critical edge'. It was the emphasis placed upon criticality that was especially important to us and we believe should be important to you as readers. Here, it is not only a matter of how criticality is defined by us but how this commitment to criticality should shape the ways in which you approach this text. We will deal with the former of these points in the section that follows, but as readers we encourage you to examine the evidence that we present and consider the theoretical influences upon it. Be sure to interrogate the interpretations that we offer and to reflect on possible alternatives to them; think, for example, about what is present and what is absent in our readings of the field. Ask yourselves how persuaded you are by the arguments and opinions that we present and the conclusions that we draw. In sum, you should be aware that we have made decisions in our research and writing and we encourage you as readers and potential future authors to enter into academic debate with us.

A Critical Introduction to Health Geography?

If we take a fairly straightforward view of what health geography is concerned with, we might suggest that it questions how the interaction of humans, materials and the environment shapes and constrains health, wellbeing, survival and flourishing. At the heart of this interaction are complex social, economic and political issues which can complicate and extend conventional debates about health. An examination of these issues and how they affect people around the world, often very differently, can unearth a myriad of health costs and benefits. For example, rising conflict in the Middle East has been quickly followed by outbreaks of polio, which has re-emerged because efforts to immunise children are being hampered (Blua 2013). Meanwhile, more than 5 billion people worldwide now have a cell phone, leading to a number of efforts to use mobile technology to revolutionise the way medical care and health information are delivered, particularly in the rich countries of the Global North (Hampton 2012). In each case, health is entangled with complex ethical, social and political concerns over the autonomy, control and care of humans. These are concerns that demand critical health geographers engage with ideas, debates and perspectives from outside of their direct fields of interest. Equally our response to them ensures that we contribute to knowledge and understanding of a multitude of health and biomedical issues that is interdisciplinary in nature.

So health geography is a broad field of enquiry, as this book amply demonstrates. Yet, we agree with Robin Kearns and Damian Collins (2010) when they state that at the core of the sub-discipline lies, or at least should lie, a concern for social justice. This is as good a place to start as any when considering the question of what a critical introduction to health geography might entail. This concept evolved from foundational principles associated with the 'social contract' (for a full history of this concept, see Rawls 1971). The social contract is the recognition that individuals have rights such as dignity and autonomy with which the state cannot unduly interfere. Individuals allow the state to rule only through laws which, at least in theory, pursue the principles of freedom and equality. This 'pact' allows society to function as a whole and gives legitimacy to the authority of the state over the individual. Of course, since these early foundational principles, different interpretative theories of social justice have developed which sit on top of the foundational principles. Governments have tended to have either a 'right' (liberal) or 'left' (social democratic) political understanding of the social contract. On the right, governments tend to interpret the social contract to mean the minimum possible role of the state: individuals should be completely untethered to pursue their own ends. The state is despised as a wasteful villain that obstructs the self-equilibrating market system. The corollary is that the state provides minimum protections to those who 'fall between the cracks'. On the left, governments tend to interpret the social contract to mean the state should provide a more supportive role and protect against the more self-destructive forces of the capitalist system.

When considering this question, critical health geographers must therefore be cognisant of the underlying political philosophies of the state as they can have significant effects on the health of individuals. A value judgement can be made about the social justice element of particular policies and their impacts on certain individuals, groups or even the popula-tion as a whole. For example, Danny Dorling's (2014) geographic work in the United Kingdom has mapped the health and distribution of wealth of its citizens and argues that as a result of the British state's commitment to neoliberal policy, including the more recent politics of 'austerity', the mere accident of being born outside the nation's wealthiest 1 per cent will have a dramatic impact on the rest of your life: it will reduce your life expectancy, as well as educational and work prospects, and affect your mental health. To Dorling's voice we can add that of Clare Bambra who, in her work with Ted Shrecker, recently argued that there are clear parallels between the health effects of neoliberalism and the 'unfettered lib-eral capitalism of the 19th century' (Shrecker and Bambra 2015, p. 17). Specifically, they argue that now as then the conditions in which people live, work and play are vital in deter-mining how long and in what state of health people live.

Collectively, this work serves as a useful example of how to be 'critical'. The value judge-ments presented by all of these scholars are drawn from thoroughly-researched, empirical findings. Based upon their generally realist epistemological positions, Dorling and Bambra recognise *what* evidence is essential to validate their argument as well as *how much* evi-dence is needed to support their conclusions. However, an important caveat here is that to be critical, one should remain equally alert to the nature of evidence itself. For example, the idea of evidence-based health care (EBHC) has quickly become a global priority. Yet, the wide-ranging critique of EBHC highlights that, although it is appropriate that the best health care is provided in the best known ways, EBHC goes far beyond this objective, becoming a powerful movement in itself that espouses a dominant scientific worldview that selectively legitimises and includes certain forms of knowledge but degrades and excludes other forms, such as qualitative ones. Critical health researchers argue that, in response, a critique is necessary for deconstructing this mode of thinking, and that resistance is ethi-cally necessary given the powerful forces in play (Holmes et al. 2007).

Another way of thinking about the criticality of this work is to focus on the philosophi-cal and social theoretical perspectives that it draws upon. As Hester Parr (2004) argued some time ago now, critical geography is, among other of its key aspects, broadly defined as research work that is relevant, interdisciplinary, cutting edge and theoretically sophisti-cated. While Dorling's and Bambra's work does not necessarily pay too much attention to some of the other characteristics of critical geography that Parr outlined (notably those that relate to the 'theoretical gymnastics' that we might associate with the 'cultural turn'), it can be argued to mirror these other elements. For example, Dorling implicitly draws on the Marxist philosophy of unequal ownership of wealth to help make sense of his empirical observations and provide new ways of understanding the complex matters of health, wealth and illness. Similarly, Shrecker and Bambra offer an account of contemporary health and health care that demands we pay close attention to the neoliberal political philosophy that underpins many of the policy decisions that are made around the world today. Being able to theoretically (re)interpret research is an important way of making sense of empirical observations, as it allows us to disentangle and articulate some of the underlying meanings and processes involved. We may not all agree with the particular theoretical and for that matter political perspectives that we encounter but it is important to recognise that academics use theory to frame how they see the world and as critical health geographers we need to question this as well as consider theoretical possibilities other than those presented to us.

Of course, to be critical does not limit us as health geographers to only addressing those topics that are most closely aligned with questions of social justice. As Lynn Staeheli and Don Mitchell (2005) note in their analysis of the politics of relevance, what counts and does not count as relevant, and by extension critical, research is defined in many ways. For example, for some of the geographers that they interviewed in their research, relevance was linked to the kinds of political commitment and wider social impact demonstrated by Dorling and Bambra in the above discussion. Outside of this, relevance can also be defined in terms of the pertinence of research – the timeliness of an issue with regard to a particular time and place, as well as in relation to questions of the applicability of research – the ability of research to be applied or to result in some kind of action. Although these two values may appear to be constraining, especially on research that is more theoretically oriented, Staeheli and Mitchell reveal that this does not necessarily have to be the case. Referring to interviews that they conducted with Michael Dear and Jennifer Wolch, whose research we refer to later on in the book (see Chapter 6 and Chapter 7), Staeheli and Mitchell note that theoretical work is not only necessary to the development of research and to its communication but also to 'bringing to light issues and ways of thinking that might change how people understand problems or evaluate what is important' (2005, p. 370). Though questions of social justice are relevant here, so too are many other social issues and the various possible responses to them of interest to health geographers.

Critical research demands that we do not simply accept the world as it is presented to us in political announcements, policy briefings or in empirically-oriented, atheoretical research. Instead, critical researchers are encouraged to familiarise themselves with relevant literature, theories and research methods, as well as be cognisant of their own values, assumptions and epistemological and ontological positions. In so doing, researchers place themselves in a position to be able to challenge social and institutional norms, models of thinking and hegemonic power relationships. With this goal in mind, critical health geographers often pay close attention to people and issues that are neglected or marginalised in mainstream society. It is observed that certain people – often deemed the most vulnerable – 'fall off the map' of policy, practice and research. We might think here of those least able to care for themselves, for example the young and the elderly, the mentally ill or physically incapacitated, or populations who are placed on society's margin because of their sexuality, race or ethnicity, class position or housing status. However we define vulnerability, and it is a complex question that deserves careful consideration, it is up to critical researchers to challenge neglect and expose the lived experience of people in their everyday encounters with social relations of power. As Blomley (2006) suggests, as critical geographers we should promote solidarity with people, particularly those who are the oppressed and victimised, and this book is certainly attuned to this ideal.

To extend this perspective on criticality a little further, another important facet of being a critical health geographer is exploring and questioning everyday practices and their complex inter-relationship with the spaces and places which we co-inhabit with other human and non-human entities. Health geographers are interested in the everyday in many different ways, for example, in terms of the decisions that people make or the routines and practices in which they partake (e.g. whether to eat '5 a day', consume alcohol or smoke tobacco products or take part in risky sexual practices) and the socio-environmental conditions under which people live and work and the differential effects of these on their ability to access health care services and health-related resources. We might also focus in on the experiences of individual citizens – often, but not only, when they are reconstituted as patients, risk groups or as healthy or diseased subjects, as well as on the significant role of health professionals, health care commissioners and policy makers and increasingly bioscientists and pharmaceutical companies in helping to shape these experiences. Crucial to our understanding of the everyday is not only that we account for those processes that (materially) structure people's experiences, but that we also recognise that these experiences are contingent upon the spaces and times within which people live. Here, it is vital that we acknowledge that the identities people assume and those that are socially ascribed to them – whether based on race/ethnicity, class status, sex and/or sexuality, ability/disability and so on – will be important in differentiating these health-related experiences and their consequences for people's health and wellbeing. Moreover, we argue throughout this book for a concern with the modes of governance – often referred to under the Foucauldian concept of biopolitics – that help to shape and reconfigure the kinds of behaviours and practices discussed, as well as our understanding of the bodies who willingly or otherwise perform them.

Finally, as critical health geographers it is important to remain alert to the differential effects of mobility and scale on health as well as on their relevance to our understanding of disease and biomedicine. Geographers sitting outside of the sub-discipline of health geography, as well as other social scientists, have been particularly attuned to these questions. The case of severe acute respiratory syndrome (SARS), which we explore in Chapter 11, is an especially good illustration of this. In their edited volume covering the epidemic, *Networked Disease: Emerging Infections in the Global City*, Harris Ali and Roger Keil draw on a quote from the former Director-General of the World Health Organization (WHO), Gro-Harlem Brundtland, which is especially helpful in highlighting the importance of scale: 'Today public health challenges are no longer local, national or regional. They are *global*' (Brundtland 2005. Cited in Ali and Keil 2009, p. xix. Emphasis added). The point being made here is one that geographers are, of course, fully alert to and that is the idea that local situations and events are increasingly closely related to global scale processes. SARS was an especially powerful illustration of this because of the rapidity with which a relatively localised epidemic – one whose origins lay in the economic and cultural practices associated with the production and consumption of civet cats in the Guangdong province of China – was transformed into the first major pandemic of the twenty first century in part because of the global cities network through which it was primarily transmitted.

The chapters in this edited volume not only offer accounts of the transmission process, they also provide important insight into wider sets of questions relating to the processes of globalisation and the hypermobility of pathogens such as the coronavirus that caused SARS, for example the interplay between human and non-human agents, the challenges that such hypermobility places upon public health strategies of containment and control, as well as the pathologisation of highly mobile human bodies and the closely related problem of their subsequent stigmatisation. Of course, it is not only infectious diseases and the pathogens that cause them that are mobile and multi-scalar in their effects and as such the target of critical health scholarship. Similarly to SARS and other emerging and re-emerging infectious diseases, it is also increasingly recognised that the so-called 'global obesity epidemic' is caused by processes – namely risk factors associated with diet and physical inactivity – that were once believed to be confined to affluent nations in the Global North but are now global in their reach. As Tim Brown and Morag Bell (2008) have commented, non-communicable diseases are considered to be transmissible across borders due to their being linked to risk behaviours, which, according to a joint report by the WHO and the Food and Agriculture Organization, 'travel across countries and are transferable from one population to another like an infectious disease' (WHO/FAO 2003, pp. 4–5. Cited in Brown and Bell 2008, p. 1575).

Applying a Critical Perspective to Our World

Drawing on this loose typology of critical research above, and the inherent lessons for how such an approach can be used, our book seeks to develop understanding by focusing on the main debates and thematic areas that we argue define critical scholarship in health geography research. From our work in the field of health geography, which for us also includes topics that might otherwise be covered under the rubric of medical and biomedical geographies, we distil five key cross-cutting critical themes that extend across all the chapters of this book. Some are more obviously relevant to, or explicit in, some chapters than in others and we do not claim that this list is exhaustive. Nonetheless, given that each contributor to this book is firmly committed to advancing critical health geography debates, we argue that the five themes serve as important rallying calls to begin to explore the myriad and diverse issues and trends with which the book engages, therefore allowing you as a reader to punctuate such debates. While the themes are not necessarily 'new', we argue first that they have entered new stages in their depth and breadth of reach, and second that they have become increasingly entangled and intersected with each other, thus creating new forms and new spaces entirely. Taken together, they therefore have a cumulative effect on the health of people around the world and, we argue, can either exacerbate or ameliorate many of the challenges people face in their everyday lives.

Neoliberalism

Whilst being an ideology rooted in earlier liberal philosophy and a blueprint for the 1970s Thatcher–Reagan government projects in Anglo-America, neoliberalism has arguably entered a new phase in terms of its breadth and reach. In the wake of the financial crisis of 2007–2008 and its prolonged aftermath, governments in many countries, particularly in the Global North, have resorted to policy measures that seek to reduce the role of government – although as argued later, it has hardly reduced bureaucratic control in many areas involving welfare and support – as well as implemented deregulation, privatisation, outsourcing and competition in public services. Governments have imposed strict fiscal discipline and cut public spending in the hope of restoring budgetary integrity and securing the confidence of investors. These measures are argued to be essential in order to pave the way to renewed economic growth.

Interestingly, this has largely been done without neoliberalism being mentioned by the political parties that drive it. Its anonymity, according to George Monbiot (2016), is both a symptom and cause of its power: 'So pervasive has neoliberalism become that we seldom even recognise it as an ideology' (Monbiot 2016). Its creeds have become internalised and reproduced with little thought. According to Monbiot's argument, the result of this internalisation has been that the rich (can) persuade themselves that they acquired their wealth through merit, ignoring the personal advantages – such as education, inheritance and class – that may have helped to secure it. Meanwhile, the poor begin to blame themselves for their failures, even when they can do little to change their circumstances. While neoliberalism has gone incognito in a very short space of time, the political dogma of 'austerity' has become the catchword for the renewed attempts to cope with 'post-crisis' uncertainties at different spatial scales (Blyth 2013, p. 2; Peck 2012, p. 626). With neoliberalism firmly positioned as the dominant economic policy script, the tension between the right and left politics mentioned above has come to be increasingly resolved in favour of right-wing austerity. David Featherstone and colleagues talk about 'austerity localism' whereby 'localism is being mobilised as part of an "anti state", "anti public" discourse to build support for an aggressive round of "roll back" neoliberalism' (Featherstone et al. 2012, p. 177).

In terms of breadth, neoliberal policy has expanded across Europe, North America, Latin America and Africa, although of course it remains always incomplete and existing in myriad different forms. In Asian nations, for example, 'coordinated market capitalism' exists whereby institutions coordinate many of the most important economic decisions and functions (e.g. wage setting, bargaining, business/labour management of social programmes) (McGregor 2001). Nonetheless, despite its hybridity, through the IMF, the World Bank, the Maastricht Treaty and the World Trade Organization, neoliberal policies have been imposed – often without democratic consent – on much of the world (see Chapters 11 and 14). In terms of its depth of reach, it has also become more firmly embedded in political and economic contexts and in terms of the level of impacts on the ground. One of the most pressing concerns relating to neoliberalism in health geography is the withdrawal of the state from health and social care. Freedom from collective bargaining and trade unions has meant the freedom to suppress wages. Freedom from tax has meant a freedom from the distribution of wealth that lifts people out of poverty and poor health. The post-war consensus that the state is best placed to provide comprehensive health care no longer has widespread credence. In the UK for example, the Institute for Fiscal Studies (2015) drew the conclusion that the Conservative manifesto of public sector cuts would reduce state and social spending to *pre-(World War II) welfare state* levels.

Under neoliberalism, state health care is seen as inefficient and private markets are seen as more cost-effective and consumer-friendly. The neoliberal agenda of health care reform includes cost cutting for efficiency, decentralising to the local or regional levels rather than the national levels and setting up health care as a private good for sale rather than a public good paid for with tax revenue (McGregor 2001). Austerity budgets have led to reductions in community services, such as the closure of day centres (Hall 2014). Meanwhile, in the Global South, some of the initiatives led by international organisations under the flag of development were counter-productive in many contexts, such as the Poverty Reduction Strategy Papers introduced by the World Bank and the International Monetary Fund in 1999, which ultimately reduced health service expenditure in several African countries (Navarro 2007, p. 354; see also discussion of SAPs in Chapter 14). Alongside the decline in state health care provision, epidemics of self-harm, eating disorders, depression, loneliness, performance anxiety and social phobia are being increasingly documented (Verhaeghe 2014). Social care users risk 'moving from a position of enforced collectivism to an enforced individualism characteristic of neoliberal constructions of economic life' (Roulstone and Morgan 2009, p. 333). Readers of this book should therefore remain alert to the idea of the political shaping of health and the politics of vulnerability. Those at the front line in health care provision often have little time to engage critically with such debates, and yet they must deal with the pragmatic challenges of reduced budgets.

Inequality

Disadvantage is patterned across a range of spatial scales from the local to the global, and within and between populations of interest. The existence of inequality relies on the social, economic, political and cultural ordering of people and place and is thus not a naturally occurring property of society but a product of the way we live now and the ways we have lived. As a cross-cutting theme in this book, inequality is both the precondition and outcome of the other themes we identify, acting reciprocally to either deepen or ameliorate experiences of disadvantage according to individual circumstance.

As indicated in the earlier discussion, Dorling's (2014) work illustrates the growth of inequality within the British context. But Britain typifies a growing trend in both Global North and South countries towards an unequal accumulation and distribution of wealth. In Stiglitz's (2015) *The Great Divide*, he traces the massive growth of deregulation, tax cuts, and tax breaks for the 1 per cent in the United States and argues that many are falling further and further behind. In a global comparison, according to the World Bank Gini coefficient (2015),[1] many of the wealthiest nations in the world such as the United States (calculated at 0.41 out of 1) and the United Kingdom (0.38) are in a race to the bottom of the global league tables of wealth inequality. Those deemed as the most unequal include nations such as Brazil (0.53), Haiti (0.59) and Colombia (0.54). According to the Organisation for Economic Co-operation and Development (OECD), Britain serves as a pertinent example, as it was once deemed one of the most equal countries in the post-war period of the 1950s.

What has driven these increases in inequalities? While there is no consensus, it is argued that one key reason has been the rise of globalisation and skill-biased (task-biased) technological change and institutional change. However, critical researchers also argue that social policy, particularly tax and benefit policy, no doubt also plays a key role in modifying these external pressures. Indeed, David Harvey's (2000) central thesis argues that inequality stems from a class-based political project rooted in the global neoliberal philosophy, thus creating new means of capital accumulation. Inequality is often employed as a proxy for social justice, discussed earlier as a key motivator for health geographic research, particularly as an indicator of 'distributional fairness' or 'distributive justice'. These terms capture how resources are differently allocated in a society and owe their prominence to early work such as Harvey's *Social Justice and the City* (1973) and David M. Smith's *Human Geography: A Welfare Approach* (1977). A range of terms have been used in the literature to describe situations of (in)equality, most notably including (dis)parity, (in)justice and (in)equity. As Paula Braveman (2006) elucidates in an annual review, there is little consensus about the practical differences between these terms but they nonetheless remain important concepts nationally and internationally to governance and policy. The enduring value of inequalities work is evidenced by the range of recent publications that describe the disadvantage of some within a society compared to others as inherently detrimental to its functioning: Richard Wilkinson and Kate Pickett's (2009) *The Spirit Level*, Danny Dorling's (2010) *Injustice* and Thomas Piketty's (2014) *Capital in the Twenty-First Century*.

In health geography, early work on inequality sought to characterise disadvantage, particularly economic disadvantage, as leading to the development and widening of a number

---

[1] The Gini coefficient is a number between 0 and 1, where 0 corresponds with perfect equality (where everyone has the same income) and 1 corresponds with perfect inequality (where one person has all the income – and everyone else has zero income). Income distribution can vary greatly from wealth distribution in a country.

of health 'gaps' between the various occupational social classes. This was the approach adopted by the UK Government in the influential *Black Report* (DHSS 1980) in which an expert committee led by Sir Douglas Black demonstrated the existence of widespread ine-qualities in population health (see Chapter 10). The report showed that at the time of its publication, people belonging to the lowest occupational social group, 'unskilled workers', had a death rate twice that of the highest occupational social group, 'professional workers'. The objective of public health policy at the time became the narrowing of the gaps between social classes in light of evidence that suggested that these gaps were widening. The narra-tive of health inequalities has continued ever since in public health policy in the United Kingdom and globally; however, we now no longer think of health inequality as being the presence of 'gaps' between the richest and poorest, rather we talk in terms of a 'social gradi-ent' of inequality in health.

The expression of health inequalities from gap to gradient owes much to the work of Sir Michael Marmot, who chaired the *Marmot Review* (see Marmot et al. 2010), and his team who evidenced that rather than a gap there was a continuous gradient in life expectancy in the continuum from most to least deprived. Academic and policy-based characterisations of inequality have been complemented by more populist accounts, such as Danny Dorling's (2013) *The 32 Stops*, which narrates inequality along the London Underground's Central Line. This project reflects work by the London Health Observatory whose diagram (see Figure 1.1) shows the inequality in male life expectancy along the London Underground's Jubilee Line. James Cheshire (2012) subsequently produced a web map called 'Lives on the Line' (see http://life.mappinglondon.co.uk/, visited on 21 April 2016) which maps life expectancy at birth and child poverty, as well as other social determinants of health, according

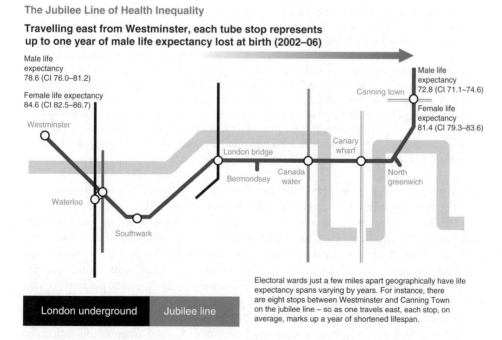

The Jubilee Line of Health Inequality

Travelling east from Westminster, each tube stop represents up to one year of male life expectancy lost at birth (2002–06)

Male life expectancy 78.6 (CI 76.0–81.2)

Female life expectancy 84.6 (CI 82.5–86.7)

Westminster

Waterloo

Southwark

London bridge

Bermondsey

Canada water

Canary wharf

Canning town

North greenwich

Male life expectancy 72.8 (CI 71.1–74.6)

Female life expectancy 81.4 (CI 79.3–83.6)

London underground   Jubilee line

Electoral wards just a few miles apart geographically have life expectancy spans varying by years. For instance, there are eight stops between Westminster and Canning Town on the jubilee line – so as one travels east, each stop, on average, marks up a year of shortened lifespan.

Figure 1.1 Male life expectancy on the Jubilee Line, London. Source: London Health Observatory, 2012. Contains public sector information licensed under the Open Government Licence v3.0.

to the London Underground network for the entirety of Greater London. Similar maps have been produced for other major British cities, and revealing the extent to which public health professionals and academic researchers have highlighted an issue that a Conservative government under the leadership of Margaret Thatcher sought to conceal with the shelving of the *Black Report* (Schrecker and Bambra 2015).

Globalisation/urbanisation

The notion that inequality solely captures differences in the allocation or distribution of resources has been useful for health geographers, wherein access to material resources can be readily quantified and compared for different groups of people and used to inform arguments about what is 'fair' or 'just'. However, a critical insight suggests that inequality should extend also to capturing less immediately tangible concerns. Doreen Massey, for instance, developed 'power geometry' (1993) as a way of connecting notions of power to the global flow of people and the differential effects of globalisation. David Harvey, again, demonstrates the relational nature of space, place and time to social and environmental justice in *Justice, Nature and the Geography of Difference* (1996). This leads us to our third cross-cutting theme, which is globalisation and, closely associated with it, urbanisation.

The growth in specialisation, information and communication technologies and mobilisation of people has become a key characteristic of the early twenty first century. In parallel with these human endeavours, global climate change continues to loom as a growing risk to the Earth's environment and to the health and wellbeing of us all. This is clearly evident from the rhetoric of international health organisations such as the WHO, whose current Director-General, Dr Margaret Chan, stated that:

> Population growth, incursion into previously uninhabited areas, rapid urbanization, intensive farming practices, environmental degradation, and the misuse of antimicrobials have disrupted the equilibrium of the microbial world. New diseases are emerging at the historically unprecedented rate of one per year. Airlines now carry more than 2 billion passengers annually, vastly increasing opportunities for the rapid international spread of infectious agents and their vectors. ... These [and other] threats have become a much larger menace in a world characterized by high mobility, economic interdependence and electronic interconnectedness. Traditional defences at national borders cannot protect against the invasion of a disease or vector. Real time news allows panic to spread with equal ease. Shocks to health reverberate as shocks to economies and business continuity in areas well beyond the affected site. *Vulnerability is universal.* (WHO 2007, p. iv. Emphasis added)

Thus, to global inequalities in wealth and the associated challenge of 'Closing the Gap' highlighted by WHO's Commission on the Social Determinants of Health, under the chairmanship of Sir Michael Marmot (Marmot 2008; see Brown and Moon 2012), we can add health problems linked to the economic, social and political consequences of an ever greater concentration of the world's population in urban centres. As the Population Division of the UN's Department of Economic and Social Affairs reported, over half of the world's population now live in urban areas and by 2050 this figure is projected to reach 66 per cent (United Nations 2015, p. 1). More significantly, some 90 per cent of this growth is estimated to occur in Asia and Africa. As Clare Herrick (2014, p. 557) states, the conditions under which many people live in the megacities that are emerging from this process of urbanisation, especially, though not only, those in the Global South, threaten to 'unravel the "urban advantage"' received by urban dwellers who are believed to benefit from better education, higher incomes and improved access to employment opportunities, health care services and so on. As she notes, the question is not so much of an 'urban advantage' but of an 'urban penalty', which returns us to debates about the health consequences of rapid urbanisation experienced in the nineteenth century (see Kearns 1991).

How we approach these questions as critical geographers will vary. Undoubtedly there are many health geographers whose focus will remain on questions of social justice and the closely aligned issue of (global) health inequalities. Others may concentrate on the discursive construction of spatially distant, hypermobile populations as the 'Other', especially when they become associated with the movement of infectious diseases such as AIDS/HIV, SARS and Ebola from 'there' to 'here' or, put differently, from 'the rest to the West' (Hall 1992). However, Herrick's call for a much greater focus on the urban in these questions of globalisation and global health is a timely and important one. This is so not only because urbanisation is helping to intensify processes that are responsible for many of the health problems that the world now faces, as exemplified in the quote from Chan. It is also because the urban has often been overlooked in the responses of what Herrick refers to as the 'Global Health' enterprise; as she argues, the urban question is an 'implicit rather than explicit area of activity, investment and activism' when it comes to addressing global health issues (2014, p. 561). Although this book does not respond to Herrick's call as effectively as it might have, we certainly recognise the importance of the issues that she raises to critical health scholarship in the future.

Biopolitics

A concept generally ascribed to the French philosopher, Michel Foucault, biopolitics describes the political governance and control of the 'bio' of people (their bodies and minds). Biopolitics has arguably become more relevant as the modes and techniques of controlling, tweaking and 'nudging' people's bodies have grown more elaborate and fine-tuned in the political orchestration of health and social care policy (see Chapter 2). Whilst biopolitics has been around for a long time – indeed since the original 'social contract' emerged – its growth in scientific, technological, bureaucratic terms has arguably surpassed previous eras in the extent and degree of subtlety to which the state can manage the every-day lives of individuals.

Nikolas Rose and Carlos Novas (2004, p. 440) suggest we might think of the ways in which biopolitics has effectively remade citizens into 'biological citizens'. They define biological citizenship as 'all those citizenship projects that have linked their conceptions of citizens to beliefs about the biological existence of human beings, as individuals, as families and lineages, as communities, as population and races, and as a species'. In this way biology is used to determine what constitutes normal, healthy bodies or citizens and those bodies seen as being unhealthy or deviant. The crafting of biological citizenship can be seen in the formation of state policies and interventions that target the population as biological beings. For example, in welfare policy, psychology now plays a central and formative role in stigmatising the existence and behaviour of various categories of poor citizens and in legitimising the measures taken to transform and activate them. Rather than blame structural causes of unemployment, these strategies can perpetuate notions of psychological failure and shift attention away from wider social and economic trends, including market failure, precarity and the scale of income inequalities, towards individual weakness. In Britain for example, recent workfare assessments have led to severe sanctioning of those who are judged to be not complying with an increasingly elaborate set of demands. Inherent in these policies is a summoning of various citizen-subjects such as the responsible citizen, the active citizen, the democratic citizen, the citizen worker and so on (Newman 2013).

Another example of biopolitics in health and social care is seen in the implementation of personalisation policy. While originating as a response to inflexible group disability services, personalisation shifts the emphasis of what *service* people want towards what kind of *life* a person wants. Inherent in this approach is the choice afforded to individuals. While this goal is of course laudable and has been shown to have positive outcomes for disabled people, its implementation during a time of austerity has led to the wholesale shift in responsibility to the individual (Power 2014). Those eligible for social care are in effect having to become managers and 'sole-traders' of their own care. This means disabled people have to now manage insurance and employment related tasks associated with arranging support as well as their own personal lives.

This individualisation mirrors other neoliberal state strategies to 'responsibilise' citizens. One of the ways in which the state can manage people is to give them more individual responsibility. Individualisation has become a key driver of health and welfare policy. People therefore become culpable for their own health, or as Foucault (see Box 11.2) might put it, the care of the self is placed in the hands of the self. However, such responsibilisation can cut both ways. Adriana Petryna (2002) explores how, following the nuclear explosion in Chernobyl in 1986, citizens drew on biological understandings of themselves as bodies affected by radiation to create a new collective identity as *poterpili* or sufferers. This new biosocial collective then used their shared status as biological citizens to make demands upon the state for compensation and health and welfare provision. In this way biological citizenship 'can thus embody a demand for particular protections, for the enactment or cessation or particular policies or actions, or, as in this case, access to special resources' (Rose and Novas 2004, p. 441). This leads us towards a final theme, resistance.

Resistance/resilience/care

While the four earlier concepts each signal different challenges and risks facing people's health, it is also worth being equally aware of the ever-present, ever-changing nature of resistance and resilience as antidotes, coping strategies and modes of counterattack to these challenges. Critical health geographers must always remain attuned to the possibilities of action and change. People do oppose, defy, repel and endure. In *Landscapes of Antagonism*, Newman (2013) reminds us that while the current climate of neoliberal cuts, austerity and state retrenchment is presented as a meta-narrative, there is also space for politics and agency – and care. She urges us to think about the co-existence of diverse governmental, economic and political projects. As Power (2014) found, the realm of social care policy for example is a lot more heterogeneous and fluid than commonly presented. Indeed, Needham (2011) argues that the design of much health and social care policy rests on 'stories'. Using the example of personalisation discussed above, Needham argues that the stories driving personalisation have evolved and mutated from often mundane sources including conversations between individuals, third-party reports, and individual accounts of innovation. Similarly, Power (2013) found that in the design and provision of support to disabled people, real-life individual 'stories' of change are often used by service managers and policy design consultants as important markers of organisational learning, and a currency with which to trade ideas with other providers, individuals and families.

Thinking about health and social care policy design and implementation in this way can open up our understanding of the multiple spaces for change and support that exist. Geoff

DeVerteuil (2014) argues that these supportive approaches are arguably downplayed by many mainstream (primarily US) accounts of urban injustice by geographers who have become largely fixated on the punitive accounts of injustice in the city – particularly within the context of the residual neoliberal welfare state. Indeed, DeVerteuil argues injustice must *co-exist with* and *depend upon* more supportive currents within urban space. These undercurrents can evolve as direct forms of resistance to the thematic trends discussed above. Harvey's (2012) work on *Rebel Cities* traces the growth in urban protest movements from Johannesburg to Mumbai, and from New York to Sao Paulo. These movements reveal deep currents of resistance to the growing inequalities of capital accumulation and control of urban 'public' space.

Equally, DeVerteuil (2015) reminds us of the daily examples of *resilience* which exist alongside more overt and direct struggles against global, national and local challenges. Inherent in this work is an appreciation of the role of the community and voluntary sector in ameliorating the external challenges experienced by different groups deemed vulnerable. People also seek to be resilient in their everyday individual lives. Health geographers have traced the 'health enabling landscapes' (Foley and Kistemann 2014) used and developed by people, including spas, yoga centres, stillness and alternative therapies retreats to achieve more positive physical and mental health. This personal attention to human flourishing is also evident in the growing demand for healthy foods and diet supplementation. These personal practices have no doubt contributed to the growing life expectancy of people in western countries, although such a trend also undoubtedly relates to the broader influence of the global pharmaceutical industry and neoliberal economic wealth accumulation in the Global North mentioned above.

Putting this last point aside, underlying all of these personal and political 'tactics' to boost health and social wellbeing, and resist the previous four trends is an ethic of care. Drawing on feminist geographers such Victoria Lawson (2007; 2009) and Linda McDowell (2004), the ethical responsibilities to care are paramount in the face of poverty and the pervading individualistic ethos in the labour market and the welfare state. This ethic ultimately guides how individuals support each other, and contributes towards greater wellbeing and human thriving. This ethic of care therefore speaks to broader issues of social justice in the way we value and encourage human lives and human flourishing.

A 'Road Map' to *Health Geographies: A Critical Introduction*

It should, we hope, be clear that the primary aim of this book is to help you to develop your credentials as a critical health geographer or, more broadly than this, as a critical health scholar. To help you with that process we have organised the remainder of this book into four substantive parts: (1) *Body, Health and Disease*; (2) *Changing Spaces of (Health) Care*; (3) *Producing Health*; and, (4) *Emerging Geographies of Health and Biomedicine*. Each of these parts and the various chapters contained within them are designed to prompt particular sets of questions as well as to promote understanding of what we think are the main contours of past, present and potential future discussion within the sub-discipline. Each chapter has identified further reading and we set out a series of questions that we hope will encourage you to think further about the topics that we outline. Of course, we recognise that these topics are not exhaustive and that their highlighting by us is based upon our own highly partial readings of the sub-discipline and of related fields of enquiry. In the spirit with which this book has been co-authored we encourage you to identify what is absent and to critically engage with that which is present, though ultimately we take full responsibility for both!

To help you organise your reading, we have described in a little more detail the chapters that are contained in each of the parts. The first part, *Body, Health and Disease*, seeks to cover territory that is already well explored in the kinds of introductory texts that we mention above. In Chapter 2, the body is identified as a key locus of health and medical concern and it is rightly the main starting point for this text. In articulating the break with medical geography, health geographers stated quite clearly that the focus should be on exploring the body in its social and environmental context. Here, consideration is given to the multiple ways in which geographers and other social scientists have approached this question, from studies that illustrate how different types of bodies (aged, gendered, raced, sexed) experience health and health care differently, to the ways in which health is embodied and to debates relating to the geographies of exclusion and ideas about what constitutes the normal/abnormal, healthy/diseased body, and we briefly touch upon more-than-human geographies towards the end of this chapter.

Alongside the body, place was also identified as being crucial to reformulating the so-called 'post-medical geography of health'. This topic is covered in Chapter 3 which focuses explicitly on the importance of place to health geography scholarship. It locates this understanding within an historical overview that identifies geographers' earlier engagement with place through reference to the disease ecology perspective of medical geography. It then explores the significance of, and shifts associated with, the turn to place that was encouraged by health geographers writing in the early 1990s. While the emphasis is placed on ideas that illuminate the power of place to promote and enhance health, the chapter also covers much more recent scholarship on non-representational theory and considers the relevance and value of this to critical health scholars. This focus on the close inter-relationship between health and place is further explored in Chapter 4 which covers the therapeutic landscape concept that has emerged as a key thematic area of interest ever since its introduction to the sub-discipline by Wilbert Gesler in the early 1990s. While it might be regarded as a central feature of the turn to place, we argue that its impact on the wider discipline and indeed beyond this is such that it warrants a separate chapter. A further ambition of this chapter is to engage with the widely used but perhaps a little more elusive concept of wellbeing.

In the next part, *Changing Spaces of (Health) Care*, we engage with questions of health and care. In Chapter 5 we consider traditional approaches to questions of health care access and provision, which have been a core issue for health geographers for many decades. This chapter also explores how geographers have responded to the neoliberal reforms that helped to reshape the health care landscape in countries such as Canada, the United Kingdom and New Zealand and also the growth of what is commonly referred to as complementary and alternative medicine. Finally, it considers recent shifts to an evidence-based approach to health systems reform that is being articulated at the international level (e.g. through the WHO) and is being used to justify reform in health systems across the world. Chapter 6 is closely aligned with this, as it focuses on the interface between health and social care. This type of care is becoming more decentralised with a renewed focus on community living and an erosion of care centres and as a result is tending to take place in multiple settings involving a myriad of different actors and new technologies such as telecare and online marketplaces for purchasing care services. Consequently, there has been a re-sculpting of roles and relationships for those involved in care work, such as volunteering, the third sector, formal services or family care giving. The chapter pays keen attention to the gendered nature of this sector as well as to the impacts of neoliberalism upon it, especially in an age of 'austerity' politics.

The final chapter in Part 2, Chapter 7, focuses specifically on the geographies of mental health care, which has been a dominant strand of scholarship within health geography that has documented and critically explored the evolution of care during and since institutional settings. Its continued relevance as a field within health geography rests with the continuing legacies of institutional care on the lives of persons with mental health issues, in terms of the on-going forms of stigma, de-personalisation and marginalisation that still shape contemporary experiences and spaces of mental health care.

We shift tack slightly in Part 3, *Producing Health*. The chapters in this part of the book work together to explore on-going debates around how health geographers and health researchers more broadly defined account for the inequalities in health that are recognised to exist in many societies today. Here, it is recognised that there is considerable emphasis placed on the importance of place and space in geographers' accounts of health inequalities and this material is covered extensively in Chapter 8. The initial focus of Part 3 is the ecological turn in public health and especially the importance of context and composition in shaping understanding of health and health inequalities. We consider the role of epidemiology, sociology and geography in re-establishing interest in this area and question how researchers and policymakers have understood how space, place and the environment may contribute to disease risk. These are questions that are explored by geographers such as Danny Dorling and Clare Bambra; however, it will be apparent that the discussion of health inequalities in these chapters is less overtly politicised. The concern that some people fare worse than others when it comes to health remains the same, it is the way in which explanations for this important social phenomenon are interpreted that differs.

Chapters 9 and 10 add novel layers of understanding to what is a fairly routine account of the social determinants of health. In the first of these chapters, we explore the recent emergence of complex systems as a possible paradigm shift in ecological approaches in population health research. Taking a systems perspective, it can be argued, has resulted as a logical outgrowth of interest in group-level contextual phenomena in shaping health and health inequalities. In Chapter 10 we consider the kinds of area-based interventions that have become increasingly common as a result of a revitalisation of interest in understanding the social determinants of health. This suggests that modification of features of the local environment may have the potential to improve an individual's health and may also reduce social and environmental inequalities in health. This often makes contextual or area-based interventions inherently appealing as they fit well with the broader socio-ecological model of health discussed elsewhere in this book. The chapter investigates challenges in the rationale, design and evaluation of these interventions and critically assesses whether such interventions have the potential to be effective.

In the final part of the book, *Emerging Geographies of Health and Biomedicine*, we explore a series of topics that by and large sit at the margins of health geographers' interests. We include these topics not only because we believe they are important areas for geographers interested in health-related issues to consider, but also because they often draw on wider sets of literatures and debates. The first of these chapters, Chapter 11, explores different infectious agents and how their distinctive characteristics impact the probability that any particular disease outbreak will reach epidemic or pandemic proportions. Throughout the chapter we consider how the ways in which infectious diseases emerge, and the ways governments and international organisations respond, echoes many of the key themes of this volume. Specifically, we examine the impact of globalisation and inequality on disease ecology, the operation of biopolitics in tackling epidemics, the role of neoliberal policies in limiting access to vaccines and antivirals, and inequalities in who bears the greatest blame for, and impact of, epidemic outbreaks. This chapter leads us quite neatly into Chapter 12 which focuses on the growing influence of the pharmaceutical industry in shaping global health outcomes. Nik Rose (2007) has suggested that the ways in which western societies approach the challenges of poor health and disease are becoming increasingly molecularised and pharmaceuticalised. As we discuss in some detail, this 'molecular gaze' has implications for how we treat disease, including placing a much greater emphasis on pharmaceutical fixes or drugs.

The final two chapters of the book explore closely inter-related topics. The first, Chapter 13, covers the question of medical tourism. Within the academic community the appropriateness of the term 'medical tourism' has proven a topic of considerable debate and disagreement. Despite the growing body of academic work exploring medical tourism, four basic issues remain: what medical tourism is, who medical tourists are, their numbers and their impact. In this chapter, we address each of these elements in turn, touching on many of the key themes of this volume including the impact of neoliberal policies and cuts to public health services, the globalisation of medical care and inequalities in access to medical tourism benefits. Finally, in Chapter 14, we focus on global health. There are two broad questions that shape this chapter: first, what are the circumstances in which a concern for global, rather than international, health arose? This is an important question and one that demands we consider the genealogy of global health. Here, we use the term 'genealogy' not simply with reference to its association with the tracing of a lineage or history. There is almost inevitably a suggestion of this when one mentions 'doing a genealogy'. In contrast, we aim to achieve two things: on the one hand, we examine global health's emergence as a specific field of enquiry, one that produces a particular form of knowledge about the present; on the other, we open up discussion about the further possibilities for geographical engagement in global health. This transformative element of genealogy relates to our second question: what might critical geographies of global health look like? This is as good a place to end as any.

References

Ali, SH & Keil, R (Eds) (2008) *Networked disease: emerging infections in the global city.* Wiley-Blackwell, Oxford.

Anthamatten, P & Hazen, H (2011) *An introduction to the geography of health.* Routledge, London.

Blomley, N (2006) Uncritical critical geography? *Progress in Human Geography* 30, 87–94.

Blua, A (2013) Advances and setbacks in global health during 2013, Radio Free Europe, viewed 16 June 2015, http://www.rferl.org/content/global-health-advances-setbacks-2013/25217407.html

Blyth, M (2013) *Austerity: the history of a dangerous idea.* Oxford University Press, Oxford.

Braveman, P (2006) Health disparities and health equity: concepts and measurement. *Annual Review of Public Health* 27, 167–94.

Brown, T & Bell, M (2008) Imperial or postcolonial governance? Dissecting the genealogy of a global public health strategy. *Social Science & Medicine* 67, 1571–79.

Brown, T & Moon, G (2012) Commentary: geography and global health. *The Geographical Journal* 178, 13–7.

Cheshire, J (2012) Featured Graphic: Lives on the line: mapping life expectancy along the London Tube network. *Environment and Planning A* 44, 1525–28.

Curtis, S (2004) *Health and inequality: geographical perspectives.* Sage, London.

Department of Health and Human Services (DHHS) (1980). Inequalities in health: report of a research working group. (The Black Report). HMSO, London.

DeVerteuil, G (2014) Does the punitive need the supportive? A sympathetic critique of current grammars of urban injustice. *Antipode* 46, 874–93.

DeVerteuil, G (2015) *Resilience in the post-welfare inner city: voluntary sector geographies in London, Los Angeles and Sydney.* Policy Press, Bristol.

Dorling, D (2010) *Injustice: why social inequality persists.* Policy Press, Bristol.

Dorling, D (2013) *The 32 stops: lives on London's Central Line.* Penguin, London.

Dorling, D (2014) *Inequality and the 1%.* Verso, London.

Dorn, ML, Keirns, CC & del Casino Jr, VJ (2010) Doubting dualisms. In: Brown, T, McLafferty, S & Moon, G (Eds) *A companion to health and medical geography.* Wiley-Blackwell, Oxford, 59–78.

Featherstone, D, Ince, A, Mackinnon, D, Strauss, K & Cumbers, A (2012) Progressive localism and the construction of political alternatives. *Transactions of the Institute of British Geographers* 37, 177–82.

Foley, R & Kistemann, T (2015) Blue space geographies: enabling health in place. Introduction to special issue on healthy blue space. *Health & Place* 35, 157–65.

Gatrell, AC & Elliott, SJ (2009) *Geographies of health: an introduction.* Wiley-Blackwell, Oxford.

Hall, E (2014) Geographies of disability and impairment. In: Cockerham, WC, Dingwall, R & Quah, SR (Eds) *The Wiley Blackwell Encyclopedia of health, illness, behavior, and society.* Wiley-Blackwell, Oxford, 686–91.

Hall, S (1992) The West and the rest: discourse and power. In: Hall, S & Gieben, B (Eds) *Formations of modernity.* Polity Press, Cambridge, 275–332.

Hampton, T (2012) Recent advances in mobile technology benefit global health, research, and care. *Journal of the American Medical Association* 307, 2013–4.

Harvey, D (1973) *Social justice and the city.* Edward Arnold, London.

Harvey, D (1996) *Justice, nature and the geography of difference.* Blackwell, Oxford.

Harvey, D (2000) *Spaces of hope.* Edinburgh University Press, Edinburgh.

Harvey, D (2012) *Rebel cities, from the right to the city to the urban revolution.* Verso, London.

Herrick, C (2014) Healthy cities of/from the South. In: Parnell, S & Oldfield, S (Eds) *The Routledge Handbook on cities of the Global South.* Routledge, London, 556–68.

Holmes, D, Gastaldo, D & Perron, A (2007) Paranoid investments in nursing: a schizoanalysis of the evidence-based discourse. *Nursing Philosophy* 8, 85–91.

Institute for Fiscal Studies (2015) A survey of public spending in the UK, viewed 16 April 2016, http://www.ifs.org.uk/bns/bn43.pdf

Jones, K & Moon, G (1987) *Health, disease and society: an introduction to medical geography.* Routledge & Kegan Paul Ltd, London.

Kearns, G (1991) Biology, class and the urban penalty. In: Kearns, G & Withers, WJ (Eds) *Urbanising Britain: essays on class and community in the nineteenth century.* Cambridge University Press, Cambridge, 12–30.

Kearns, RA (1993) Place and health: towards a reformed medical geography. *The Professional Geographer* 46, 67–72.

Kearns, RA & Collins, DC (2010) Health geography. In: Brown, T, McLafferty, S & Moon, G (Eds) *A companion to health and medical geography.* Wiley-Blackwell, Oxford, 15–32.

Kearns, RA & Gesler, WM (2002) *Culture, place and health.* Routledge, London.

Kearns, RA & Moon, G (2002) From medical to health geography: novelty, place and theory after a decade of change. *Progress in Human Geography* 26, 605–25.

Lawson, V (2007) Geographies of care and responsibility. *Annals of the Association of American Geographers* 97, 1–11.

Lawson, V (2009) Instead of radical geography, how about caring geography? *Antipode* 41, 210–3.

London Health Observatory (2012) Health inequalities, viewed 21 April 2016, http://www.lho.org.uk/LHO_Topics/National_Lead_Areas/HealthInequalitiesOverview.aspx.

Marmot, M (2008) *Closing the gap in a generation.* World Health Organization, Geneva.

Marmot, MG, Allen, J, Goldblatt, P, Boyce, T, McNeish, D et al. (2010) *Fair society, healthy lives: strategic review of health inequalities in England post-2010*. The Marmot Review. London.

Massey, D (1993) Power-geometry and a progressive sense of place. In: Bird, J, Curtis, B, Putnam, T, Robertson, G & Tickner, L (Eds) *Mapping the futures: local cultures, global change*. Routledge, London, 59–69.

Mayer, JD & Meade, MS (1994) A reformed medical geography reconsidered. *The Professional Geographer* 46, 103–6.

McDowell, L (2004) Work, workfare, work/life balance and an ethic of care. *Progress in Human Geography* 28, 145–63.

McGregor, S (2001) Neoliberalism and health care. *International Journal of Consumer Studies* 25, 82–9.

Meade, MS & Emch, M (2010) *Medical geography. Third Edition*. Guilford Press, New York.

Monbiot, G (2016) *How did we get into this mess?* viewed 21 April 2016, http://www.monbiot.com/2007/08/28/how-did-we-get-into-this-mess/

Navarro, V (2007) *Neoliberalism, globalization, and inequalities: consequences for health and quality of life*. Baywood Publishers, Amityville, NY.

Needham, C (2011) Personalization: from story-line to practice. *Social Policy & Administration* 45, 54–68.

Newman, J (2013) Landscapes of antagonism: local governance, neoliberalism and austerity. *Urban Studies* 51, 3290–305.

Parr, H (2004) Medical geography: critical medical and health geography? *Progress in Human Geography* 28, 246–57.

Peck, J (2012) Austerity urbanism: American cities under extreme economy. *City* 16, 626–55.

Petryna, A (2002) *Life exposed: biological citizens after Chernobyl*. Princeton University Press, Princeton, NJ.

Philo, C (2000) The birth of the clinic: an unknown work of medical geography. *Area* 32, 11–9.

Philo, C (2007) A vitally human medical geography? Introducing Georges Canguilhem to geographers. *New Zealand Geographer* 63, 82–96.

Piketty, T (2014) *Capital in the twenty-first century*. Harvard University Press, Cambridge, MA.

Power, A (2013) Understanding the complex negotiations in fulfilling the right to independent living for disabled people. *Disability & Society* 28, 204–17.

Power, A (2014) Personalisation and austerity in the crosshairs: government perspectives on the remaking of adult social care. *Journal of Social Policy* 43, 1–18.

Rawls, JA (1971) *Theory of justice*. Harvard University Press, Cambridge, MA.

Rose, N (2007) *The politics of life itself: biomedicine, power, and subjectivity in the twenty-first century*. Princeton University Press, Princeton, NJ.

Rose, N & Novas, C (2004) Biological citizenship. In: Ong, A & Collier, S (Eds) *Global assemblages: technology, politics, and ethics as anthropological problems*. Blackwell, Oxford, 439–63.

Rosenberg, M (2016) Health geography II: 'dividing' health geography. *Progress in Human Geography* 40, 546–54.

Roulstone, A & Morgan, H (2009) Neo-liberal individualism or self-directed support: are we all speaking the same language on modernising adult social care? *Social Policy and Society* 8, 333–45.

Schrecker, PT & Bambra, C (2015) *How politics makes us sick: neoliberal epidemics*. Palgrave Macmillan, London.

Smith, DM (1977) *Human geography: a welfare approach*. Edward Arnold, London.

Staeheli, LA & Mitchell, D (2005) The complex politics of relevance in geography. *Annals of the Association of American Geographers* 95, 357–72.

Stiglitz, J (2015) *The great divide: unequal societies and what we can do about them*. W.W. Norton and Co, New York.

United Nations, Department of Economic and Social Affairs, Population Division (2015). World Urbanization Prospects: The 2014 Revision, (ST/ESA/SER.A/366).

Verhaeghe, P (2014) *What about me?: the struggle for identity in a market-based society*. Scribe, Brunswick, Australia.

Wilkinson, R & Pickett, K (2009) *The spirit level. Why equality is better for everyone*. Oxford University Press, Oxford.

World Bank (2015) *GINI index (World Bank estimate)*. World Bank, Washington, DC.

WHO (2007) *The world health report, 2007. A safer future: global public health security in the 21st century*. WHO, Geneva.

Part I

Body, Health and Disease

Chapter 2

The Body in Health Geography

Introduction

Writing some time ago, Ed Hall, a British health geographer, commented that '[e]veryone is talking about the body' (Hall 2000, p. 21). He qualified this statement almost immediately; everyone, that is, but health geographers. Hall was writing only a relatively short while after the previously discussed debate about the turn to the post-medical geography of health (see Chapter 1). As noted, of importance to some scholars, especially here Michael Dorn and Glenda Laws (1994), was the desire to draw health geographers' attention to the importance of the body to our understanding of health, disease, medicine and so on. However, for Hall, as for other geographers writing before or at around the same time (e.g. Longhurst 1997, 2001; Moss and Dyck 1999, 2003; Parr 2002), what followed was itself quite narrow in terms of its engagement with the body. As he argued, while the body had come into view through health geographers' focus on representation, what remained absent were its 'blood, brain and bones': put differently, its materiality and embodiment.

This chapter takes its lead from Hall's paper and explores the debates to which he was responding. It will focus on a set of core themes, beginning with arguments relating to the idea that health geographers' research was at the time *disembodied*. By this we mean that the body – as the subject of biomedical and health-related discourses, as something that is shaped by and experiences health and disease and as a 'messy fluid' object with its own spatiality (Parr 2002, p. 243) – was argued to be missing from most geographical accounts. It was against these disembodied geographies that many critically-oriented health geographers reacted and in ways that mirrored theoretical currents running through the wider discipline at the time. The following sections reflect these currents and focus on questions of representation, materiality and embodiment before drawing the chapter to a conclusion. While presented as individual sections, the debates in each do not take place in isolation but are intimately connected to each other. Moreover, attending to these debates around the body at the beginning of this book should help you to better understand the contested

Health Geographies: A Critical Introduction, First Edition. Tim Brown, Gavin J. Andrews, Steven Cummins, Beth Greenhough, Daniel Lewis, and Andrew Power.
© 2018 John Wiley & Sons Ltd. Published 2018 by John Wiley & Sons Ltd.

nature of this object of geographical investigation and its importance to the production of critically oriented health geography scholarship.

Disembodied Geographies

The idea that the research of many health, and we should add here medical, geographers was disembodied reflects the belief that the sub-discipline 'traditionally understood the body simply as a "site invaded by a disease with a specific aetiology"' (Hall 2000, p. 21; see Box 2.1). Although Hall does not explicitly refer to them in the paper, his attention here was focused on those areas of the sub-discipline that primarily rely on positivist approaches (see Gatrell and Elliott 2009; Meade and Emch 2010). Given the critique that subsequently emerged, a useful illustration of this approach can be drawn from geographical accounts of HIV/AIDS that were developed in the late 1980s and early 1990s. Work in this tradition not only mapped the spatial diffusion of the epidemic, it also provided understanding of its spatial distribution. For example, we learn about the predominant routes along which HIV infection was argued to have travelled and the speed with which it spread, the prevalence rates of the various strains of the virus within different geographical regions, and its distribution within particular subgroups of populations (e.g. class, ethnicity, gender, sexuality and so on).

For some geographers, especially those arguing from a Marxist political economy or more broadly structuralist perspective, such spatial patterning of disease can offer important

---

Box 2.1   Key Concepts: Disembodied Geographies

To talk of disembodied geographies is to refer to approaches that obscure or overlook the central role that the body plays in our interpretation of people's relationships with their socio-natural environments. As a starting point to understanding the significance of this, it is worthwhile reading geographical accounts of the body that emerged in the 1990s. For example, in her essay *(Dis)embodied Geographies*, Robyn Longhurst discussed the tendency within western masculinist rationality for men to presume that they can 'transcend their embodiment' (1997, p. 491). Because of this presumed ability to separate mind from body (the Cartesian dualism) – and especially from emotions, feelings, desires, experiences and the like – it is suggested that white, heterosexual men position themselves and the knowledge they produce as superior to that of others. Feminist geographers such as Longhurst and other critically-oriented scholars interested in, for example, questions of 'race' and sexuality have sought to destabilise this form of dualistic thinking and the masculinist, racialised, heteronormative assumptions upon which it is based. The importance of this debate here is that the body appeared as an 'ideal starting point for a critique of universality, objectivity or moral absolutism' (Longhurst 2001, p. 18). With this in mind, disembodied geographies not only appear to reinforce western masculinist rationalities, they also by implication fail to take account of the enormous variation in bodies, the spatial- and temporal-specific experiences associated with bodies of difference and of questions of emotion, desire and so on. It is because of the initial failure to account for the body and everything that we have come to associate with it that it might be argued that some approaches in health and medical geography are disembodied.

insights into questions of the social inequalities in health. Not only do they allow geographers to demonstrate the inequitable distribution of diseases or poor health within populations, they also help to build explanations for these patterns that draw attention to questions of power and the maldistribution of resources within societies (see Jones and Moon 1987; Curtis 2004; Gatrell and Elliott 2009). Returning to the specific example of HIV/AIDS, the work of Deborah and Rodrick Wallace is helpful here because it drew on geographical concepts to explore the socio-spatial patterning of the virus *and* it considered the influence of social and political context upon the disease diffusion process. Wallace and Wallace demonstrated, for example, how the spread of the virus was shaped as much by a policy of 'planned shrinkage' or 'redlining' implemented by city administrators – which saw key public services withdrawn from or at least radically reduced in predominantly African American and Latino neighbourhoods such as Brownsville, East New York and the South Bronx – as it was by patterns of particular risk-related behaviours (Wallace and Wallace 1990).

This consideration of what might be termed the political ecology of HIV/AIDS in New York City is a relatively rare example of research in this vein; critical accounts have tended to come from outside of the spatial science or positivist tradition rather than from within it. Yet, although we might view research such as this as *critical* because of its reference to the political and social contexts that shaped the emergence of HIV infection in these particular neighbourhoods, there is little reference to the body here. Indeed, it might even be argued that the ways in which the bodies of those infected by HIV are represented in this research are highly problematic. For example, in one paper Rodrick Wallace concludes: 'it seems likely the large and growing reservoir of heterosexual AIDS in "*third world*" urban ghetto populations of the Bronx and elsewhere could significantly affect the rate of heterosexual transmission within "*developed*" populations' (1988, p. 28. Emphasis added). The association with populations that are predominantly African American and Latino with the 'third world' and other, presumably white, heterosexual populations with the 'developed' world is highly suggestive and mirrors the kind of racialised logics that underpinned early AIDS discourse (Jarosz 1992; Craddock 2000a).

It was against this backdrop that an especially powerful critique of medical geography's early contribution to understanding of the HIV/AIDS epidemic emerged. The critique, which was in part initiated by Michael Brown's 1995 paper *Ironies of distance*, raised particular concerns about the epistemological and ontological implications of viewing bodies as merely the containers for disease. Rather than positioning such accounts within a political ecology framework, Brown argued from a social constructionist perspective and pointed to the ways in which spatial science legitimated a 'heightened focus on the virus and its travel across space' and reduced 'the already marginalized gay body to a mere *vector for illness*' (1995, p. 161. Emphasis added). Additionally, Brown's concern was the failure of health and medical geographers to consider the epidemic as something that was lived or, more broadly speaking, embodied. As he argued, gay men and their experiences of the epidemic, whether as activists and health educationalists, as people living with AIDS or as carers of those that lived with and died from AIDS-related infections, were the subject of an 'erasure'. What Brown offered in his research was a rich and nuanced understanding of the impact of HIV/AIDS on the bodies of gay men and the spaces (concrete as well as metaphorical) that they inhabited as well as on the individual and collective responses to the epidemic and the politics that surrounded this (Brown 1997).

Our reason for drawing your attention to Brown's work is because of its particular critique of the disembodied approach to early geographical accounts of HIV/AIDS. It was especially powerful because it drew critical health geographers' attention to the limitations of a spatial science approach to an epidemic that other scholars had termed an 'epidemic of signification' because of its marking out of specific bodies as the 'Other' (see Treichler 1987). For Brown, as for other critical scholars (e.g. Brown 2000; Craddock 2000a), it is not enough to map an epidemic such as this as it travels through time and space. Rather, it was argued that greater attention needs to be given to the socially constructed nature of epidemics and to the ways in which *specific* bodies and places are set against hegemonic ideas of what is normal. Here, it is useful to draw on a definition of the body that was offered to social geographers by Gill Valentine (2001). As Valentine discusses, the body not only marks the boundary between 'self' and 'Other' – that is, between what is viewed as normal and what is viewed as abnormal or different – it is also the 'site of pleasure and pain around which social definitions of wellbeing, illness, happiness and health are constructed' and the '*primary* location where our personal identities are constituted and social knowledges and meanings inscribed' (2001, p. 15. Emphasis in original). In the sections that follow, we draw out these different elements of the body and explore their relevance to critical health geographies.

Representational Geographies: Pathologising Bodies and Spaces

As we have noted, mapping or tracing the disembodied body's movement through space and time, as medical geographers have done through their analyses of the diffusion of disease pathogens such as HIV, can be revealing; and it might be argued that many critical geographers have been too quick to dismiss the potential of this kind of work. Nonetheless, such accounts do not consider the ways in which bodies, especially diseased or unhealthy ones, are imbued with meaning or how the spaces through which these specific bodies travel or the places they inhabit are similarly problematised. When we observe representations of diseased or sick bodies broadcast on the news, reported upon in newspapers or circulated in snippet accounts published on social media sites such as YouTube or Twitter, one question that we need to ask ourselves is what is it that we are viewing? On a fairly simplistic level, it is a view of a material body that is placed before us, a body that is sick and perhaps even dying. However, as critically minded geographers it is important that we pay attention to the wider meanings relating to diseased and sick bodies that are communicated through discourse (see Box 2.2).

Much of the work in this tradition explores historical accounts of disease. Susan Craddock (1999, 2000b), for example, examines representations of the Chinese in medical, public health and media discourses relating to San Francisco in the nineteenth century. Craddock's is a detailed analysis of shifts that emerged in the textual and visual representation of Chinese immigrants, especially following epidemics of smallpox that occurred in 1868, 1876, 1881 and 1887. As she notes, in the first of these epidemics, which resulted in the highest rates of mortality in the city with over 760 deaths in a population of approximately 150,000, the Chinese did not figure in speculation over the cause of the epidemic. By the time of the next epidemic in 1876 this picture had changed dramatically; in part, Craddock argues, because of a steep rise in the numbers of Chinese living in the city (from about 4,000 in 1869 to nearly 30,000 by 1876). As Craddock states, the association of Chinese bodies with smallpox was so dominant that the 'average San Francisco resident could not "see" the Chinese body outside the construction of its physiognomy, language, clothing, and hygiene as not only pathological, but fatally infectious' (1999, p. 365). What

Box 2.2   Key Thinkers: Sander Gilman

The scholar who has perhaps done most to make visible the situated understandings of deviance and sickness is Sander Gilman. Through several works, Gilman argues that iconographies of disease, madness and deviance play critical roles in depicting as well as producing meanings of the 'Other'. Whether focusing on photographs, paintings or medical illustrations, Gilman argues compellingly that representations are key to deciphering the often divergent but related social understandings as opposed to medical definitions of what is pathological. They portray not the 'realities' of disease, but rather the social understandings of what constitute realities of illness and pathology. Unlike Foucault, who focuses more on understanding madness, disease and deviance as integral parts of particular regimes of knowledge and governance (e.g. Foucault 1978), Gilman focuses attention on universal reasons why societies create the 'Other', in part through depictions of illness. As he argues in the introduction to his book *Difference and Pathology* (1985, p. 23):

> Our understanding of the pathological is rooted in an awareness of the human organism's fragility – not simply its mortality, though that has always and everywhere inspired fear of the ultimate loss of control, but its susceptibility to disease, pollution, corruption, and alteration, things that we experience in our own bodies and observe in others. Every group has laws, taboos, and diagnoses distinguishing the 'healthy' from the 'sick'. The very concept of pathology is a line drawn between the 'good' and the 'bad'. This accounts for the power that metaphors of illness have.

Although Gilman consistently focuses on the significance of race, ethnicity and sexuality in the production of pathologies, other scholars have extended his analyses to encompass critical race, queer and feminist theories probing the interactions of social constructions in shaping understandings of the 'sick' body, and the material and symbolic implications of these understandings for those produced as pathological.

(Adapted from Craddock and Brown 2010)

Craddock highlights are repeated references to what were presented as the immoral and unsanitary behaviours of the Chinese – for example, their association with opium consumption, prostitution and gambling (see Figure 2.1); these were behaviours that were argued to set them apart from white, Anglo-Saxon American norms.

Importantly for geographers, Craddock's work exemplifies the significant role that racialised representations of Chinese immigrants played in the concurrent pathologisation of place and space. Returning to her account of smallpox, what Craddock highlights are the processes through which the places that the Chinese inhabited – their homes, their streets and their neighbourhoods – were themselves marked out as 'Other' and, most importantly, as pathological. Referring, for example, to an 1880 report by the city's public health officers, Craddock reveals that Chinatown was 'designated a "laboratory of infection"' (Craddock 2000b, p. 80). These extremely powerful representations of Chinese bodies and spaces informed public health interventions that were put in place to contain the smallpox outbreak. As Craddock describes, these included placing restrictions on the numbers of Chinese occupying housing through the implementation of a Cubic Air Law, as well as more invasive

Figure 2.1 'A hard job,' the front cover from the *San Francisco Illustrated Wasp* published in August, 1878. Reproduced with permission from UC Berkeley, Bancroft Library.

strategies such as the enforced fumigation and cleansing of Chinatown and the reconstruction of buildings, streets and homes that were regarded as unsanitary. Referring to the language used by public health officials to justify these forms of intervention – with Chinatown described not only as a 'laboratory of infection' but also as a 'cancer' in the city and as a 'plague spot' – Craddock concludes that this not only exemplifies the pathologisation of Chinese bodies and spaces but also points implicitly towards the necessity of '*excision*' (1999, p. 366. Emphasis added).

Craddock's interpretive work unpacks the time- and place-specific relations of power that are often enacted through discourses associated with epidemic diseases. A more recent illustration of the importance of considering the ways in which diseased bodies are represented comes from the outbreak of Ebola virus disease in West Africa in 2014–15. As with previous outbreaks of infectious disease, whether cholera, smallpox and typhoid in the nineteenth century, HIV/AIDS in the twentieth century or SARS in the twenty first century, there is something about an outbreak of highly infectious disease that results in the production of discourses that reproduce dominant ideas about social normativity. On the one hand, it is their association with *contagion*. As the feminist theorist, Margaret Shildrick (2001, pp. 154–5), notes:

> Among the several meanings of the word contagion – all of which are deeply negative in their import – is the notion of a disease process spread by touch, or even by proximity. We understand that a contaminated object is one to be avoided or kept at a safe distance, lest we too become infected, our bodies opened up to the forces of disintegration.

In this reading, while contagion refers to an epidemiological process, it should be understood as more than an 'epidemiological fact' (Wald 2008, p. 2). As this suggests, a body infected with a highly contagious virus such as Ebola is to be avoided or set apart from normal society and is the subject of public health regimes that aim to contain the spread of disease through the careful management of contaminated bodies (see Chapter 11).

As demonstrated in Craddock's work, social constructions relating to ideas about race, ethnicity, sexuality and so on are consistently present in discourses surrounding the diseased and sick body; it is these other forms of social differentiation that help to mark some bodies out from the norm and as diseased or pathological. In the case of Ebola, it is the association of non-white African (African heritage) bodies with poverty, underdevelopment and with dominant western representations of the *Third World* more broadly that are evident in the associated discourses. Hélène Joffe and Georgina Haarhoff provide an insight into this in their detailed account of the reporting of an earlier outbreak of Ebola virus disease in British media accounts of the mid 1990s (Joffe and Haarhoff 2002). As they reveal, media representations of the Ebola outbreak, especially those emanating from the nation's 'tabloid' newspapers, presented it as an African problem and tended to emphasise specific, and by inference abnormal, cultural practices, especially the eating of monkey flesh. Moreover, Joffe and Haarhoff highlight that there were a number of ways through which the newspapers constructed the outbreak as a threat to their readership: by speculating about the possible globalisation of Ebola, by explicit reference to its impact on the bodies of those infected (e.g. reference to the liquefying of organs) and by comparison with AIDS, an already known 'killer disease' (2002, p. 961–2).

Although the language employed in these media representations was less explicitly racialised than in Craddock's analysis of the smallpox outbreaks in San Francisco, there is evidence in them of what the cultural commentator and journalist, Cindy Patton, has referred to as 'tropical thinking' (Patton 2002, p. 36). As Craddock observes of Patton's concept, the 'tropical' here does not only refer to a place but to a 'designation, a signal that the *Third World* is the location of disease while the *First World* body is the locus of health, biologically threatened when boundaries disappear or fail' (2008, p. 192. Emphasis added). Using this construct here enables us to offer a critical reading of representations of epidemic disease such as Ebola because they imply that the disease and by association those bodies associated with it belong 'there' (the Third World) and not 'here' (the First World). Moreover, the specific bodies associated with the outbreak of epidemic disease, in the case of the Ebola outbreak of 2013–2016, largely West African ones, are stigmatised and marginalised because they are represented as the conduits through which a disease such as this is, or at least is potentially, able to travel across borders. We can begin to judge the impact of representing or labelling bodies in this way through reference to the 'I AM' social media campaign that aimed to counter the stigmatisation and discrimination associated with the Ebola outbreak in 2013–2016. Appearing on social media sites such as Facebook and Twitter, the latter under the hash tag #iamaliberiannotavirus, the campaign featured images of Liberians living in the USA holding up placards reading 'I AM a Liberian, not a virus' (*The Guardian*, 22 October 2012). The campaign was initiated by parents who recognised that their children were being marginalised and stigmatised at school because of their Liberian ethnicity and because of the anxieties that Ebola continues to generate.

From Representation and Governance to Materiality and Embodiment

As mentioned in the introduction to this chapter, Ed Hall, in his response to the debates around the body in health geography, argued that what was missing was a concern for materiality and embodiment. Indeed, Hall was really quite critical of the social constructionist approach to the body discussed above, suggesting that in such accounts the 'body is of little interest in itself. It is its representation, meaning and symbolism that matter; the material body is not understood to play an active part in social relations' (2000, p. 23). In making this particular critique, Hall was eluding to a key set of debates that raged within feminist writing on the body in the early 1990s. Feminist theorists such as Susan Bordo (2003) and Judith Butler (1990, 1993), both of whom were heavily influenced by Foucault, viewed the materiality of the body as a product of the actions of discourses upon it. As the former noted in her highly influential *Unbearable Weight*, 'our bodies are trained, shaped and impressed with the stamp of prevailing historical forms of selfhood, desire, masculinity, femininity' (2003, p. 165–6). Similarly, Butler, through her concept of performativity, understood as the repeated or iterative discursive acts that 'congeal over time to produce the appearance of substance' (Butler 1990, p. 33), draws our attention to the ways in which bodies are stylised, how identities are made in relation to discourse and how the force of social and cultural norms means that some bodies appear more natural, more desirable and even less disgusting than others.

This particular reading of the action of discourse upon women's bodies, and we could extend this to other types of bodies, has been taken up in various ways by a range of critically oriented health geographers. For example, Pamela Moss and Isabel Dyck have alerted us to the bodily and material experiences of impairment and disability within the often exclusionary environments of the workplace, shop, city and even home (e.g. Moss and Dyck 1999, 2003). As an illustration of their argument, Moss and Dyck turned to insights that can be drawn from the accounts of women diagnosed with *myalgic encephalomyelitis* (ME) or chronic fatigue syndrome. In their interpretive analysis, they suggested that the process of medical diagnosis, which would usually take place within a highly medicalised context such as a clinic or hospital, should be viewed as a discursive practice that produces and reproduces specific meanings about the body – as 'diseased', 'ailing', or 'malfunctioning' and the identity of the person with ME as 'ill', 'abnormal', or 'disabled' (1999, p. 377). As they argue, although we can challenge or resist such bodily inscriptions, 'diagnosis etches onto a material body a representation of what it is to be ill, have an ill body, and be socially constructed as ill'. Such an analysis clearly draws on the idea that sick bodies and the social identities produced of them are at least in part the products of discourses such as these.

In a similar vein, Andrea Litva, Kay Peggs and Graham Moon (2001) drew on the work of Bordo and Butler to consider the influence of bodily control and body management discourses on young women's perspectives of their health and appearance. Although only a narrowly defined study, focused on a small group of students in a single British university, it revealed how the young women interviewed were less concerned with the health of their 'inner bodies' as might be defined by biomedicine and were more attentive to the physical appearance of their 'outer bodies', which was thought of primarily in terms of dominant notions of 'beauty' that are produced and consumed within social and cultural discourses. Litva and colleagues' study points us in two important theoretical directions: first, towards insights from research into the sociology of the body and specifically to the focus on the idea of the body as a project that 'should be worked at and accomplished as part of an *individual's* self-identity' (Shilling 1993, p. 4. Emphasis in original). Such a reading of the body has attracted the attention of critical health geographers, for example in analyses of gym culture (e.g. Andrews, Mark and Andrew 2005). More significant, however, is a parallel stream of research that locates this concern with body management or *self-care* within the Foucauldian concept of governmentality.

Geographers have been particularly attentive to governmentality, a concept developed in Foucault's 1977–78 series of lectures on *Security, Territory, Population* (Foucault 2007) and subsequently reworked by a much broader range of inter-disciplinary scholars. Its importance to health geographers can be identified as being the attention that it draws to governmental strategies and associated technologies that are brought to bear on populations with a view to securing their health and vitality. As Foucault stated, the purpose of government in this understanding of governmentality is to 'improve the condition of the population, to increase its wealth, its longevity, and its health' (2007, p. 105), an ideal that is achieved in part through what he referred to as the 'conduct of conduct'. A particularly pertinent illustration of this form of governmentality and how it helps to foster healthy subjectivity can be found in the discourse of the new public health. As Alan Petersen and Deborah Lupton suggest:

> The new public health is, if nothing else, a set of discourses focusing on bodies, and on the regulation of the ways in which these bodies interact within particular arrangements of time and space… the discourses of the new public health also seek to transform the awareness of individuals in such a way that they become more *self-regulating* and *productive*. (1996, p. 12. Emphasis added)

When thought about in this way, the 'new' public health, as distinguished from the 'old' public health that emerged out of the sanitary reform movement of the nineteenth century, is regarded as a set of health-related imperatives that seek to encourage within populations transformative practices that can be enacted across an array of places or settings: for example, eat five a day, perform at least 30 minutes of physical activity, practise safe sex, reduce alcohol intake, stop smoking and so on.

We need, as mentioned earlier in this chapter, always to be aware of the time- and place-specific contexts within which these discourses emerge and especially of the influence of the political rationalities that inform differing forms of government. In the case of the new public health, it has been widely argued that this is representative of neoliberal governmentality with its emphasis upon: the individualisation of health-related risks, strategies of community empowerment, and entrepreneurial and market-oriented approaches to achieving desired improvements in population level health and wellbeing (Brown and Burges Watson 2010). We can see this in the examples of the kinds of transformative practices associated with the new public health mentioned above, and it is upon these aspects of neoliberal governmentality that much health geography scholarship in this area has been focused. For example, Tim Brown (2000) considered the promotion of safe sex practices in public health discourses associated with the management of HIV/AIDS in the United Kingdom; Damian Collins and colleagues (2006) explored the risks of ultraviolet radiation exposure and associated prevention strategies in primary schools in Auckland, New Zealand; and, more recently, the US geographer, Eric Carter, has focused on the 'Blue Zones Project', a health promotion strategy originating in the US state of Iowa that provides advice on healthy living and is associated with 'nudging' its population into making healthy lifestyle choices (see Carter 2015). Additionally, as Evans and Colls (2009) suggest, Foucault's governmentality has proven especially useful in critical obesity studies and particularly those that focus upon education as a form of governmental technology.

Although these and similar studies are disparate in terms of temporal and geographical focus, what connects them is a concern with the governmental strategies evoked in the name of the new public health and with the possibilities that this has for the production of healthy subjectivity and healthy spaces. Yet, as with Bordo's and Butler's work, the body that emerges in this kind of interpretive approach fails to accommodate its *weightiness* or in Hall's terms its 'blood, brain and bones'. Hall argued that there are a number of possible responses that might help to overcome these concerns. First, he proposed that much more attention needed to be paid to the shaping and the reshaping of the 'internal geography' of the body and not only through attention to the kinds of materiality produced by the discourses of biomedicine. Second, Hall proposed that we acknowledge that the depths of our bodies and not only their surfaces are constantly interacting with, responding to and being reshaped by the socio-spatial or more broadly socio-environmental contexts in which we place them or in which they are placed. For Hall, such an approach would allow geographers to take account of the 'physicality of the body... its fleshy reality' as well as of the 'complex interaction between society and biology' (2000, p. 28).

Materiality and the body

To help us think through Hall's questioning of approaches that emphasise discursive constructions of the body, we turn initially to David Bell and Gill Valentine's (1997) *Consuming Geographies: We Are What We Eat* in which they consider the relationship between food, place and identity (Bell and Valentine 1997, p. 25). In this text, Bell and Valentine draw heavily on the likes of Bordo, Butler and Foucault to discuss the representation of the body in popular, scientific and governmental discourses. As they note, geographically and historically specific norms are circulated within these discourses that help to establish particular sized bodies as the ideal or normative body. However, there is more to Bell and Valentine's reading than this. Drawing on the work of sociologists such as the previously mentioned Deborah Lupton (1996), they also point to the processes through which the interior of the fat body as well its external surfaces is problematised. As they argue, 'we are not only symbolically what we eat, but also literally what we eat' (1997, p. 45). Of particular importance here is the emphasis placed upon the nutritional properties of foods and of the ways in which their specific elements – proteins, carbohydrates, fats, fibre, minerals and vitamins, sugars and so on – interact with the biochemistry of the body to promote health and protect against disease or alternatively result in harm. Thus, bodies are not only social objects constituted through the performance of discourse but they are also biological objects with a materiality that lies outside of language and sociality; the biological body is, in this reading, extra-discursive.

This particular understanding of materiality has been picked up in a number of ways in more recent geographical work, especially that which relates to questions of obesity and health. As mentioned above, a growing number of geographers have engaged critically with obesity and challenged some of the normative ideas surrounding its problematisation as a health issue. Of concern for these scholars is not only the discursive construction of fat bodies as sick bodies and associated attempts to evoke regimes of self-care that reproduce societal norms surrounding the thin and fit body (see Evans 2006, 2010; Herrick 2007, 2011), but also the scientific knowledge that underpins obesity and the associated medicalisation of fatness. The US geographer, Julie Guthman, perhaps stands out amongst these scholars with regards to her ongoing critical engagement with these debates. As she argues in her text *Weighing In*, the medicalisation of fatness as obesity is a double-edged sword. On the one hand, medicalisation can bring comfort to people experiencing poor health and wellbeing associated with obesity because medical interventions might be offered to treat the diagnosed condition. However, on the other, it can result in people being subjected to medical scrutiny regardless of their desires. Questioning, for example, the term *morbidly obese*, Guthman notes that this is 'surely designed to elicit revulsion' and acts to diminish 'the subjectivity of fat people, making them victims, not agents, of their own embodiment' (2011, p. 26).

Importantly, here, Guthman's critical engagement with the discourses of obesity focuses on the fat body as a biological as well as a discursive entity; one whose permeable boundaries allow its insides as well as its surfaces to interact with, and be changed by, the external environments in which it is located. On the face of it, an approach such as this appears to mirror explanations for obesity found in geographical accounts that emphasise the environmental determinants of health and focus on the idea of obesogenic environments (Smith and Cummins 2009). However, Guthman argues that such explanations tend to 'black-box' the body and treat the environment as causal rather than as interactive. In place of this form of explanation, Guthman adopts a political ecology of health perspective but one that is attuned to the idea that human bodies are sites where the 'biological and the social constantly remake each other' (2011, p. 97). This perspective, which builds upon work in the field of science and technology studies (STS), encourages geographers to engage with emerging explanations of obesity, some of which consider the possibility that exposure to environmental stressors can shape bodily function at the genetic level and that such changes are inheritable. As Paul Jackson and Abigail Neely (2015) suggest, the epigenetic effects that Guthman (see also Guthman and Mansfield 2013) refers to invite health geographers to rethink assumptions about the relationships between the body, environment and health.

Embodying fleshy, (dis)abled and sick bodies

Where Guthman offers one way for health geographers to engage with the materiality of bodies, Rachel Colls' (2007) focus on what she refers to as the intra-active capacities of fat and how it is embodied offers another. Colls' engagement with the materiality and embodiment of fat bodies, similarly to Guthman's, runs contrary to dominant discourses relating to overweight and obesity which tend to equate them only with ill health. In contrast, however, Colls is less interested in offering alternative explanations for obesity. Rather, her concern lies with exploring women's embodied experience of their fatness and with their capacities to understand fat in ways that sit outside of the discursive constructions of it. As she notes, of the three layers of adipose tissue that sit below the skin (superficial, deep and visceral), it is the deep layer of fat that is most often the site of medical and cosmetic intervention *and* that part of the fat body that we can 'grab, squeeze, feel moving when we run and walk and also manage and manipulate through bodily practices' (Colls 2007, p. 358). Drawn from her analysis of personal descriptions of fat bodies in the writing of women engaged in the size acceptance movement, what Colls explores are accounts of fat that highlight its productive capacities. Fat, in one account, is described as pouring, folding, hanging, growing; as Colls notes, the fat body in this understanding is not 'passive or inert' but has its 'own momentum' and 'capacities to act' (2007, p. 359).

In drawing attention to these women's accounts of their embodied experience of fat, Colls not only raises questions of dominant discourses that medicalise fatness as obesity, she also questions the kinds of passive bodies produced through discursive approaches to the body. As she argues, 'exposing the "constructedness" of bodies' can result in a view of bodily matter as passive and this 'only serves to impose particular discursive regimes upon fat bodies as lazy, incapable of self-control and irresponsible' (2007, p. 358; see also Evans 2006). Colls' concern is that the focus on representations of fatness rather than its embodiment raises the possibility of fat bodies being known only through discursive constructions of them. Thus, in making an argument for analyses that consider fat as bodily matter she is making space for the production of subject positions that are 'premised on fatness rather than on its absence' (2007, p. 358). Whilst this argument is not without its challenges, the crucial point that Colls is making is that there are other ways of knowing the materiality of fat bodies. Of course, it is not only fat bodies that are medicalised and constituted as 'Other' in this way. As Hall (2014) notes, people with emotional and behavioural problems or chronic illness, older adults and so on have in recent years been included within the field of disability geographies because of their shared, if different, experience of socio-spatial contexts as disabling and exclusionary.

Importantly, here, health geographers' engagement with disabled bodies has also involved paying attention to the question of embodiment (see Box 2.3). As Vincent J. del Casino Jr explains, 'how one experiences and lives with a certain disease (or illness) is dependent on where he or she is, when he or she is, and how he or she conceptualizes his or her relationship to that condition' (2010, p. 189). Developing this point further, he argues that health geographers need to invest their research with a 'historical imagination' in order to come to trace the embodied experience of ill health and to understand diseases as 'fluid processes that change over time and place'. People living with a physical impairment, with a mental health condition, with chronic ill health or with a life-threatening disease will experience change in their bodies as well as in the socio-spatial environments they inhabit. Health geographers have explored the embodied experience of people living with this myriad of conditions and in so doing have documented the various ways in which they experience and negotiate changes to their everyday life spaces. Returning to the work of Moss and Dyck, for example, we are alerted to the idea that diagnosis with a condition such as ME is not only about the impact of discourse on the surface of bodies; it is not solely about the process of bodily inscription. Rather, through detailed ethnographic work they highlighted how women with ME reclaimed their diagnoses through challenging medical authority or renegotiating work-related tasks and reorganising their working environments.

Box 2.3   Key Themes: Embodiment and Disability Geographies

Rather than being viewed through the lens of the biomedical model, it has become accepted following the activism of the disability rights movement and disability scholars that the label disability is a product of 'social relations, practices and organization of society and space' that marginalise and disable those with physical and mental illnesses and impairments (Chouinard 2010, p. 245). Since this acknowledgement, much has been written about the nature of disability as a socially constructed category and the role that geographers can play in generating understanding of the socio-spatial relations that shape people's experiences of being disabled (see Butler and Parr 1999; Chouinard et al. 2010). For scholars such as Hall, it is not enough to consider the question of disability through the lens of social constructionism. As he argues, 'disability is an excellent example… [for] thinking about the body as embodied and material' (2000, p. 24; Hall 2014). In making this observation Hall was arguing for an alternative to a purely biomedical perspective on disability – one that saw it as the product of biological abnormality – and a purely socially constructed one. Both, he argued, fail to take account of the lived, experienced body. In his work, and in that of others, considerable attention has been paid to the ways in which disability is embodied not only as it is constructed through discourse but in terms that seek to go beyond this level of surface inscription. Of particular importance in geographical accounts are the quotidian experiences of the disabled body, the ways in which people notice their impairments and respond to them in different socio-spatial settings. While much of this work remains centred on the experience of being disabled in the wealthy countries of the Global North, recent attention has been paid to resource-poor countries in the Global South (e.g. Chouinard 2014).

As Moss and Dyck (1999) suggest, this is just one example of how the women in their study engaged in embodied practices that helped them to manage their conditions and re-negotiate the discursive constructions of it.

Conclusion: More-than-human Bodies

In order to conclude this chapter we would like to point to questions that require some additional attention. The materiality of bodies matters in the constitution of health geographies. It matters to the medical profession, whose biomedical gaze, Foucault (1973) argues, seeks to reduce us to a series of objective scientific observations. It matters to us too, as living human subjects, who feel pain and pleasure, comfort and discomfort, the wrack of a cough and the excruciating pain of a broken collarbone, the fatigue and disorientation brought about by fever. We should also remember, as Longhurst encourages us to do, that the boundaries of our bodies are not stable, fixed or impermeable; rather, they are 'fragile, insecure, and increasingly difficult to keep intact' (2001, p. 1). Put differently, bodies are leaky and messy and subject to flows across the boundaries that we seek to secure through social and cultural practices of all kinds. Although we have not been able to cover much of this messiness in the chapter, it is important as critical health geographers that we acknowledge it because these are the bodies we inhabit.

Furthermore, our bodies are also the means through which we see, sense and engage with the world; they are interactive, they are the bodies we 'do'. As Annemarie Mol and John Law question, if 'the body we *have* is the one known by pathologists after our death, while the body we *are* is the one we know ourselves by being self-aware, then what about the body we *do*?' (2004, p. 45. Emphasis in original). An attention to the materiality of bodies and how this is shaped by, but not limited to, their social construction alludes to broader concerns with the socio-material construction of geographies or what Sarah Whatmore (2002) has termed more-than-human geographies. The phrase more-than-human, while more frequently used to challenge the anthropocentricism of the societies, communities and economies we study as human geographers, also draws attention to how the materiality of human bodies is also objectified, naturalised and thereby excluded from geographical analysis. The challenge for health geographers is how to draw this understanding of bodies into their analyses of health, disease and illness (Jackson and Neely 2015).

Questions for Review

1. What is meant by the term 'pathological' in this chapter? Think of examples that help to illustrate your understanding.
2. Consider the ways in which the human body can be described as material and embodied and discuss the significance of this understanding to critical health geographies.
3. If you were asked to design a research project to explore the body in health geography, what are the research methods that you would use and the challenges that you might face?

Suggested Reading

Dorn, M & Laws, G (1994) Social theory, body politics, and medical geography: extending Kearns's invitation. *Professional Geographer* 46, 106–110.

Hall, E (2000) 'Blood, brain and bones': taking the body seriously in the geography of health and impairment. *Area* 31, 21–29.

Mol, A & Law, J (2004) Embodied action, enacted bodies: the example of hypoglycaemia. *Body & Society* 10, 43–62.

References

Andrews, GJ, Mark, IS & Andrew, CS (2005) Towards a geography of fitness: an ethnographic case study of the gym in British bodybuilding culture. *Social Science & Medicine* 60, 877–91.

Bell, D & Valentine, G (1997) *Consuming geographies: we are what we eat*. Routledge, London.

Bordo, S (2003) *Unbearable weight: feminism, western culture, and the body*. University of California Press, Berkeley, CA.

Brown, M (1995) Ironies of distance: an ongoing critique of the geographies of AIDS. *Environment and Planning D: Society and Space* 13, 159–83.

Brown, M (1997) *RePlacing Citizenship: AIDS activism and radical democracy*. Guilford Press, New York.

Brown, T (2000) AIDS, risk and social governance. *Social Science & Medicine* 50, 1273–84.

Brown, T & Burges Watson, DL (2010) Governing un/healthy populations. In: Brown, T, McLafferty, S & Moon, G (Eds) *A companion to health and medical geography*. Wiley-Blackwell, Chichester, 477–93.

Butler, J (1990) *Gender trouble: feminism and the subversion of identity*. Routledge, London.

Butler, J (1993) *Bodies that matter: on the discourse limits of "sex"*. Routledge, New York.

Butler, R & Parr, H (Eds) (1999) *Mind and body spaces: geographies of illness, impairment and disability*. Routledge, London.

Carter, ED (2015) Making the Blue Zones: neoliberalism and nudges in public health promotion. *Social Science & Medicine* 133, 374–82.

Chouinard, V (2010) Impairment and disability. In: Brown, T, McLafferty, S & Moon, G (Eds) *A companion to health and medical geography*. Wiley-Blackwell, Chichester, 242–57.

Chouinard, V (2014) Precarious lives in the global south: on being disabled in Guyana. *Antipode* 46, 340–58.

Chouinard, V, Hall, E & Wilton, R (Eds) (2010) *Towards enabling geographies: 'disabled' bodies and minds in society and space*. Ashgate, Aldershot.

Collins, DC, Kearns, RA & Mitchell, H (2006) "An integral part of the children's education": placing sun protection in Auckland primary schools. *Health & Place* 12, 436–48.

Colls, R (2007) Materialising body matter: intra-action and the embodiment of 'Fat' *Geoforum* 38, 353–65.

Craddock, S (1999) Embodying place: pathologizing Chinese and Chinatown in nineteenth-century San Francisco. *Antipode* 31, 351–71.

Craddock, S (2000a) Disease, social identity, and risk: rethinking the geography of AIDS. *Transactions of the Institute of British Geographers* 25, 153–68.

Craddock, S (2000b) *City of plagues: disease, poverty and deviance in San Francisco*. University of Minnesota Press, Minneapolis, MN.

Craddock, S (2008) Tuberculosis and the anxieties of containment. In: Ali, SH & Keil, R (Eds) *Networked disease: emerging infections in the global city*. Wiley-Blackwell, Oxford, 186–200.

Craddock, S & Brown, T (2010) Representing the un/healthy body. In: Brown, T, McLafferty, S & Moon, G (Eds) *A companion to health and medical geography*. Wiley-Blackwell, Oxford, 301–21.

Curtis, S (2004) *Health and inequality: geographical perspectives*. Sage, London.

Del Casino Jr, V (2010) Living with and experiencing disease. In: Brown, T, McLafferty, S & Moon, G (Eds) *A companion to health and medical geography*. Wiley-Blackwell, Chichester, 188–204.

Dorn, M & Laws, G (1994) Social theory, body politics, and medical geography: extending Kearns's invitation. *Professional Geographer* 46, 106–10.

Evans, B (2006) 'Gluttony or sloth': critical geographies of bodies and morality in (anti)obesity policy. *Area* 38, 259–67.

Evans, B (2010) Anticipating fatness: childhood, affect and pre-emptive 'war on obesity'. *Transactions of the Institute of British Geographers* 35, 21–38.

Evans, B & Colls, R (2009) Measuring fatness, governing bodies: the spatialities of the body mass index (BMI) in anti-obesity politics. *Antipode* 41, 1051–83.

Foucault, M (1973) *The birth of the clinic*. Tavistock, London.

Foucault, M (1978) *The history of sexuality, Vol. 1: an introduction*. Random House, New York.

Foucault, M (2007) *Security, territory, population: lectures at the College de France 1977–78*. Palgrave Macmillan, New York.

Gatrell, A & Elliott, S (2009) *Geographies of health: an introduction. Second Edition*. Wiley-Blackwell, Chichester.

Gilman, SL (1985) *Difference and pathology: stereotypes of sexuality, race, and madness*. Cornell University Press, Ithaca, NY.

Guthman, J (2011) *Weighing in: obesity, food justice, and the limits of capitalism*. University of California Press, Berkeley, CA.

Guthman, J & Mansfield, B (2013) The implications of environmental epigenetics: a new direction for geographic inquiry on health, space, and nature-society relations. *Progress in Human Geography* 37, 486–504.

Hall, E (2000) 'Blood, brain and bones': taking the body seriously in the geography of health and impairment. *Area* 31, 21–29.

Hall, E (2014) Geographies of disability and impairment. In: Cockerham, WC, Dingwall, R & Quah, SR (Eds) *The Wiley Blackwell Encyclopedia of health, illness, behavior and society. First Edition.* Wiley-Blackwell, Chichester.

Herrick, C (2007) Risky bodies: public health, social marketing and the governance of obesity. *Geoforum* 38, 90–102.

Herrick, C (2011) *Governing health and consumption: sensible citizens, behaviour and the city.* Policy Press, Bristol.

Jackson, P & Neely, AH (2015) Triangulating health: toward a practice of a political ecology of health. *Progress in Human Geography* 39, 47–64.

Jarosz, L (1992) Constructing the dark continent: metaphor as geographic representation of Africa. *Geografiska Annaler. Series B. Human Geography* 74, 105–15.

Joffe, H & Haarhoff, G (2002) Representations of far-flung illnesses: the case of Ebola in Britain. *Social Science & Medicine* 54, 955–69.

Jones, K & Moon, G (1987) *Health, disease and society: an introduction to medical geography.* Routledge & Kegan Paul Ltd, London.

Litva, A, Peggs, K & Moon, G (2001) The beauty of health: locating young women's health and appearance. In: Dyck, I, Lewis, ND & McLafferty, S (Eds) *Geographies of women's health.* Routledge, London, 248–64.

Longhurst, R (1997) (Dis)embodied geographies. *Progress in Human Geography* 21, 486–501.

Longhurst, R (2001) *Bodies: exploring fluid boundaries.* Routledge, London.

Lupton, D (1996) *Food, the body and the self.* Sage, London.

Meade, M & Emch, M (2010) *Medical geography. Third Edition.* Guilford Press, New York.

Mol, A & Law, J (2004) Embodied action, enacted bodies: the example of hypoglycaemia. *Body & Society* 10, 43–62.

Moss, P & Dyck, I (1999) Body, corporeal space, and legitimating chronic illness: women diagnosed with ME. *Antipode* 31, 372–97.

Moss, P & Dyck, I (2003) *Women, body, illness: space and identity in the everyday lives of women with chronic illness.* Rowman & Littlefield, New York.

Parr, H (2002) Diagnosing the body in medical and health geography: 1999–2000. *Progress in Human Geography* 26, 240–51.

Patton, C (2002) *Globalizing AIDS.* University of Minnesota Press, Minneapolis, MN.

Petersen, A & Lupton, D (1996). *The new public health: health and self in the age of risk.* Sage, London.

Shildrick, M (2001) Vulnerable bodies and ontological contamination. In: Bashford, A & Hooker, C (Eds) *Contagion.* Routledge, London, 153–67.

Shilling, C (1993) *The body and social theory.* Sage, London.

Smith, DM & Cummins, S (2009) Obese cities: how our environment shapes overweight. *Geography Compass* 3, 518–35.

Treichler, P (1987) AIDS: cultural analysis/cultural activism. *October* 43 (Winter), 31–70.

Valentine, G (2001) *Social geographies: society and space.* Prentice Hall, Harlow.

Wald, P (2008) *Contagious: cultures, carriers, and the outbreak narrative.* Duke University Press, Durham, NC.

Wallace, R (1988) A synergism of plagues: "planned shrinkage", contagious housing destruction, and AIDS in the Bronx. *Environmental Research* 47, 1–33.

Wallace, R & Wallace, D (1990) Origins of public health collapse in New York City: the dynamics of planned shrinkage, contagious urban decay and social disintegration. *Bulletin of the New York Academy of Medicine* 66, 391–434.

Whatmore, S (2002) *Hybrid geographies: natures, cultures, spaces.* Sage, London.

Chapter 3

Health and Place

Introduction

The interrelationship between health and place has long been of interest, with philosophers, clinicians and early scientists referring to the influence of one on the other throughout antiquity. Indeed, a rapid pass through a few thousand years of thinking on health and disease reveals varied engagements with and references to particular types of places (Barrett 2000). As historical reviews note, some of the earliest mentions of place in the context of health can be found in the fifth century BCE in Hippocrates' *Airs, Waters and Places*. This document provided guidance for travelling physicians on what to expect when entering a new location and conveyed in simple terms that health and disease were a product of their environment (Barrett 2000). It is not only in western thought where health and place were argued to be closely entangled; the US medical geographer, Frank Barrett, notes, for example, how works in ancient Chinese (*Huang Di nei jing su wen*) and Indian medicine (Ayurveda) from the same period sought to explain local variations in health and disease in very similar ways to Hippocrates. Insights from this early period in human history informed medical geography as it emerged in the eighteenth and nineteenth centuries and we can still trace this influence in contemporary debates. In this sense, it might be argued that there has simply been no period of a 'placeless' medical or health geography.

The influence of such early ideas on contemporary health and medical geography is well covered in the literature (Gesler 1991; Barrett 2000; see also Dorn et al. 2010), therefore this chapter focuses on debates surrounding the call for a place-centred approach to health that emerged in the 1980s and early 1990s and which represent a critical moment in the history of the sub-discipline. To this end, in the sections that follow we consider the differing ways in which place has been conceptualised in research generally labelled as belonging to either health or medical geography (see Box 3.1). Although we recognise the limitations of the 'two traditions' approach, especially as there is a tendency in doing so to produce uncritical and largely problematic genealogies of the discipline (Dorn et al. 2010),

Health Geographies: A Critical Introduction, First Edition. Tim Brown, Gavin J. Andrews, Steven Cummins, Beth Greenhough, Daniel Lewis, and Andrew Power.
© 2018 John Wiley & Sons Ltd. Published 2018 by John Wiley & Sons Ltd.

Box 3.1   Key Concepts: Understandings and Attributes of Place

Understanding of Place	Attributes and Assumptions
Place as a noun	Known, assumed, not itself theorised
Place as a location	Precise, static, mappable
Place as a social construction	Occupied and felt; imbued with meaning
Place as relational	Networked, fluid, changing, co-dependent
Place as active, lively	Acted, sensed, moving, energetic

---

this dualism was inscribed in accounts of the time. As Michael Dorn and colleagues note, the health geography versus medical geography dualism was entrenched in the shift to a post-medical geography of health, a point reflected in Robin Kearns' (1993) call for the renaming of medical geography as 'medical geography' and the 'geography of health'. However, we do not wish simply to rehearse old debates, rather the chapter uses this sub-disciplinary discussion (one might say 'navel gazing') as a stepping stone to consider other more recent reflections on health and place, notably here those emanating from within non-representational theory.

Medical Geography: Place as Location

It was the emergence of 'regional geography' in the nineteenth and early twentieth centuries that launched and defined the early discipline of human geography. In this particular academic tradition, health occasionally gained a mention in scholarship in the description of specific regions but few studies were focused solely on single concerns such as this, no matter how important they might have been. Health was thus considered as one of the many facets and features of regions as complex places. Notably, however, the underlying environmental determinism in early regional geography laid an important theoretical foundation for medical geography that arguably reverberates in certain strands of research to the present day. When a 'new regional geography' emerged in the 1980s, greater critical attention was given to regional economic and social structures. Following from this, medicine and health gained greater prominence as empirical fields of inquiry, particularly with regards to local needs for, and local planning of, health care, place-based policy and local determinants of health (Jones and Moon 1993).

Where regional geography largely ignored health concerns, the next iteration of place in geographical thinking had a much more profound impact on medical geography. The so-called 'quantitative revolution' or 'empirical turn' in the parent discipline was a key development that looked for spatial patterns in collective human existence – some of its explicit 'geometries'. Under this project, place took on an applied role in conjunction with space. Based on a positivistic philosophical understanding, space was thought of as an underlying template for human agency, as a featureless, neutral surface upon which life unfolds. However, when 'things' (such as people, homes, facilities or political boundaries) are located and quantified at places (places being points or locations), space begins to mean more and represent substantial features of, and challenges in, human life. This is because place then allows space to become distinguishable and dividable. On one level, *at* places, rates, volumes and other localised measures become visible and calculable (such as levels of morbidity and mortality, which we saw from at least the mid nineteenth century with the production of vital statistics relating to population health and the territory of the state. See Foucault 2009; Elden 2007). On another level, *between* places, times, distances, movements and differences also become visible and calculable (such as the spread of disease. See Cliff et al. 2000). In many respects, this tradition had as an objective the search for fundamental laws for spatial relationships in disease, health and health care.

Although sometimes critiqued for being an unreflexive, atheoretical mapping exercise, concerned only with the measurement, calculation and spread of 'things' (see Chapter 2), it might equally be argued that research from within this tradition has been informed by specific theoretical traditions and perspectives that guide and frame inquiries and help interpret findings; early positivistic medical geography found particular guidance, for example, in disease ecology (May 1959; Brown and Moon 2004). As Joseph Oppong and Adam Harold (2010) describe, disease ecology provided, and still provides, explanations for the geographical distribution of diseases by studying the factors and principles that influence their spatio-temporal patterns. The underlying assumption is that diseases and pathogens can only be fully understood if considered in the context of the places or ecologies in which they are found. In this approach, places can be composed of environmental conditions (including climate and levels of pollution or other environmental toxins), built features (including building types and neighbourhood properties) or localised social contexts (such as demographic variables) (see Meade and Earickson 2000). As we shall discuss later in this chapter, a new political ecology of health has emerged in recent years and adds a layer of theoretical complexity to this form of explanation.

On the other hand, another strand of research closely aligned with spatial science traditions has concerned itself with describing and explaining distributive features in the supply of health care services (over international, national, regional and localised areas) and their relationships to usage, health patterns and health outcomes (Joseph and Phillips 1984; Eyles 1990; Mohan 1998). A political economy perspective has theoretically framed and informed much of this research, considering how economic and political structures and processes determine and influence spatial patterns and the health outcomes that follow. In the context of the pervasive 'efficiency agenda' in local governmental and health service planning, Sara McLafferty (1982), for example, analysed the distribution of hospital closures in New York City and found areas with low income and high mortality to have been hardest hit.

More recently, developing this even further and more critically moving beyond basic considerations of the 'shape' of services, studies have paid much closer attention to specific features that form provision, such as administrative boundaries and local markets (Joseph and Chalmers 1996; Cloutier-Fisher and Skinner 2006) and health policy/regulation (Joseph and Kearns 1996; Norris 1997). These developments have led to this field of research – the 'geography of health care' – being recognised as a body of work that contributes directly to mainstream health service and academic debates on rationing, efficiency and equity in service planning and provision. Meanwhile, with regard to both research on the distributive features of disease and research on the distributive features of health care services, methodological scholarship has paid attention to some of the core 'ingredients' of spatial analysis (Gesler 1986), for example exploring the potential of multilevel statistical modelling (Duncan et al. 1993, 1996, 1998) and geographic information systems (GIS) (Higgs and Gould 2001; McLafferty 2003; Higgs et al. 2005) in articulating spatial relationships.

In the last two decades, even though place is still essentially thought of as a location in much research in medical geography, a far greater appreciation of what is found in and influential in places, and the complex processes involved, has led to much more sophisticated understandings and analysis. No more so is this evident than in geographical research focused on the social determinants of health. For example, for a substantial period in the 1980s debates existed as to whether health in place is more greatly influenced by the characteristics of local people (social composition, e.g. ethnicity, gender, marital or employment status, income, debt) or by the services and facilities available to them (social context) (see Chapter 8). Since the late 1990s, however, geographers have highlighted weaknesses in both compositional and contextual explanations for health (Macintyre et al. 2002). Instead, it is argued that 'collective' dimensions might be more important than basic demographics or how many and what type of services are present. Indeed, this collective dimension to area-based explanations for health emphasises the social and cultural norms of particular people in particular places – the sharing of traditions, values and interests within places. These, for example, could be ethnic, regional, religious, political, historical or cultural in character and/or class based. Specifically the concept of social capital has been introduced as an explanation for these collective social dimensions (Mohan et al. 2005; Wakefield and Poland 2005), inching the understanding of place ever closer to a social constructionist perspective.

Health Geography

The 'disease geographer' and the 'health services geographer' strands within medical geography research that the above discussion alludes to have been reified in some accounts of the sub-discipline (Dorn et al. 2010; *cf.* Kearns and Joseph 1993); this is perhaps most apparent in the debate that surrounded the so-called post-medical turn to health of the early 1990s. We have already begun to engage with aspects of this debate in our discussion of spatial science accounts of epidemic diseases in Chapter 2. In this section, we engage much more directly with the post-medical turn because it has helped to shape the next twenty-plus years of academic research by self-identified geographers of health.

Health and place: A critical debate

Building on research on topics such as 'sense of place' (Eyles 1985), 'perceptions of health' (Eyles and Donovan 1986) and 'culture and health' (Gesler 1991), geographers such as Robin Kearns (1991, 1993, 1994), Graham Moon (1990; Jones and Moon 1993) and Alun Joseph (Kearns and Joseph 1993) began to articulate a number of concerns with what they regarded as the reductionist approach to place in much medical geography research. For example, in his discussion of the conceptions of space and community in British health policy, Moon (1990) tackled what he saw as the tension between geographical understandings of absolute space (i.e. space as a container) and relative space (i.e. space as an entity that is shaped by human agency and structural forces). Importantly, Moon's discussion led him to focus on the sociological conception of the *locale* which he described as 'simultaneously a fixed geographical location and also a *place* with meaning where social interaction occurs' (Moon 1990, p. 169. Emphasis in original). What followed was an encouragement for geographers not only to calculate and map the patterns of disease and health, as well as of health care services, that existed in place, but to give much greater consideration to questions of human agency and experience as well as to the socio-structural forces that shaped and were shaped by place.

Although Moon was central to the foundation of the journal *Health & Place* in 1995 and co-authored important disciplinary perspectives on the subject (e.g. Jones and Moon 1993), it is Robin Kearns who is most often associated with defining the early contours of the post-medical turn (see Box 3.2). An early articulation of his perspective on health and place can be found in an analysis of place-based experiences of primary care settings amongst Maori populations living in the Northland district of New Zealand (Kearns 1991). Kearns uses this paper to articulate both the theoretical and associated methodological innovations of his approach and in so doing sets the tone for further discussion in the wider sub-discipline. More specifically, he argued for an approach to the study of health and health care that recognised the 'health of place' (1991, p. 520). By this he meant research that not only acknowledged the relevance of sense of place to understanding people's perceptions but also the experiences of health in place, experiences that were and are shaped by wider cultural, political and social structures as well as by the form that health care settings take. Clearly, such analysis could not be supported by research adopting a positivistic epistemology; rather, as Kearns argued, it required 'immersion in a community, a research stance that has variably been called participant observation and thick description' (1991, p. 520).

Kearns' 1991 paper signalled a turn towards very different theoretical and methodological approaches to those conducted in the majority of medical geography research, a turn that demanded that the sub-discipline pay much closer heed to developments taking place

---

Box 3.2   Key Thinkers: Robin Kearns

Within health geography, Robin Kearns, a geographer based in the University of Auckland, had a particularly significant effect on the 'post-medical' turn to health. It was Kearns who first coined this phrase in his 1993 paper and it was he who most explicitly argued for a two traditions approach. As Kearns noted, 'I suggest that two interrelated streams be identified in the medicine/health/geography nexus: *medical geography* and the *geography of health*' (1993, p. 145). For Kearns, at least at this juncture, this meant separating research into two fields: (1) medical geography that focused on the spatial and ecological aspects of disease (i.e. disease ecology, disease diffusion and so on) as well as on the spatial aspects of health care (e.g. location allocation modelling); and (2) the geography of health that focused on the 'dynamic relationship between health and place and the impacts of health services and the health of population groups on the vitality of place'. Kearns' agenda-setting paper was massively influential and there can be little argument that it helped to shape the field from this point forwards. However, it is important to place Kearns within the academic milieu in which he was operating. Like many other geographers at this time, he was a regular attendee at the Association of American Geographers/Institute of British Geographers sponsored Symposium in Medical Geography (now the International Symposium in Medical Geography) and the ideas presented in the 1993 paper in part reflect discussion and debate that took place at these highly influential meetings and in the post-conference debates that inevitably followed (see Kearns 1995).

in the wider discipline of geography. Informed by the 'new' cultural geography of the period, Kearns called for geographers to incorporate a 'place-sensitive', 'post-medical' perspective into their scholarship (Kearns 1993). With regard to the former, he meant moving beyond previous preoccupations with distributional aspects of disease and medicine by examining the meaning and significance of places (re-imagined as social and cultural constructions) in health and health care. With regard to the latter, he considered moreover that they might problematise medical categorisation, assumptions and power and realise health as both a positive mental and physical state of wellbeing and happiness (see also Jones and Moon 1987). Following some initial scepticism (e.g. Mayer and Meade 1994), as well as complementary advice (Dorn and Laws 1994) and further explanation (Kearns 1994), understanding has since developed in geography that health and health care are deeply affected by places and the ways in which places are reacted to, felt and represented. It is to this wider scholarship that we now turn.

Social constructions of health and place

At one level, health care settings are argued to possess basic agency (for example, hospitals are settings that provide access to institutional medicine; community clinics provide access to primary health care and so on). Underlying this basic agency, however, are far more intimate processes that are recognised to be at play whereby 'people make places' and 'places make people'. Armed with such ideas of place, a new generation of health geographers have sought to understand how place plays a central role in a variety of processes that impact on health and health care. One longstanding approach has been, and continues to be, to develop qualitative methods to observe in depth the health and illness lives of individuals and groups and to unlock the social and political structures imposed upon them and their experiences and agency within these (Gesler and Kearns 2002). Research in this vein initially drew on the humanistic tradition and especially phenomenological accounts of place produced by geographers such as Edward Relph (1976) and Yi-Fu Tuan (1976, 1979). As Wilbert Gesler and Robin Kearns note, humanistic approaches aim to 'understand personal experiences and feeling and how people attach meaning to their surroundings' (2002, p. 23). In this understanding, places are recognised to evoke a broad range of emotions and feelings that might shape a person's health-related experiences, both positively and negatively. For example, some places are experienced by some people as sites of health and healing (e.g. a gymnasium or a clinic) or refuge (e.g. mental asylums or homeless shelters) and others' experience may be one that is stigmatising, health-damaging and perhaps even dangerous (e.g. Parr 2008).

Alongside humanistic approaches to the analysis of people's subjective experiences of health, disease and place, there emerged a closely-related body of research influenced by the 'new' cultural geography that explored health landscapes as 'texts' (for a discussion see Gesler and Kearns 2002). The metaphor of text is an important one here as it signals the adoption of an interpretive approach to research, that is, one that treats landscapes not as only those features of a place that are experienced sensorially but as something that is imbued with social meaning. The role of the researcher – in our case health geographers – is to attempt to read or interpret such 'texts' and to consider what they reveal about the inter relationship between health and place. We shall discuss health geographers' engagement with landscapes in much more detail in Chapter 4; however, it is important to acknowledge that what we can say about landscapes, whether healthy or otherwise, as researchers is 'mediated by how we are acculturated to see the world, what our society believes is important, and by our individual experiences' (Gesler and Kearns 2002, p. 120). Although suggestive of the problem of relativism – that is, the meaning we derive from texts can only be understood within their specific social and cultural contexts – what Gesler and Kearns are alerting us to is the idea that our reading of texts is not absolute or fixed but is spatially and temporally, as well as socially and culturally, situated.

This approach to exploring health and place has been taken up in several different ways. Given the influence of both humanistic approaches and the 'new' cultural geography on early exponents, the initial research focus lay with exploring the health-related or healing properties that have been attributed to places or specific features of places throughout human history. This particular perspective has developed into the now well-established concept of therapeutic landscapes and often focuses quite explicitly on human–nature interactions and the longstanding belief that particular properties of 'natural' landscapes promote healing (see Chapter 4; Williams 2007). Although therapeutic landscapes research often draws upon people's experiences and feelings of healing places, this approach also explores written (e.g. literary texts) and visual materials (e.g. art work). Such an approach might involve analysing literary texts such as Gesler's (2005) examination of Thomas Mann's 1933 novel *The Magic Mountain* or François Tonnellier and Sarah Curtis' (2005) analysis of Honoré de Balzac's much earlier novel *Le Médecin de campagne* ('*The Country Doctor*') published in 1833. In both of these cases, emphasis was placed on the ways in which ideas about human health and healing, as well as about disease and death, were constructed in the texts and how they were associated with particular features of the landscapes the authors were writing about. As Gesler suggests, even a fictional text such as Mann's *The Magic Mountain* can reveal a great deal about how people experience health and disease and the meanings that are attached to the places that we inhabit.

Where much of the above research often involved developing a constructive dialogue between humanistic geography and the 'new' cultural geography, other strands of research have been informed by post-structuralist perspectives. Partly a response to the structuralism of Saussurean linguistics, post-structuralism recognises texts as historically specific and spatially variable components of the social worlds that we inhabit. From this perspective – although we should really say 'perspectives' given the range of theorists contributing to post-structuralism – texts are generally regarded as meaning-making resources produced and circulated within society that have the capacity to constitute social reality. A crucial difference between this and humanistic approaches to landscapes as texts is that the former not only considered texts as being involved in meaning-making (i.e. symbolising health and healing) but also in the formation of subject identities (e.g. class, able bodied/disabled, ethnicity/race, gender, sexuality) and in associated relations of power. Not only does such an approach recognise that texts, often viewed as being produced by powerful social institutions, are involved in the formation of identities but it also recognises that these identities are contested and resisted through counter-discourses (e.g. through the politics of disability, feminism, sexuality, class, race based activists and scholars).

For critical geographers interested in health and disease, reading texts through a post-structuralist lens produced very different interpretations of healthy and diseased landscapes. We have already explored the latter in Chapter 2 where we engaged with Susan Craddock's work on the pathologising of place. Other examples of research adopting a post-structuralist approach include analyses of health care landscapes, such as Robin Kearns and Ross Barnett's work on an emerging consumerism in the New Zealand hospital system (1997, 2000). In this example, the authors were concerned with interpreting what they referred to as the 'corporate colonisation' of the health care system, or the idea of 'McHospitalisation' (2000, p. 81). Their analysis involved interpreting a range of texts (e.g. official documents and media accounts) and images from newly constructed hospitals and considered what they tell us about the dynamic interrelationship between health and place. We will pick this up in Chapter 4, but the important point to raise here is that their interpretive approach was able to highlight the influence of neoliberalism on the health care landscape in New Zealand and the associated transformation of 'patients' into 'consumers'. Similarly, Meghann Ormond and Matt Sothern (2012) in much more recent research consider how patients are constituted as 'active, cosmopolitan consumers' in the texts of international medical travel guidebooks. In their research, the contemporary health care landscape in countries such as Canada, the United States, Britain and other parts of Western Europe is constructed as 'dysfunctional', 'failing' and dangerous to the health of the 'savvy' patient-consumer.

Health and place as relational

One criticism of the aforementioned understandings that has emerged in recent years is that, although they recognise the rich and complex composition and production of places, they generally portray them as somewhat discrete and static phenomena. Places tend to be conceptualised as stable, parochial centres of meaning resulting from social inscription, whilst little attention is paid to relationships that might exist beyond them. In response, relational thinking complicates the conventional assumption that places possess 'intrinsic' qualities. Simply put, it implies a twist in how place is theorised, evoking an image of places emerging not only 'in situ', but also through their connections within networks of 'translocal interactions'. In other words, places are highly related to, and produced by, many other places at multiple scales. Relational ideas such as these in geography emerged as part of a broader 'relational turn' in the social sciences. So whilst relational debates in sociology, for example, have centred on individuals, groups and organisations, in geography, given its particular conceptual focus, relationality centres foremost on places as networked and performed articulations of social relations (Darling 2009).

Notably, relational accounts of place also lay emphasis on temporality as they consider places to be ever developing and changing over time. Indeed, as 'bundles of inter-relations', places are considered only temporarily accomplished, forever 'coming into being'. Thus, as Martin Jones (2009) suggests, the research agenda for relational scholarship centres upon ideas and theories of places that portray them as forever encountered, performed and fluid. Indeed, various aspects of such relational thinking are usefully explained by Steven Cummins and colleagues (2007) who emphasise that: (i) whilst a conventional view of place focuses on fixed boundaries, a relational view focuses on fluid boundaries; (ii) whilst a conventional view of place focuses on its content, a relational view focuses on influxes that change that content; (iii) whilst a conventional view of place focuses on residence, a relational view focuses on mobility; (iv) whilst a conventional view of place focuses on certain times and places, a relational view focuses on many and their change; (v) whilst a conventional view of place focuses on common understandings and constructions between individuals and groups, a relational view focuses on variable understandings between individuals and groups.

Scholars have offered ideas for infusing relational notions of place into health-related research, notably in the context of talking about complexity and complexity theory (see

Chapter 9). More generally, however, outside dedicated commentaries, the emergence of 'relational health geography' is evidenced more subtly in the way that relationality has been used to frame a growing number of studies. These include, for example, considerations of health system processes and community outcomes (e.g. Durie and Wyatt 2007), political ecologies of health (e.g. King 2010), therapeutic, enabling and restorative environments (e.g. Curtis et al. 2009) and infectious disease and public health (e.g. Craddock 2000; Keil and Ali 2006, 2007; Brown and Bell 2008). Such works have enriched understandings of health and place by demonstrating the relational connections constituting health experiences. Most recently some health geographers have started to move beyond 'mapping' relationalities (articulating places as 'nodes' in wider 'networks') and have embraced further understandings that place is itself relationally performed. As Ben Anderson and Paul Harrison (2010, p. 16) state, 'it is not enough to simply assert that phenomena are relationally constituted or invoke the form of the network, rather it becomes necessary to think about the specificity and performative efficacy of different relations and different relational configurations'. In embracing this understanding they have started to engage with non-representational theory and we consider this particular theoretical innovation in the following sections.

'Taking-place': Place as lively and acted

We know well from many published books and articles that as an overall approach, non-representational theory brings something slightly different to the table of contemporary human geography (see Thrift 1997; Lorimer 2005, 2008; Cadman 2009; Anderson and Harrison 2010; Vannini 2015). The approach has arisen through its own set of fundamental realisations on what it is to be human. Commenting on these, Derek McCormack notes:

> Central to this [non-representational] work are a number of claims: that we do not always consciously reflect upon external representations – signs, symbols, etc. – when we make sense of the world; that thinking does not necessarily involve the internal manipulation of picture-like representations; that intelligence is a distributed and relational process, in which a range of actors (bodies, texts, devices, objects) are lively participants. (2008, p. 1824)

Thus, not wanting to drill down to theorise or explain the world away, nor aiming to find meanings in places or patterns over spaces and, rightly or wrongly, arguing against the 'static(ness)' and 'touchy-feely(ness)' of mainstream representational and social constructionist approaches, its mission is instead to view, directly engage and present the world as a lived, immediate, continually moving performance (Thrift 2004). Moreover, acknowledging this action as being at the forefront, rather than as the background, of people's lives, the focus of its inquiries lies with the thousands of modest, unsaid, unplanned and often involuntary practices that together make life. As Nigel Thrift (2008) explains, research might reverberate then what actually happens *in* and *as* space-time; how life presents, shows, manifests and feels in its most basic forms (often prior to it being fully cognitively realised), and how this physical and sensory part of life informs, and is informed by, consciously enacted 'known' social, institutional, political and economic processes (see also Thrift 1997).

No one philosophy or philosopher has underpinned non-representational theory; rather, its development has largely involved re-reading many of those that have already informed social constructionism and other traditions drawn upon by critically-minded geographers. As Louisa Cadman (2009) explains, first, non-representational theory has involved re-reading Martin Heidegger's phenomenology, but instead of focusing on meanings derived from being 'embedded-in-the-world', it focuses on the consequences of humans being unavoidably 'thrown-into-the-world'. This has helped foster a realisation that how humans live and make the world is just as important as how they might cognitively reason it (Cadman 2009). Second, there has been a re-engagement with vitalist philosophy, primarily to help escape phenomenology's human-centred view of the world. This has led to an understanding that scholars might avoid the enduring dualism in research of 'subjects versus objects', and instead of focusing on what objects *are to* humans, focus on the fundamental energies and liveliness of humans and humans acting with objects (Cadman 2009). Third, and building on this, there has been a re-reading of some post-structuralist ideas and thought – particularly the works of Jacques Derrida and others – looking beyond their ideas on the significance and meaning of things (and thus places), to their ideas on the materiality, force encounters and relations of and between things (in places) (Cadman 2009). As this initial explanation indicates, non-representational theory is not strictly one theory, rather it is a number of ways of understanding the active world and doing research on and with it.

Non-representational theory for health geographers

Amongst health geographers, one of the authors of this book, Gavin Andrews, has been most active in drawing attention to the possibilities that this approach affords researchers. He has achieved this by pulling out a number of its core features for discussion (Andrews 2014; Andrews et al. 2014). The first of these features requires that we pay attention to what is referred to as the onflow of life: the moving, physical, processional frontier of existence as it continually rolls out creating space and time (Pred 2005; Thrift 2008). Before existence is recognised or even registered by humans, existence 'happens'. The moment is constantly being created, with 'onflow' providing a set of moving, physical conditions and capacities on which all conscious life is placed and builds. To ignore onflow and immediately dig for life's meaning – as exclusively social constructionist approaches tend to do – is to underplay life's physicality (which is inescapable), to view life as stopped (which it never can be), to provide a fixing (that is always false) and present life in an afterthought (which it never is), and miss much of what it actually involves. Attempting to describe onflow, Andrews (2014, p. 166) suggests:

> In a health care context an onflow could involve, for example, the unfolding of time and space of a primary health care reception area and waiting room. People walking in, some sitting, others walking out, some coughing, doors opening and shutting, calls from staff that direct, phones ringing and computers bleeping, a television flashing the daily news in the corner. These are moments that are constantly being created, each creating potential for, and leading into, the next. These transitions become so seamless, that life becomes one unrolling moment.

A second feature is to focus on body senses and sensation, but not just on an individual level, rather as something co-produced and shared between bodies and as something that might resonate widely. This particular feature has led to the exploration of 'affect' as an explanatory concept and testing ground in research. In basic terms, affect is the ability of a body through expression and movement to be affected and to affect. In collective terms, affect can spread like a mobile energy, like a virus, amongst people, manifesting to them less-than-fully consciously on a somatic register as a 'feeling state' and spatially as an environmental intensity; a vague but intense atmosphere (Thrift 2004). One might thus think about the sensation of affect as a highly variable yet constantly occurring part of people's lives in which they participate – a part that is endlessly streaming, sandwiched in-between, but complexly related to, what is physically happening, and what they observe, reason and know to have happened. As Emma Rowland (2014) posits, affect has thus challenged the traditional notion that the mind always controls the body. Instead it brings to the fore the possibility that they work together on a less-than-fully conscious level, constantly changing and altering each other in tune with their environment. Notably, in terms of well-being, affect potentially impacts on individuals in either positive or negative ways, through its bearing on their energy, capacity for engagement and involvement. Indeed, Giles Deleuze (1988) argues that whilst negative affection ('sadness affect') acts like a debilitating toxin that weighs a person down and reduces their capacity to operate physically and mentally, positive affection ('joy affect') acts as a nutrition that lifts a person, propels them forwards and increases their capacity to operate physically and mentally. Describing an affective activity in action, Andrews (2014, p. 167) notes:

> In fitness activities such as running, much of what is important to a participant might be the affective feels of moving in space and time; the acceleration, speed, deceleration, driving arms, burning lungs and legs. With other bodies, the togetherness of running beside other runners, the boost of overtaking another runner, the energy sapping weight of being overtaken by another runner. Moreover, the shared sensation of bodies moving together through urban space and time might provide a physical unity that underlies runners' personal and collective commitment to overcome physical obstacles and, on another conscious level, when participating for charity, overcome the obstacles that concern the people and causes the runners might be collectively supporting.

A third feature of non-representational theory is to focus on practice and performance. This contrasts with a preoccupation in other types of research with the mind (ideas, motivations, values, beliefs, attitudes and so on) (Vannini 2015). Thus practice and performance is about the expressive and purposeful engagement of bodies and bodies and objects, whether they be expected or unexpected, intentional or unintentional. In this endeavour, as Cadman (2009) suggests, the objective is not necessarily to look for signs and meanings in body performativity (such as in Judith Butler's well known 'formulations') and might just as well be about a very basic and active performativity including timings and spacings between events and things. Coming out of these understandings of practice and performance have been new forms of engagement and expectations with regard to ethics and society. The idea of hope, for example, becomes more about how it might have potential, move forward and be acted (rather than remaining unfulfilled or utopian – Cadman 2009; Popke 2009). The idea of being political, on the other hand, moves beyond political thinking to the diffusion of political physicality and creating and acting new realities (Cadman 2009; Thrift 2004). Discussing the importance of practice and performance in health care, Andrews (2014, p. 167) notes:

> In a surgical medical procedure the nurses and doctors time and limit their actions and movements to the finest of degrees. They all have different roles and parts to play but work and act together like a single entity. In home care, a formal carer might make their way around a client's home, in ways and with motions that reflect the highly regulated and standardized nature of their practice. This might contrast and collide with the ways and motions of the client/home-owner and, their friends and family who share the same time and space.

A fourth feature is to approach life with a fascination and wonderment for its immediacy; with an appreciation of, and excitement to witness the happenings that occur in people's life worlds, and all the movement and energy they involve (Thrift 2008; Vannini 2009, 2015). As Vannini (2015) notes, non-representational researchers are aware of an ongoing and quickly changing moment that moves out of view once they focus too hard, but are nonetheless enticed enough by it to know it deserves some academic comprehension. This feature is thus a particular disposition that the researcher has, not unlike that in mindfulness practices and techniques.

A fifth feature is, through methodological engagement, to simultaneously 'witness', 'act into' and 'change and boost' the active world and help it 'speak back'. Although a non-representational methodological toolkit has yet to be developed by scholars, an openness to experiment and produce case-specific methodological hybrids is key to inquiries so that researchers do not go too far down contemplative and interpretative paths and attempt to present what occurs. 'Witnessing' is thus to pay attention to all occurrences, even those that might seem trivial. By doing this, it is hoped that the emerging data might have a fidelity to, and as close a resemblance as possible with, events that took place. One approach to maximise witnessing is to use more than one method, for example combining photography and film with traditional written field notes to help show a situation and provide more than one sensory insight (see Larsen 2008). 'Acting into', on the other hand, denotes a close relationship between the researcher and what is happening in the field, and a blurring of the role of observer and what is observed (Dirksmeier and Helbrecht 2008). Indeed, as Vannini (2015) argues, with non-representational theory, method is itself a performance that does not study social reality through the acquisition of data, as much as perform a social reality and live the data. Interviewing, for example, can be as much about the interaction itself as the stories told, and participant observation can be modified to become 'observant participation' which is about doing the same thing as those observed, getting more embroiled and invested in the effort and experience, and even actively intervening to change happenings (Dewsbury 2009). This last point leads to 'changing and boosting' and 'speaking back'. Creating new realities is a key priority to researchers, both in the field and in forms of knowledge translation. This has led particularly to the development of arts-based methods and a more general agenda towards an activist and public scholarship.

Although health geography has not drawn on non-representational theory to the same extent as some other sub-disciplines of human geography, interest is undoubtedly increasing. Some studies engage squarely with the aforementioned concerns and features of non-representational theory. Others engage partially and/or do not explicitly claim a heritage or spot within the emerging tradition. Yet others, meanwhile, might combine both representational and non-representational approaches. Hence, as Hayden Lorimer (2005) would say, the field might be thought of more loosely as 'more-than-representational'. Empirically there has been a focus on medicine and health care and also on community contexts: in terms of the former, for example, networking, feelings and performances in the virtuality of holistic practice (Andrews 2004; Paterson 2005; Andrews and Shaw 2010; Andrews et al. 2013; Lea et al. 2015), and with non-human actors in bioscience and biopolitics (e.g. Braun 2007; Greenhough 2011a, 2011b; Greenhough and Roe 2011; Jackson and Neely 2015); and in terms of the latter, for example, networking, 'feels' and performances in enabling and therapeutic situations (e.g. Conradson 2005; Tucker 2010; Foley 2011; Philo et al. 2014), including in arts and musical contexts (Anderson 2006; Andrews et al.

2011; Atkinson and Rubidge 2013; McCormack 2013; Simpson 2014). Theoretically, there has been a focus on key thinkers, and on specific concepts and approaches; for example on how the work of Georges Canguilhem (Philo 2007), Gilles Deleuze (Duff 2014) and Michel Foucault (Philo 2012) might hold potential to anchor scholarship in this area and, more generally, on how Actor-Network Theory might be drawn on to elucidate the co-active roles of humans and technologies in health and health care (e.g. Hall 2004; Timmons et al. 2010; Greenhough 2011a, 2011b; Andrews et al. 2013).

Non-representational theory does however have its critics, their arguments being highly relevant to health geographers. As Colls (2012) argues, certain scholars have taken issue with what they see as the universalist nature of the new tradition (e.g. Tolia-Kelly 2006) that fails to differentiate bodies and see people through important social and demographic categories such as gender, ethnicity, disability and age (Jacobs and Nash 2003). Moreover, other scholars have taken issue with what they perceive as the voiding of political content and intent (Pain 2006), its masculinist, technocratic distancing and abstraction (Bondi 2005; Thien 2005), distancing of deep feelings and emotions (Thien 2005) and the ways in which people make sense of their lives (Bondi 2005). Colls (2012) argues, however, that these problems and shortfalls need not be so acute, because non-representational theory does not require that existing understandings, approaches and areas of research be jettisoned. Specifically, Colls sees potential in developing a 'nomadic consciousness' between the representational and non-representational, both between studies and even within single studies where subject matter allows. This approach reflects the simple reality that in life less-than-fully conscious movement and sensing 'overflows' conscious thought and action (where power, meaning, identity and such things come into play). Indeed, as suggested earlier, as much as non-representational theory is concerned with movement and sensing, it is also an injunction for thinking about how humans consciously shape them and are shaped by them.

Conclusion

This chapter has described how place has a long and varied history in geographical thinking on health and health care. Although understood and defined differently, generally speaking the experiential and human dimensions of place have gradually come to the fore in scholarship. Indeed, since the early 1990s, as health geography has emerged, place has become recognised as a complex social and cultural construction from which meanings, identities and attachments flow. Now, in the current century, as relational and non-representational approaches have come to the fore, place is also recognised as something that is networked, dynamic, immediate – that 'happens'.

Importantly, these debates on place and transitions in understandings have not been limited to medical and health geography, and beyond the sub-discipline they have been influential in informing the character of 'spatial turns' amongst many other health-focused disciplines and fields of inquiry including nursing studies (Andrews 2016), social gerontology (Andrews et al. 2013), population and public health (Brown and Duncan 2000, 2002) and the sociology of health and fitness (Kelly 2003; Van Ingen 2003). The following chapters draw on these understandings in the context of specific empirical concerns and critical perspectives.

Questions for Review

1. How has place been conceptualised and understood differently in health geography? What are the key phases in the development of this thinking?
2. Through what processes might a place – such as a hospital – be socially constructed?
3. Through what processes might a place – such as a hospital – be relational and performed?

Suggested Reading

Andrews, GJ, Evans, J, Dunn, JR & Masuda, JR (2012) Arguments in health geography: on sub-disciplinary progress, observation, translation. *Geography Compass* 6, 351–83.

Andrews, GJ, Chen, S & Myers, S (2014) The 'taking place' of health and wellbeing: towards non-representational theory. *Social Science & Medicine* 108, 210–22.

Barrett, FA (2000) *Disease & geography: the history of an idea.* Atkinson College, York University.

Kearns, RA (1993) Place and health: towards a reformed medical geography. *The Professional Geographer* 46, 67–72.

Meade, MS & Earickson, R (2000) *Medical geography.* Guilford, New York.

References

Anderson, B (2006) Becoming and being hopeful: towards a theory of affect. *Environment and planning D: Society and Space* 24, 733–52.

Anderson, B & Harrison, P (2010) *Taking place: non-representational theories and geography.* Ashgate, Aldershot, UK.

Andrews, GJ (2004) (Re)thinking the dynamic between healthcare and place: therapeutic geographies in treatment and care practices *Area* 36, 307–18.

Andrews, GJ (2014) Co-creating health's lively, moving frontiers: brief observations on the facets and possibilities of non-representational theory. *Health & Place* 30, 165–70.

Andrews, GJ (2016) Geographical thinking in nursing inquiry, part one: locations, contents, meanings. *Nursing Philosophy* 17, 262–81.

Andrews GJ & Shaw D (2010) 'So we started talking about a beach in Barbados': visualization practices and needle phobia. *Social Science & Medicine* 71, 1804–10.

Andrews, GJ, Evans, J & McAlister, S (2013) 'Creating the right therapy vibe': relational performances in holistic medicine. *Social Science & Medicine* 83, 99–109.

Andrews, GJ, Kearns, RA, Kingsbury, P & Carr, ER (2011) Cool aid? Health, wellbeing and place in the work of Bono and U2. *Health & Place* 17, 185–94.

Andrews, GJ, Chen, S & Myers, S (2014) The 'taking place' of health and wellbeing: towards non-representational theory. *Social Science & Medicine* 108, 210–22.

Atkinson, S & Rubidge, T (2013) Managing the spatialities of arts-based practices with school children: an inter-disciplinary exploration of engagement, movement and well-being. *Arts & Health* 5, 39–50.

Barrett, FA (2000) *Disease & geography: the history of an idea.* Atkinson College, York University.

Bondi, L (2005) Making connections and thinking through emotions: between geography and psychotherapy. *Transactions of the Institute of British Geographers* 30, 433–88.

Braun, B (2007) Biopolitics and the molecularization of life. *Cultural Geographies* 14, 6–28.

Brown, T & Bell, M (2008) Imperial or postcolonial governance? Dissecting the genealogy of a global public health strategy. *Social Science & Medicine* 67, 1571–79.

Brown, T & Duncan, C (2002) Placing geographies of public health. *Area* 34, 361–69.

Brown, T & Duncan, C (2000) London's burning: recovering other geographies of health. *Health & Place* 6, 363–75.

Brown, T & Moon, G (2004) From Siam to New York: Jacques May and the 'foundation' of medical geography. *Journal of Historical Geography* 30, 747–63.

Cadman, L (2009) Autonomic non-representational theory/non-representational geographies. In: Kitchin, R & Thrift, N (Eds) *The international encyclopedia of human geography*. Elsevier, Oxford, 456–63.

Cliff, AD, Haggett, P & Smallman-Raynor, M (2000) Island epidemics. Oxford University Press, Oxford.

Cloutier-Fisher, D & Skinner, MW (2006) Levelling the playing field? Exploring the implications of managed competition for voluntary sector providers of long-term care in small town Ontario. *Health & Place* 12, 97–109.

Colls, R (2012) Feminism, bodily difference and non-representational geographies. *Transactions of the Institute of British Geographers* 37, 430–45.

Conradson, D (2005) Freedom, space and perspective: moving encounters with other ecologies. In: Davidson, J, Bondi, L & Smith, M (Eds) *Emotional geographies*. Ashgate, Aldershot, 103–16.

Craddock, S (2000) *City of plagues: disease, poverty and deviance in San Francisco*. University of Minnesota Press, Minneapolis, MN.

Cummins, S, Curtis, S, Diez-Roux, A & Macintyre, S (2007) Understanding and representing 'place' in health research: a relational approach. *Social Science & Medicine* 65, 1825–38.

Curtis, S, Gesler, W, Priebe, S & Francis, S (2009) New spaces of inpatient care for people with mental illness: a complex "rebirth" of the clinic? *Health & Place* 15, 340–48.

Darling, J (2009) Thinking beyond place: the responsibilities of a relational spatial politics. *Geography Compass* 3, 1938–54.

Deleuze, G (1988) *Spinoza: practical philosophy*. City Lights Books, San Francisco.

Dewsbury, JD (2009) Performative, non-representational and affect-based research: seven injunctions. In: Delyser, D, Aitken, S, Craig, M, Herbert, S & McDowell, L (Eds) *The Sage Handbook of qualitative geography*. Sage, London, 321–34.

Dirksmeier, P & Helbrecht, I (2008) Time, non-representational theory and the 'performative turn' – towards a new methodology in qualitative social research. *Forum: Qualitative Social Research* 9. Available at: http://www.qualitative-research.net/index.php/fqs/article/view/385/840. Accessed 9 November, 2016.

Dorn, M & Laws, G (1994) Social theory, body politics, and medical geography: extending Kearns's invitation. *The Professional Geographer* 46, 106–10.

Dorn, ML, Keirns, CC & del Casino Jr, VJ (2010) Doubting dualisms. In: Brown, T, McLafferty, S & Moon, G (Eds) *A companion to health and medical geography*. Wiley-Blackwell, Oxford, 59–78.

Duff, C (2014) Assemblages of health: Deleuze's empiricism and the ethology of life. Springer, Netherlands.

Duncan, C, Jones, K & Moon, G (1993) Do places matter? A multi-level analysis of regional variations in health-related behaviour in Britain. *Social Science & Medicine* 37, 725–33.

Duncan, C, Jones, K & Moon, G (1996) Health-related behaviour in context: a multilevel modelling approach. *Social Science & Medicine* 42, 817–30.

Duncan, C, Jones, K & Moon, G (1998) Context, composition and heterogeneity: using multilevel models in health research. *Social Science & Medicine* 46, 97–117.

Durie, R & Wyatt, K (2007) New communities, new relations: the impact of community organization on health outcomes. *Social Science & Medicine* 65, 1928–41.

Elden, S (2007) Governmentality, calculation, territory. *Environment and Planning D: Society and Space* 25, 562–80.

Eyles, J (1985) *Senses of place*. Silverbook Press, Warrington, UK.

Eyles, J (1990) How significant are the spatial configurations of health care systems? *Social Science & Medicine* 30, 157–64.

Eyles, J & Donovan, J (1986). Making sense of sickness and care: an ethnography of health in a West Midlands Town. *Transactions of the Institute of British Geographers* 11, 415–27.

Foley, R (2011) Performing health in place: the holy well as a therapeutic assemblage. *Health & Place* 17, 470–79.

Foucault, M (2009) *Security, territory, population: lectures at the College de France 1977-78.* Palgrave Macmillan, New York.

Gesler, WM (1986) The uses of spatial analysis in medical geography: a review. *Social Science & Medicine* 23, 963–73.

Gesler, WM (1991) *The cultural geography of health care.* University of Pittsburgh Press, Pittsburgh.

Gesler, WM (2005) Therapeutic landscapes: an evolving theme. *Health & Place* 11, 295–7.

Gesler, WM & Kearns, RA (2002) *Culture/place/health.* Routledge, London.

Greenhough, B (2011a) Assembling an island laboratory. *Area* 43, 134–8.

Greenhough, B (2011b) Citizenship, care and companionship: approaching geographies of health and bioscience. *Progress in Human Geography* 35, 153–71.

Greenhough, B & Roe, EJ (2011) Ethics, space, and somatic sensibilities: comparing relationships between scientific researchers and their human and animal experimental subjects. *Environment and Planning D: Society and Space* 29, 47–66.

Hall, E (2004) Social geographies of learning disability: narratives of exclusion and inclusion. *Area* 36, 298–306.

Higgs, G & Gould, M (2001) Is there a role for GIS in the 'new NHS'? *Health & Place* 7, 247–59.

Higgs, G, Smith, DP & Gould, M (2005) Findings from a survey on GIS use in the UK National Health Service: organisational challenges and opportunities. *Health Policy* 72, 105–17.

Jackson, P & Neely, AH (2015) Triangulating health: toward a practice of a political ecology of health. *Progress in Human Geography* 39, 47–64.

Jacobs, J & Nash, C (2003) Too little, too much: cultural feminist geographies. *Gender, Place and Culture* 10, 265–79.

Jones, K & Moon, G (1987) *Health, disease and society: an introduction to medical geography.* Routledge & Kegan Paul Ltd, London.

Jones, K & Moon, G (1993) Medical geography: taking space seriously. *Progress in Human Geography* 17, 515–24.

Jones, M (2009) Phase space: geography, relational thinking, and beyond. *Progress in Human Geography* 33, 487–506.

Joseph, AE & Chalmers, AL (1996) Restructuring long-term care and the geography of ageing: a view from rural New Zealand. *Social Science & Medicine* 42, 887–96.

Joseph, AE & Kearns, RA (1996) Deinstitutionalization meets restructuring: the closure of a psychiatric hospital in New Zealand. *Health & Place* 2, 179–89.

Joseph, AE & Phillips, DR (1984) *Accessibility and utilization: geographical perspectives on health care delivery.* Sage, London.

Kearns, RA (1991) The place of health in the health of place: the case of the Hokianga special medical area. *Social Science & Medicine* 33, 519–530.

Kearns, RA (1993) Place and health: towards a reformed medical geography. *The Professional Geographer* 46, 67–72.

Kearns, RA (1994) Putting health and health care into place: an invitation accepted and declined. *The Professional Geographer* 46, 111–5.

Kearns, RA (1995) Medical geography: making space for difference. *Progress in Human Geography* 19, 251–9.

Kearns, RA & Barnett, JR (2000) "Happy Meals" in the Starship Enterprise: interpreting a moral geography of health care consumption. *Health & Place* 6, 81–93.

Kearns, RA & Barnett, R (1997) Consumerist ideology and the symbolic landscapes of private medicine. *Health & Place* 3, 171–80.

Kearns, RA & Joseph, AE (1993) Space in its place: developing the link in medical geography. *Social Science & Medicine* 37, 711–7.

Keil, R & Ali, H (2006) Global cities and the spread of infectious disease: the case of severe acute respiratory syndrome (SARS) in Toronto, Canada. *Urban Studies* 43, 491–509.

Keil, R & Ali, H (2007) Governing the sick city: urban governance in the age of emerging infectious disease. *Antipode* 39, 846–73.

Kelly, S. E. (2003). Bioethics and rural health: theorizing place, space, and subjects. *Social Science & Medicine* 56, 2277–88.

King, B (2010) Political ecologies of health. *Progress in Human Geography* 34, 38–55.

Larsen, J (2008) Practices and flows of digital photography: an ethnographic framework. *Mobilities* 3, 141–60.

Lea, J, Cadman, L & Philo, C (2015) Changing the habits of a lifetime? Mindfulness meditation and habitual geographies. *Cultural Geographies* 22, 49–65.

Lorimer, H (2005) Cultural geography: the busyness of being 'more-than-representational.' *Progress in Human Geography* 29, 83–94.

Lorimer, H (2008) Cultural geography: nonrepresentational conditions and concerns. *Progress in Human Geography* 32, 551–9.

Macintyre, S, Ellaway, A & Cummins, S (2002) Place effects on health: how can we conceptualise, operationalise and measure them? *Social Science & Medicine* 55, 125–39.

McCormack, DP (2008) Geographies for moving bodies: thinking, dancing, spaces. *Geography Compass* 2, 1822–36.

McCormack, DP (2013) *Refrains for moving bodies: experience and experiment in affective spaces.* Duke University Press, Durham, NC.

McLafferty, S (1982) Neighborhood characteristics and hospital closures: a comparison of the public, private and voluntary hospital systems. *Social Science & Medicine* 16, 1667–74.

McLafferty, S (2003) GIS and health care. *Annual Review of Public Health* 24, 25–42.

May, JM (1959) *The ecology of human disease.* MD Publishing, New York.

Mayer, JD & Meade, MS (1994) A reformed medical geography reconsidered. *The Professional Geographer* 46, 103–6.

Meade, M & Earickson, RJ (2000) *Medical geography.* Guilford, New York.

Mohan, J (1998) Explaining the geography of health care: a critique. *Health & Place* 4, 113–24.

Mohan, J, Twigg, L, Barnard, S & Jones, K (2005) Social capital, geography and health: a small-area analysis for England. *Social Science & Medicine* 60, 1267–83.

Moon, G (1990) Conceptions of space and community in British health policy. *Social Science & Medicine* 30, 165–71.

Norris, P (1997) The state and the market: the impact of pharmacy licensing on the geographical distribution of pharmacies. *Health & Place* 3, 259–69.

Oppong, JR & Harold, A (2010) Disease, ecology and environment. In: Brown, T, McLafferty, S & Moon, G (Eds) *A companion to health and medical geography.* Wiley-Blackwell, Chichester, 181–95.

Ormond, M & Sothern, M (2012) You, too, can be an international medical traveler: reading medical travel guidebooks. *Health & Place*, 18, 935–41.

Pain, R (2006) Paranoid parenting? Rematerializing risk and fear for children. *Social and Cultural Geography* 7, 221–43.

Parr, H (2008) *Mental health and social space: towards inclusionary geographies.* Blackwell, Oxford.

Paterson, M (2005) Affecting touch: towards a felt phenomenology of therapeutic touch. In: Davidson, J, Bondi, L & Smith, M (Eds) *Emotional geographies.* Ashgate, Aldershot, 161–73.

Philo, C (2007) A vitally human medical geography? Introducing Georges Canguilhem to geographers. *New Zealand Geographer* 63, 82–96.

Philo, C (2012) A 'new Foucault' with lively implications – or 'the crawfish advances sideways.' *Transactions of the Institute of British Geographers* 37, 496–514.

Philo, C, Cadman, L & Lea, J (2014) New energy geographies: a case study of yoga, meditation and healthfulness. *Medical Humanities* 36, 35–46.

Popke, J (2009) Geography and ethics: nonrepresentational encounters, collective responsibility and economic difference. *Progress in Human Geography* 33, 81–90.

Pred, R (2005) *Onflow: dynamics of conscious experience*. MIT Press, Boston.

Relph, E (1976) *Place and placelessness*. Pion, London.

Rowland, EJ (2014) *Emotional geographies of care work in the NHS*. PhD Thesis, Department of Geography, Royal Holloway University of London.

Simpson, P (2014) A soundtrack to the everyday: street music and the production of convivial, healthy public spaces. In: Andrews, GJ, Kingsbury, P, Kearns, RA (Eds) *Soundscapes of wellbeing in popular music*. Ashgate, Aldershot.

Thien, D (2005) After or beyond feeling? A consideration of affect and emotion in geography. *Area* 37, 450–6.

Thrift, N (1997) The still point: resistance, expressive embodiment and dance. In: Pile, S & Keith, M (Eds) *Geographies of resistance*. Routledge, London, 124–51.

Thrift, N (2004) Intensities of feeling: towards a spatial politics of affect. *Geografiska Annaler B* 86, 57–78.

Thrift, N (2008) *Non-representational theory: space, politics, affect*. Routledge, London.

Timmons, S, Crosbie, B & Harrison-Paul, R (2010) Displacement of death in public space by lay people using the automated external defibrillator. *Health & Place* 16, 365–70.

Tolia-Kelly, D (2006) Affect – an ethnocentric encounter? Exploring the 'universalist' imperative of emotional/affectual geographies. *Area* 38, 213–7.

Tonnellier, F & Curtis, S (2005) Medicine, landscapes, symbols: "The Country doctor" by Honore de Balzac. *Health & Place* 11, 313–21.

Tuan, YF (1976) Humanistic geography. *Annals of the Association of American Geographers* 66, 266–76.

Tuan, YF (1979) *Space and place: the perspective of experience*. University of Minnesota Press, Minneapolis, MN.

Tucker, I (2010) Everyday spaces of mental distress: the spatial habituation of home. *Environment and Planning D: Society and Space* 28, 526–38.

Van Ingen, C (2003) Geographies of gender, sexuality and race reframing the focus on space in sport sociology. *International Review for the Sociology of Sport* 38, 201–16.

Vannini, P (2009) Non-representational theory and symbolic interactionism: shared perspectives and missed articulations. *Symbolic Interaction* 32, 282–6.

Vannini, P (2015) Non-representational research methodologies: an introduction. In: Vaninni, P (Ed) *Non-representational methodologies: re-envisioning research*. Routledge, London.

Wakefield, SE & Poland, B (2005) Family, friend or foe? Critical reflections on the relevance and role of social capital in health promotion and community development. *Social Science & Medicine* 60, 2819–32.

Williams, A (2007) *Therapeutic landscapes*. Ashgate, Aldershot.

Part II

Changing Spaces of (Health) Care

Chapter 4

Landscapes of Wellbeing

Introduction

Wellbeing is an idea important in political, economic, social and health realms and to a range of scientific and social scientific academic disciplines, human geography being no exception. Continuing a tradition set in place in the parent discipline, wellbeing has also been an important consideration of the reformed 'health geography', particularly over the past two decades. In the first half of this chapter, we consider how wellbeing has been broadly understood over time: its origin, empirical application and various critiques. In the second half, we move on to consider the specific and well-used sub-disciplinary concept of 'therapeutic landscapes', which is often employed by health geographers to describe a particular type of wellbeing experience associated with healing, recovery, restoration and place. In both cases the chapter looks to the future, pointing to the ways in which researchers have suggested that wellbeing and therapeutic landscapes might be understood and researched in the next generation of scholarship. In general this involves understanding them as active phenomena and, performed by bodies and objects in the moment.

Wellbeing: Its Emergence and Development

One of the first places from which wellbeing emerged and which launched it as a medical and popularly understood concept, was the World Health Organization's constitution, which famously defined health as 'a state of complete physical, mental and social well-being and not merely the absence of disease or infirmity' (WHO 1948). This was an important watershed moment because, for the very first time, and at the very highest levels of officialdom, it was recognised that the human condition included a positive state or experience that was definable and important unto itself. More recently, WHO has further positioned

Health Geographies: A Critical Introduction, First Edition. Tim Brown, Gavin J. Andrews, Steven Cummins, Beth Greenhough, Daniel Lewis, and Andrew Power.

wellbeing as part of mental good health and stability: 'defined as a state of well-being in which every individual realizes his or her own potential, can cope with the normal stresses of life, can work productively and fruitfully, and is able to make a contribution to her or his community' (WHO 2015, p. 1). As we shall see, such baseline statements have tended to inform, or at least foreground, the many different ways in which wellbeing is understood and mobilised. Indeed, wellbeing is now a concept that reoccurs across societies and is substantiated through public health discourses, government policy and economic activity, including patterns of production and consumption. Because of all this attention, wellbeing is part of the popular culture, being in the thoughts and conversations, and driving the actions, of people the world over.

A general consensus across approaches to, and conceptualisations of, wellbeing is that it is fundamentally about 'being-well' – contented, healthy and in a good place in life. However, although familiar, this is only a simple lay 'dictionary' understanding. As Gavin Andrews and colleagues (2014a) describe, beyond this, wellbeing is defined and utilised in multiple ways. At one level, wellbeing has surfaced as a subject in the language and statements of policy makers as something to be achieved and maintained through individual as well as collective action (see Atkinson et al. 2012). A materialist understanding has formed here – that improving a population's financial prosperity, and the range and quality of goods and services that people are able to purchase, increases wellbeing; the idea being simply that these goods and services can satisfy people's basic needs (such as food, shelter and good health) and assist them to live successfully. However very different, almost diametrically opposing, ideas exist on how this might be accomplished. While the political left has mobilised the idea of 'social wellbeing' to bolster arguments for the development of welfare systems (for example the UK Labour Party from the 1950s to at least the mid 1990s), the political right has utilised the idea of 'economic wellbeing' to support its neoliberal agenda for the distribution of resources through markets (for example, the UK Conservative Party since the 1980s).

At another level, connecting further to advanced capitalist economies, as well as with so-called 'emerging' ones, is a prevailing materialist mindset that associates the accumulation of wealth and consumption with wellbeing. Indeed, both creating and feeding a ravenous public appetite for all manner of goods and services, the private sector uses wellbeing in advertising products, and designs, promotes, circulates and sells specific commodities connected to wellbeing-promoting experiences and lifestyles (MacKian 2009). We are constantly told through advertising that particular foods, supplements, shampoos, clothing, vehicles, holidays, cosmetics, decorations and numerous household products are all critical to enhancing our wellbeing.

Lastly, related to all this but in a more personal and holistic sense, wellbeing exists in the minds and agency of significant numbers of people as a personal goal, and part of achieving and living the 'good life' (in other words, involving moral judgement, what they recognise to be a personally and socially 'responsible' life from both health and sustainability standpoints) (MacKian 2009; Kearns and Andrews 2010). This priority originated partly in the 'new age'/'spirituality' movement of the 1960s and 1970s, and, since the 1980s, has (re)surfaced in consumer trends towards complementary medicine (with its holistic attention to the mind and body). More recently, it has become associated with, and motivated by, the rise in the self-help and fitness movement which, although having many earlier historical and geographical precedents, really took off in most developed countries after the 1970s, and expanded into the mainstream culture it is today. Across both new age and fitness cultures it is believed that, as both a status and feeling, wellbeing can be attained through being responsible for, and assisting oneself mentally and physically (MacKian 2009).

It is not surprising that mirroring this widespread political, commercial and public concern for wellbeing, academics have also developed an interest in the concept (although they often use the term 'human happiness' instead to denote subjective wellbeing) (Duncan 2005, 2013; Stevenson and Wolfers 2008). Indeed, in this respect wellbeing is now just as much a well-used intellectual idea, appearing often across science, social science, and humanities literatures (Diener et al. 1999; de Chavez et al. 2005; Sointu 2005). Geography is no exception in this regard; the concept is frequently found across a broad range of empirical inquiry here (for reviews see Fleuret and Atkinson 2007; Kearns and Andrews 2010; Smith and Pain 2010; Atkinson et al. 2012).

If one looks hard enough and adopts very inclusive criteria, it is possible to find an interest in wellbeing in almost all historical paradigms and traditions in human geography. For example, studies of environment and heredity in geographical debates of the inter-war period were concerned with questions of wellbeing as much as they were with eugenics and 'race' (Gruffudd 1995). The British geographer, H. J. Fleure, for example, stated that '[t]hinking, then, of man [*sic*] as a continuous source of life and of effort, we realise that his effort tends to accomplish three essential functions, namely nutrition, reproduction, and the increase of well-being, or life, new life, and good life' (1919, p. 94). Here, Fleure questioned the influence of the environment on the human capacity to achieve wellbeing or the 'good life', a concern that saw him explore issues of acclimatisation and degeneration as well as race. However, many of these types of early engagements with wellbeing submerged the concept within much broader objectives; thus, wellbeing cannot be viewed as a particularly central motivation or feature of early geographical debates.

Although still not particularly reflexive or focused, a more explicit engagement with wellbeing can be traced to the early 1970s in three emerging areas of scholarship: two theoretically driven, the other largely empirically driven. In terms of the former, a concern for wellbeing arose in radical Marxist geography's objective to expose the structures and causes of social and economic inequality in cities (Harvey 1973; Castells 1983). The idea here is that human wellbeing can be maximised through liberating workers from their exploited positions in unequal labour relations, allowing them to maximise their skills and ensuring that they are compensated fairly in line with their true productive value. Moreover, a concern for wellbeing arose in humanistic geography's desire to uncover the essence of human conditions and experiences (Tuan 1977). Indeed, the argument here is that if humans, and what is meaningful and significant to them, are meant to be front and centre of research inquiry, what makes them happy and content and maximises their creative potential are also important considerations. Meanwhile, in terms of the latter, a concern for wellbeing also arose within the establishing welfare geography of the same period (Conradson 2012). Here, set within a general concern for social and spatial inequalities in wealth, life chances and resources across populations, early discussions of 'life satisfaction' and 'quality of life' emerged, and in particular their measurement within defined areas (e.g. Smith 1973). In sum, given these three engagements and their timing in relation to the broader history of the discipline, one might argue that wellbeing at one stage existed at the very 'heart' of the majority of post-positivistic human geography.

Although Marxist, humanistic and welfare geography have, in more recent decades, either been superseded or dissolved into the broader disciplinary mix of approaches, there has been an increasing concern for wellbeing and an expanding empirical engagement with its spatial components and manifestations. While this can be traced across many subject fields – such as environmental justice, geopolitics, geographies of war, public geographies and many others – it is particularly evident across the sub-disciplines of social geography and health geography (Kearns and Andrews 2010). Initially at least, rather than refining geography's engagements with wellbeing and deepening conceptual understandings of it, researchers working in these two sub-disciplines broadened its empirical application. For example, in addition to more traditional foci (e.g. the environmental influences on wellbeing – see Chapter 8, or the impact of social care policy and practice – see Chapter 6) their research started to cover areas such as alternative medicines and lifestyles (e.g. Williams 1998; Andrews 2003), happiness, friendship and spirituality (e.g. Bunnell et al. 2012; MacKian 2012), as well as cultural practices such as in art and music (e.g. Parr 2006; Andrews et al. 2014b).

Notably, in addition to the above engagement with what might be considered the more positive aspects of wellbeing, researchers in health and social geography have considered the negative or 'wellbeing reducing' aspects of life. There has been a long-term focus on what is unjust and causes hardship for people, such as inequality, poverty, isolation and exclusion (i.e. what detracts from a person's wellbeing and the ways in which they live with, or escape, the life situations that challenge them). As Robin Kearns and Damian Collins (2010) have cautioned, in turning to wellbeing geographers must remain alert to social inequalities and the broader structural factors that help shape a person's life chances (see also Schrecker and Bambra 2015). Moreover, they must continue to adopt a place-sensitive perspective that emphasises the ways in which local processes – including those relating to the unequal and often inequitable experience of power relations (relating to age, class, gender, race/ethnicity, sexuality and so on) – shape the 'meaning of wellbeing, and the opportunities for it to be realized' (2010, p. 27). In this sense, then, there was a call from Kearns and Collins for health geographers concerned with wellbeing to retain critical agendas.

Given the diversity of the aforementioned topics, one challenge with considering wellbeing in geography becomes deciding the 'cut off' point with regard to what does and does not constitute a specifically wellbeing focus. Moreover, much of this broad engagement with wellbeing, although insightful into particular empirical situations and contexts, rarely defines, explores or evaluates the concept itself. Indeed, most often wellbeing is itself only a partial consideration and/or the understanding of wellbeing is assumed, the term being used in its most everyday/lay sense (Pain and Smith 2010). The difficulty with this approach is that one never moves towards a better understanding of wellbeing beyond a creeping empirical coverage of its manifestation: one only adds to a long and increasing list of places where and when wellbeing, as quite rudimentarily understood, does or does not arise. Subsequently, incorrect assumptions can be made. Rachel Pain and Sarah Smith (2010) note, for example, that the mere incidence of known facilitators or detractors of wellbeing does not necessarily mean that wellbeing will be increased or decreased in a given context. Indeed, curing a disease does not mean that a person or population feels healthy, and providing an environment deemed to be therapeutic does not necessarily provide everybody with a sense of healing and recovery. The result then of empiricism underpinned by only a general notion of wellbeing is that wellbeing explains almost anything, yet nothing explains wellbeing (Pain and Smith 2010; Andrews et al. 2014a).

Wellbeing in health geography: Recent critical engagements

The engagement with wellbeing has deepened theoretically in recent years through the scholarship of a small number of researchers who have begun to consider the concept far more directly. Underlying their work has been a basic realisation that 'place matters' to the contexts, unravelling and experience of wellbeing (Kearns and Collins 2010; Pain and Smith 2010). We mentioned previously that, in a literal sense, wellbeing implies *being* well, but as Robin Kearns and Gavin Andrews (2010) observe, *being* as a state of existence can only be achieved through place (everyone and everything necessarily being somewhere in space and time). From observations such as these emerges the fundamental question, what is wellbeing and how does it occur? In terms of answers, a consensus seems to be that wellbeing is a state of mental and physical health and welfare attained in some way by fulfilling personal needs. Indeed, Sébastien Fleuret and Sarah Atkinson (2007) draw on classical psychological theory (see Maslow 1954) to describe a three-tiered hierarchy of needs, topped by those that are vital to human existence (e.g. clean air and water, food and shelter), and followed by those that are spiritual and emotional in orientation (e.g. knowing people and sharing identity with them) as well as those that are more materialistic and consumer-related (e.g. going on vacations, owning a car). There is recognition amongst scholars, however, that needs-based theories of wellbeing are inadequate on their own as they do not recognise human variability either in terms of desires, values and preferences (realised in choices) or in terms of capacities and restrictions (realised as limitations) (Fleuret and Atkinson 2007). Indeed, this understanding connects to recent debates on social capital in health and human geography, with regard to how wellbeing is unlocked and mobilised through collective understandings and mutually supportive collective activities (e.g. Mohan and Mohan 2002; Wakefield and Poland 2005).

In terms of a continuing critique, Fleuret and Atkinson develop a research agenda on wellbeing that sets out three further questions that, they feel, need to be answered by geographers and others. First, where do different forms of wellbeing arise? Second, how do space and/or the nature of place influence wellbeing in specific situations? Third, how are wellbeing, space and place contested? Fleuret and Atkinson engage with the first and second of these questions by developing a potential empirical research programme around four spaces where wellbeing is created: (i) spaces of human capacity (that assist and amplify wellbeing); (ii) integrative spaces or networks (that spread wellbeing); (iii) spaces of security (that provide refuge and support); and (iv), therapeutic spaces (that facilitate healing). In a recent edited collection, Sarah Atkinson, Sara Fuller and Jo Painter (2012) actively take up this agenda and programme. Whilst certain chapters consider the qualities of place that are thought to produce or change wellbeing, others probe different assumptions on wellbeing and highlight power imbalances and other inequalities. Meanwhile, others consider specific approaches and routes to wellbeing such as through activism, nationhood and international development.

As Andrews and colleagues (2014a) argue, whilst it is encouraging that geographers are now deconstructing wellbeing and analysing it directly, arguably they could go further. The emphasis of their scholarship has been on how wellbeing is achieved as a state of life, and is associated with meaning (how it has meaning or is reached through things that have meaning). However, research has yet to consider two areas. The first is the processual aspects of how wellbeing arises in space-time. In other words, research currently pays attention to spatial constitutions and configurations that are thought to be engaged by individuals where and when wellbeing arises (Conradson 2012), but it is time to push inquiry further and think about these spatial constitutions and configurations as active performances – how they 'take place'. The second area is how wellbeing feels, both on fully conscious and less-than-fully conscious experiential levels, particularly in the moment. With regard to both these areas, the suggestion is that wellbeing emerges often unexpectedly in everyday situations, as a basic but very familiar 'feeling state'; a sense of happiness and contentment

---

Box 4.1   Key Themes: Types of Wellbeing

Wellbeing can be thought of in terms of typologies associated with particular political philosophies; for example, we might think of economic wellbeing as something associated with neoliberalism or social wellbeing as a concern of the political left. Similarly, emotional or psychological wellbeing is most often associated with the philosophy of the so-called 'new age movement'. Wellbeing can also be considered in terms of something that humans (and of course non-humans) possess or feel. As such, wellbeing is something that is measured and categorised within social science research and by governments concerned with the 'wellbeing' of the populations in their territories. For example, in the United Kingdom, the Coalition Government, which was made up of the Conservative party and the Liberal Democrats, introduced a programme on *Measuring National Well-being* at the beginning of their period in power (2010–2015). Delivered by the Office for National Statistics (ONS), the UK's leading producer of official statistics, the programme was set up to 'develop and publish an accepted and trusted set of National Statistics which help people understand and monitor well-being'. The ONS suggest that wellbeing can be described as '"how we are doing"' as individuals, as communities and as a nation, and how sustainable this is for the future' (ONS 2015, p. 1). A snapshot report published in March 2015 by the ONS, the third in a series, revealed that of the indicators of wellbeing measured – which include 41 headline measures organised into 10 domains (e.g. Health, Where we live, What we do, Our relationships and so on) – 33 per cent had improved, 42 per cent had remained the same and 5 per cent had deteriorated. For example, healthy life expectancy had improved over the period 2010–11 to 2013–14 but levels of moderate intensity exercise had deteriorated between 2012–13 and 2013–14 (the latter perhaps indicating the limited lifespan of the Olympic legacy). In addition to considering what such data tell us about the state of wellbeing in a nation, as critical health geographers we might ask what such a programme of research tells us about questions of inequality as well as about forms of (neoliberal) biopolitical rule that operate in a society.

---

that arises and then passes. In such situations, wellbeing stems from interactions between humans and non-humans and, from a post-humanistic standpoint, might be considered a result of particular environmental assemblages (see Box 4.1).

Therapeutic Landscapes: Definitions and Beginnings

In this and subsequent sections, we move our attention from health geography's engagement with the broad idea of 'wellbeing' to its focus on the more specific yet closely related concept of therapeutic landscapes. The notion of 'therapeutic' has been subject to multiple and often very broad definitions across academic disciplines and health specialties. In general practice medicine, for example, it relates to almost any treatment a doctor prescribes or recommends (known as 'therapeutic intervention'): in nursing, to both short and long term interpersonal interactions (known as 'therapeutic communication' and 'the therapeutic relationship'); and, in mental health care, to a shared team approach to care (known as 'therapeutic community'). However, for a great deal of research across the health and social sciences, therapeutic is used to describe a particular feeling, related variously to experiences such as 'healing', 'relaxation', 'restoration', 'contentment' and 'being at peace'. It is this understanding of therapeutic, and its relation to feelings and experiences of wellbeing in place, that geographers have spoken to when developing the concept of 'therapeutic landscapes'. In doing this they have been able to simultaneously focus and 'ground' their studies of wellbeing.

The therapeutic landscapes concept was first introduced to geographers in a position paper by the American health geographer, Wilbert Gesler, twenty five years ago (Gesler 1992); this paper was quickly followed up with the publication of an illustrative case study one year later (see Gesler, 1993). Gesler was attempting to bring medical geography – at that time predominantly a positivistic quantitative endeavour – up to speed with the 'new cultural geography' of the period. Taking a broad theoretical sweep, Gesler drew on, and blended, humanistic geography (and the ideas of 'sense of place' and 'symbolic places') and structuralism (and the ideas of 'territoriality' and 'hegemony') in his arguments for research that would pay attention to the psychological, social, cultural and economic processes in how the healing process works out in place, and in how certain places become known for their healing qualities. Gesler's idea was clearly to encourage a new research agenda, yet even he could not have predicted exactly how influential his concept would become. By 2017 his original 1992 paper had been cited over 700 times by other academic publications and the therapeutic landscapes concept has been the subject of many review articles (e.g. Smyth 2005), edited collections (Williams 1999, 2007a), and dedicated single-authored books on healing (e.g. Foley 2010). In this regard, the concept is, without doubt, a fundamental feature of the turns from medical geography towards broader health geography and from quantitative methods to qualitative and mixed methods approaches. With this in mind, the following sub-sections provide further discussion of therapeutic landscapes and how the concept has been mobilised empirically, developed and also critiqued.

Therapeutic landscapes: Substantive areas of empirical inquiry

Although there are many ways of categorising the empirical interests of therapeutic landscape research, broadly speaking two 'person-focused' themes have emerged alongside three 'place-focused' ones. With regard to the former, research has considered different life contexts and changes through which therapeutic landscapes are encountered or sought. For example, studies have considered the experiences of migrants and refugees, and specifically the importance of place-making practices, in the creation of therapeutic landscapes for promoting restoration and recovery (e.g. Gastaldo et al. 2004; Sampson and Gifford 2010). Research in this vein has also considered the formation of therapeutic landscapes that act to support people through the emotional experiences associated with illness and corresponding treatment journeys (e.g. Donovan and Williams 2007; English et al. 2008). On another level, 'people-centred' research has considered different belief systems that map onto place and are often associated with, and perhaps give rise to, therapeutic landscapes. Studies have considered, for example, the cultural norms amongst developing world populations (e.g. Sperling and Decker 2007) and in first nations/indigenous people and populations (e.g. Wilson 2003; Wendt and Gone 2012), and the theories and philosophies underpinning holistic medicine and lifestyles and how these help to constitute therapeutic landscapes (e.g. Andrews 2004; Hoyez 2007a, 2007b; Lea 2008).

Of the place-focused themes, the first explores what might be broadly termed 'natural environments', with studies in this area considering the convergence between settings that support some degree of engagement with 'nature' and the promotion of health and healing (e.g. parks and gardens, woodland and wilderness spaces; see Palka 1999; Milligan et al. 2004; Milligan and Bingley 2007). There is a close link between this research and the emerging general focus across many disciplines on the therapeutic qualities of green spaces and it is this interconnection that has arguably seen the concept adopted in a much wider range of academic debates as well as in policy discourses (e.g. Maas et al. 2006; Lee and Maheswaran 2011; Ward-Thompson 2011).

The second place-focused theme, 'designed and built spaces', is far better represented in terms of research outputs and is concerned with the creation and promotion of therapeutic landscapes through medical and political ideas, economic conditions and private sector ideology and enterprise. Particular attention has been paid here to the promotion of healing through improvements in design a range of health care settings; for example, through the use of colour, light and art in hospitals (e.g. Gesler et al. 2004; Curtis et al. 2007; Gesler and Curtis 2007) and within primary health care spaces (Crooks and Evans 2007; Evans et al. 2009). Outside of health care settings, the importance of design to the idea of therapeutic landscapes has also been explored through attention to a range of other settings, including children's health camps (Kearns and Collins 2000), former mental asylums (Moon et al. 2006), contemporary spas (Little 2013) and sites of community heritage (Power and Smyth 2016). As the above topics suggest, a full range of geographical scales can be found in this literature, with studies focusing in on the home (Williams 2002; Donovan and Williams 2007), on specialist spaces such as spiritual retreats (Gesler 1996, 2003; Conradson 2007; Williams 2010), through to work on neighbourhoods and even towns (e.g. Andrews and Kearns 2005; Wilton and DeVerteuil 2006; Foley et al. 2011).

A third and final place-focused theme extends this spatiality further; that is, certain research has focused on 'imagined places' (the virtuality and multiplicity of place). Here, the emphasis is on places that are not necessarily materially present or existent but are imaginary, often purposefully created for escape, relaxation or for the promotion of psychological resilience. Studies in this area have considered, for example, places evoked in fictional writing (Gesler 2000; Baer and Gesler 2004; Tonnellier and Curtis 2005; Williams 2007b), places evoked in therapy sessions (Andrews 2004), soundscapes arising in popular music (Andrews et al. 2011; Andrews et al. 2014b; Evans 2014) and past places that are mobilised in the memories of mobile populations such as migrants (e.g. Gastaldo et al. 2004).

Therapeutic landscapes: Progressive development

Progress has clearly occurred in therapeutic landscape research, we would argue, through two 'eras', the first being 1992 to approximately 2005, characterised by incremental empirical development, and the second being approximately 2005 onwards (characterised by piecemeal critical interventions).

The first era, 1992–2005

As Smyth (2005) describes, the first era of therapeutic landscape research is constituted by three consecutive but overlapping sub-phases of research. The first looked at exceptional, obvious, important, longstanding and mostly well-known places such as Lourdes in France,

Bath in England and Hot Springs Dakota in the United States. These places were positioned for the most part as unchanging therapeutic backdrops affecting generations of visitors (Gesler 1996, 1998; Geores 1998). This approach is reflected by Gesler's (1993, p. 171) original description of therapeutic landscapes as 'places which have attained an enduring reputation for achieving physical, mental, and spiritual healing'. In contrast, the second phase, realising the shortfalls in the first (see Wilson 2003), involved the concept of therapeutic landscapes being applied to a much wider variety of normal/everyday/common places, including greater emphasis on human and market interactions with place (for example, to health care settings, considering the preferences of 'consumers' and the corporate ideology of 'providers'; Kearns and Barnett 1999a, 1999b, 2000). The third phase meanwhile, mirroring the emerging 'relational turn' in the parent discipline at the time, emphasised networks of various kinds in therapeutic landscapes, for example of care and support between people and/ or of types and scales of settings and/or of types of medicine (e.g. Andrews 2004; Del Casino 2004). This critical phase foregrounded and informed the second and current era in therapeutic landscape research, and continues to resonate today.

The second era, 2005 onwards

The second era of therapeutic landscape research has typically involved individual authors presenting a critique of the existing literature before moving on to address gaps in inquiry they just highlighted, often through focused empirical research. This era has, though, arguably seen most critical progress. At one level, studies have addressed the lack of attention in research to existing (known) processes and structures in society such as gender (Love et al. 2012; Little 2013), global connections and relations (Hoyez 2007a, 2007b) and 'nature' as an active participant in the co-construction of therapeutic experiences (Lea 2008). At another level, studies have considered the anti-therapeutic effects of certain places and/or the possibility that unplanned, dangerous and sometimes unpleasant experiences and places can actually be part of the therapeutic landscape (having opposite and/or both effects). For example, we might all be able to think of some urban environments that are fun yet also 'edgy' and threatening (Laws 2009); woodlands that are therapeutic as well as isolating, scary and potentially dangerous (Milligan 2007; Milligan and Bingley 2007); places of internment that incorporate both brutal and safe spaces (DeVerteuil and Andrews 2007); places of sexual pleasure, that are 'safe' spaces but, at the same time, are 'risky' in terms of the transmission of infectious disease (Andrews and Holmes 2007). The list here is seemingly endless: smoking spaces that are mentally therapeutic and physically harmful (Wood et al. 2013); first nations' reserves that are both spiritually uplifting yet contaminated with pollutants (Smith et al. 2010); sunbathing on beaches which is fun and relaxing yet also a cancer risk (Collins and Kearns 2007); and zoos that are fun and ambient for human visitors but traumatic for captive animals (Hallman 2007).

This second era of research has also seen some precise attention to how therapeutic landscapes might arise and work, again largely through the 'note a gap then fill that gap' approach in research. Studies have considered for example media mechanisms and roles (MacKian 2008), psychoanalytic explanations and processes (Evans et al. 2009; Rose 2012), psychological relationality between place and the self (Conradson 2005; Evans et al. 2009), the performed relationality of bodies and objects in specific assemblages (Foley 2010, 2011; Andrews 2014), individual and shared movement in space-time (Doughty 2013; Gatrell 2013), and the importance of rhythms and sounds (Conradson 2007; Evans 2014).

Finally, the second era has witnessed a greater degree of inter- and even trans-disciplinarity in the application of the therapeutic landscape concept. This has always had some precedent as other disciplines have developed their own 'versions' of therapeutic landscapes, for example in design and architecture (Day et al. 2000), environmental psychology (Reser 1995; Winkel and Holahan 1985; Whitehouse et al. 2001) and more recently anthropology (Hampshire et al. 2011; Naraindas and Bastos 2011). The difference, however, is that these disciplines are now actively debating and mixing their ideas with geographers (and vice versa) as exemplified by chapters in Williams' 2007 edited collection (Williams 2007a). This said, beyond the social sciences, therapeutic landscapes has yet to be connected to many aligned concepts and debates in the health sciences, namely therapeutic interventions, therapeutic communication, therapeutic relationships and therapeutic community (Andrews and Evans 2008). Indeed, these are important concepts as they drive numerous areas of contemporary clinical practice and help determine the treatment and experiences of patients during health care.

Therapeutic landscapes: Critiques

Therapeutic landscapes has had its detractors, perhaps not always voicing their opinions in print, but often in conversations at meetings and conferences. There are scholars who think it should have been a 'one and done' paper in 1992 and/or that things have not progressed as they could have. One line of criticism surrounds the title itself: that on one level there has never been a full examination and explanation of the meaning of 'therapeutic' (it being subject to very different historical and contemporary interpretations) and that, on another level, 'landscape' is the wrong metaphor as it evokes something remote, 'elsewhere', apart from the body.

Even more concerning for some is the lack of 'internal' theoretical progression beyond a creeping empirical coverage, the term therapeutic landscape being reapplied again and again as a basic descriptive 'bumper sticker' to legitimize studies (Andrews 2004). The concern here is that, as a consequence of this labelling, theory rarely moves beyond specific ideas relating to the specific empirical subject of the day. As a result then, almost everything is explained by therapeutic landscapes but nothing explains therapeutic landscapes. Indeed, Alison Williams, in the introduction to her 2007 edited collection, celebrates the concept's growth, flexibility and wide-ranging potential (Williams 2007a). However, one could easily claim that all of these assets arise precisely because the term therapeutic landscapes is so general, it being very easily attached as a basic descriptor without saying too much else. Indeed, Williams notes that therapeutic landscapes is one of the few unique contributions that health geographers have made to the human geography. However, given the aforementioned issues and shortfalls, some might consider this to be a sign of the sub-discipline's theoretical weaknesses rather than of its strengths (for a discussion on theory in health geography see Kearns and Moon 2002; Andrews et al. 2012). A generic problem, that is to some extent insurmountable, is that therapeutic landscapes is only a concept. As such, it is always going to be limited in what it can say, in contrast, for example, to methodologies, or theoretical traditions, which are often more substantive, intricate and well explained.

Certainly the therapeutic landscapes concept seems to have lost some momentum in recent years, perhaps because of an inevitable weariness that comes with anything that is no longer new and is well used. This is particularly observable in academic conversations, at meetings, in its increasing absence in the new work of graduate students and in the lack of dedicated conference sessions. In some quarters, therapeutic landscapes has even become a topic of derision. In terms of the future then, just as Gesler (1992, 2005) drew therapeutic landscapes out of the emerging cultural geography and social constructionism of the period to help health geography 'catch up with the parent discipline', scholars might now draw a new line of therapeutic landscape inquiry out of the post-human, new materialist, relational and more-than representational thinking at the forefront of contemporary human geography once again to help health geography catch up (Duff 2011). Thus, a new generation of critical health geographers could rejuvenate the concept, lest it fade away into the rich history of the sub-discipline.

Conclusion

The idea of wellbeing is longstanding both in academic research and society at large. Mirroring this, geographers have over the years engaged in multiple ways, developing different understandings as to how wellbeing is produced and is realised spatially. They have also developed their own concepts and ideas related to wellbeing, one of the most notable and popular of these being therapeutic landscapes. As we have discussed in this chapter, the therapeutic landscapes concept has gone through various stages of development since its initial introduction in the writing of Wilbert Gesler. For some scholars, it has continued value, especially as researchers have begun to apply it beyond the obvious sites and places with which it was initially associated. Yet it does remain a contested and controversial concept and it is thus important to consider the arguments raised against it as well as those put forward in its favour. Indeed, it might be argued that critical scholarship has made important contributions to the understanding of wellbeing in general, and the therapeutic landscapes concept in particular, and that this must continue if geographers are to develop these areas further.

Questions for Review

1. How has wellbeing been recognised and valued differently by society?
2. How have geographers understood wellbeing and in what ways has it been embedded in their research?
3. How and in what ways are places therapeutic to people and populations?

Suggested Reading

Atkinson, S, Fuller, S & Painter, J (Eds) (2012) *Wellbeing and place*. Ashgate, Aldershot.
Gesler, WM (1992) Therapeutic landscapes: medical issues in light of the new cultural geography. *Social Science & Medicine* 34, 735–46.
Smyth, F (2005) Medical geography: therapeutic places, spaces and networks. *Progress in Human Geography* 29, 488–95.
Williams, A (Ed) (2007) *Therapeutic landscapes*. Ashgate, Aldershot.

References

Andrews, GJ (2003) Placing the consumption of private complementary medicine: everyday geographies of older peoples' use. *Health & Place* 9, 337–49.

Andrews, GJ (2004) (Re)thinking the dynamics between healthcare and place: therapeutic geographies in treatment and care practices. *Area* 36, 307–18.

Andrews, GJ (2014) Co-creating health's lively, moving frontiers: brief observations on the facets and possibilities of non-representational theory. *Health & Place* 30, 165–70.

Andrews, GJ & Evans, J (2008) Understanding the reproduction of health care: towards geographies in health care work. *Progress in Human Geography* 32, 759–80.

Andrews, GJ & Holmes, D (2007) Gay bathhouses: transgressions of health in therapeutic places. In: Williams, A (Ed) *Therapeutic landscapes*. Ashgate, Aldershot, 221–32.

Andrews, GJ, & Kearns, RA (2005) Everyday health histories and the making of place: the case of an English coastal town. *Social Science & Medicine* 60, 2697–713.

Andrews, GJ, Evans, J, Dunn, JR & Masuda, JR (2012) Arguments in health geography: on subdisciplinary progress, observation, translation. *Geography Compass* 6, 351–83.

Andrews, GJ, Chen, S & Myers, S (2014a) The 'taking place' of health and wellbeing: towards non-representational theory. *Social Science & Medicine* 108, 210–22.

Andrews, GJ, Kearns, RA, Kingsbury, P & Carr, ER (2011) Cool aid? Health, wellbeing and place in the work of Bono and U2. *Health & Place* 17, 185–94.

Andrews GJ, Kingsbury P, Kearns RA (Eds) (2014b) *Soundscapes of and wellbeing in popular music*. Ashgate, Aldershot.

Atkinson, S, Fuller, S & Painter, J (Eds) (2012) *Wellbeing and place*. Ashgate, Aldershot.

Baer, LD & Gesler, WM (2004) Reconsidering the concept of therapeutic landscapes in JD Salinger's The Catcher in the Rye. *Area* 36, 404–13.

Bunnell, T, Yea, S, Peake, L, Skelton, T & Smith, M (2012) Geographies of friendships. *Progress in Human Geography* 36, 490–507.

Castells, M (1983) Crisis, planning, and the quality of life: managing the new historical relationships between space and society. *Environment and Planning D: Society and Space* 1, 3–22.

Collins, D & Kearns, R (2007) Ambiguous landscapes: sun, risk and recreation on New Zealand beaches. In: Williams, A (Ed) *Therapeutic landscapes*. Ashgate, Aldershot, 15–32.

Conradson, D (2005) Landscape, care and the relational self: therapeutic encounters in rural England. *Health & Place* 11, 337–48.

Conradson, D (2007) The experiential economy of stillness: places of retreat in contemporary Britain. In: Williams, A (Ed) *Therapeutic landscapes*. Ashgate, Aldershot, 33–47.

Conradson, D (2012) Wellbeing: reflections on geographical engagements. In: Atkinson, S, Fuller, S & Painter, J (Eds) *Wellbeing and place*. Ashgate, Aldershot, 15–34.

Crooks, VA & Evans, J (2007) The writing's on the wall: decoding the interior space of the hospital waiting room. In: Williams, A (Ed) *Therapeutic landscapes*. Ashgate, Aldershot, 165–80.

Curtis, S, Gesler, WM, Fabian, K, Francis, S & Priebe, S (2007) Therapeutic landscapes in hospital design: a qualitative assessment by staff and service users of the design of a new mental health inpatient unit. *Environment and Planning C: Government and Policy* 25, 591–610.

Day, K, Carreon, D, & Stump, C (2000) The therapeutic design of environments for people with dementia a review of the empirical research. *The Gerontologist* 40, 397–416.

de Chavez, AC, Backett-Milburn, K, Parry, O & Platt, S (2005) Understanding and researching wellbeing: its usage in different disciplines and potential for health research and health promotion. *Health Education Journal* 64, 70–87.

Del Casino, VJ (2004) (Re)placing health and health care: mapping the competing discourses and practices of 'traditional' and 'modern' Thai medicine. *Health & Place* 10, 59–73.

DeVerteuil, G & Andrews, G (2007) Surviving profoundly unhealthy places: the ambivalent, fragile and absent therapeutic landscapes of the Soviet gulag. In: Williams, A (Ed) *Therapeutic landscapes*. Ashgate, Aldershot, 273–87.

Diener, E, Suh, EM, Lucas, RE & Smith, HL (1999) Subjective well-being: three decades of progress. *Psychological Bulletin* 125, 276–302.

Donovan, R & Williams, A (2007) Home as therapeutic landscape: family caregivers providing palliative care at home. In: Williams, A (Ed) *Therapeutic landscapes*. Ashgate, Aldershot, 199–218.

Doughty, K (2013) Walking together: the embodied and mobile production of a therapeutic landscape. *Health & Place* 24, 140–6.

Duff, C (2011) Networks, resources and agencies: On the character and production of enabling places. *Health & Place* 17(1), 149–56.

Duncan, G (2005) What do we mean by "happiness"? The relevance of subjective wellbeing to social policy. *Social Policy Journal of New Zealand* 25, 16–31.

Duncan, G (2013) Politics, paradoxes and pragmatics of happiness. *Culture, Theory and Critique* 55, 1–17.

English, J, Wilson, K & Keller-Olaman, S (2008) Health, healing and recovery: therapeutic landscapes and the everyday lives of breast cancer survivors. *Social Science & Medicine* 67, 68–78.

Evans, JD (2014) Painting therapeutic landscapes with sound: on land by Brian Eno. In: Andrews G J, Kingsbury P, Kearns RA (Eds) *Soundscapes of and wellbeing in popular music*. Ashgate, Aldershot, 173–90.

Evans, JD, Crooks, VA & Kingsbury, PT (2009) Theoretical injections: on the therapeutic aesthetics of medical spaces. *Social Science & Medicine* 69, 716–21.

Fleure, HJ (1919) Human regions. *Scottish Geographical Magazine* 35, 94–105.

Fleuret, S & Atkinson, S (2007) Wellbeing, health and geography: a critical review and research agenda. *New Zealand Geographer* 63, 106–18.

Foley, R (2010) *Healing waters: therapeutic landscapes in historic and contemporary Ireland*. Ashgate, Aldershot.

Foley, R (2011) Performing health in place: the holy well as a therapeutic assemblage. *Health & Place* 17, 470–9.

Foley, R, Wheeler, A & Kearns, R (2011) Selling the colonial spa town: the contested therapeutic landscapes of Lisdoonvarna and Te Aroha. *Irish Geography* 44, 151–72.

Gastaldo, D, Andrews, GJ & Khanlou, N (2004) Therapeutic landscapes of the mind: theorizing some intersections between health geography, health promotion and immigration studies. *Critical Public Health* 14, 157–76.

Gatrell, AC (2013) Therapeutic mobilities: walking and 'steps' to wellbeing and health. *Health & Place* 22, 98–106.

Geores, ME (1998) Surviving on metaphor: how "Health = Hot springs" created and sustained a town. In: Kearns, RA & Gesler, WM (Eds) *Putting health into place: landscape, identity and well-being*. Syracuse University Press, Syracuse, NY, 36–52.

Gesler, WM (1992) Therapeutic landscapes: medical issues in light of the new cultural geography. *Social Science & Medicine* 34, 735–46.

Gesler, WM (1993) Therapeutic landscapes: theory and a case study of Epidauros, Greece. *Environment and Planning D: Society & Space* 11, 171–89.

Gesler, WM (1996) Lourdes: healing in a place of pilgrimage. *Health & Place* 2, 95–105.

Gesler, WM (1998) Bath's reputation as a healing place. In: Kearns, RA & Gesler, WM (Eds) *Putting health into place: landscape, identity and well-being*. Syracuse University Press, Syracuse, NY, 17–35.

Gesler, WM (2000) Hans Castorp's journey-to-knowledge of disease and health in Thomas Mann's The Magic Mountain. *Health & Place* 6, 125–34.

Gesler, WM (2003) *Healing places*. Rowman & Littlefield, Lanham, MD.

Gesler, WM (2005) Therapeutic landscapes: an evolving theme. *Health & Place* 11, 295–7.

Gesler, WM & Curtis, S (2007) Application of concepts of therapeutic landscapes to the design of hospitals in the UK: the example of a mental health facility in London. In: Williams, A (Ed) *Therapeutic landscapes*. Ashgate, Aldershot, 149–64.

Gesler, WM, Bell, M, Curtis, S, Hubbard, P & Francis, S (2004) Therapy by design: evaluating the UK hospital building program. *Health & Place* 10, 117–28.

Gruffudd, P (1995) Remaking Wales: nation-building and the geographical imagination, 1925-1950. *Political Geography* 14, 219–39.

Hallman, B (2007) A "family-friendly" place: family leisure, identity and wellbeing – the Zoo as therapeutic landscape. In: Williams, A (Ed) *Therapeutic landscapes*. Ashgate, Aldershot, 133–45.

Hampshire, KR, Porter, G, Owusu, SA, Tanle, A & Abane, A (2011) Out of the reach of children? Young people's health-seeking practices and agency in Africa's newly-emerging therapeutic landscapes. *Social Science & Medicine* 73, 702–10.

Harvey, D (1973) *Social justice and the city*. University of Georgia Press, London.

Hoyez, AC (2007a) The 'world of yoga': the production and reproduction of therapeutic landscapes. *Social Science & Medicine* 65, 112–24.

Hoyez, AC (2007b) From Rishikesh to Yogaville: the globalization of therapeutic landscapes. In: Williams, A (Ed) *Therapeutic landscapes*. Ashgate, Aldershot, 49–64.

Kearns, RA & Andrews, GJ (2010) *Geographies of wellbeing*. In: Smith, SJ, Pain, R, Marston, SA & Jones III, JP (Eds) *The SAGE handbook of social geographies*. Sage, London, 309–28.

Kearns, RA & Barnett, JR (1999a) Auckland's starship enterprise: placing metaphor in a children's hospital. In: Williams, A (Ed) *Therapeutic landscapes: the dynamic between place and wellness*. University Press of America, Lanham, MD, 169–200.

Kearns, RA & Barnett, JR (1999b) To boldly go? Place, metaphor, and the marketing of Auckland's Starship Hospital. *Environment and Planning D: Society & Space* 17, 201–26.

Kearns, RA & Barnett, JR (2000) "Happy Meals" in the Starship Enterprise: interpreting a moral geography of health care consumption. *Health & Place* 6, 81–93.

Kearns, RA & Collins, DC (2000) New Zealand children's health camps: therapeutic landscapes meet the contract state. *Social Science & Medicine* 51, 1047–59.

Kearns, RA & Collins, DC (2010) Health geography. In: Brown, T, McLafferty, S & Moon, G (Eds) *A companion to health and medical geography*. Wiley-Blackwell, Oxford, 15–32.

Kearns, RA & Moon, G (2002) From medical to health geography: novelty, place and theory after a decade of change. *Progress in Human Geography* 26, 605–25.

Laws, J (2009) Reworking therapeutic landscapes: the spatiality of an 'alternative' self-help group. *Social Science & Medicine* 69, 1827–33.

Lea, J (2008) Retreating to nature: rethinking 'therapeutic landscapes.' *Area* 40, 90–8.

Lee, ACK & Maheswaran, R (2011) The health benefits of urban green spaces: a review of the evidence. *Journal of Public Health* 33, 212–22.

Little, J (2013) Pampering, well-being and women's bodies in the therapeutic spaces of the spa. *Social & Cultural Geography* 14, 41–58.

Love, M, Wilton, R & DeVerteuil, G (2012) 'You have to make a new way of life': women's drug treatment programmes as therapeutic landscapes in Canada. *Gender, Place & Culture* 19, 382–96.

Maas, J, Verheij, RA, Groenewegen, PP, De Vries, S & Spreeuwenberg, P (2006) Greenspace, urbanity, and health: how strong is the relation? *Journal of Epidemiology and Community Health* 60, 587–92.

MacKian, SC (2008) What the papers say: reading therapeutic landscapes of women's health and empowerment in Uganda. *Health & Place* 14, 106–15.

MacKian, SC (2009) Wellbeing. In: Kitchin, R & Thrift, R (Eds) *International encyclopedia of human geography*. Elsevier, Oxford, 235–40.

MacKian, SC (2012) *Everyday spirituality: social and spatial worlds of enchantment*. Palgrave Macmillan, Basingstoke.

Maslow, AH (1954) *Personality and motivation*. Longman, Harlow.

Milligan, C (2007) Restoration or risk? Exploring the place of the common place. In: Williams, A (Ed) *Therapeutic landscapes*. Ashgate, Aldershot, 255–72.

Milligan, C & Bingley, A (2007) Restorative places or scary spaces? The impact of woodland on the mental well-being of young adults. *Health & Place* 13, 799–811.

Milligan, C, Gatrell, AC & Bingley, A (2004) 'Cultivating health': therapeutic landscapes and older people in northern England. *Social Science & Medicine* 58, 1781–93.

Mohan, G & Mohan, J (2002) Placing social capital. *Progress in Human Geography* 26, 191–210.

Moon, G, Kearns, RA & Joseph, A (2006) Selling the private asylum: therapeutic landscapes and the (re) valorization of confinement in the era of community care. *Transactions of the Institute of British Geographers* 31, 131–49.

Naraindas, H & Bastos, C (2011) Healing holidays? Itinerant patients, therapeutic locales and the quest for health: Special Issue for Anthropology & Medicine. *Anthropology and Medicine* 18, 1–6.

Office for National Statistics (2015) Statistical bulletin: Measuring National Well-being: Personal Well-being in the UK, 2014 to 2015, viewed 7 December 2016. http://www.ons.gov.uk/ons/rel/wellbeing/measuring-subjective-wellbeing-in-the-uk/analysis-of-experimental-subjective-well-being-data-from-the-annual-population-survey-april-september-2011/report-april-to-september-2011.html

Pain, R & Smith, SJ (2010) Introduction: geographies of wellbeing. In: Smith SJ, Pain R, Jones, J-P and Marston, S (eds) (2010) *Handbook of social geography*. Sage, London, 299–308.

Palka, E (1999) Accessible wilderness as a therapeutic landscape: experiencing the nature of Denali National Park, Alaska. In: Williams, A (Ed) *Therapeutic landscapes: the dynamic between place and wellness*. University Press of America, Lanham, MD, 29–51.

Parr, H (2006) Mental health, the arts and belongings. *Transactions of the Institute of British Geographers* 31, 150–66.

Power, A & Smyth, K (2016) Heritage, health and place: the legacies of local community-based heritage conservation on social wellbeing. *Health & Place*, 39, 160–7.

Reser, JP (1995) Whither environmental psychology? The transpersonal ecopsychology crossroads. *Journal of Environmental Psychology* 15, 235–57.

Rose, E (2012) Encountering place: a psychoanalytic approach for understanding how therapeutic landscapes benefit health and wellbeing. *Health & Place* 18, 1381–7.

Sampson, R & Gifford, SM (2010) Place-making, settlement and well-being: the therapeutic landscapes of recently arrived youth with refugee backgrounds. *Health & Place* 16, 116–31.

Schrecker, T & Bambra, C (2015) *How politics makes us sick: neoliberal epidemics*. Palgrave Macmillan, Basingstoke.

Smith, DM (1973) *An introduction to welfare geography. Occasional paper II*. Department of Geography and Environmental Studies, University of the Witwatersrand Johannesburg.

Smith, K, Luginaah, I & Lockridge, A (2010) 'Contaminated' therapeutic landscape: the case of the Aamjiwnaang First Nation in Ontario, Canada. *Geography Research Forum* 30, 83–102.

Smyth, F (2005) Medical geography: therapeutic places, spaces and networks. *Progress in Human Geography* 29, 488–95.

Sointu, E (2005) The rise of an ideal: tracing changing discourses of wellbeing. *The Sociological Review* 53, 255–74.

Sperling, JM & Decker, JF (2007) The therapeutic landscapes of the Kaqchikel of San Lucas Toliman, Guatemala. In: Williams, A (Ed) *Therapeutic landscapes*. Ashgate, Aldershot, 233–53.

Stevenson, B & Wolfers, J (2008) Economic growth and subjective well-being: reassessing the Easterlin paradox. *Brookings Papers on Economic Activity* Spring, 1–87.

Tonnellier, F & Curtis, S (2005) Medicine, landscapes, symbols: "The Country doctor" by Honore de Balzac. *Health & Place* 11, 313–21.

Tuan, YF (1977) *Space and place: the perspective of experience.* University of Minnesota Press, Minneapolis, MN.

Wakefield, SE & Poland, B (2005) Family, friend or foe? Critical reflections on the relevance and role of social capital in health promotion and community development. *Social Science & Medicine* 60, 2819–32.

Ward-Thompson, C (2011) Linking landscape and health: the recurring theme. *Landscape and Urban Planning* 99, 187–95.

Wendt, DC & Gone, JP (2012) Urban-indigenous therapeutic landscapes: a case study of an urban American Indian health organization. *Health & Place* 18, 1025–33.

Whitehouse, S, Varni, JW, Seid, M, Cooper-Marcus, C, Ensberg, MJ, Jacobs, JR & Mehlenbeck, RS (2001) Evaluating a children's hospital garden environment: utilization and consumer satisfaction. *Journal of Environmental Psychology* 21, 301–14.

WHO (1948; 2015) *Mental health: a state of well-being,* viewed 11 March 2016, http://www.who.int/features/factfiles/mental_health/en/

Winkel, GH & Holahan, CJ (1985) The environmental psychology of the hospital: is the cure worse than the illness? *Journal of Prevention & Intervention in the Community* 4, 11–33.

Williams, A (1998) Therapeutic landscapes in holistic medicine. *Social Science & Medicine* 46, 1193–203.

Williams, A (Ed) (1999) *Therapeutic landscapes: the dynamic between wellness and place.* University Press of America, Lanham, MD.

Williams, A (2002) Changing geographies of care: employing the concept of therapeutic landscapes as a framework in examining home space. *Social Science & Medicine* 55, 141–54.

Williams, A (Ed) (2007a) *Therapeutic landscapes.* Ashgate, Aldershot.

Williams, A (2007b) Healing landscapes in the Alps: Heidi by Johanna Spyri. In: Williams, A (Ed) *Therapeutic landscapes.* Ashgate, Aldershot, 65–73.

Williams, A (2010) Spiritual therapeutic landscapes and healing: a case study of St. Anne de Beaupre, Quebec, Canada. *Social Science & Medicine* 70, 1633–40.

Wilson, K (2003) Therapeutic landscapes and First Nations peoples: an exploration of culture, health and place. *Health & Place* 9, 83–93.

Wilton, R & DeVerteuil, G (2006) Spaces of sobriety/sites of power: examining social model alcohol recovery programs as therapeutic landscapes. *Social Science & Medicine* 63, 649–61.

Wood, VJ, Curtis, SE, Gesler, WM, Spencer, IH, Close, HJ, Mason, JM & Reilly, JG (2013) Spaces for smoking in a psychiatric hospital: social capital, resistance to control, and significance for 'therapeutic landscapes'. *Social Science & Medicine* 97, 104–11.

Chapter 5

(Re)Locating, Reforming and Providing Health Care

Introduction

Places have always been important to health care, not only at the macro-scale, in terms of how and where services and resources are located and how they are distributed, but also at the meso- and micro-scales, in terms of the nature and experience of how health care is produced and consumed. Recognising this, geographers have long considered the geographical aspects of health care, employing a wide range of perspectives, methods and theories across their studies. This chapter considers a range of subjects – from issues related to access and utilisation to policy and structural reforms – that have fundamentally changed the landscape of health care. Attention is paid in particular to emerging 'alternative' forms and paradigms of health care and to the spatial features in its provision and practice. Finally, the chapter considers critically the shift to evidence-based health care and the many ways in which place is implicated in this powerful project.

Locating Health Care

The study of health care has been a central concern of medical and health geography. Within this field, a longstanding predominantly quantitative research tradition has concerned itself with areal differentiation and patterning, reporting how health care facilities, services and other resources are spatially distributed across local, regional, national and international scales, and the consequences of these distributions on service utilisation and health outcomes (e.g. Joseph and Phillips 1984; Ricketts 2010); commentators noting for example the 'friction of distance' and a 'distance decay' in service utilisation (i.e. increasing distance, decreasing usage) (Stock 1983) and potential modifiers (Joseph 1979). Whilst some of this research – often published by self-identifying medical geographers – recognises

Health Geographies: A Critical Introduction, First Edition. Tim Brown, Gavin J. Andrews, Steven Cummins, Beth Greenhough, Daniel Lewis, and Andrew Power.
© 2018 John Wiley & Sons Ltd. Published 2018 by John Wiley & Sons Ltd.

the fundamental nature and importance of 'space' (thus elevating it in the analysis), some of it – often published by mainstream health service researchers – treats space and other geographical phenomena as extrinsic, albeit important, properties of health systems (thus placing them alongside other non-spatial properties in the analysis). Notably this research is based on an ethical argument that it is a morally correct action to maximise accessibility to health services and that part of this involves working towards an optimal spatial allocation of them (Meade and Earickson 2000; Barnett and Copeland 2010); this, indeed, being part of a broader sub-disciplinary concern for underserviced populations (Jones and Moon 1987; Boyne and Powell 1991; Ricketts 2010).

Underpinning geographical research on the accessibility and utilisation of services are specific theories and approaches for finding and providing the optimal allocation of services. As Ross Barnett and Alison Copeland (2010) note, there are generally four themes that are emphasised in this research: the geographical bases of service organisation, locational variations in the provision of health care services, the allocation of resources on the basis of need, and variations in utilisation of services. To this end, location-allocation modelling, which involves rigorous analysis of spatial allocation, has been employed to identify the location of services within any given territory and at a range of geographical scales, to identify the flows of people using the services and to consider this in terms of space-time (i.e. the distances from services and the time taken to access them) (Tomintz and Garcia-Barrios 2014). However, as Melinda Meade and Robert Earickson (2000) and Mark Rosenberg (1988) explain, such approaches are far from perfect as they do not account for a range of factors including irrational provider and consumer behaviours, varying barriers and facilitators over space (such as transport), inconsistency in service quality and the problems of providing for very remote populations. Further, Barnett and Copeland suggest that much of the research in this area has tended to prioritise the search for empirical regularities in provision and utilisation rather than to consider the political and economic structures that frame such provision or people's experiences of the services that are provided.

Whilst these interests and perspectives on accessibility and utilisation have remained strong in the sub-discipline (see Ricketts 2010; Tomintz and Garia-Barrios 2014), two key developments in this field since the early 1990s have challenged the above approach. First, as Gavin Andrews and Joshua Evans (2008) describe, studies have displayed ever greater degrees of theoretical, methodological and analytical sophistication and have thus built more expansive bodies of knowledge. Second, moving beyond considerations of the 'shape' and 'use' of services, studies have paid much closer attention to the features that form provision, such as administrative boundaries and local markets and health policy and regulation. In combination, and as encouraged by David Phillips and Yola Verhasselt (1989), important contexts to health care provision and utilisation have increasingly been accounted for in research including human resource issues, population health goals and medical, political and social movements. These developments – often framed within a political economy perspective – have arguably led to this particular field of geography being taken far more seriously in health services research as a whole. Indeed, it is increasingly recognised as a body of work that contributes directly to mainstream health service and academic debates on rationing, efficiency and equity in service planning and provision.

Notably however, despite these developments, a number of commentaries published over the last few years have questioned the assumptions of conventional geographical accessibility and utilisation research, and have suggested ways to strengthen and develop it. For example, Meade and Earickson (2000) note that, in addition to distance, accessibility and utilisation might also be a product of a number of complex variables including availability of services (their basic existence), means of access (including income and cost), discriminatory and non-discriminatory systems and practices (for example in relation to age, gender and ethnicity/race), and knowledge and attitude of consumers (including health seeking behaviours). Moreover, Neil Hanlon (2009) and Nadine Schuurman (2009) argue the need in accessibility and utilisation research to consider the full range of health care services in communities beyond those that are physician-led, that is, to consider who provides services and how services are organised. This, Hanlon argues, is because accessibility and utilisation are related to, and even reinforce, social exclusion and inclusion in communities more broadly. More fundamentally, though much earlier, Sarah Curtis and Ann Taket (1996) argued the need to consider far more thoroughly the relative merits of market versus planned or collectivist ideology and systems for meeting needs and producing spatial allocations of resources, a point re-emphasised by Barnett and Copeland in their recent review (2010). Meanwhile, above and beyond these questions, other scholars have debated how far spatial configurations of services really matter and to whom, and whether geographers' research contributions are recognised across the health sciences and by policy makers to the extent that they would like to think they are (e.g. Eyles 1990; Powell 1995; Mohan 1998).

Reforming Health Care

In the past twenty years a second substantive strand of geographical research on health care has emerged, moving beyond locational considerations outlined previously to consider the nature of places themselves as social and cultural phenomena. Notably, this emergence has come at precisely the same time that the range of settings and locations for health care has been expanding, and existing health care settings themselves transitioning and diversifying. Hence, in this section we outline these changes, referencing geographical work along the way. As Andrews and Evans (2008) have noted, a common feature of much health care that has emerged, especially in the world's richest countries, over the last twenty years is a particular spatial character. In contrast to post-war provision that saw health care services provided primarily in hospitals (primary health care being the only sector to be provided in significant volume outside of these), a spatial diffusion of health care services has taken place through both a growth in smaller and more specialised community-based settings and a corresponding increase in the number of larger institutions providing secondary care beyond the boundaries of their main institutional buildings (see also Andrews et al. 2012). In many respects health care is now provided 'here, there and everywhere'; that is, health providers are seen as having responded to a neoliberal logic, which replaces 'patients' with 'consumers' and seeks to provide services closer to sites of everyday consumption (see McKeever and Coyte 2002).

The extent to which this change has been motivated by financial concerns to improve health care experiences and outcomes, or by shifts in political ideology (notably the emergence of an anti-collectivist ethos in the period since neoliberalism become hegemonic) is perhaps debatable (*cf.* Schrecker and Bambra 2015). Nonetheless, it has involved a transfer of responsibility to people and places at two scales. The first is communities and neighbourhoods. Once viewed by policy makers and administrators as areas on maps to be 'serviced', communities and neighbourhoods have now been re-positioned by them as social terrains of health care (a position that we will return to later), which have health needs but also the ability and inclination to support and care for each other (Prince et al. 2006; Andrews and Evans 2008). The second is to families and homes. Once viewed as places too unpredictable and unsafe for medicine, mirroring patient preferences, homes have emerged as the priority environment for an ever-increasing range of treatments and care (Milligan 2000, 2009; Dyck et al. 2005). Crucially, underpinning these trends is a wide range of new technologies. These facilitate care remote from hospitals through improving communication. Contemporary examples include telehealth and telephone triage, remote monitoring and intervention, robotic surgery and distance acute and rehabilitative care (Andrews and Evans 2008; Andrews et al. 2012).

Both of these aforementioned trends are underpinned by geographical concepts and ideas that have become central to public policy and administrative initiatives (Andrews et al. 2012). Falling under the rubric the 're-scaling of statehood' under neoliberalism (see Brenner 2004) two of these initiatives are most notable. The first is geographical decentralisation of the administration of health care within universal, publicly-funded systems. Indeed, one of the more common administrative transformations has been the move towards greater 'local control' in the operation of public programs. There are several terms used to describe these changes including 'regionalisation', 'devolution', 'decentralisation' and 'deconcentration' (see Secker et al. 2006). Often the switch to more local control over decision-making is associated with a reduction in funding, justified by fiscal necessity to make 'efficiencies' (Hurley et al. 1994, 1995), critics regarding them instead as attempts to offload political responsibility and accountability for potentially controversial allocation decisions (Lomas 1997). Second under the re-scaling of statehood is increasing 'place-based policy'. This has been particularly popular in the UK where, for example, a number of area-based initiatives have been rolled out (see Powell and Moon 2001; Halliday and Asthana 2005). Another example is 'aging-in-place' and its preference for home as a long-term setting, illustrating a further alliance between medical, political and public opinion on where long-term care is best provided. In the push towards decentralisation this new spatial logic has been, in many cases, uncritically applied, particularly with regard to community. For example, according to Young (1990), discourses of 'community' are based on 'an ideal of community', a utopian vision. The affective value of the term community is exploited, but it presumes that subjects can understand one another and their role within 'community' social relations and fails to recognise that alienation and violence equally exist as 'community' social relations (see also Dunn and Eyles 2012).

Evidently then, just as health geography has emerging terrains to consider in terms of disease prevention and public health, the sub-discipline can be critical of spatial assumptions that underpin them in policy. Primary health care, for example, has been the subject of considerable recent research attention in this vein, itself having been extended in terms of its scope and in terms of the settings it is produced within. Chapters in Valorie Crooks and Gavin J. Andrews' (2009) edited volume, *Primary health care: people, practice, place*, consider a range of issues including: landscapes of care – from clinics to local community – in the context of GP, nursing and complementary and alternative medicine practice (see Agarwal 2009; Crooks and Agarwal 2009; Hollenberg and Bourgeault 2009; Lapum et al. 2009); voluntary and unpaid providers (Yantzi and Skinner 2009); and services for difficult to reach populations (Conradson and Moon 2009). Moreover, the nature of community participation (Gold 2009) and policy change and structural reforms pertaining to this particular sector have been of particular and broader interest (Barnett and Barnett 2009; Gold 2009). Indeed, this research showcases a much more developed understanding and richer description of the nature of social life and relations within which such services operate (see also Barnett et al. 1998; Evans et al. 2009; Lee et al. 2010).

Changing Places: Institutions and Neoliberal Thinking

As Wilbert Gesler and Robin Kearns (2002) observe, the past twenty years has witnessed the infusion of neoliberal thinking, policies and structures in health care, and
health geography has very much concerned itself with how this has played out in, and
impacted on, places. Indeed, underpinning a vast range of initiatives across many
countries has been a market-based ideology involving competitive thinking and practices (including a greater involvement of marketing, advertising and the private sector)
and a general sense of health being a form of utility, with health care being regarded as
a consumer item (Curtis and Taket 1996). Similar to the community initiatives outlined
previously, underlying the neoliberal agenda has been an objective to make health care
providers more efficient and accountable for their spending – often via competition (in
the United Kingdom, for example, reflected variously in successive initiatives such as
the NHS internal market, GP fundholding, Primary Care Groups, Primary Care Trusts,
and now Clinical Commissioning Groups; see Box 5.1). Although governments and
other forms of officialdom have undoubtedly played a very significant role in this infusion, their efforts have also been foregrounded by wider social trends: first, a growing
consumer culture involving materialism, the commodification of social life and health
(Crawford 1980); and, second, a blurring of traditional social divisions (such as class)
and the enhanced consumption cleavages based around taste. These have changed the
outlooks and expectations of those entering health care settings and more generally the
attitudes of the public observing them, even from afar.

In terms of research, there has been a sustained interest in health geography on the
broad transformations health care settings have gone through over time and as a result of
these political economic as well as social and cultural forces, in other words, an interest in
what powerful economic and political interests consider health care settings should be and
represent and what they have done to make this a reality. In particular, studies have argued
how corporate principles in health care translate spatially into 'consumption landscapes'
(Gesler and Kearns 2002), whereby either health care institutions allow the market to colo-
nise them or they themselves more thoroughly embrace and manipulate their own market
position (Kearns and Barnett 1992; Moon and Brown 1998, 2000). In much of this work,
scholars have approached health care landscapes as 'texts' that they can read, decode and
construct arguments on their meaning and significance (Kearns and Barnett 1997; see
Chapter 3). In terms of the market 'colonising', Robin Kearns and Ross Barnett (1997), for
example, argue that large public hospitals are often highly conspicuous and functional parts
of urban and rural landscapes and, with their considerable size and regularity, make an
immediate impression on the external observer. Modernist designs and architecture can
create a sense of 'placelessness' whilst older designs can feel cold, uncaring and even frightening. Nevertheless, an emerging move has been, through design that often mimics private
sector consumer spaces, to manipulate the design and decoration of hospitals so that they
feel 'warmer' and more therapeutic to those who frequent them (Gesler 2003; Gesler et al.
2004; Curtis et al 2007; Evans et al. 2009). Beyond this, health care spaces are increasingly
being opened up directly to commercial enterprise to make them appear more exciting,
engaging and even adventurous. Studies, for example, have considered debate and conflict
in the locating of fast food restaurants, shops and the explicit use of mall designs in hospital
entrances and atria (Kearns and Barnett 1999, 2000; Adams et al. 2010). Indeed, as studies
have shown, this often results in competing arguments between differently invested groups
with different visions of what health care settings should be.

Box 5.1   Key Themes: Health Care Restructuring

During the twentieth century, there were several phases of health system restructuring. The first saw the establishing of health care and social insurance systems throughout the 1940s and 1950s in most advanced industrialised societies and somewhat later, if at all, in poorer countries. Following this was a phase of exceptional growth, both in terms of the range of health care services provided and the percentage of the total population covered by social insurance schemes. However, it is generally accepted that health services restructuring refers to the widespread re-examination of, and reform to, such health care provision following the global economic slow-down of the mid 1970s. Framed by a broader ideological debate about the relationship between the state, the market and civil society, this re-examination raised questions about the sustainability of health care systems which were characterised by their ever-increasing cost to national economies.

A useful illustration of this can be found in the Clinton administration's attempts to reform the US health care system in the early 1990s. The need for reform is demonstrated both by the proportion of the population that was uninsured, which by 1990 had reached approximately 13 per cent or 33.4 million people, and by the total expenditure on health care as a percentage of GDP, which was 12.1 per cent or $666 bn only a year later. Clinton's Health Security plan sought to remedy both issues simultaneously, by implementing a national health insurance scheme and by introducing government-structured market competition. Yet the plan for a national insurance scheme floundered in Congress and the ensuing introduction of managed care, which has been characterised as a form of 'unmanaged competition', was implemented by employers rather than the state. What this example highlights is the need to recognise that restructuring is not simply a technical response but one that is influenced by an array of actors operating within a particular health care landscape.

The above illustration also reveals that such change is ideologically and politically mediated. For many commentators, contemporary restructuring debates have been influenced by the neoliberal ideology of the 'New Right', according to which the once dominant Keynesian model of welfare provision is regarded as overly bureaucratic, inflexible and inefficient because of its reliance on the state. Fostered under the Reaganite and Thatcherite administrations of the late 1970s and 1980s, the anti-collectivist principles of neoliberalism have resulted in quite substantial change across the health care sector. For example, in countries such as the United Kingdom, New Zealand and Russia there has been a shift towards the principles of market competition as the most effective mechanism for controlling costs and delivering efficient and flexible health care services. This shift is not limited to advanced, industrial economies, for such is the dominance of neoliberalist ideology that international organisations such as the WHO measure the performance of national health care systems according to the extent to which they have adopted a market-oriented approach.

Adapted from Brown (2009)

With regard to 'embracing' and 'manipulating' a market position, it has been noted how hospitals themselves increasingly deploy commercial language and, through corporate branding and marketing, their own self-promotional strategies. Here, for example, the intent can be to de-emphasise negative identity with institutional medicine and, at the same time, promote achievements in positive ways to donors, politicians, private business, potential clients and the general public (Kearns and Barnett 1999, 2000; Kearns et al. 2003; Moon et al. 2005, 2006; Joseph et al. 2009). Indeed, geographers have talked about how, using these self-promotional strategies, health care institutions have become locally, nationally and internationally 'famous' even when, as in the case of mental health asylums, they might have had controversial pasts, being highly involved in oppressive institutionali-sation practices (Kearns et al. 2003; Moon et al. 2005, 2006; Joseph et al. 2009). On a related note, geographers have also articulated how communities develop attachments to, and responsibility for, their local 'famous' hospitals and, through an identity politics and activism, oppose government and other officialdom in support of them, particularly when they are threatened with deep cuts or even complete closure (e.g. Moon and Brown 2001; Brown 2003).

New geographies of health care work

The forms of structural, financial, technological and conceptual changes in health care outlined in previous sections have also had far-reaching consequences for workers as individuals and as cohorts, and their workplaces (see Andrews 2006; Andrews and Evans 2008). Greater professional scope has occurred with each professional extending their responsibilities and practices, and each profession – such as nursing – introducing new specialist sub-categories. In unison, the blurring of traditional professional boundaries has also occurred. For example, on the one hand, health professionals have been required to be more financially accountable whilst, on the other hand, managers and administrators increasingly impact upon clinical decision-making at the planning level (Hanlon 2001). In other developments, the composition of health care teams has been extended, with health professionals working with patients and informal and voluntary care providers who each possess greater roles and responsibilities. Consequently, moral and duty boundaries sepa-rating these groups have shifted, and new authority relationships have developed between them. New challenges have also arisen with regard to professional competence, safety and accountability, and new models for regulating geographically dispersed and technology-dependent health care work are being followed. At the micro-scale, technology changes social relationships within workplaces, making professionals more physically and narratively – and in some cases morally – distant from each other and their patients as their tasks become orientated around monitoring equipment rather than building interpersonal relationships (Sandelowski 2002; Malone 2003; Andrews 2006; Andrews and Evans 2008). More gener-ally, because it has increasingly become unnecessary for health professionals and patients to be co-present during their interactions, distance work for diagnostic, therapeutic, acute, palliative and rehabilitative care has become more common.

As described by Gavin Andrews and Joshua Evans (2008), and later John Connell and Margaret Walton-Roberts (2016), an emerging strand of research in health geography is concerned with these changes on workers and on professional health care work and the workforce more broadly. At a macro-level, one group of studies is focused on decision makers, considering the geographical dimensions to, or consequences of, decision-making across cohorts of workers (for example, family or hospital-based doctors or service managers). These decisions are often narrowly defined in nature, involving specific financial, planning or clinical concerns, and are often reactions to policy and/or broad system changes (Carr-Hill et al. 1994; Moon et al. 2002; Iredale et al. 2005). Also at the macro-scale, broad population-based studies focus on the supply of labour or career decision-making and the consequences of these for local communities (Barnett 1988; Cutchin 1997; Baer 2003; Farmer et al. 2003; Guagliardo et al. 2004; Laditka 2004). In more recent years, however, this macro-scale perspective has been joined by a place-sensitive micro-scale perspective on the nature of work and workplaces. The topics considered include, for example, hospital strategic management (Hanlon 2001) and the interpersonal and spatial dynamics that make and characterise specific specialities including general/family practice (Rapport et al. 2006, 2007), labour and delivery (Burges Watson et al. 2007), neonatal intensive care (Brown and Middleton 2005), mobile dialysis (Lehoux et al. 2007) and mental health care (Curtis et al. 2007).

Alternative forms of health care

Related to many of the aforementioned debates is the fact that the biomedical response to the organisation and provision of health care services has never been the only game in town. Vastly pre-dating it is so-called 'traditional' medicine (TM), which typically refers to treatments associated with Ayurvedic medicine (India), Kampoh medicinal preparation (China) and other theories, beliefs, and experiences indigenous to different human cultures (see Barrett 2000). The study of TM is an interdisciplinary field but also was an important interest of early medical geography, with Charles Good's landmark paper setting an agenda that heavily influenced and directed subsequent research. Good (1977) highlighted the substantial health problems facing many countries in Africa, Asia and Latin America, with the lack of conventional services in many areas but, at the same time, the widespread availability and use of TM. He noted that integration with TM would allow vast human resources to be unlocked and improvements to patient access made, and indicated the potential for collaboration from the national scale to the scale of individual facilities. Mirroring the perspectives and concerns of medical geography in the 1970s, the research agenda that Good proposed was focused mainly on accessibility and utilisation of TM, investigating matters including spatial arrangements in urban and rural areas, factors in seeking TM and various obstacles related to distance. However, he did also note the need to investigate how integration of TM potentially relates to wider national and regional health goals and planning.

More recent geographical research has studied TM more critically, with a richer notion of place, and in contemporary contexts. Vincent Del Casino's (2004) research on the renewal of TM in Thailand, for example, discusses its partial integration within the state-run health system to address the care needs of people living with HIV/AIDS. Del Casino highlights how different knowledges are produced and contested at the level of localised settings; thus TM is regulated, formalised and systematised through its 're-placing' at the micro-space of the hospital and through its 'proper' arrangement with the hospital. There is also a substantive critical geographical literature specifically focused on aboriginal health beliefs, aboriginal medicine and culturally appropriate orthodox medicine and care (e.g. Newbold 1997; DeVerteuil and Wilson 2010; Kornelsen et al. 2010; Wilson et al. 2011). Given the significant health challenges facing aboriginal communities and the way they have been historically neglected, marginalised and even attacked by institutions of government (particularly in countries like Australia and Canada), this scholarship is particularly important in terms of informing contemporary health policy and practice.

Related to TM, a significant trend in nations where the biomedical model has dominated in terms of the provision of health care services is the emergence of 'new' forms of holistic health care collectively termed complementary and alternative medicine (CAM). Despite an initial critical response from some scholars because of concerns with the individualistic tendencies of CAM (e.g. Crawford 1980), the growth of therapies provided by this new sector has been exponential. Emerging in line with the growth of this sector has been a wide range of research from social and health scientists, studying, for example, the structure of provision (Andrews and Hammond 2004), patterns in consumption (Kelner and Wellman 1997; Molassiotis et al. 2005), issues regarding evidence base and effectiveness (Barry 2006) and regulation and integration (Walker and Budd 2002). Indeed, geography has played its part in these multidisciplinary endeavours. The argument for geographical research on CAM goes back twenty five years to Anyinam (1990), who argued for quantitative inquiry paying attention to local, regional and national distributions of therapists, their relationships to biomedical services, referral networks and practice catchment areas. Those studies that directly answered this call mainly considered spatial trends in CAM at the regional level. Notably, for example, Robert Verheij and colleagues (1999) considered distributive trends in CAM provision in Holland, and Alison Williams (2000) considered distributive trends in CAM provision in two Canadian provinces (see also Williams et al. 2011). Other foundational geographical work has identified the prevalence and use of CAM in a number of national settings, for example in the United States (Eisenberg et al. 1998; Kessler et al. 2001; Barnes et al. 2004; Tindle et al. 2004), the United Kingdom (Thomas et al. 2001), Australia (MacLennan et al. 1996; Xue et al. 2007), Italy (Menniti-Ippolito et al. 2002), Norway (Hanssen et al. 2005; Steinsbekk et al. 2007, 2011), Denmark (Hanssen et al. 2005) and Sweden (Al-windi 2004), including demographic profiles at national levels (Wiles and Rosenberg, 2001; Adams et al. 2003). Collectively, this body of research has demonstrated consistent or growing rates of use. Indeed, surveys provide usage estimates ranging from 30 per cent to 75 per cent of the general public, the wide variation being due in part to the particular questions asked in surveys such as CAM use over different durations and periods (Kessler et al. 2001; Adams et al. 2003). In terms of demographics, despite increasing prevalence rates across many demographic groups and a narrowing of the gap between them, it does appear that CAM users are still more likely to be white, female, middle-aged, have a higher income and level of education and be employed (Adams et al. 2003; Graham et al. 2005; Hsiao et al. 2006). In terms of provision, although, as we shall see later, CAM is being integrated with conventional medicine, it remains predominantly a large scale 'cottage industry'; therapists own small businesses and sell their services to privately paying clients (Andrews 2003).

To some extent, the emergence of a place-sensitive geography of health since the 1990s has involved a more comprehensive engagement with CAM; scholars have considered more intimately the ways in which therapies are performed and consumed within particular kinds of places and how CAM is shaped by these geographies. Specifically, these studies have focused on how geographical concepts play a part in the core ideas and principles of CAM (Williams 1998; Andrews et al. 2013), how CAM can become locked in territorial struggles with orthodox bio-medicine (King 2012), who uses CAM in particular places and the meanings of those places (Andrews 2003) and how CAM jumps traditional spatial boundaries of practice into everyday life through its diversity and media exposure (Doel and Segrott 2003a, 2003b). Moreover, issues have been investigated with regard to the professionalisation and regulation of CAM in particular jurisdictions (Clarke et al. 2004; Doel and Segrott 2004) and within CAM practices and practice environments (Andrews et al. 2003; Andrews 2004; Doel and Segrott 2004; Andrews and Shaw 2010, 2012). More generally, four cross-cutting themes are identifiable in this literature.

The first of these is 'place and healing'. A key focus of this work (informed by humanistic geography) is to think through how the characteristics of places such as the therapist's clinic might have therapeutic qualities, promote the healing process and help define the performance of CAM therapies. Alison Williams (1998), Anne-Cécile Hoyez (2007) and Gavin Andrews (2003, 2004), for instance, have applied the concept of therapeutic landscapes to CAM to explore how the places where CAM is practised may produce feelings of health and wellbeing or promote healing (on therapeutic landscapes see Chapter 4). Reflecting Wilbert Gesler's proposition that therapeutic landscapes work on both physical and psychological levels, Williams suggests that practitioners create therapeutic landscapes both because of the physical attributes of the spaces in which they deliver care and due to the strong interpersonal relationships that are built within them. Thus, through the work that they do, CAM practitioners can create 'authentic' or 'caring' environments that promote the healing process. Moreover, CAM clients may come to attach particular meanings to the clinic where they receive treatment, and a sense of place can develop (Williams 1998; Andrews 2003).

The second theme is 'tools' (both imagined and material). Work by Andrews (2004), Andrews et al. (2013) and Williams (1998) has taken the concept of the therapeutic landscape in new directions by considering how these places might not only be comprised of physical space but also include spaces in the imagination. Specifically, Andrews and Williams explore the ways in which many CAM therapists purposefully use imagination and visualisation in their work, asking clients to visualise their own bodies as well as imagine distant spaces as part of the healing process (see also Andrews and Shaw 2010, 2012). Meanwhile other studies have examined the spaces in which CAM is performed, and how such spaces are produced, arranged and contested. Marcus Doel and Jeremy Segrott (2004), for example, explore the materialisation of CAM and the importance of materials within therapeutic practice. They view CAM less in terms of unified therapies and more in terms of unique events in which practice depends upon the articulation of bodies and materials. Moreover, Doel and Segrott argue that a professional image is achieved in large part through attending to space – to the ambience of the clinic (clean towels, good quality decoration) and the furnishing of the waiting room (comfortable seating and the presentation of a diverse set of objects, from framed qualification certificates to potted plants) (see also Mizrachi et al. 2005; Andrews et al. 2013).

The third theme is 'other spaces, spatial diffusion'. Whilst the provision of therapies by independent practitioners in private clinics remains dominant, recent years have seen the diffusion of CAM into a range of new spaces, particularly through the increased consumption of self-treatment remedies and materials. Homeopathic preparations, aromatherapy oils, acupuncture pens, crystals and a vast range of manuals, self-help books, MP3s and other sources of information are all now freely available for those with the financial means to pay. Janine Wiles and Mark Rosenberg (2001) suggest that the growth in the use of CAM is linked to the growing importance of health and the body in western society and the 'constant (re)formulation and negotiation of situated identities' (p. 221). They suggest that CAM consumption takes place within a range of everyday geographies and that the study of CAM should be situated within the 'geographies of consumption'. The newly dispersed geography of CAM therefore takes place in domestic space, work space, retail space and the mass media (including magazines and the internet) alongside the therapist's clinic (see also Doel and Segrott 2003a, 2003b).

A fourth and final theme is 'integration', often focused on the changing relationship between orthodox medicine and CAM and the ways in which CAM is entering spaces of orthodox medicine (e.g. Del Casino 2004; Fadlon 2004; Andrews and Shaw 2010, 2012).

Nissim Mizrachi and colleagues (2005), for example, describe the introduction of CAM practitioners into an Israeli hospital. Whilst the biomedical profession allowed CAM to enter its territory, it maintained its position and professional boundaries and excluded and marginalised CAM practitioners in highly spatialised ways. The authors provide several examples of such spatialised exclusion and marginalisation and suggest that one way in which biomedicine exercises professional power is by locating the knowledge of CAM outside of the formal structure of the hospital, something which again is expressed spatially in relation to the equipment such practitioners use. Another example of research on integration is a study by Andrews and Shaw (2012) which considers visualisation as an untrained, unregulated, organically occurring yet highly holistic technique employed by nurses as part of their everyday 'conventional' practice. Hence, their study challenges the notion that two discrete paradigms (biomedicine and CAM) of health care exist, there being considerable fluidity between them.

Place and the Evidence-Based Agenda

In order to round off this chapter we shift our attention to the idea of evidence-based health care (EBHC), which originated at McMaster University in Canada in the 1990s and has very quickly become a global priority. Based on the observation that too much health care practice was based on tradition, intuition, anecdotal evidence and guesswork – a reality that, it was thought, affected the safety, effectiveness and efficiency of care – EBHC stresses that all clinical practice should be supported by rigorous scientific research (Guyatt et al. 1992; Sackett et al. 1996). In terms of the nature of this evidence, emphasis is laid on the scientific method in its production and systematic reviews to summarise findings across studies (Broom and Adams, 2012). EBHC is a phenomenon that ranges ever wider. Originally focused on clinical practice – as reflected in the often used alternative terms evidence-based medicine (EBM), evidence-based practice (EBP) and evidence-based nursing (EBN) – it has recently extended to include such concepts as evidence-based policy. Notably, in addition, in recent years EBHC and its derivatives have been supported and applied at a global scale through non-governmental organisations – most notably the World Health Organization (WHO) – becoming involved centrally in making and applying evidence-based recommendations, and setting goals and standards based on them, particularly in developing world countries and contexts (WHO 2001; Aronson 2004; Bryce et al. 2005; Gilks et al. 2006).

More recently, the 'sister concept' of knowledge translation (KT) has emerged. It is based on the observation that although evidence might be produced by research, it does not necessarily find its way into practice, often reaching only as far as academic journals and their readers and informing self-serving circular debates. Thus, as a natural extension and facilitator of EBHC, KT involves finding approaches to enhance EBHC by closing the gap between what researchers know and what health professionals do (Grol 2000; Davis et al. 2003). Although many scholars have written in depth about theoretical models of, and processes in, KT (Kitson et al. 1998; Lavis et al. 2003), in practice KT involves the dissemination of research findings to health professionals and, beyond this, communication and problem solving between researchers and health professionals. Over time, KT strategies have expanded to include more accessible and straightforward forms of publication, websites that show research findings and online forums that facilitate inter-professional communication, stake holder dialogues, public talks, social media and arts-based dissemination.

The wide-ranging critique of EBHC acknowledges that it is appropriate that the best health care is provided in the best known ways, but considers that EBHC goes far beyond this objective, becoming a powerful movement in itself that espouses a dominant *epistemé* or world view. For certain scholars, it is a world view that selectively legitimises and includes certain knowledge but degrades and excludes other knowledge (Holmes and O'Byrne 2012). More specifically, for Dave Holmes and colleagues, EBHC supports a hierarchy of evidence, at the top of which lies the double blind randomised controlled trial (RCT) with social science survey research (economic evaluation, cost analysis and so on) lagging some way behind the RCT in the hierarchy. Meanwhile qualitative research – previously excluded in the first historical phase of EBHC and now marginally included in a second phase –still has an inferior status (Holmes and O'Byrne 2012). Moreover, it is argued that the EBHC movement is supported by both the state and academia. Of the former, government bodies that control funding, thus determining which methodologies and empirical subjects get priority, make EBHC an institutionalised 'state science' (Holmes et al. 2006; Murray et al. 2008). Of the latter, scientists with vested interests – whose research is compatible with EBHC and whose careers benefit from it – act as 'gatekeepers' (Holmes et al. 2006; Murray et al. 2007).

Particularly troubling for critics such as Dave Holmes and colleagues, is that such is the power and dominance of EBHC that it is uncritically taken for granted in academia as the 'correct path'. They argue that, in response, a post-modern critique is necessary to deconstruct this mode of thinking; that resistance is necessary given the powerful forces in play (Holmes and Gagnon 2008) and that challenging concepts dictated by EBHC is crucial for professional integrity and independence of thought (Holmes et al. 2007). Moreover, Holmes and colleagues also argue that the critique of EBHC is not just evident in critical research. They suggest it also arises 'on the ground' in the everyday actions of health care workers who, despite the constant EBHC rhetoric surrounding them, value other forms of knowledge, drawing liberally on wide-ranging sources and their own experiences (Holmes et al. 2009; Andrews and Shaw 2010). These workers ultimately realise that EBHC oversimplifies their work (as a set of tasks) and their workplace (as a regular space) whereas they are both unique and complex. Meanwhile other critiques mention that EBHC quality marks have been misappropriated by vested interests, that the volume of evidence produced has become unmanageable, that statistically significant findings do not translate to practice, and that EBHC encourages technically driven solutions over patient-centred care (Greenhalgh et al. 2014).

With these issues in mind, Gavin Andrews and Joshua Evans (2008) developed an agenda for health geography with regard to EBHC and KT; an agenda that might be attractive to scholars with a wide range of interests, methods and theoretical and philosophical positions. With regard to EBHC, Andrews and Evans argue that attention might be paid in research to the impact of place on the creation and use of evidence. Here, three approaches are possible. The first approach involves consideration of '*place as evidence*'. At one level, places can be created or adjusted as distinct practice and/or design interventions (for example, this has been done previously with respect to places for childbirth and breastfeeding support – McKeever et al. 2002; Hodnett et al. 2005, 2009). At another level, as noted earlier, place can frame 'natural experiments' (Petticrew et al. 2005), whereby non-controlled existing interventions are rigorously observed and evaluated (for example, this has been conducted previously with respect to community-based interventions for diet – see Cummins et al. 2005). The second approach considers the '*place specificity of evidence*', examining how evidence is produced within, and exported from, places. With respect to RCTs, for example, the personal, professional and technical aspects of each clinical setting are unique, thus rendering clinical interventions set within clinical settings also somewhat unique and hence the generalisability of their findings questionable (Angus et al. 2003). The third approach, connecting to the critical work by Holmes and colleagues, considers '*EBP: the control of space and knowledge*', specifically, the ways in which it is reproduced and enforced in both academic and clinical spaces, how it moves clinical action and debate and the extent to which geography is included as a form of 'legitimate' knowledge. Indeed, Sibley (1995) argues that, just as forms of social and spatial exclusion occur in society, equally social and spatial knowledge – and those who produce it – can be excluded. With regard to KT, as Andrews and Evans (2008) posit, three critical approaches are also possible. First, efforts could be made by health geographers to translate evidence – that is, to '*do KT*' themselves – involving the KT strategies mentioned above, and others. Second, a more critical approach could be taken. This would consider '*the introduction of evidence into places*'. Indeed, the nature of how research evidence is collected and applied differs between individuals, teams, institutions and localities. Moreover, economic, social, cultural, political and historical forces specific to settings help or hinder KT. Both of these processes need to be understood. Third, also part of a critical approach, there is a need to pursue '*the geography of knowledge translation*' – that is, the application of theories of place, scale, mobility and diffusion in considering ways that KT has been rationalised and implemented.

Conclusion

This chapter has described how place is important in terms of the ways in which health care is provided, used and experienced. In particular, it considered how place (as location) is critical to the accessibility and utilisation of services and ultimately population health, and how a range of non-institutional community settings have been opened up for treatment and care. Further, it described how institutional spaces are increasingly designed and manipulated with the market in mind, how place impacts upon health care work, and how new forms of holistic health care are both creating new places of practice and being integrated into conventional ones. Finally, it considered critically how place impacts on the ways in which the evidence that informs health care practice is produced, circulated and used.

Questions for Review

1. What are the main spatial changes that have occurred in health care provision and what are their motivating factors?
2. How is place integral to 'alternative' forms of health care?
3. How can place impact upon the production and use of evidence for health care practice?

Suggested Reading

Andrews, GJ & Evans, J (2008) Understanding the reproduction of health care: towards geographies in health care work. *Progress in Human Geography* 32, 759–80.

Eyles, J (1990) How significant are the spatial configurations of health care systems? *Social Science & Medicine* 30, 157–64.

Joseph, AE & Phillips, DR (1984) *Accessibility and utilization: geographical perspectives on health care delivery.* Sage, London.

Kearns, RA & Barnett, R (2000) "Happy Meals" in the Starship Enterprise: interpreting a moral geography of health care consumption. *Health & Place* 6, 81–93.

References

Adams, A, Theodore, D, Goldenberg, E, McLaren, C & McKeever, P (2010) Kids in the atrium: comparing architectural intentions and children's experiences in a pediatric hospital lobby. *Social Science & Medicine* 70, 658–67.

Adams, J, Sibbritt, D, Easthope, G & Young, A (2003) The profile of women who consult alternative health practitioners in Australia. *Medical Journal of Australia* 179, 297–300.

Agarwal, G (2009) Geographies of family medicine: describing the family doctor's practice-based landscape of care. In: Crooks, VA & Andrews, GJ (Eds) *Primary health care: people, practice, place.* Ashgate, Aldershot, 115–30.

Al-Windi, A (2004) Determinants of complementary alternative medicine (CAM) use. *Complementary Therapies in Medicine* 12, 99–111.

Andrews, GJ (2003) Placing the consumption of private complementary medicine: everyday geographies of older peoples' use. *Health & Place* 9, 337–49.

Andrews, GJ (2004) (Re)thinking the dynamics between healthcare and place: therapeutic geographies in treatment and care practices. *Area* 36, 307–18.

Andrews, GJ (2006) Geographies of health in nursing. *Health & Place* 12, 110–18.

Andrews, GJ & Evans, J (2008) Understanding the reproduction of health care: towards geographies in health care work. *Progress in Human Geography* 32, 759–80.

Andrews, GJ & Hammond, R (2004) Small business complementary medicine: a profile of British therapists and their pathways to practice. *Primary Health Care Research and Development* 5, 40–51.

Andrews, GJ & Shaw, D (2010) "So we started talking about a beach in Barbados": visualization practices and needle phobia. *Social Science & Medicine* 71, 1804–10.

Andrews, GJ & Shaw, D (2012) Place visualization: conventional or unconventional practice? *Complementary Therapies in Clinical Practice* 18, 43–8.

Andrews, GJ, Peters, E & Hammond, R (2003) Receiving money for medicine: some tensions and resolutions for community-based private complementary therapists. *Health and Social Care in the Community* 11, 155–68.

Andrews, GJ, Evans, J, Dunn, J & Masuda, J (2012) Arguments in health geography: on sub-disciplinary progress, observation, translation. *Geography Compass* 6, 351–83.

Andrews, GJ, Evans, J & McAlister, S (2013) 'Creating the right therapy vibe': relational performances in holistic medicine. *Social Science & Medicine* 83, 99–109.

Angus, J, Hodnett, E & O'Brien-Pallas, L (2003) Implementing evidence-based nursing practice: a tale of two intrapartum nursing units. *Nursing Inquiry* 10, 218–28.

Anyinam, C (1990) Alternative medicine in western industrialized countries: an agenda for medical geography. *The Canadian Geographer/Le Géographe canadien* 34, 69–76.

Aronson, B (2004) Improving online access to medical information for low-income countries. *New England Journal of Medicine* 350, 966–8.

Baer, LD (2003) A proposed framework for analyzing the potential replacement of international medical graduates. *Health & Place* 9, 291–304.

Barnes, PM, Powell-Griner, E, McFann, K & Nahin, RL (2004) Complementary and alternative medicine use among adults: United States, 2002. *Seminars in Integrative Medicine* 2, 54–71.

Barnett, JR (1988) Foreign medical graduates in New Zealand 1973-1979: a test of the 'exacerbation hypothesis'. *Social Science & Medicine* 26, 1049–60.

Barnett, JR & Barnett, P (2009) Reinventing primary care: the New Zealand case compared. In: Crooks, VA & Andrews, GJ (Eds) *Primary health care: people, practice, place*. Ashgate, Aldershot, 149–65.

Barnett, JR & Copeland, A (2010) Providing health care. In: Brown, T, McLafferty, S & Moon, G (Eds) *A companion to health and medical geography*. Wiley-Blackwell, Oxford, 497–520.

Barnett, JR, Barnett, P & Kearns, RA (1998) Declining professional dominance?: trends in the proletarianisation of primary care in New Zealand. *Social Science & Medicine* 46, 193–207.

Barrett, FA (2000) *Disease & Geography: the history of an idea*. York University Press, Toronto.

Barry, CA (2006) The role of evidence in alternative medicine: contrasting biomedical and anthropological approaches. *Social Science & Medicine* 62, 2646–57.

Boyne, G & Powell, M (1991) Territorial justice: a review of theory and evidence. *Political Geography Quarterly* 10, 263–81.

Brenner, N (2004) *New state spaces: urban governance and the rescaling of statehood*. Oxford University Press, New York.

Broom, A & Adams, J (Eds.) (2012) *Evidence-based healthcare in context: Critical social science perspectives*. Ashgate, Aldershot.

Brown, SD & Middleton, D (2005) The baby as virtual object: agency and difference in a neonatal intensive care unit. *Environment and Planning D: Society & Space* 23, 695–715.

Brown, T (2003) Towards an understanding of local protest: hospital closure and community resistance. *Social & Cultural Geography* 4, 489–506.

Brown, T (2009) Health services restructuring. In: Kitchin, R & Thrift, N (Eds) *The international encyclopedia of human geography*. Elsevier, Oxford, 51–7.

Bryce, J, Boschi-Pinto, C, Shibuya, K & Black, RE (2005) WHO estimates of the causes of death in children. *The Lancet* 365, 1147–52.

Burges Watson, D, Murtagh, MJ, Lally, JE, Thomson, RG & McPhail, S (2007) Flexible therapeutic landscapes of labour and the place of pain relief. *Health & Place* 13, 865–76.

Carr-Hill, RA, Sheldon, TA, Smith, P, Martin, S, Peacock, S & Hardman, G (1994) Allocating resources to health authorities: development of method for small area analysis of use of inpatient services. *BMJ* 309, 1046–9.

Clarke, DB, Doel, MA & Segrott, J (2004) No alternative? The regulation and professionalization of complementary and alternative medicine in the United Kingdom. *Health & Place* 10, 329–38.

Connell, J & Walton-Roberts, M (2016) What about the workers? The missing geographies of health care. *Progress in Human Geography* 40, 158–76.

Conradson, D & Moon, G (2009) On the street: primary health care for difficult to reach populations. In: Crooks, VA & Andrews, GJ (Eds) *Primary health care: people, practice, place*. Ashgate, Aldershot, 237–57.

Crawford, R (1980) Healthism and the medicalization of everyday life. *International Journal of Health Services* 10, 365–88.

Crooks, VA & Agarwal, G (2009) Considering the clinic environment: implications for practice and primary health care. In: Crooks, VA & Andrews, GJ (Eds) *Primary health care: people, practice, place*. Ashgate, Aldershot, 187–202.

Crooks, VA & Andrews, GJ (Eds) (2009) *Primary health care: people, practice, place*. Ashgate, Aldershot.

Cummins, S, Petticrew, M, Higgins, C, Findlay, A & Sparks, L (2005) Large scale food retailing as an intervention for diet and health: quasi-experimental evaluation of a natural experiment. *Journal of Epidemiology and Public Health* 59, 1035–40.

Curtis, S & Taket, E (1996) *Health and societies: changing perspectives*. Hodder Arnold, London.

Curtis, S, Gesler, W, Fabian, K, Francis, S & Priebe, S (2007) Therapeutic landscapes in hospital design: a qualitative assessment by staff and service users of the design of a new mental health inpatient unit. *Environment and Planning C: Government and Policy* 25, 591–610.

Cutchin, MP (1997) Physician retention in rural communities: the perspective of experiential place integration. *Health & Place* 3, 25–41.

Davis, D, Evans, M, Jadad, A, Perrier, L, Rath, D, Ryan, D et al. (2003) The case for knowledge translation: shortening the journey from evidence to effect. *BMJ* 327, 33–5.

Del Casino, VJ (2004) (Re) placing health and health care: mapping the competing discourses and practices of 'traditional' and 'modern' Thai medicine. *Health & Place* 10, 59–73.

DeVerteuil, G & Wilson, K (2010) Reconciling indigenous need with the urban welfare state? Evidence of culturally-appropriate services and spaces for Aboriginals in Winnipeg, Canada. *Geoforum* 41, 498–507.

Doel, MA & Segrott, J (2003a) Beyond belief? Consumer culture, complementary medicine, and the dis-ease of everyday life. *Environment and Planning D: Society and Space* 21, 739–59.

Doel, MA & Segrott, J (2003b) Self, health and gender: complementary and alternative medicine in the British mass media. *Gender, Place and Culture* 10, 131–44.

Doel, MA & Segrott, J (2004) Materializing complementary and alternative medicine: aromatherapy, chiropractic, and Chinese herbal medicine in the UK. *Geoforum* 35, 727–38.

Dunn, JR & Eyles, JD (2012) Deconstructing devolution: the discursive use of 'community' in Canadian health care regionalization policy. *Crunch Working Paper 12-01*. Hamilton, Canada.

Dyck, I, Kontos, P, Angus, J, McKeever, P & Poland, B (2005) The home as a site of long-term care: meanings and management of bodies and spaces. *Health & Place* 11, 173–85.

Eisenberg, DM, Davis, RB, Ettner, SL, Appel, S, Wilkey, S, Van Rompay, M & Kessler, RC (1998) Trends in alternative medicine use in the United States, 1990-1997: results of a follow-up national survey. *Journal of the American Medical Association* 280, 1569–75.

Evans, JD, Crooks, VA & Kingsbury, PT (2009) Theoretical injections: on the therapeutic aesthetics of medical spaces. *Social Science & Medicine* 69, 716–21.

Eyles, J (1990) How significant are the spatial configurations of health care systems? *Social Science and Medicine* 30, 157–64.

Fadlon, J (2004) Meridians, chakras and psycho-neuro-immunology: the dematerialising body and the domestication of alternative medicine. *Body and Society* 10, 69–86.

Farmer, J, Lauder, W, Richards, H & Sharkey, S (2003) Dr. John has gone: assessing health professionals' contribution to remote rural community sustainability in the UK. *Social Science & Medicine* 57, 673–86.

Gesler, WM (2003) *Healing places*. Rowman & Littlefield, Lanham, MD.

Gesler, WM & Kearns, RA (2002) *Culture/place/health*. Routledge, London.

Gesler, WM, Bell, M, Hubbard, P & Francis, S (2004) Therapy by design: evaluating the UK hospital building program. *Health & Place* 10, 117–28.

Gilks, CF, Crowley, S, Ekpini, R, Gove, S, Perriens, J, Souteyrand, Y & De Cock, K (2006) The WHO public-health approach to antiretroviral treatment against HIV in resource-limited settings. *The Lancet* 368, 505–10.

Gold, L (2009) Cloaked selective primary health care? Local observations of rural primary health care clinics in Perú. In: Crooks, VA & Andrews, GJ (Eds) *Primary health care: people, practice, place*. Ashgate, Aldershot, 93–111.

Good, CM (1977) Traditional medicine: an agenda for medical geography. *Social Science & Medicine* 11, 705–13.

Graham, R, Ahn, A, Davis, R, O'Connor, B, Eisenberg, D & Phillips, R (2005) Use of complementary and alternative medical therapies among racial and ethnic minority adults: results from the 2002 National Health Interview Survey. *Journal of the National Medical Association* 97, 535–45.

Greenhalgh, T, Howick, J & Maskrey, N (2014) Evidence based medicine: a movement in crisis? *BMJ* 348, g3725.

Grol, R (2000) Twenty years of implementation research. *Family Practice* 17, s32–5.

Guagliardo, MF, Ronzio, CR, Cheung, I, Chacko, E & Joseph, JG (2004) Physician accessibility: an urban case study of pediatric providers. *Health & Place* 10, 273–83.

Guyatt, G, Cairns, J, Churchill, D, Cook, D, Haynes, B, Hirsh, J et al (1992) Evidence-based medicine: a new approach to teaching the practice of medicine. *Journal of the American Medical Association* 268, 2420–25.

Halliday, J & Asthana, S (2005) Policy at the margins: developing community capacity in a rural Health Action Zone. *Area* 37, 180–8.

Hanlon, NT (2001) Sense of place, organizational context and the strategic management of publicly funded hospitals. *Health Policy* 58, 151–73.

Hanlon, NT (2009) Access and utilization reconsidered: towards a broader understanding of the spatial ordering of primary health care. In: Crooks, VA & Andrews, GJ (Eds) *Primary health care: people, practice, place.* Ashgate, Aldershot, 43–56.

Hanssen, B, Grimsgaard, S, Launsø, L, Fønnebø, V, Falkenberg, T & Rasmussen, NK (2005) Use of complementary and alternative medicine in the Scandinavian countries. *Scandinavian Journal of Primary Health Care* 23, 57–62.

Hodnett, ED, Downe, S, Edwards, N & Walsh, D (2005) Home-like versus conventional institutional settings for birth. *Cochrane Database of Systematic Reviews,* viewed 11 March 2016, http://onlinelibrary.wiley.com/doi/10.1002/14651858.CD000012.pub2/full

Hodnett, ED, Stremler, R, Weston, JA & McKeever, P (2009) Re-conceptualizing the hospital labor room: the PLACE (Pregnant and Laboring in an Ambient Clinical Environment) pilot trial. *Birth* 36, 159–66.

Hollenberg, D & Bourgeault, I (2009) New health geographies of complementary, alternative and traditional medicines in primary health care. In: Crooks, VA & Andrews, GJ (Eds) *Primary health care: people, practice, place.* Ashgate, Aldershot, 167–83.

Holmes, D & Gagnon, M (2008) Practice to evidence and evidence to practice: misunderstanding the epistemic incommensurability. *Journal of Evaluation in Clinical Practice – International Journal of Public Health Policy and Health Services Research* 14, 663–4.

Holmes, D & O'Byrne, P (2012) Resisting the violence of stratification: imperialism, war machines and the evidence-based movement. In: Broom, A & Adams, J (Eds) *Evidence based healthcare in context: critical social science perspectives.* Aldershot, Farnham, 43–60.

Holmes, D, Gastaldo, D & Perron, A (2007) Paranoid investments in nursing: a schizoanalysis of the evidence-based discourse. *Nursing Philosophy* 8, 85–91.

Holmes, D, Murray, S & Perron, A (2009) "Insufficient" but still "necessary"? EBPM's dangerous leap of faith. *International Journal of Nursing Studies* 46, 749–50.

Holmes, D, Murray, S, Perron, A & Rail, G (2006) Entertaining fascism? *International Journal of Evidence Based Health Care* 4, 189–90.

Hoyez, AC (2007) The 'world of yoga': the production and reproduction of therapeutic landscapes. *Social Science & Medicine* 65, 112–24.

Hsiao, A, Wong, M, Goldstein, M, Anderson, R, Brown, E et al (2006) Variation in complementary and alternative medicine (CAM) use across racial/ethnic groups and the development of ethnic-specific measures of CAM use. *Journal of Alternative and Complementary Medicine* 12, 281–90.

Hurley, J, Birch, S & Eyles, J (1995) Information and efficiency in geographically decentralized healthcare systems. *Social Science & Medicine* 41, 3–11.

Hurley, J, Lomas, J & Bhatia, V (1994) When tinkering is not enough: provincial reform to manage health care resources. *Canadian Public Administration* 37, 490–514.

Iredale, R, Jones, L, Gray, J & Deaville, J (2005) 'The edge effect': an exploratory study of some factors affecting referrals to cancer genetic services in rural Wales. *Health & Place* 11, 197–204.

Jones, K & Moon, G (1987) *Health, disease and society: an introduction to medical geography.* Routledge & Kegan Paul, London.

Joseph, AE (1979) The referral system as a modifier of distance decay effects in the utilization of mental health care services. *The Canadian Geographer/Le Géographe canadien* 23, 159–69.

Joseph, AE & Phillips, DR (1984) *Accessibility and utilization: geographical perspectives on health care delivery.* Sage, London.

Joseph, AE, Kearns, RA & Moon, G (2009) Recycling former psychiatric hospitals in New Zealand: echoes of deinstitutionalisation and restructuring. *Health & Place* 15, 79–87.

Kearns, RA & Barnett, JR (1992) Enter the supermarket: entrepreneurial medical practice in New Zealand. *Environment and Planning C: Government and Policy* 10, 267–81.

Kearns, RA & Barnett, JR (1997) Consumerist ideology and the symbolic landscapes of private medicine. *Health & Place* 3, 171–80.

Kearns, RA & Barnett, JR (1999) To boldly go? Place, metaphor and the marketing of Auckland's Starship hospital. *Environment and Planning D: Society and Space* 17, 201–26.

Kearns, RA & Barnett, JR (2000) "Happy Meals" in the Starship Enterprise: interpreting a moral geography of health care consumption. *Health & Place* 6, 81–93.

Kearns, RA, Barnett, JR & Newman, D (2003) Placing private health care: reading Ascot hospital in the landscape of contemporary Auckland. *Social Science & Medicine* 56, 2303–15.

Kessler, RC, Davis, RB, Foster, DF, Van Rompay, MI, Walters, EE et al (2001) Long-term trends in the use of complementary and alternative medical therapies in the United States. *Annals of Internal Medicine* 135, 262–68.

Kelner, M & Wellman, B (1997) Health care and consumer choice: medical and alternative therapies. *Social Science & Medicine* 45, 203–12.

King, B (2012) "We pray at the church in the day and visit the Sangomas at night": health discourses and traditional medicine in rural South Africa. *Annals of the Association of American Geographers* 102, 1173–81.

Kitson, A, Harvey, G & McCormack, B (1998) Enabling the implementation of evidence-based practice: a conceptual framework. *Quality in Health Care* 7, 149–58.

Kornelsen, J, Kotaska, A, Waterfall, P, Willie, L & Wilson, D (2010) The geography of belonging: the experience of birthing at home for First Nations women. *Health & Place* 16, 638–45.

Laditka, JN (2004) Physician supply, physician diversity, and outcomes of primary health care for older persons in the United States. *Health & Place* 10, 231–44.

Lapum, J, Chen, S, Peterson, J, Leung, D & Andrews, GJ (2009) The place of nursing in primary health care. In: Crooks, VA & Andrews, GJ (Eds) *Primary health care: people, practice, place.* Ashgate, Aldershot, 131–48.

Lavis, JN, Robertson, D, Woodside, JM, McLeod, CB & Abelson, J (2003) How can research organizations more effectively transfer research knowledge to decision makers? *Milbank Quarterly* 81, 221–8.

Lee, JY, Kearns, RA & Friesen, W (2010) Seeking affective health care: Korean immigrants' use of homeland medical services. *Health & Place* 16, 108–15.

Lehoux, P, Daudelin, G, Poland, B, Andrews, GJ & Holmes, D (2007) Designing a better place for patients: professional struggles surrounding satellite and mobile dialysis units. *Social Science & Medicine* 65, 1536–48.

Lomas, J (1997) Devolving authority for health care in Canada's provinces: emerging issues and prospects. *Canadian Medical Association Journal* 156, 817–23.

MacLennan, AH, Wilson, DH & Taylor, AW (1996) Prevalence and cost of alternative medicine in Australia. *The Lancet* 347, 569–73.

Malone, R (2003) Distal nursing. *Social Science & Medicine* 56, 2317–26.

McKeever, P & Coyte, PC (2002) Here, there and everywhere. *University of Toronto Bulletin March* 25, 16.

McKeever, P, Stevens, B, Miller, KL, MacDonell, JW, Gibbins, S et al (2002) Home versus hospital breastfeeding support for newborns: a randomized controlled clinical trial. *Birth* 29, 258–65.

Meade, MS & Earickson, R (2000) *Medical geography.* Guilford, New York.

Menniti-Ippolito, F, Gargiulo, L, Bologna, E, Forcella, E & Raschetti, R (2002) Use of unconventional medicine in Italy: a nation-wide survey. *European Journal of Clinical Pharmacology* 58, 61–4.

Milligan, C (2000) Bearing the burden: towards a restructured geography of caring. *Area* 32, 49–58.

Milligan, C (2009) *There's no place like home: place and care in an aging society.* Ashgate, Aldershot.

Mizrachi, N, Shuval, J & Gross, S (2005) Boundary at work: alternative medicine in biomedical settings. *Sociology of Health and Illness* 27, 20–43.

Mohan, JF (1998) Explaining geographies of health care: a critique. *Health & Place* 4, 113–24.

Molassiotis, A, Fernadez-Ortega, P, Pud, G, Ozden, G, Scott, J et al (2005) Use of complementary and alternative medicine in cancer patients: a European survey. *Annals of Oncology* 16, 655–63.

Moon, G & Brown, T (1998) Place, space and health service reform. In: Kearns, RA & Gesler, WM (Eds) *Putting health into place.* Syracuse University Press, Syracuse, NY, 270–88.

Moon, G & Brown, T (2000) Governmentality and the spatialized discourse of policy: the consolidation of the post-1989 NHS reforms. *Transactions of the Institute of British Geographers NS* 25, 65–76.

Moon, G & Brown, T (2001) Closing Barts: community and resistance in contemporary UK hospital policy. *Environment and Planning D: Society and Space* 19, 43–59.

Moon, G, Joseph, AE & Kearns, RA (2005) Towards a general explanation for the survival of the private asylum. *Environment and Planning C: Government and Policy* 23, 159–72.

Moon, G, Kearns, RA & Joseph, AE (2006) Selling the private asylum: therapeutic landscapes and the (re)valorization of confinement in the era of community care. *Transactions Institute British Geographers NS* 31, 131–49.

Moon, G, Mohan, J, Twigg, L, McGrath, K & Pollock, A (2002) Catching waves: the historical geography of the general practice fundholding initiative in England and Wales. *Social Science & Medicine* 55, 2201–13.

Murray, S, Holmes, D, Perron, A & Rail, G (2007) No exit?: Intellectual integrity under the regime of 'evidence' and 'best-practices'. *Journal of Public Health Policy and Health Services Research* 13, 512–16.

Murray, S, Holmes, D & Rail, G (2008) On the constitution and status of 'evidence' in the health sciences. *Journal of Research in Nursing* 13, 272–80.

Newbold, KB (1997) Aboriginal physician use in Canada: location, orientation and identity. *Health Economics* 6, 197–207.

Petticrew, M, Cummins, S, Ferrell, C, Findlay, A, Higgins, C et al. (2005) Natural experiments: an underused tool in public health? *Public Health* 119, 751–7.

Phillips, DR & Verhasselt, Y (1989) The future relevance of medical geography for health planning, health and development in the Third World. *GeoJournal* 19, 129–34.

Powell, M (1995) On the outside looking in: medical geography, medical geographers and access to health care. *Health & Place* 3, 73–89.

Powell, M & Moon, G (2001) Health Action Zones: the 'third way' of a new area-based policy? *Health and Social Care in the Community* 9, 43–50.

Prince, R, Kearns, R & Craig, D (2006) Governmentality, discourse and space in the New Zealand health care system, 1991-2003. *Health & Place* 12, 253–66.

Rapport, F, Doel, MA, Greaves, D & Elwyn, G (2006) From manila to monitor: biographies of general practitioner workspaces. *Health: An Interdisciplinary Journal for the Social Study of Health, Illness and Medicine* 10, 233–51.

Rapport, F, Doel, MA & Elwyn, G (2007) Snapshots and snippets: general practitioners' reflections on professional space. *Health & Place* 13, 532–44.

Ricketts, TC (2010) Accessing health care. In: Brown, T, McLafferty, S & Moon, G (Eds) *A companion to health and medical geography.* Wiley-Blackwell, Oxford, 521–39.

Rosenberg, MW (1988) Linking the geographical, the medical and the political in analysing health care delivery systems. *Social Science & Medicine* 26, 179–86.

Sackett, DL, Rosenberg, JA & Gray, RB (1996) Evidence based medicine: what it is and what it isn't. *BMJ* 312, 71–2.

Sandelowski, M (2002) Visible humans, vanishing bodies, and virtual nursing: complications of life, presence, place, and identity. *Advances in Nursing Science* 24, 58–70.

Schrecker, T & Bambra, C (2015) *How politics makes us sick: Neoliberal epidemics*. Palgrave Macmillan, Basingstoke.

Schuurman, N (2009) The effects of population density, physical distance and socio-economic vulnerability on access to primary health care in rural and remote British Columbia, Canada. In: Crooks, VA & Andrews, GJ (Eds) *Primary health care: people, practice, place*. Ashgate, Aldershot, 57–73.

Secker, B, Goldberg, M, Gibson, B, Wagner, F, Parke, B et al (2006) Just regionalization: rehabilitating care for people with disabilities and chronic illness. *BMC Medical Ethics* 7, 9–13.

Sibley, D (1995) *Geographical exclusion, society and difference in the West*. Routledge, London

Steinsbekk, A, Adams, J, Sibbritt, D, Jacobsen, G & Johnsen, R (2007) The profiles of adults who consult alternative health practitioners and/or general practitioners. *Scandinavian Journal of Primary Health Care* 25, 86–92.

Steinsbekk, A, Rise, MB & Johnsen, R (2011) Changes among male and female visitors to practitioners of complementary and alternative medicine in a large adult Norwegian population from 1997 to 2008 (The HUNT studies). *BMC Complementary and Alternative Medicine* 11, 61.

Stock, R (1983) Distance and the utilization of health facilities in rural Nigeria. *Social Science & Medicine* 17, 563–70.

Thomas, KJ, Nicholl, JP & Coleman, P (2001) Use and expenditure on complementary medicine in England: a population based survey. *Complementary Therapies in Medicine* 9, 2–11.

Tindle, HA, Davis, RB, Phillips, RS & Eisenberg, DM (2004) Trends in use of complementary and alternative medicine by US adults: 1997-2002. *Alternative Therapies in Health and Medicine* 11, 42–9.

Tomintz, MN & Garcia-Barrios, VM (2014) Location–allocation planning. In: Cockerham, WC, Dingwall, R & Quah, SR (Eds) *The Wiley Blackwell Encyclopedia of health, illness, behavior, and society*. Wiley-Blackwell, Oxford, 1298–1300.

Verheij, RA, de Bakker, DH & Groenewegen, PP (1999) Is there a geography of alternative medical treatment in The Netherlands? *Health & Place* 5, 83–97.

Walker, LA & Budd, S (2002) UK: the current state of regulation of complementary and alternative medicine. *Complementary Therapies in Medicine* 10, 8–13.

Wiles, J & Rosenberg, MW (2001) "Gentle caring experience": seeking alternative health care in Canada. *Health & Place* 7, 209–24.

Williams, AM (1998) Therapeutic landscapes in holistic medicine. *Social Science & Medicine* 46, 1193–203.

Williams, AM (2000) The diffusion of alternative health care: a Canadian case study of chiropractic and naturopathic practices. *The Canadian Geographer/Le Géographe canadien* 44, 152–66.

Williams, AM, Kitchen, P & Eby, J (2011) Alternative health care consultations in Ontario, Canada: a geographic and socio-demographic analysis. *BMC Complementary and Alternative Medicine* 11, 47.

Wilson, K, Rosenberg, MW & Abonyi, S (2011) Aboriginal peoples, health and healing approaches: the effects of age and place on health. *Social Science & Medicine* 72, 355–64.

World Health Organization (2001) WHO evidence-based recommendations on the treatment of tobacco dependence. World Health Organization, Geneva.

Xue, CC, Zhang, AL, Lin, V, da Costa, C & Story, DF (2007) Complementary and alternative medicine use in Australia: a national population-based survey. *The Journal of Alternative and Complementary Medicine* 13, 643–50.

Yantzi, NM & Skinner, MW (2009) Providers of care in the home: sustainable partners in primary health care. In: Crooks, VA & Andrews, GJ (Eds) *Primary health care: people, practice, place*. Ashgate, Aldershot, 221–36.

Young, IM (1990) The ideal of community and the politics of difference. In: Nicholson, L. (Ed.) *Feminism/postmodernism*. Routledge, New York, 104–32.

Chapter 6

Spaces of Care

Introduction

This chapter follows on from Chapter 5, shifting the focus to the interface between health and social care. On the interface is positioned a myriad of different actors with different roles including family caregivers, social workers, support workers, volunteers and advocates. Of these, family carers generally provide the greatest extent of social care and are positioned within a dynamic, complex relationship with the contemporary welfare state. The division of responsibility between the state's own 'market' of care, the private sector and the family can vary significantly from country to country on account of different ideological, cultural and political debates (Barnes 2012). Indeed, there are ever-shifting boundaries in terms of *how* the roles of different carers are each defined and *on whom* expectations and obligations lie. As this chapter explores, the relative carving out of these boundaries is particularly driven by the contemporary context of reduced government spending and provision of services, welfare reform, and a persistent and widespread guiding political philosophy of neoliberal austerity. It will trace some of the changing boundaries in care, in terms of the different 'social ecologies' and inter-dependencies that exist between family carers and those within the formal support workforce and the voluntary sector, as well as the different spaces and places of care that exist within the current (post) welfare state.

The chapter first maps out the different forms of care that exist, and who provides care, who receives it, and indeed who contests it. It explores how care provision is embodied by different people within various roles and contexts. Mapping the boundaries of care reveals a deeply gendered and ideological phenomenon. The chapter then turns to examine the ever-changing landscape of care in which these actors provide caring roles and explores where care is provided and how space can shape its practices. Within this context, we consider how, more recently, the concept and practices of 'care', particularly in high-income countries such as Sweden, France, the Netherlands, the United Kingdom, Canada and the United States, have become increasingly hidden within the landscape, in terms of the

Health Geographies: A Critical Introduction, First Edition. Tim Brown, Gavin J. Andrews, Steven Cummins, Beth Greenhough, Daniel Lewis, and Andrew Power.
© 2018 John Wiley & Sons Ltd. Published 2018 by John Wiley & Sons Ltd.

withdrawal of conventional sites of care such as day care centres, as well as becoming more hidden from official policy discourse. The latter is increasingly moving towards new guiding philosophies of independence, choice and autonomy. Thus, in the final section we ask, is care still important in these nations? Is there an ethic of care that can still help inform ways of understanding how individuals support each other, and contribute towards greater wellbeing and human thriving?

Care: Mapping the Boundaries of an Ideological Term

Care is an enduring and contested concept in health and social support provision. It comprises a set of values, which are often highly normative and embedded in historical cultural norms and expectations, as well as a set of practices which are often necessary for human survival and flourishing. It can include the provision of personal assistance (e.g. bathing, lifting, feeding), cognitive support and advice (e.g. supported decision-making) as well as emotional and pastoral support and advocacy. Each of these different practices – and the meanings associated with them – can vary by care relationship and the actors involved. As mentioned, it involves a myriad of different individuals from family caregivers to volunteers to professional support workers. With this in mind, this section examines care in these three different contexts, identifying how the underlying values have been created and invoked and how they in turn shape the practices and understandings of care. So, in a sense, we begin by trying to map out the conceptual 'spaces' of care.

First, as stated above, family caregivers make up the largest and most fundamental sector in health and social care, in terms of the numbers of people involved and the hours spent providing support and care (as compared to doctors, qualified nursing staff, scientific and technical staff and managers; Milligan and Power 2010). Moreover, the market value of family caregiving according to carer groups in the United States and United Kingdom is estimated to outweigh the national health budgets in those countries. Yet many people may not see themselves as 'carers', given that many of the roles associated with the term are tied up in the ordinary, everyday family roles of looking after loved ones. Known collectively as the 'informal' sector, it comprises parents, children, siblings and spouses, and to a lesser extent neighbours and friends.

Second, alongside family carers, the voluntary and statutory sectors both play a central role in the geographies of care. These sectors collectively have been described as offering a patchwork quilt of services. The state often provides funding for day care centres, group homes and long-stay hospitals, personal assistants, social workers, general practitioners, nurses, care assistants and key workers. Meanwhile, the voluntary sector comprises respite centres, carer groups, community drop-ins, intermediate care facilities and day care centres.

This patchwork quilt of services emerged largely as a response to deinstitutionalisation from the late 1970s to early 2000s, which is explored further in the next chapter. In many countries around the world including Greece, Spain and the Global South, a very different blend of service provision exists, with a strong reliance on the voluntary sector and non-governmental organisations. With the exception of large institutions, a similar picture existed in the United Kingdom and the United States until the mid to late twentieth century. What unfolded was a vast yet often patchy landscape of 'care spaces', with the philosophy of 'community care' taking centre stage. It is important to remember though that forms of charitable provision pre-dated and worked alongside the institutions (Bartlett and Wright 1999), and many philanthropic efforts were involved in establishing hospitals for people who were disabled (e.g. Simpson's Hospital for Blind and Gouty Men, established 1791,

Dublin). Voluntary organisations in their myriad forms were also inherently involved in providing support and alms in the community. Groups were often initially founded by parent- and family-run support groups as well as doctors and other professionals who set up disability-specific groups such as the Leonard Cheshire Association, the National Spastics Society (subsequently Scope), Rehab and so on, each with their own particular specialty and targeted user group. In time, many of these groups became wholly or partly funded by the state to provide core services to people under their remit.

Care in the community has therefore always been a mixed economy in contrast to primary care which, since World War II in the United Kingdom at least, has been chiefly financed and delivered by the state (Lewis 1999). Although community care involved significant voluntary sector effort and family care provision from the outset, nonetheless it had a discernible quorum of local statutory services, often funded and managed by municipalities/local authorities and/or health agencies. Across the United Kingdom, Europe and in many areas within the United States, the statutory and voluntary sector work alongside each other to varying extents, within the patchwork quilt of services.

Of course, the extent to which the voluntary sector has become increasingly professionalised, operating more as a 'shadow state', has been well documented in some jurisdictions (Wolch 1990). This concept refers to the blurring of boundaries between state and voluntary sectors, as the latter is becoming increasingly professionalised and taking on a more central role in support provision, compared to the supplementary role envisaged in the post-World War II welfare settlement in many European and North American countries (see Box 6.1 for more details).

Voluntary or 'community' groups thus have a complex inter relationship with the state, with different groups existing along a spectrum from local parent-led and community charities to large, highly bureaucratised service delivery organisations (Milligan 2007; Skinner and Power 2012). Similarly, the way in which the voluntary sector in health and social care has evolved has been closely intertwined with the family care sector. Many disability and

---

Box 6.1 Key Concepts: Shadow State

A major part of the political economic critique of the restructuring of public services in the 1980s was Wolch's (1990) pivotal conceptualisation of the voluntary sector as a 'shadow state'. The term 'shadow state' refers to the repositioning of the voluntary sector, particularly in health and social care, from providing a complementary or supplementary role to being seen as an alternative or, in some cases, a primary provider of health and community care services. This was seen as a major shift in policy from the state being the main provider. Underpinning this work was a wider belief that public welfare retrenchment was eroding the centralist and universalist foundations of support services. And in turn, many scholars argued it would lead to a more fragmented, decentralised and ad hoc provision of support, reliant on a piecemeal voluntary sector.

Wolch's conceptualisation of the shadow state also provides a critical appraisal of how far voluntary sector providers have come to look more like public sector providers. In particular, she notes the increasing professionalisation of much of the voluntary sector and its corporate positioning alongside the state. The phenomenon of the shadow state has arguably become more pervasive since the 2000s, as public service restructuring has become a defining feature of welfare state reform across Europe, North America, and elsewhere.

older people's representative organisations were founded by parents or spouses: for example, learning disability organisations were often founded by 'parent and friends groups' (Power 2010); similarly the Alzheimer's Society in the United Kingdom and United States has been primarily led by spouses (Alzheimer's Society n.d.). We return to examine this sector later in the chapter, describing how it has responded to more recent welfare reform efforts.

It is thus possible to discern active engagement by parents and friends in the various groups and associations providing care. So, even within the wider 'landscape of care', the significant offering of time and resources 'informally' by family members is evident throughout. We thus now return to consider family care within this wider context of community care and go on to consider the ways in which family carers – in particular women – occupy or at least are ambiguously situated within care in the community.

Family caregiving

The involvement of women in family caregiving is well documented and, as such, the geography of (family) care finds its roots in feminist sociology from the early 1980s, which took a burgeoning interest in the concept of care (Finch and Groves 1983; Ungerson 1990). One of the key aspects explored within this caregiving literature is the 'cycle of caring' (Twigg and Atkin 1994) phenomenon, where women are affected by the moral principles and expectations within families to take on care roles, leading to on-going caring cycles as different family members move through the life course (children and older relations). In effect, women were taking on multiple caring roles within the family.

In response to the commonly held assumptions about the maternal nurturing instincts of women, Hilary Land and Hilary Rose (1985) articulated the concept of 'compulsory altruism' to illustrate how women in many cases do not *choose* to become carers. This vein of work derives its underlying philosophy largely from first-wave feminism emerging in the late 1960s and focusing on the much broader patriarchal processes and expectations on women. This literature has explored the unpaid basis of care work (Ungerson 1990). The unpaid caregivers in this sector of care work are often referred to by the media as 'an army of unpaid carers' (Lakhani 2012, no pagination).

More broadly, one of the dominant themes that emerged from much of this earlier caregiving literature is carer burden. The emphasis here is on how the restructuring of health and social care provision has led to care falling disproportionately on female members of the family; as a result, many commentators identify burnout as a common experience of carers. To illustrate the supposed burden on carers, a report by the Carers Trust in the United Kingdom argued that many carers are isolated, depressed, physically exhausted and financially strained as they struggle to cope with caring for sick and disabled relatives without adequate support (Lakhani 2012). In response to many of these experiences, carers have recognised their political voice, and their agenda has become increasingly promulgated. This has led to the collective identification of 'carers' as a political category with the evolution of a generation of carer organisations such as Carers UK, the Carers Association (in Ireland), and the Family Caregiver Alliance (in the United States).

The concept of burden has faced a powerful critique, particularly from disability studies, as many disabled people argue that it denotes the care recipient as dependent and helpless – 'a burden'. In this sense, being 'cared for' is argued to be more synonymous with dependency, being helpless and being a subject of pity (Oliver and Barnes 1998). This raises important questions over the future evolution of how we think of care and whether it should still be valued as a concept.

In any case, this early work on caregiving – and the coining of the term 'informal caregiver' in the literature – also coincided with the broader context of social care policy in the 1980s, in particular the erosion of state-run institutions and 'care' facilities. This period saw the emergence of 'community care', which at the time was welcomed by many proponents of social care reform as it was envisaged that care recipients (people with disabilities, mental health issues, chronic illness, or frailty in old age) would take up more active and valued roles in their neighbourhoods. For many policy makers, though, particularly in countries that had led the way with deinstitutionalisation, such as the United States, Canada and the United Kingdom, it was presumed that community care would mean care *by* the community, rather than *in* the community (DHSS 1981). This was a very important distinction. In other words, the state arguably failed to provide the range of formal services to enable independent living in the community to become a reality. Thus, there was a renewed expectation that persons in need of support would stay at home and, by implication, this need fell disproportionately on female members of the family. Christine Milligan (2000), one of the first human geographers to write about family caregiving, examines some of the reasons why care has historically fallen disproportionately on female members of the family. Alongside the patriarchal gender divide associated with the labour force breadwinner role and the household maker/carer role, she also takes account of the greater longevity of women, the increased mortality of men in the twentieth century and the fact that, in general, women often marry men who are older than they are.

Internationally, this picture of women caring is also evident across global care 'chains' (Parreñas 2000; Hochschild 2001; Yeates 2005; Vullnetari 2008). The term refers to the increasing geographic dispersion of extended family members, usually from poorer Global South or Eastern European countries, to care for older and disabled people in the Global North. This is driven by a range of factors including the low cost of sourcing carers from these countries, the ability to control labour and racial/ethnic stereotypes of people from the Global South as model minorities with certain expected behaviours and expectations. Work in this vein also highlights the 'left behind' generation of older people as a result of the 'care drain' within the migrant origin countries (see Figure 6.1).

Despite the strong gendered lines on which caregiving is drawn, geographers such as Stuart Aitken have also examined the awkward spaces of fathering within family life. Aitken (2012) unpacks the daily emotional practices that are negotiated, contested and resisted between parents in different spaces, exploring the complex identity politics around 'house-husbands' and 'Mr Moms'. Rather than seeing the greater presence of male caregivers as leading to a mutual or shared care identity between men and women (referred to as the 'universal caregiver model'), Nancy Fraser (2006) found that even the most active fathers tend to see their role as 'helping out' their partners rather than taking the main responsibility for childcare themselves. Others such as Hilary Arksey and Caroline Glendinning (2005) have found that men who are caring for people with complex needs are more likely to draw boundaries around the extent of intimate care they will or will not undertake. Also, older male carers in married relationships are often more likely to accept domestic help, as it is often perceived as substituting domestic labour previously provided by their wives.

While this broader account of voluntary and family caregiving reveals the main discernible trends in the informal care literature (including human geography work within this field), a closer look reveals how the experiences of caregiving can differ geographically from nation to nation, due to the welfare practices and policies that have evolved in different jurisdictions. While little work has been done at the international comparative level, one exception is the comparative landscapes of care case studies in the United Kingdom, United States and Ireland by Andrew Power (2010). 'Landscapes of care' is taken to mean the

Figure 6.1   The 'left behind' generation from global care chains, as evidenced in Albania. Reproduced with permission of Julie Vullnetari.

differing historical cultural and political norms that have evolved regarding caregiving across different countries, how carers themselves have been defined and (by implication) the material service sector on the ground. In the United States for example, there remains much resistance to recognising carers as a distinct 'client group'. Rather, social care policies in this jurisdiction have been and continue to be firmly based on a rights perspective for the care recipient. With the strength of the independent living movement since the 1960s as well as the wider liberal philosophy, the ethos has been to assume (read: not support) the natural role of the family in providing care. As an indirect outcome, family caregivers remain relatively at the margins.

Meanwhile, in the United Kingdom, although the early foundation of the NHS and welfare state was built on the assumption of family care as a principal resource, there has been much greater recognition of the carer role from the 1990s. The then government instigated an agenda of 'Caring about the Carers' (Department of Health 1999) and since this time there has been a more explicit effort to recognise the rights of carers and include them within assessments of needs.

Finally, in Ireland, given the dominant conservative and religious context from the late nineteenth to mid twentieth century, a strong moral duty of care was placed upon the voluntary and family sector. Indeed, the Catholic Church was resistant to the state 'interfering' in the lives of families. As a result, consecutive governments from the 1920s to the late 1970s kept social care at arm's length. Church and religious voluntary provision (e.g. St. Vincent de Paul) filled the gap. As the Church's grip loosened in the latter two decades of the twentieth century, Ireland became a relatively paternalistic state in relation to supporting carers, with an enduring charitable ethos to care for the 'needy' and 'special', over a focus on rights to independent living. As a result, carers are often supported by statutory payments, yet can remain frustrated by low expectations by the state and society regarding those in their care.

More generally, this work serves to demonstrate how carers occupy an ambiguous position within the social care system, in effect being 'squeezed' by the demands (and separate calls for rights) of care recipients who are often seen as the primary client. In addition, carers are often perceived in contradictory ways by the state (in terms of how welfare policy frames the value of family care) and the formal professional care sector (which can define family roles in different ways). This blurring of boundaries can have important consequences for the geographies of those involved in caring. This ambiguous position is the subject of a seminal paper by a sociologist, Julia Twigg (1989), who identifies three different models of carers (see Box 6.2): carers as resources; carers as co-workers; and carers as co-clients. Twigg's typology has helped geographers think about the relationship between carers and space.

Box 6.2   Key Thinkers: Julia Twigg

Carers as *resources*

In Twigg's first model, care is seen as informal, and presumed as *prior* to formal. In this sense, family members are not subject to the formal laws of supply and demand. Due to societal norms over kinship, the pattern of the availability of informal carers remains in any extensive sense beyond the influence of agencies.

Carers as *co-workers*

The social and political construction of the term 'carer', and the rapid growth of its use within social service departments and other social care agencies is itself part of the process whereby kin and friendship relations are semi-professionalised and brought within the orbit of the formal system. Carers here become co-workers in the care enterprise. This model is often used by policy efforts designed to boost good carer morale with the context that it clearly contributes both to the likelihood that care will continue to be offered, and to the quality of the care that is offered.

Carers as *co-clients*

Here, carers are seen as legitimate cases for welfare intervention. Carers become fully integrated into the concerns of agencies and welfare policy. Given the societal norms expressed with caring, this model totally changes the normative assumptions of the caregiving relationship. Moreover, it has been argued that carer payments can undermine the voluntary nature of caregiving (Ungerson 1990). In particular, it has been this model which has invoked contested debates over the substitute client group, with disability groups most vehement that carers do not detract from their goals to achieve a right to independent living.

One of the main reasons Twigg's paper has sustained such an interest in geographers has been the varying ways in which the different models can play out across space. As Twigg maintains, there is no single model of the relationship between agencies and informal carers; rather, a series of models or frames of reference is in operation. Each model can map out in different ways: for example, in terms of how many hours a carer might have to spend at home, the availability of respite and day care provision at their disposal, the financial ability to visit different sites in the community (e.g. coffee shops), the ability to work part-time and so on. All these are dependent on how the state and its many different actors and institutions recognise caregiving. It is this attention to the everyday geographies of carers that we turn to in the next section.

Tracing the Everyday Spaces of Care

Geographers have chronicled the complex and varied everyday spatial aspects of caregiving: in the home, in the community and in public spaces. These wider spaces of care comprise a complex array of in-between care-related places such as voluntary shelters, day-care centres and group homes. Across all these spaces, geographers have been attuned to the embodied dimensions of care and sought to examine the experiences of care recipients on the ground.

One of the first strands of this work that evolved within geography focuses on the changing spaces of the home which arise from caring within this private space. Once again, Milligan's work is relevant here, as her paper *Bearing the Burden* (2000) argues that with the movement of care away from institutional spaces such as nursing homes and long-stay hospitals to the 'homespace', it may be creating a blurring of the boundaries between what has traditionally been public/institutional space, and the homespace. Her work traces the increasing presence of qualified care workers, telecare technology, ramps and medical devices within and around the home, in effect leading to an institutionalisation of the home for the family.

Similarly, Janine Wiles (2003) examines the changing routines that can occur when long-term caring takes place within the domestic sphere of the home, resulting in careful monitoring of noise, reduced visits by friends and more structured routines. These factors raise delicate moral and ethical questions for families involved in caregiving work.

These delicate negotiations are taken up further in Rachel Herron and Mark Skinner's (2013) work, which traces the implications of emotions within and across multiple scales at which care relationships, expectations and responsibilities are negotiated in the care of older people in rural Ontario (Canada). These scales include the interpersonal, household and community. In the words of one of the research participants, 'the doing [care] is not the issue… it's the emotional overlay… if everyone was happy, I'd be happy too. It's not that big a deal I mean I worked full time before; this is just like working full time in a different way' (family carer. Cited in Herron and Skinner 2013, p. 188). This emotional aspect, they argue, needs to be more fully recognised in the development of support policies in order to be more contextually sensitive and, ultimately, have the potential to build more ethical (rural) conditions of care.

Meanwhile, the everyday spatial aspects of caregiving have been considered through the lens of social/urban geographers who have scrutinised the spaces of care and welfare within the city. Many of these settings, such as drop-in centres and day care centres, offer places for people to 'just be', away from the world. David Conradson (2003), using homeless shelters as his focus, believes that designated spaces of care have a lot more to offer than basic survival; they allow a space for homeless people to just 'be' away from stigma. Hester Parr

(2000) refers to this form of service as a 'space of licence' where normal rules do not apply and everyone is welcome regardless of their background. These services are also referred to as 'spaces of refuge' (Dean 1999), away from the threatening elements of the outside world. These 'spaces of care' also serve other purposes: to utilise facilities (relevant for those with more complex and multiple impairments); to socialise; to kill time; and to gain information (Waters 1992).

As Geoffrey DeVerteuil (2014) argues, however, the supportive approaches to how vulnerable groups are managed on the ground are arguably downplayed by many mainstream (primarily US) accounts of urban injustice by geographers who have become largely fixated on the accounts of punitive injustice in the city – particularly within the context of the residual neoliberal welfare state'. Indeed, DeVerteuil argues that injustice must *co-exist with* and *depend upon* more supportive currents (such as The Salvation Army for example; see Figure 6.2) within urban space. In this sense, caregiving at a very fundamental level thus allows the neoliberal punitive ideology of welfare to continue. In a similar vein, the work by Paul Cloke, Jon May and Sarah Johnsen (2010) challenges conventional accounts of urban homelessness to trace the complex and varied attempts to care for homeless people.

The final strand of work in this area examines how caregiving continues across mainstream public space in terms of the management of both the care tasks outside of private or purpose-built spaces of care and perceptions by members of the public of those who may be perceived

Figure 6.2 'Supportive currents' within US cities. Photo Credit: Sombilon Art & Photography. Creative Commons Licence.

as different. One example of this work is by Sara Ryan (2005) who focuses on the complex and on-going interactions between parents of learning disabled children and members of the public. She points to the on-going spatial coping strategies and interventions used by mothers to appease negative reactions to children who may not be able to conform to appropriate ways of behaving and using space. In this case, caregiving becomes more than physical supportive acts and involves complex relational practices and coping strategies. Similarly, Andrew Power (2008) has focused on how carers are often 'caught in the middle' between promoting the independence of young adults with learning disabilities and being overprotective, which can manifest itself in the continual management of their spatial practices.

Linda McKie, Sue Gregory and Sophie Bowlby (2001, 2002) take up this theme of the complex and on-going interactions involved in caring across space by using the concept of caringscapes to describe the multifarious everyday experiences of caring and working. These experiences can involve a complex temporal and spatial interplay of physical manoeuvres most obviously linked by processes of 'getting to work on time' and 'leaving work in time to pick the kids up' or 'making time' to check up on the frail elderly parent. Caringscapes can thus be thought of as shifting and changing multi-dimensional terrain that comprises people's caring possibilities and obligations: routes that are influenced by everyday scheduling, combining caring work with paid work and the paid work of carers (McKie et al. 2001, 2002).

This section has considered the geographies of caring within the context of community care, where a complex patchwork quilt of services has evolved and competing philosophies of how to care for the carers have unfolded. The following section turns its attention to a more recent transformation of adult social care, where there has been a wholesale shift *away* from care in both policy and practice. It examines how it has impacted on the wider landscape of care provision and care itself as a concept. It explores some of the more recent impacts on family carers, the voluntary sector and care workers.

Eroding Places of Care in a Post-welfare State

The spaces and boundaries of care provide a useful context for examining how the care landscape has been changing from the earlier period of community care provision. The focus here is on how care has evolved in more recent times. The philosophy of personalisation, discussed in this section, has now taken centre stage in numerous countries including the United Kingdom, United States, France, the Netherlands and Sweden. This section also draws on geographic work that examines the relative impacts of this unfolding transformation on the different people providing and receiving care. In particular, the concept of compulsory altruism is ever more relevant today, with both austerity and localism (a renewed focus on local community involvement rather than the state) resulting in greater expectations of families and communities, with an increasingly residual role of the state.

This new era in care marks a shift from both the institutional care of the nineteenth and early twentieth century and the 'community care' landscape from the 1970s comprising publicly funded nursing homes, long-stay residential homes and day care centres – towards a new 'post-welfare' geography of care in the twenty first century (Power and Bartlett 2016). This latter evolution of health and social care has seen a new ideologically driven reform agenda over 'choice' and 'control', tightening of eligibility, more stringent assessments and day care centre and nursing home closures (Power et al. 2013; see Figure 6.3).

Figure 6.3   A disappearing landscape of day care? Source: Steve Snodgrass, https://www.flickr.com/
photos/stevensnodgrass/5826326649/in/photolist. Used under CC BY 2.0 https://creativecommons.
org/licenses/by/2.0/

While it is acknowledged that community care was always a mixed economy, as has
already been discussed, it nonetheless had a discernible involvement by the state in the
provision of core services. Since this time, though, there has been a significant erosion of
collective formal services (Roulstone and Morgan 2009; Mencap 2012). This is arguably a
'downstream' effect of increasing pressures from the independent living movement to make
services more 'person-centred' and health and social care restructuring from government,
purportedly to cultivate meaningful lives for people in the community.

Independent living philosophy has now largely become crystallised around the idea of
personalisation and its 'choice' agenda (known as self-determination or consumer directed
care in the United States), although we would acknowledge that independent living refers
to a wider vision for rights and inclusion than choice alone. This shift has been led by a
strong independent living movement in the United States, Canada, Sweden, France and the
United Kingdom (Power et al. 2013).

The individualised focus is a central pillar of personalisation. Originating out of person-
centred planning, personalisation has prioritised a shift from provider- and professional-
led services, which many proponents of reform considered were leading to inflexible and
inappropriate support arrangements, towards personal 'control' over decision-making as
well as access to funding. 'Personal budgets' (or self-directed funding) have become the key
mechanism by which people entitled to state support can now exercise their right to plan
and manage their support. It can give people the ability to decide who provides support,
how it is provided and *where*. This mirrors the wider growth in private medicine and emergence of personal health care, and a sense in which care of the self is increasingly meaning
the *responsibility of the self*, as explored in Box 11.2 in Chapter 11.

Numerous – indeed countless – variants of self-directed funding models exist across the
jurisdictions identified earlier in this section. In the United States, for example, different
states have established their own funding mechanisms with different rules of entitlement
and spending flexibility, in response to their own local historical, social, and political contexts,

and strength of their independent living lobbies. One of the larger programmes, *Cash and Counselling*, exists across 15 states.

Alongside these changes, formal services have also seen the rise of austerity measures in the wake of the late-2008 economic downturn, as evidenced by cuts to social care funding in many countries giving rise to the closure of services. This period of austerity, as already discussed earlier in this book, is also of course ideologically driven, being informed by the liberal economics' view of the need to reduce state spending with the belief that it 'purges' the system and allows markets to adjust during adverse economic conditions (Lowndes and Pratchett 2011). Its increasing utilisation in the post global financial crisis period in Canada, the United States, the United Kingdom and many European countries (often compulsorily enforced) has demonstrated the growing dominance as a doctrine of late twentieth century neoliberalism. Yet austerity programmes remain controversial; counter-arguments centre on their inefficacy as a stimulus for economic growth, as well as their adverse impact on the poorest segments of the population (Global Unions 2013).

The implementation of the guiding philosophy of personalisation in many countries with neoliberal regimes has thus occurred during difficult economic 'austere' conditions, with both political projects of personalisation and austerity operating simultaneously (Power 2014). Indeed, some work has critically appraised the recent restructuring of health and social care under the auspices of personalisation as a cost-saving agenda (Ferguson 2007; Houston 2010).

Geographers have begun to examine the new geographies of care that are unfolding within this context. With the rising acceptance of independent living and personalisation in many countries, particularly Anglo-American and Scandinavian countries where de-institutionalisation has been achieved, the spaces of caregiving have increasingly become fragmented and 'place-less,' as people expect to live meaningful lives in the community. Care thus takes place in shared spaces in the community such as libraries, museums and allotments (Morse and Munro 2015; Power and Bartlett 2015).

Ed Hall (2005) has examined the blurring of boundaries between social inclusion and social exclusion for persons with learning disabilities within the context of day care centre closures and greater expectations for former service users to take up valued lives in the community and occupy positions in the open labour market, thus becoming effectively coerced into inclusion. In effect, Hall argues that to feel part of the wider community a person with a disability may at times experience greater feelings of social exclusion, while simultaneously being constrained from collective and interdependent forms of support.

In addition, while volunteering has been a long and enduring practice throughout the history of welfare, in more recent times there has been a championing of localism in public services alongside personalisation in countries such as Sweden and the United Kingdom. Community volunteers and families are being increasingly called upon to take more active and supportive roles to care for their communities and its local institutions (e.g. libraries) in the midst of a shrinking statutory role in welfare provision. These 'caring' activities include working in community groups, drop-in centres and libraries, and taking part in voluntary fundraising as well as in host-family and home share arrangements, offering in-home support to persons with disabilities.

The political project of localism stems to a large extent from a broader neoliberal philosophy, which has become more distilled within the context of austerity, where the state is seeking to withdraw increasingly from the provision of 'public' amenities and services. Carving out an increased 'volunteer space' within the interface between health and social care has thus become a more central feature of many contemporary governments (see Box 6.3 for

> **Box 6.3**   Key Themes: The 'Big Society' in the United Kingdom
>
> The 'Big Society' became the watchword of the Conservative party manifesto and official banner of its government in coalition with the Liberal Democrats (2001–2015). Underpinning the term was a 'morally-driven' political commitment to greater civic participation. Under the banner, the government implemented a more distilled version of austerity and localism than many other jurisdictions. The Big Society agenda sought to redefine the relationship between voluntarism and society by calling on individuals to play a larger role in volunteering. This political project deploys a narrative associated with the middle-class volunteer of the Victorian 'golden age' of voluntarism and of all parts of society contributing regardless of class, religion or gender. It also emphasises and seeks to champion the ubiquity of 'everyday' volunteering, as seen in support of libraries and school activities and sports for instance. It draws on a particularly British ideology of responding with pride to the hardship associated with fiscal (and other) crises similar to the wartime rhetoric of 'keep calm and carry on'. Although the use of the term 'Big Society' diminished in official public discourse as a result of strong resistance and critical reaction (North 2011), nonetheless the underlying philosophy of austerity localism (Featherstone et al. 2012) has remained. With a Conservative majority being elected in the 2015 general election, these trends of austerity and supporting voluntarism – and the associated cuts to public services – are likely to continue. In other national contexts, such as Canada and the United States, this rhetoric has become a typical narrative alongside (and perhaps associated with) the wider welfare retrenchment and restructuring of the voluntary sector and is having profound material outcomes for voluntarism and the shape of the voluntary sector.

example). An example of this is seen in learning disability services (Power et al. 2013), which are seeking to involve increasing numbers of home share volunteers, who 'host' a person with a learning disability in their home (often for a stipend or paid rent) in an effort to cultivate more meaningful lives in the community for their clients.

In terms of the impact of personalisation and austerity localism within the landscape of 'community care', it is evident that support and assistance have become more decentralised, tending to take place in/across multiple settings, as people move through life, e.g. journeys to work, in work places (with colleagues and customers) and in public places (e.g. local community halls). The need to be flexible and responsive to 'clients' or 'consumers' has thus become the main driving force behind the shaping of the social care market. The market has in many cases become more decentralised as a result, as services try to compete for individuals' self-directed funding, block contract agreements between the state and providers increasingly becoming a thing of the past.

Care is thus becoming more decentralised with a renewed focus on community living and an attrition of care centres. As a result, care is tending to take place in multiple settings involving a myriad of different actors and new technologies such as telecare and online marketplaces for purchasing care services (Hall 2005; Milligan et al. 2011). Consequently, there has been a re-sculpting of roles and relationships for those involved in care work, such as volunteering, the third sector, formal services and family caregiving.

Related to this, transport is becoming one of the core issues facing both home care workers (including visiting therapists, nurses, and home support workers) and clients/recipients of support. Care workers often have to make their own way by car to multiple clients' homes (McCann et al. 2005). Meanwhile, recipients often must rely on public transport because service providers can no longer fund transit. These issues can often be exacerbated by pressures on carers' time and can cause additional stress for carers, care recipients and families, thus ultimately reducing the quality of care being provided.

With the focus on the cultivation of care 'markets' and personalisation, there is also growing demand for brokerage, co-ordination and advocacy services. These areas have seen marked growth in Canada, New Zealand and Australia. 'Local Area Co-ordination' has become a recognisable support model in the Australian context and has attracted much policy interest in Scotland and elsewhere (Hall and McGarroll 2012). Local area co-ordinators work together with older and disabled people and families to develop innovative solutions to re-imagine the possibilities of 'a good life' in the community. Meanwhile, people often require additional support in the use of direct payments and the co-ordination of care from brokerage services. However, brokerage still remains ad hoc in many of these countries (Roulstone and Morgan 2009).

In terms of how this is playing out within the informal family care sector, there are contradictory forces that are undermining – and to some extent resisting – expectations of familial responsibility. The feminisation of the workforce towards the end of the twentieth century, increased geographical mobility and changing family structures are just some of the factors that can mitigate against statutory expectations of an increase in the caring role of women (Milligan 2000).

Nonetheless, the combined impacts of day care centre closures and tightening eligibility for statutory support mean that the home remains a pivotal site of care as Alan Roulstone and Hannah Morgan (2009) have found; their study reveals that many disabled people now occupy their homes for longer periods in the wake of day care centre closures. These increasing ties to the home thus make Christine Milligan's earlier work on care in the home ever more relevant. Moreover, the increasing use of new technologies such as telecare and online marketplaces for purchasing care services heightens the phenomenon of the institutionalisation of the home space.

An End to Care?

More broadly, given the changing lexicon associated with the emphasis towards individualised choice and control, 'care' has become a term that has fallen out of favour amongst many users of support services, particularly amongst disabled adults (primarily those with physical disabilities) and persons with mental health issues. In particular, disability studies scholars argue that the concept of care is too closely tied up with need and dependency and as such has become a contested term for many persons who may require support at different stages in the life course.

The concept of 'care' has thus become increasingly hidden from professional codes of practice and is losing favour among the 'care professions' such as social workers, personal assistants, occupational therapists and clinicians. This is arguably a reaction to the way people were previously 'cared for' by the state in the past, in a way that was often anything but caring, particularly when said care forced people into separate and institutional lives. In this sense, care became synonymous with dependency, being helpless and being a subject of pity. For this reason, the terms care and care-*giving* have become gradually less visible within social care policy discourse.

In its place, there have been increasing calls for the use of terms such as 'help', 'assistance' and 'support', which are argued by many to be less loaded than 'care'. Allied with the concept of support has been an evolving lexicon of choice and control, prioritising autonomous decision-making and control over one's own support. As we saw, this shift has been led by a strong independent living movement in the United States, Canada, Sweden and the United Kingdom and has become a central policy agenda. Although the policy is rooted in such disability movements, critiques of how it has been implemented point to how it has been driven by a desire to shift responsibility onto citizens, often with little support, as well as being associated with a cost-saving agenda (Roulstone and Morgan 2009; Power 2013). Thus, it is unclear in this context of self-management and autonomy how personalisation and caregiving can cohere.

Paradoxically, despite the term 'care' losing favour among certain client groups such as disabled people, within contemporary social policy there has been a renewed focus on the privatisation of caregiving and increasing reliance on the family. With the rise of austerity politics in many countries, which seek to reduce budget deficits in an attempt to allow markets to adjust during adverse economic conditions, policy makers have been looking increasingly towards individuals and families within the community to become more involved in local caregiving and volunteering work. This has manifested itself on the ground by restricted eligibility criteria for social care users and regional commissioning bodies (e.g. local authorities) now only providing support for those in 'critical' and 'substantial' need. As a result more individuals have to rely on the care and support of relatives, friends and neighbours and local voluntary associations. Again, geographers have been centrally involved in debates in this re-making of the welfare state.

The neglect of the concept of care within social policy has led some scholars such as Marion Barnes to make renewed claims for an 'ethic of care' to be reinstated within welfare and broader social policy (Barnes 2012; see Figure 6.4). She draws on the work of Jean Tronto and other moral theorists to articulate six core principles of care: attentiveness, responsibility, competence, responsiveness, trust and respect. Without an ethic of care at the core of support policy, those in need of support, she argues, can become susceptible to a more commodified, transaction-like, and potentially abusive relationship with support professionals. In this context, care work should be assessed by how much the practices involved are considered 'care full' (Barnes 2012). It is clear therefore that care speaks to broader issues of social justice in the way we value and encourage human lives and human flourishing in areas as extensive as policing, education, the labour market, urban governance and the environment.

In the context of caregiving, geographers who have contributed to this debate over the contested understanding of the term include Sophie Bowlby and colleagues (2010) and Andrew Power (2008), who have argued against seeing it as inferring dependence but rather recognising the interdependence inherent in all personal relationships. This work has questioned the assumption that the experiences of a care-*giver* should be presented as a dyadic relationship with a care-*receiver*, and that this is a one-way relationship. Rather, their work emphasises the interdependent and reciprocal nature of caregiving relationships. The concept of interdependence also allows us to examine the way in which care takes place outside the private sphere of the home.

Conclusion

In terms of future directions in care research, it is clear that growing numbers of older people will place greater demands on informal caregiving. On the supply side, delayed marriages, declining fertility rates and evolving family structures (from extended intergenerational family units or traditional nuclear families to single-parent households

Figure 6.4   Time to CARE from a rooftop in Detroit, MI. Reproduced with permission of Mike Boening Photography (www.mikeboening.com).

or people living alone) mean that there are fewer family members to provide informal care. How families, voluntary organisations, the private sector and the state will reconfigure care arrangements and renegotiate the 'care contract' will be forced to evolve in new ways. As support budgets devolve to the level of individuals and the privatisation of care continues, providing rights to support workers, particularly personal assistants, will become an important issue as many will likely see more precarious working conditions such as zero volume contracts and rising transport costs, exacerbated by having to call on separate clients across the community. Given this continually evolving landscape of care, and the resulting spaces and places which its different actors must access, occupy, shape and use, geographers are well placed for examining how these issues will continue to play out.

Questions for Review

1. What role do you think place plays in shaping the practices of care?
2. Do you agree with the contention that care, as an emotionally-rooted supportive practice, will continue to decline? Justify your answer.
3. In what ways do caregiving politics and identity politics intersect most commonly? Does the intersectionality affect the valuing of care?

Suggested Reading

Barnes, M (2012) *Care in everyday life: an ethic of care in practice.* Policy Press, Bristol.

Milligan, C (2000) Bearing the burden: towards a restructured geography of caring. *Area* 32, 49–58.

Power, A (2008) Caring for independent lives: geographies of caring for young adults with intellectual disabilities. *Social Science & Medicine* 67, 834–43.

Twigg, J (1989) Models of carers: how do social care agencies conceptualise their relationship with informal carers? *Journal of Social Policy* 18, 53–66.

References

Aitken, S (2012) *The awkward spaces of fathering.* Ashgate, Aldershot.

Arksey, H & Glendinning, C (2005) Choice in the context of informal care-giving. *Health and Social Care in the Community* 15, 165–75.

Barnes, M (2012) *Care in everyday life: an ethic of care in practice.* Policy Press, Bristol.

Bartlett, P & Wright, D (Eds) (1999) *Outside the walls of the asylum: the history of care in the community 1750-2000.* The Athlone Press, London.

Bowlby, S, McKie, L, Gregory, S & Macpherson, I (2010) *Interdependency and care over the lifecourse.* Routledge, London.

Cloke, PJ, May, J & Johnsen, S (2010) *Swept up lives?: re-envisioning the homeless city* (RGS-IBG Book Series). John Wiley & Sons, London.

Conradson, D (2003) Geographies of care: spaces, practices, experiences. *Social & Cultural Geography* 4, 451–54.

Dean, H (1999) (ed) *Begging questions: street-level economic activity and social policy failure.* Policy Press, Bristol.

Department of Health (1999) *Caring about carers: a national strategy for carers.* HMSO, London.

DeVerteuil, G (2014) Does the punitive need the supportive? A sympathetic critique of current grammars of urban injustice. *Antipode* 46, 874–93.

DHSS (1981) *Care in the community: a consultative document on moving resources for care in England.* HMSO, London.

Featherstone, D, Ince, A, Mackinnon, D, Strauss, K & Cumbers. A (2012) Progressive localism and the construction of political alternatives. *Transactions of the Institute of British Geographers* 37, 177–82.

Ferguson, I (2007) Increasing user choice or privatizing risk? The antinomies of personalisation. *British Journal of Social Work* 37, 387–403.

Finch, J & Groves, D (1983) *Labour of love: women, work and caring.* Routledge, London.

Fraser, N (2006) After the family wage: a postindustrial thought experiment. In: Zimmerman, MK, Litt, JS & Bose, CE (Eds) *Global dimensions of gender and carework.* Stanford University Press, Stanford, CA, 305–9.

Global Unions (2013) *Global Unions' Statement to he 2013 Spring Meetings of the IMF and World Bank Washington,* 19-21 April 2013

Hall, E (2005) The entangled geographies of social exclusion/inclusion for people with learning disabilities. *Health and Place* 11, 107–15.

Hall, E & McGarrol, S (2012) Bridging the gap between employment and social care for people with learning disabilities: Local Area Co-ordination and in-between spaces of social inclusion. *Geoforum* 43, 1276–86.

Herron, R & Skinner, M (2013) The emotional overlay: older person and carer perspectives on negotiating aging and care in rural Ontario. *Social Science & Medicine* 91, 186–93.

Hochschild, AR (2001) Global care chains and emotional surplus value. In: Hutton, W & Giddens, A (Eds) *On the edge: living with global capitalism.* Vintage Books, London, 130–46.

Houston S (2010) Beyond homo economicus: recognition and self-realization and social work. *British Journal of Social Work* 40, 841–57.

Lakhani, N (2012) Britain's army of unpaid carers 'being pushed to breaking point'. *The Independent*, Tuesday 08 May 2012.

Land, H & Rose, H (1985) *In defence of welfare.* Tavistock, London.

Lewis, J (1999) Reviewing the relationship between the voluntary sector and the state in Britain in the 1990s. *Voluntas* 10, 255–70.

Lowndes, V and Pratchett, L (2012) Local governance under the coalition government: austerity, localism and the 'Big Society'. *Local Government Studies* 38, 21–41.

McCann, S, Ryan, AA & McKenna, H (2005) The challenges associated with providing community care for people with complex needs in rural areas: a qualitative investigation. *Health & Social Care in the Community* 13, 462–9.

McKie, L, Bowlby, S & Gregory, S (2001) Gender, caring and employment in Britain. *Journal of Social Policy* 30, 233–58.

McKie, L, Gregory, S & Bowlby, S (2002) Shadow times: the temporal and spatial frameworks and experiences of caring and working. *Sociology* 36, 897–924.

Mencap (2012) *Stuck at home: the impact of day service cuts on people with a learning disability.* Mencap, London.

Milligan, C (2000) Bearing the burden: towards a restructured geography of caring. *Area* 32, 49–58.

Milligan, C (2007) Geographies of voluntarism: mapping the terrain. *Geography Compass* 1, 183–99.

Milligan, C & Power, A (2010) The changing geography of care. In: Brown, T, McLafferty, S & Moon, G (Eds) *A companion to health and medical geography.* Wiley-Blackwell, Chichester, 567–86.

Milligan, C, Roberts, C & Mort, M (2011) Telecare and older people: who cares where? *Social Science & Medicine* 72, 347–54.

Morse, N and Munro, E (2015) Museums' community engagement schemes, austerity and practices of care in two local museum services. *Social & Cultural Geography*, online first.

North, P (2011) Geographies and utopias of Cameron's Big Society. *Social & Cultural Geography* 12, 817–27.

Oliver, M & Barnes, C (1989) *Disabled people and social policy: from exclusion to inclusion.* Longman, London.

Parr, H (2000) Interpreting the 'hidden social geographies' of mental health: ethnographies of inclusion and exclusion in semi-institutional places. *Health & Place* 6, 225–37.

Parreñas, RS (2000) Migrant Filipina domestic workers and the international division of reproductive labor. *Gender and Society* 14, 560–80.

Power, A (2008) Caring for independent lives: geographies of caring for young adults with intellectual disabilities. *Social Science & Medicine* 67, 834–43.

Power, A (2010) *Landscapes of care: comparative perspectives on family care-giving*, Ashgate, Aldershot.

Power, A (2013) Making space for belonging: critical reflections on the implementation of personalised adult social care under the veil of meaningful inclusion. *Social Science & Medicine* 88, 68–75.

Power, A (2014) Personalisation and austerity in the crosshairs: government perspectives on the remaking of adult social care. *Journal of Social Policy*, 1–18.

Power, A & Bartlett, R (2015) Self-building safe havens in a post-service landscape: how adults with learning disabilities are re-claiming the welcoming communities agenda, *Social & Cultural Geography*, online first.

Power, A, Lord, J & DeFranco, A (2013) *Active citizenship & disability: towards the personalisation of support.* Cambridge University Press, Cambridge.

Roulstone, A & Morgan, H (2009) Neo-liberal individualism or self-directed support: are we all speaking the same language on modernising adult social care. *Social Policy and Society* 8, 333–45.

Ryan, S (2005) 'People don't do odd, do they? ' mothers making sense of the reactions of others towards their learning disabled children in public places. *Children's Geographies* 3, 291–305.

Skinner, MW & Power, A (2011) Voluntarism, health and place: bringing an emerging field into focus. *Health & Place* 17, 1–6.

Twigg, J (1989) Models of carers: how do social care agencies conceptualise their relationship with informal carers? *Journal of Social Policy* 18, 53–66.

Twigg, J & Atkin, K (1994) *Carers perceived: policy and practice in informal care.* Open University Press, Milton Keynes.

Ungerson, C (1990) *Gender and caring: work and welfare in Britain and Scandinavia.* Harvester Wheatsheaf, London.

Vullnetari, J & King, R (2008) 'Does your granny eat grass?' On mass migration, care drain and the fate of older people in rural Albania. *Global Networks* 8, 139–71.

Yeates, N (2005) *Global care chains: a critical introduction.* Global Migration Perspectives Paper 44. Global Commission on International Migration, Geneva.

Waters, J (1992) *Community or ghetto? An analysis of day centres for single homeless people.* CHAR, London.

Wiles, J (2003) Daily geographies of caregivers: mobility, routine, scale. *Social Science & Medicine* 57, 1307–25.

Wolch, JR (1990) *The shadow state: government and voluntary sector in transition.* The Foundation Center, New York.

Chapter 7

Post-Asylum Geographies

Introduction

The geographies of care, as explored in the last chapter, has been a strong sub-field within geography since the 1970s. This chapter focuses specifically on the geographies of mental health care, which has been a dominant strand of scholarship within health geography that has documented and critically explored the evolution of care from and since the height of institutional care provision in the nineteenth century. Its continued relevance as a field within health geography rests with the continuing legacies of institutional care on the lives of persons with mental health issues, in terms of the on-going forms of stigma, de-personalisation and marginalisation that still shape contemporary experiences and spaces of mental health care.

In this chapter we first take a look at the initial scholarship on asylum geographies – a substantial area of historical inquiry evidenced through the work of Chris Philo, Michael Dear, Jennifer Wolch and others. It traces how geographers have contributed to our understandings of the spatial manifestations of care within the institutional setting, in terms of the impact of an asylum's dominant and imposing structures on the landscape and on the imaginations of people within and outside these sites. We draw partly on a themed special issue 'Post-Asylum Geographies' in the journal *Health & Place* (2000), which demonstrates the significance of mental asylum spaces, making a testimony to Chris Philo's words that such 'monolithic institutions comprise rich reservoirs of geographical knowledge': they tell us about the particular and complex relationships between people and care (Parr et al. 2003, p. 341).

The chapter then examines the wellsprings of reform that prompted a rejection of asylums as a form of 'care' in the 1970s and 1980s and the resulting de-institutionalisation of persons with mental health issues and their relocation into the community. It identifies a number of geographic case studies from different jurisdictions, including the United States,

Health Geographies: A Critical Introduction, First Edition. Tim Brown, Gavin J. Andrews,
Steven Cummins, Beth Greenhough, Daniel Lewis, and Andrew Power.
© 2018 John Wiley & Sons Ltd. Published 2018 by John Wiley & Sons Ltd.

Canada and the United Kingdom, exploring the fledgling efforts made by policy makers, care professionals and advocates to reposition former mental health 'inmates' (a term we do not use lightly here but one that denotes the *de facto* incarceration of people that took place in asylums) into the community, as well as the subsequent landscapes of despair that emerged in many cases with community care because those persons dislocated from such former sites were not fully supported.

In terms of the contemporary geographies of mental health that have emerged since de-institutionalisation, the chapter draws on the work of geographers such as Graham Moon, Hester Parr, Geoffrey DeVerteuil and Chris Philo amongst others to explore the continuing legacies left behind from the asylum. The focus here is on the experiences of service users and the wider community as well as on the changing nature of the carceral environment itself since de-institutionalisation.

Within this contemporary geography, the chapter considers mental health in both the urban and rural context. Within the contemporary urban context, it draws on the geographic work to disentangle the post-welfare geographies that exist for many persons living with mental health conditions on the fringes of society today. Emphasis is placed on the emergence of service-dependent ghettoes and associated forms of socio-spatial stigmatisation. Within the rural setting, where institutions would have commonly been located (for reasons discussed later in this chapter), the chapter examines the important effects of living with mental health issues within smaller, more remote communities.

Throughout the chapter we engage with notions of stigma and exclusion as well as ideas about confinement, containment and 'othering'. Case studies examine the life worlds of service users in different environments and the fate of the psychiatric asylum. So, we pose two important questions in exploring the geographies of asylums: first, what vision did those behind them have?; and, second, how was mental health defined as a result?

Asylum Geographies

The international context

This section explores the asylum in terms of the ideas behind it, the physical forms it took, the practices that took place within it and, relatedly, how mental health became defined by it. For the purposes of the book, the chapter seeks to examine how the legacies of this landscape of care have left 'traces' (a term we return to in Post-asylum geographies) in how mental health is envisioned today. Prior to the emergence of asylums, the care of mentally disturbed individuals in pre-industrial society rested almost entirely on the family (Bartlett and Wright 1999). Those without the support of family relied on early forms of 'indoor relief' found in alms houses and workhouses (poorhouses). Indeed, the overwhelming majority of the 'insane' (the terminology of the day) were still to be found at large in the community. Those who could not be kept at home often wandered free, begging for food and shelter or committed to *gaols* (prisons). This particular narrative invokes a feeling of wastelands; however other accounts such as Andrew Scull's (1979) *Museums of Madness* characterise a more open and tolerant pre-industrial society, in contrast to the absolute restrictive incarceration that emerged in the Victorian period.

While society may have been more tolerant, or at least indifferent, nonetheless in Europe a few small Christian institutions dedicated to sheltering the insane were already evident in the early Middle Ages. London's Bethlem Royal Hospital, later known as Bedlam (a term later coined to describe a state of disarray), in the fourteenth century was the most famous. A growing market economy in the 1600s and 1700s saw the development of private sector asylums. Physical restraints such as chains and manacles were often used. Families paid for secrecy and discretion, and private 'madhouses' left few records (Porter 1992). Quaker businessman William Tuke founded the York Retreat in the 1790s. It was the first asylum to shun physical restraint and coercion. Its influential methods became known as moral treatment; this relied on a strict, well-run household where patients were expected to dine at the table, consider the consequences of their actions, and clean and garden (Digby 1985).

With growing industrialisation and urbanisation across Europe from the late eighteenth century, demand from government grew for a wider infrastructure of asylums. These sites were promoted by the newly developing psychiatric profession as therapeutic sites of care for individuals and families coping with the stresses and strains of a rapidly urbanised and industrialised, noisy environment (Scull 1979). From the early nineteenth century, a landscape of publicly-funded provincial asylums emerged across the United Kingdom, Europe, Scandinavia and North America, as well as in the Russian Empire. Those deemed 'insane' or in some cases 'non-conforming' were committed to asylums. Since this time, over the course of the next century, the role of the state continued to extend into the spheres of individual and family life.

Public funding poured into asylum construction between 1800 and the early 1900s. The Victorians placed their faith in bricks-and-mortar solutions to social problems associated with the accelerating pace of modern life (Porter and Wright 2003). This period thus represented the 'golden age' of asylums (illustrated by the image of the colossal St. Loman's hospital in Figure 7.1) in terms of its peak in levels of institutional investment, size of buildings, numbers admitted and the strength of the psychiatric profession in colonising mental health care. Asylums were often totally self-sufficient; both staff and patients were involved in working their own farms and abattoirs, undertakers, tailors and shoemakers (see Box 7.1). They became a catch-all for persons deemed too difficult for society to handle, including those with mental health issues (referred to as 'the insane' or 'lunatics' in Victorian times), brain injuries and learning disabilities (also referred to as intellectual or developmental disabilities, patients being known as 'idiots' or 'imbeciles'). These sites were also used as a containment area for many social problems thought to bring shame to the family, with women often committed for becoming pregnant out of wedlock (Scheper-Hughes 1979). Its 'golden age' in care provision, we would argue, could at the same time have been characterised as its 'dark ages' in terms of the levels of de-personalisation, deprivation and at times cruelty that often became a feature of life inside – a fate that subsequently emerged in exposés and scandals in the 1960s, covered later in the chapter.

A key geographic theme in the history of asylums was its links to the colonial regime. The logic of the asylum according to Saris (1996) must be understood in the context of colonial understandings of disordered persons, disordered living spaces, disordered landscapes and the importance of state appendages in the redemption of such disorder. In particular, Ireland was seen as a testing ground for asylums in the Victorian period by the British government, pre-dating Britain's subsequent bureaucratically organised state-supported institutional provision in England, with the passage of the Irish Lunatic Asylums for the Poor Act 1817. This resolved that the prisons and poorhouses in Dublin, Cork, Waterford and Limerick should no longer accommodate 'idiots' and 'lunatics'. Instead, the legislation led to the creation of a system of provincial asylums – one in each province: Leinster, Munster, Connaught and Ulster (see Figure 7.1).

Figure 7.1 St. Loman's Hospital (formerly Mullingar District Lunatic Asylum), Mullingar, Ireland (built 1847). Photo credit: Andrew Power. Reproduced with permission of photographer.

Box 7.1 Key Thinkers: Chris Philo

Chris Philo is Professor of Geography at the Department of Geographical and Earth Sciences, University of Glasgow. He is regarded as one of the most pioneering geographers in the sub-field of mental health geography. In particular, his work examines the historical geographies of 'madness' and mental health and mental health care provision. His PhD was carried out at Sidney Sussex College, Cambridge University, and was awarded in 1992. His PhD and subsequent research reconstructed the origins of a more systematic (although *never* all-encompassing) institutionalisation of 'madness' following legislation of the early 1700s onwards. He is particularly interested in the work of Michel Foucault and has sought to extend and localise Foucault's history of madness to England and Wales. Some of this work was published in the 1987 paper cited in the section – The 'therapeutic instrument'. Since this time, he has become a prolific scholar in this sub-field and in 2004 published his complete findings from extensive archival work in a c.700 page monograph, *The Geographical History of Institutional Provision for the Insane from Medieval Times to the 1860s in England and Wales* (Edwin Mellen Press).

With the subsequent famine (1845–1850), which caused almost irreparable damage to the fabric of Irish society, Ireland quickly became the site with the largest institutional population per capita in the world (Finnane 1981). Additional asylums were built across the country such as the Mullingar District Lunatic Asylum (as shown in Figure 7.1) and the institutional infrastructure quickly became overburdened. The extensive development of asylums in Ireland has prompted a wide range of different scholarship to explore this unique case study, which considered the spaces of the institution itself and its impact on the local landscape, including work by anthropologists (Scheper-Hughes 1979; Saris 1996), historians (Finnane 1981), psychiatrists (Browne 2008), former patients (Greally 2008) and geographers (Power et al. 2013).

More generally, successive colonial governments responded to concerns about the growing number of citizens with mental illness and the housing of these people in prisons (Brunton 2001. Cited in Kearns et al. 2012, p. 178) and poorhouses. The subsequent Victorian county asylum period saw the emergence of a comprehensive provincial asylum system across the United Kingdom as well as in Canada, New Zealand and the United States (Rothman 1971). In Canada, for example, the institutionalisation of people with mental health issues began in the mid 1800s in the British North American colonies. British Columbia subsequently followed suit, with the founding of a large Provincial Lunatic Asylum in New Westminster in 1878, later known as Woodlands School (Power et al. 2013).

The global spread of asylums is also evident across Europe. Indeed, French intellectual Michel Foucault's work *Madness and Civilisation* (1965) traced the 'great confinement' that emerged particularly in France. Its reach, as mentioned, also included Russia and its legacies are now found across the Eastern EU accession countries where custodial treatment in these settings still persists. For example, the Mental Disability Advocacy Centre (MDAC) (2003) carried out research in the Czech Republic, Hungary, Slovakia and Slovenia on those countries' continued use of caged beds at the turn of the twenty first century. Caged beds are used within many mental health institutions as a means of confinement and restraint for adults and children.

Meanwhile, in the Global South, where 650 million disabled people are located (Goodley et al. 2012), the use of institutions is on a much smaller scale. Nonetheless, in many cases the use of asylums still takes up the largest proportion of the mental health budget. Kenya, for example, has little provision for mental health; the government spends only 0.01% of its health budget on mental health (MindFreedom Kenya 2008). However, much of this budget is used to fund a small infrastructure of psychiatric hospitals, including Mathari hospital, the only referral public mental hospital in Kenya. In the context of mental health care in Kenya, then, mutual caring and support in the community is the norm and it is often felt that there is no need for persons with mental health issues or disabilities to live physically and financially apart from their families (Kamundia 2013). Community based mental health care services in Kenya are therefore limited and lack adequate funding to reach a wider portion of the population affected. People thus live in their homes without formal support and without meaningful engagement in the community, or as homeless people (particularly in urban areas) or are institutionalised in the few psychiatric hospitals (Kamundia 2013).

Internationally, it is clear that asylums continue to be very much evident on the landscape today. Their continued presence reinforces the legacies of mental health history in nations that have de-institutionalised or are in the difficult process of managing this transition. The following section draws on geographic work that traces the local operations of these sites and their impacts on the immediate environment.

The 'therapeutic instrument'

According to Jamie Saris (1996), institutions held great sway at the outset in terms of the transformative belief they instilled in local people. The building itself was seen by the asylum designers at the time to be a critical tool for rehabilitating those deemed 'lunatic'.

> The provision of a suitable building is in fact a most essential condition to any judicious form of treatment. The treatment of the lunatic is to be accomplished not merely *in* but *by* the Asylum, which may be looked upon as a great therapeutic instrument itself, without which the efforts of the physicians could accomplish little. (Fogerty 1867, p. 39. Cited in Saris 1996, p. 543)

Indeed, the asylum was seen as a carefully constructed apparatus of the bureaucratic state that advertised its ability to change certain classes of persons on *precisely* the idea that it was a physical manifestation of transformative order (Saris 1996). One of the most important contributions to this area of scholarship within geography is from Chris Philo (see Box 7.1). Since 1987, his work has traced how asylums were considered 'natural' in Britain during Victorian times for people with mental illness as they were advised to be removed from the 'normal round' of people and places in the community. As can be seen from an analysis of psychiatric medical journals of the mid nineteenth century, in particular *Transactions of the Association for the Promotion of Social Science* (c.1850), the medical profession assumed that 'mental derangement' was caused by environmental factors and saw fit to remove the patient from 'all the influences and all the associations' of the home:

> It seems to have been too much forgotten that in every case of insanity the first object should be, as in other maladies, the recovery of the patient: and that is often impossible without *a removal of the patient from home*. All the influences and all the associations of home become perverted, in the large majority of cases, in this unhappy malady. (Cited in Philo 1987, p. 402. Emphasis added)

Parr et al. (2003) describes how people taken to an asylum for the first time were often in a state of shock, or experiencing an acute phase of mental illness. Their memories were of how frightening and disorientating entry to an asylum could be for patients, who recall having to go through 'rites of hospital passage' such as getting used to the new routines and temporal rhythms. Also, the lack of privacy in the wards was noted, thus undermining the extent to which these spaces were seen by patients as sites of refuge; peaceful, caring and calm. The growing numbers entering these settings and the emerging carceral nature of their care thus marked a shift in emphasis from a therapeutic instrument towards an apparatus of control.

Nonetheless, despite these restrictive living arrangements, Philo also traces how over time more complicated social relations emerged for patients with greater opportunities for informal sociality in the halls, reception areas and the asylum café. Also, to varying extents, there were efforts within Britain to separate out those with mental health and developmental disabilities with the evolution of a more specific medical bureaucracy for these different groups of people.

More widely, in terms of how the building was envisaged by the local population, Saris' (1996) ethnographic study at an asylum still in operation in Ireland found that stigma was associated with the building itself, given its symbolic value in people's minds. Quoting a local man, we hear how the symbolic site of the asylum had imposed itself on local people:

> In the country parts, now, going to 'the mental' would be the worst thing that could happen to you. You were never treated the same after that. I know for myself growing up that there was something about that place that changed people. I would never look the same on someone who had 'spent the fortnight,' as we used to say. (Research participant, Saris 1996, p. 539)

Similar accounts of 'malicious gossip' arising from *outside* a local asylum called Craig Dunain in the Scottish highlands are explored in Parr et al. (2003), thus creating an interpretive geography for those unfamiliar with the asylum and thus continuing to cultivate the sense of fear and dread about the place. Parr et al.'s account draws heavily upon the ideas of Foucault to inform our understanding of both historical geography and the historical geography of madness. Foucault's work in *Madness and Civilization* on the great 'carceral' confinement traced the enduring conceptual distinction made during this time between the mad and the rational which was enshrined through the physical separation in the institution.

Drawing on Philo's and Saris' 'interpretive geography', it is clear that the image of going to 'that place' and spending a particular amount of time inside, rather than the application of a diagnostic category (or even a more generalised notion of crazy) *per se*, became a source of stigma in itself. In Scheper-Hughes' (1979) anthropological work in Ireland, she found that rural isolation and small village life in Ireland, mixed with strong Catholic moral codes, meant that there were a lot of 'social admissions' to institutions from families fearful of losing face, including 'loose women' and 'difficult' family members. In many ways, given the provincial, semi-rural location of institutions, the physical distance between people's homes and the asylum must have also fuelled fearful feelings about these places. As Robin Kearns and Graham Moon (2002) point out, they were inherently spatial in terms of their semi-rural, stately-home like settings.

The buildings were often designed by leading Victorian Gothic architects such as John Notman, for example. They soon became associated with a nineteenth century asylum 'type' architectural design, of imposing and majestic appearance. These places of confinement became great signatures of power for the state. Indeed, when they started appearing on the rural landscape in the nineteenth century, the countryside was not given to large buildings, with the exception of widely scattered manor houses (Saris, 1996). These asylums were intentionally sited on the outskirts of provincial centres in semi-rural or rural settings (Brunton 2003). Indeed, the ruralised asylum sought to adopt a scenic location open to the beauties of external nature, with the sites often complete with rolling grounds, nearby woods, duck ponds and scenic views (Brown 1937. Cited in Parr et al. 2003, p. 347).

While many of the early institutions were known for their size, an important point was that the intensive, strict routinisation of time and place and de-personalisation of life within them contributed to the institutionalisation of life inside. According to the European Coalition for Community Living (ECCL 2008, p. 6):

> An institution is any place in which people [...] are isolated, segregated and/or compelled to live together. An institution is also any place in which people do not have, or are not allowed to exercise control over their lives and their day-to-day decisions. An institution is not defined merely by its size.

Goffman's (1959) concept of 'total institution' is useful in this respect in that it provided a complete social, personal and economic ordering of a person's life (see Box 7.2).

Box 7.2   Key Concepts: Total Institution

The term 'total institution' was coined by Irving Goffman, who was a pioneering scholar (this time a sociologist but nonetheless influential within geography) of asylums. The term is used to convey the merging of spheres of work, recreation and sleep into one, whereby all these activities are undertaken in the same place, at the same time and under the same central governing body. The activities (work, recreation and sleep) are undertaken with others who are required to do the same thing, and the activities are also timetabled, planned and imposed on those inside. Second, in a total institution, people are excluded from decisions concerning them. As Foucault (1965) argued, knowledge of patients is created, controlled and shared amongst care staff, therefore ensuring they have power over people in their care. Moreover, a specialist knowledge was generated by the mental health professions (primarily led by psychiatry) around the treatment of mental health conditions including electro-convulsive treatment (ECT), lobotomy and, later, psychotropic drugs. Meanwhile, patients have no knowledge about the staff other than that which the staff choose to share. In addition, staff can leave at the end of their working day, where patients are deprived of normal social supports that are available in the community; thus their needs are handled in a bureaucratic way.

Despite mental health hospitals being characterised as 'total institutions' and usually situated on the hinterlands, their 'distance' from the local community was often softened through familiarity. They were often locally recognised as an 'important place' in the neighbouring area (Kearns et al. 2012). Indeed, as Kearns and colleagues point out, not only were these 'mental hospitals' (as they later became known) highly visible but they also provided significant levels of employment. Moreover, Alun Joseph and Robin Kearns (1996) also revealed how, despite being 'other worldly spaces' and lacking in close proximity, they nonetheless were often closely embedded within the moral, social and political–economic geographies of the localities where they were situated (see also Parr and Philo 1996; Radford and Park 1993). Indeed, local people often regarded them as meaningful entities, loaded with significance beyond their care functions, and usually the institution had its own 'diaspora' made up of a network of individuals intimately linked by their experiences of the institution.

In terms of the geography of *where* people being admitted came from, work by John Giggs in Nottingham found that the highest rates of first-time admissions to Nottingham's sole psychiatric hospital almost all originated from a single, compact census tract extending no more than one mile from the centre of the central business district (1973, p. 58). His conclusions suggest a causal connection between the incidence of schizophrenia and social–environmental variables characteristic of low-status areas, especially the 'inner-city slum areas' of Nottingham (Giggs 1973, p. 71). Giggs states how powerful social and economic factors combine to form a milieu in which schizophrenia is likely to develop. He argues that here, as in other large cities, there are pathogenic areas that seem to destroy mental health. This theory has become part of a recurring debate within geography (Joseph 1979; Dean and James 1981) over the drift and feeder hypotheses and is returned to later in the chapter.

A Failed Ideal and the Grassroots of Reform

While the institution was designed to offer aid to all with mental health difficulties and other impairments, over time that aid became so distasteful (for reasons discussed in this section) according to Saris (1996) that only the truly desperate would make the 'rational' move to avail themselves of it. By the late 1960s and early 1970s, asylums had begun to fall out of favour as a result of reports of over-crowding, de-personalisation and at times deplorable conditions, with the methods of 'care' (e.g. ECT, lobotomies) associated with these sites becoming outmoded amongst an increasingly questioning public.

In 1972, Geraldo Rivera made a TV programme for NBC that exposed the appalling conditions in Willowbrook, a large asylum in New York. Many have considered Rivera's exposé the single most important event to give impetus to the shift away from institutional services. Lawsuits were filed on behalf of the people living in institutions and their relatives in a dozen states, including New York (Willowbrook), Michigan (Plymouth), Alabama (Partlow) and Pennsylvania (Pennhurst). Initially these lawsuits focused on improving conditions within the institutions. However, the Pennhurst case was the first that transformed into a judgement which claimed that no amount of money could remedy the degree of isolation and segregation which it was claimed led directly to abuse and neglect and that should be abolished (Power et al. 2013).

Meanwhile, in Canada on 5 March 1971, Frederick Sanderson, a resident of the Rideau Regional Hospital in Smiths Falls, Ontario, hanged himself; this led to a government review that found the conditions in which he had lived to be 'deplorable'. In response to the scandal and the wider public concern, the Ontario Premier commissioned the Williston Report (1971) which was presented to the minister of health. The report recommended phasing out, as quickly as possible, the large hospital institutions.

Similarly, in the United Kingdom, the move from institutions was driven largely by concerns over the quality of care inside these settings. In 1961, Enoch Powell delivered his famous 'water tower' speech (see Figure 7.2), summarised in the following quote, which captured the imagination of the general population and catalysed a debate over the closure of these settings:

> There they stand, isolated, majestic, imperious, brooded over by the gigantic water-tower and chimney combined, rising unmistakable and daunting out of the countryside – the asylums which our forefathers built with such immense solidity to express the notions of their day. Do not for a moment underestimate their powers of resistance to our assault. (Powell 1961, no pagination)

Public awareness of the conditions in these settings grew further as a result of a series of institutional scandals that provided evidence of abuse from Ely Hospital in Cardiff, South Wales (Crossman 1969), and the Longcare Inquiry into widespread abuse at two large residential homes for adults with learning disabilities in Stoke Poges, Buckinghamshire (Adult Protection 1998). At the same time, Peter Townsend (1962), an influential British social scientist, published a book that exposed the poor quality of care within certain institutions for the aged. However, Powell in his speech also referred to the 'colossal undertaking' required to overcome 'the sheer inertia of mind and matter' involved in closing these settings. This acknowledgement proved to be accurate as it was only by 1986 that the government of Margaret Thatcher adopted a new policy of 'care in the community' after the Audit Commission published a report called 'Making a Reality of Community Care' (1986) which outlined the advantages of home care.

Figure 7.2 Kalamazoo Psychiatric Hospital, Michigan. Photo credit: Graham Moon. Reproduced with permission of photographer.

The period of social care policy in the 1980s thus saw the emergence of 'community care' in Anglo-American countries, which was welcomed by many proponents of social care reform as it was envisaged that care recipients would take up more active and valued roles in their neighbourhoods. For many policy makers though, it was envisioned that community care would mean care *by* the community, rather than *in* the community (DHSS 1981). The background context to this caveat is important. While the scandals fuelled support for closures of institutions, the cost of institutional support was another important driver for their closure. In each of the countries leading the de-institutionalisation movement – the United Kingdom, Sweden, United States and Canada – the government projected excessive public expenditures if the populations of mental hospitals continued to grow. For national governments, they often consumed an overwhelming proportion of the national mental health care budget (Hall and Joseph 1988) and became one of the predominant bureaucratic systems of control alongside prisons over the 'unruly' in society.

Interestingly, in comparison to the United States, Sweden and Canada, cost evaluations in the United Kingdom showed that the institutions were so poorly funded in the first place that community care would cost more (Power et al. 2013). Nonetheless, mental hospitals began to close in all these nations in the 1970s and 1980s. According to Graham Moon et al. (2015), de-institutionalisation in Britain took a period of 30 years, with many delayed closures and re-developments by property developers and retention as Priory hospitals. Such hospitals were transferred to or established by the Priory Group, a private treatment provider of acute mental health rehabilitation services. Other mental hospitals were converted to 'short-stay' treatment centres – a policy enabled by new psychiatric drugs.

In other parts of the world, however, the landscape of asylums has proven more resilient to change, as evidenced by case studies in France and Ireland (Power et al. 2013), as well as in Eastern Europe and Kenya as mentioned earlier in the chapter. These jurisdictions illustrate the continued prominence of large institutional settings around the globe. In most of these countries, mental health and disability groups have been calling for their closure. Moreover, with the internationalisation of disability policy (e.g. the United Nations Convention of Rights for Persons with Disabilities), many governments themselves want to close them. However, many obstacles exist including care worker unions, parents' groups (such as in Ontario, Canada, where parents' groups were very resistant to the closure of the provincial asylum because they felt a life in the community was too threatening for their sons or daughters), reorganisation fatigue and the costs of dual-funding community care and institutions during transition.

Meanwhile, the Anglo-American (and to a lesser extent Scandinavian) experience of de-institutionalisation has inspired much geographic work that has traced the evolution of the new post-asylum landscape of care. This work is explored in more detail in the next section, drawing on the work of geographers who have chronicled the spaces and places forged in the wake of institutional provision of care.

Post-Asylum Geographies

Significant work in geography has looked at landscapes of de-institutionalisation. Here it is evident that from the outset, the movement of people from mental hospitals to the community has been beleaguered by setbacks, experiences of stigma and exclusion as well as cultural politics associated with 'othering'. Our focus here is the post-asylum era, the voices of service users and the changing nature of the carceral environment itself.

Geographic work on de-institutionalisation can be traced back to the 1970s. Julian and Eileen Wolpert (1974) in a paper for the critical geography journal *Antipode* drew attention to the ghettoisation of people with mental health issues and intellectual disabilities and their facilities in poor inner-city areas:

> The massive discharge of tens of thousands of mental disabled people in the past decade has added a new indigent group to the inner cities of our large metropolitan areas... The former asylum residents, not unpredictably have become ghettoized in those sections of the city which have run down boarding houses, and seedy residential hostels, the dumping grounds for their disadvantaged and their caretakers. (Wolpert and Wolpert 1974, p. 63)

A later paper by Julian Wolpert, Michael Dear and Randi Crawford (1975) coined the term 'asylum without walls' to describe the marginalisation of people with mental health issues affected by the spatial concentration of community mental health care facilities in lower-income urban neighbourhoods.

Michael Dear and Jennifer Wolch's seminal text *Landscapes of Despair: From Deinstitutionalisation to Homelessness* (1987) comprehensively traced the period following the first wave of de-institutionalisation from the late 1960s to the 1980s in Canada. They found the development of 'service dependent ghettos' made up of concentrated group homes and halfway houses in inner-city areas as a result of land-use planning and the relative powerlessness of people with mental health issues. This process also left many 'ex-patients' to fend for themselves, becoming homeless or living in temporary lodging homes. Indeed, the lack of bed space prompted the government to pass the Homes for Special Care Act (1964) to provide more accommodation for discharged persons with psychiatric disabilities.

Christopher Smith (1976, Smith and Giggs 1988) also contributed significantly to debates over the unfolding landscape of mental health services at this time. Drawing on the US context, he traced the growing privatisation of mental health services in the wake of institution closures and the challenges facing former institution residents including high levels of community opposition to their new residential proximity. Smith also sought to challenge the automatic link being made by Dear between de-institutionalisation and high levels of homelessness. He found that, empirically, the majority of homeless persons had not come from former institutions but from members of the general public who had been marginalised by broader economic restructuring and social displacement (e.g. divorce leading to the loss of income and housing).

Despite earlier efforts to ensure that community care facilities could support people, as noted above, the locus of care for many shifted to the service ghettoes whose imprints on cities powerfully reinforced the stigma associated with mental health. John Radford and Deborah Park (1993) claimed that the geographies of asylums possess an enduring legacy which continues to have social, political and economic significance. This significance became understood as the original debates over the gradual closures by local people, staff, residents and their families gave way to wider tensions relating to societal expectations and norms of space.

Robin Kearns and colleagues (2012) cite Anderson's (2010) notion of 'traces' to capture the transcendent role of stigma. For Anderson, traces are material remnants (e.g. buildings) as well as non-material consequences (e.g. events and emotions). These two traces are inextricably linked with the tainted reputation rooted in the palpable markers (stigmata). In the case of closed psychiatric hospitals, Kearns et al. (2012) contend that the tainted reputation forms the primary trace upon which more physical triggers of memory are dependent and which largely determine their interpretation. The psychiatric hospital sites accrue further stigma through the modes of care that became associated with the buildings, including ECT, caged beds and lobotomies. These modality-based forms of stigma thus reinforced the tainting of the buildings in the mindsets of the general public. Moreover, these traces continued to contaminate new, smaller mental health facilities in the community, as illustrated by Michael Dear and Martin Taylor's (1982) work, *Not on our street*, which concerned itself with the territorial exclusivity found in residential neighbourhoods which resisted locating facilities in their areas.

Meanwhile, other geographic work has traced the fate of the former psychiatric asylums that became available to relevant authorities following closure. Collective work by Graham Moon, Alun Joseph and Robin Kearns (Moon et al. 2006; Kearns et al. 2010; Joseph et al. 2012; Moon et al. 2015) has identified four key fates in the post-asylum period: retention, trans-institutionalisation, residential redevelopment and dereliction. Importantly, in each case, the 'traces' left from these sites have either been purposively erased or left to instil a mythological status.

Retention of these sites is often derived from delayed closures, where land is retained and health administrative roles have been housed and mental health services have been repackaged. Alternatively, the sites have been used as the elite alternative to seeking respite from the community. One example, Priory Hall, has become a site for the sophisticated selling of the therapeutic landscape for niche markets. The rebranding of these retained sites is evident; in many cases there has been a removal of all mention of the 'traces' of the former mental hospital and any association with the former patients.

Trans-institutionalisation is also evident for many former patients of asylums, in that they are still going as inpatients to facilities within these buildings or else for health care administration. The concept of trans-institutionalisation also refers to the phenomenon of people with mentally ill health who are discharged from, or no longer admitted to, mental hospitals, instead frequently finding themselves in prisons, boarding houses and nursing homes rather than their own homes (Gleeson and Kearns 2001).

The *residential redevelopment* of former psychiatric sites provides a particularly important lens for examining the lasting legacies of former mental health care. It is within this context that 'strategic forgetting' can take place (Kearns et al. 2010), where prospectors and developers minimise all mention of the building's former inhabitants and purposely blur the narratives associated with its history (see Figure 7.3).

It is within the context of the final key fate of *dereliction* that their old and isolated locations, their decaying country manor facades, their long dark empty corridors and their

Figure 7.3   Apartments at Knowle former asylum. Photo credit: Graham Moon. Reproduced with permission of photographer.

ECT treatment rooms have all generated symbolic and even mythological status, and 'ghost tours' around their 'haunted' spaces have been developed. Hence, the stigma associated with the deteriorating condition of many buildings is augmented by the detritus associated with abandonment (see Figure 7.4).

The ways in which mental health stigma has unfolded, as examined within this body of work, is telling given the extensive othering that has marginalised those with mental health issues. Despite the impressive Victorian Gothic architecture of asylums and the thousands of people who lived and died in their custody, there has been little memorialisation of former patients or preservation of the heritage of these historical landmarks. Rather, their 'trace' is often all but purposively removed. This is a critical omission in terms of the potential for memories to be lost and the failure to respectfully honour ex-patients and inform future generations about the outcomes of mass-congregated care. Indeed, the lack of effort to create respectful monuments of their lives offers a glimpse of how mental ill health is envisaged (and still feared by many) today.

It is important to note, however, that not all post-asylum fates have contributed to negative perceptions and stereotypes of mental health issues. Philo (2003) traces how the outside spaces of Craig Dunain asylum still hold special significance for many former workers and residents following its closure – the duck pond, the bowling green, the golf course and nearby wood. In this sense, these landmarks represent a therapeutic landscape for many local people to enjoy the fresh air and green spaces, to walk the dog or to preserve quiet moments (see Parr 2008).

Figure 7.4   Tokani derelict asylum, New Zealand. Photo credit: Robin Kearns. Reproduced with permission of photographer.

Placing Contemporary Mental Health

As well as geographic work on the urban 'landscapes of despair' and the socio-spatial redeployments of former asylum sites, geographic studies (primarily from America and the United Kingdom) have also sought to investigate the intimate social and spatial worlds of the people caught up in contemporary mental health care, in both urban and rural environments.

In urban environments, Geoffrey DeVerteuil's work in this field considers intra-urban residential mobility of a cohort with schizophrenia. Pointing to an extensive 'psychiatric geography', DeVerteuil and colleagues (2007) trace how individuals with schizophrenia continue to cluster in disadvantaged and socially disorganised inner-city locations. Their research offers support to the social selection-drift theory – that individuals drift into deprived, service-rich inner-city areas, rather than inner-city residents being more susceptible to poor mental health *per se*, as advocated by Giggs (1973) and others. Part of the drift may be explained by the push factors of unemployment, dependence on income assistance and poverty, all of which are higher for people with schizophrenia and other severe mental illnesses than for the general population. They work in tandem with many pull factors including low-cost housing and the clustering of mental health services.

Other social/health geographers including Rob Wilton, Hester Parr and Chris Philo have furthered past work by Michael Dear and Jennifer Wolch by examining the 'intimate social and spatial worlds' of people with mental health issues. Dear and colleagues (1999) argue that mental health problems are often constructed as noxious, thus contributing to urban geographies of othering in the city. Wilton (1998) extends Dear's arguments by developing a 'psycho-geography' of mental health, which draws on the work of David Sibley (1995) to map out how and why social distancing between the so-called 'same and other' occurs. He argues that there is a fear of close proximity to people with mental health issues, which can de-stabilise and 'pollute' people's self-identities, thereby creating an impulse to distance oneself from the threat of pollution.

Case studies have also examined the experiences of contemporary mental health service users *within* the designated sites of mental health care within the city. Parr (2000) in the context of the community 'drop in' refers to this form of service as a 'space of licence', a place where normal rules in theory do not apply and everyone is welcome regardless of their background. As discussed in Chapter 6, these services are also referred to as 'spaces of refuge' (Dean 1999) or 'spaces of sanctuary', away from the threatening elements of the outside world.

Beneath the surface though, geographers have also been able to discern more subtle, complex social dynamics that are less than inclusionary which operate within such sites. Parr's (2000) ethnographic study uncovers more intricate understandings of the social geographies of de-institutionalised mental patients within an inner-city 'drop in' centre. Her work examines the complex interplay of norms, transgressions, boundary formation and personal identities of the users of such a setting. Her work reveals the presence of insider/outsider relations amongst the users, with the distancing of some as *too* transgressive, *too* 'ill' (judged by other users as being too noisy and using violent gestures, arguments, and excessive and repetitive bodily movement). Her insights thus disrupt our understanding of people with mental health issues as a homogenous social grouping that is straightforwardly excluded from 'the mainstream' to marginal spaces. Rather, we discover that the mainstream exclusionary social processes somehow 'leak' or 'filter' into marginal spaces and groupings wherein social interactions amongst the users also become marked with considerations of difference, distance, borders and boundaries. This intimate account reveals the extent of internalised oppression that can exist amongst people with mental health issues, thus marking the extent of the dead hand of history of asylums on former and present psychiatric patients.

Meanwhile David Conradson's (2003) and Josh Evans' (2011) work focuses on substance misuse and homeless shelters, which are sites where a complex interplay often exists, as discussed earlier, between disruptive livelihood outcomes and poor mental health. It is important to note once again Smith's earlier assertion that de-institutionalisation was not the sole cause of homelessness in the 1970s and 1980s. However, it is equally important to note that in contemporary homeless shelter settings many of those who are homeless also have mental health conditions and/or substance abuse issues. Indeed, according to Sarah Curtis (2004), many people with mental illness living in the community are unable to find and retain adequate and affordable housing and they are at high risk of becoming homeless. Likewise, the stresses of homelessness may give rise to or exacerbate mental health issues. It is important though not to reinforce the myth that *all* homeless people have mental health issues; this would only further unintentionally stigmatise the homeless population.

Given this complex and contested relationship between experiences of mental health and homelessness, homeless shelters therefore still represent relevant places for understanding the treatment of people with mental ill health within a broader context of spatial 'othering' and control of disordered bodies on the fringes of citizenship. On the one hand, Conradson (2003) believes that homeless shelters have a lot more to offer than basic survival; they allow a space for homeless people to just 'be', away from stigma. On the other hand, Evans (2011) illustrates the subtle surveillance, control and biopolitical dimensions that also take place within these settings. His conceptualisation offers an account of a more punitive welfare space where users are imbued with Giorgio Agamben's (1998) notion of 'bare life'. For Evans, this concept is deployed to illustrate the human status of homeless service users as being barred from any political existence or being recognized as citizens, a process Agamben (1998) calls 'abandonment'. This is evidenced by the subtle moral coding and policing of behaviour and of who is to be 'cared for' within these settings.

Alongside this work on mental health in the city, Parr et al. (2004) have examined the experiences of people with mental health issues and their families in rural areas, drawing on their research in the Scottish Highlands. Their work disentangles the effects of geographical distance, social proximity, stoic cultures and rural gossip networks, all of which have a part to play in shaping the 'place' of people both living with and caring for mental health issues in such places.

Community care in the context of mental health often means small-scale care facilities (e.g. drop-in centres) and a patchwork of formal 'care' provision including general practitioners (GPs), community psychiatric nurses (CPNs), social workers and psychiatrists. Alongside this is a nexus of care from family carers, friends and neighbours. However, beyond this, the work of Parr and Philo shows how being located in a sparsely populated rural area can give rise to a very different experience of living with mental health issues; here, often attention is more fully drawn to people deemed 'other' or 'deviant' because their identifiers lack the anonymity of strangers (or even neighbours) in the city. Parr and Philo (2004) thus argue that rural places are often made up of people who are *physically distant* from neighbours but more *socially proximate*. This social proximity means that neighbours five miles apart might know intimately each other's personal histories and biographies, family relationships and so on. This can give rise to a very different geography of mental health, where the sheer visibility of rural residents' lives enables routine surveillance and the sustenance of community gossip networks.

The outcome of this is that behaviours associated with mental health issues can often be interpreted narrowly as infractions against local codes of conduct.

Through the work of Parr and Philo, the notion of 'community care' is critically examined, as the rural context of Highland communities offers an important comparative lens for unpacking the 'imagined geography' associated with the term: the idea that communities are a resource of willing people supposed to be able to care for each other. This 'moral landscape' is often perpetuated by policy makers, journalists and even academics, as discussed by Rob Gleeson and Robin Kearns (2001).

Parr and Philo (2004) remind us that rural places have exactly the opposite social-geographical relationships found in inner-city locations, which are often made up of fragmented individuals and groups, all leading disparate lives, and as such are places that might be characterized as *physically proximate* but *socially distant*. Thus, the general view of mental health issues as a social contaminant is often a result of two differing practices: the closeness in everyday urban life can spur efforts at distancing while intimacy in rural life can go hand-in-glove with repulsion.

Clearly then, the legacies of institutional care continue to shape the everyday micro-spaces of persons with mental health issues, as well as the experiences and spaces of contemporary mental health care. The on-going forms of stigma, de-personalisation and marginalisation are found in the mainstream, thus blurring the boundaries between inclusion and exclusion.

Conclusion

While mental health care is an expansive and complex field of study, geographic work on the legacies of asylums, the forms of care utilised and the hidden social geographies of mental health have provided important insights and lessons for how we think of mental health care today. As stated in the opening section, the use of institutions still remains prevalent around the world and there continue to be on-going pressures to *re*-institutionalise people in new congregated-care settings. Moreover, recent examples of abuse (e.g. Winterbourne View in the United Kingdom; see DH 2012) remind us of the recalcitrant nature of change in a sector that has remained under-resourced and under-prioritised. Furthermore, despite the closure of institutions in some nations including the United Kingdom, Canada and the United States, there remain institutional practices and technologies all around the world, including inappropriate inpatient settings, inflexible schedules and de-personalising group services.

In this chapter we have sought to examine the critical insights from health geography to the sub-field of mental health care. It remains an important sub-field within health geography as it provides a lens for understanding the extent of social construction behind the illness, and the relationships of power and knowledge (and 'care') at play between the care profession, the state and individuals.

These critical insights into health geography more generally allow us to appreciate the potency of place in shaping the lived realities of people with socio-medico-defined illnesses. They allow us to examine critically the cultural and institutional imprints on how treatment regimes and local indifference and discrimination are normalised and justified. They show us how this area of health care, compared with others you will read about in this book, is neglected and ignored and less prioritised over others (hence often being deemed a 'Cinderella service'), a health 'care' sector which itself has been given little attention or 'care'.

Questions for Review

1. To what extent do you think the traces of historical care still shape contemporary mental health care?
2. How does our contemporary social geography of post-modern urban life exacerbate people's risks of mental health issues and undermine the supports available?
3. How can 'therapeutic' or 'health-enabling' spaces help support people's recovery from mental ill health?

Suggested Reading

Dear, M & Wolch, J (1987) *Landscapes of despair*. Princeton University Press, Princeton, NJ.

Kearns, RA, Joseph, AE & Moon, G (2010) Memorialisation and remembrance: on strategic forgetting and the metamorphosis of psychiatric asylums into sites for tertiary educational provision. *Social & Cultural Geography* 11, 731–49.

Parr, H (2008) *Mental health and social space: towards inclusionary geographies*. Blackwell, Oxford.

Philo, C (1987) 'Fit localities for an asylum': the historical geography of the 'mad-business' in England viewed through the pages of *The Asylum Journal*. *Journal of Historical Geography* 13, 398–415.

Philo, C (2004) *A geographical history of institutional provision for the insane from medieval times to the 1860s in England and Wales: the space reserved for insanity*. Edwin Mellen Press, Lewiston and Queenston, USA and Lampeter, Wales, UK.

References

Adult Protection (1998) *Independent longcare inquiry*, viewed 21 November 2016, http://www.hampshiresab.org.uk/wp-content/uploads/1998-Independent-Longcare-Inquiry-Buckingham.pdf

Agamben, G (1998) *Homo sacer: sovereign power and bare life*. Stanford University Press, Stanford, CA.

Anderson, J (2010) *Understanding cultural geography: places and traces*. Taylor and Francis, Oxford.

Audit Commission (1986) *Making a reality of community care*. HMSO, London.

Bartlett, P & Wright, D (Eds) (1999) *Outside the walls of the asylum: the history of care in the community 1750-2000*. The Athlone Press, London.

Browne, I (2008) *Music and madness*. Atrium, Cork.

Brunton, W (2001) *A choice of difficulties: national mental health policy in New Zealand, 1840-1947*. PhD thesis, University of Otago, Dunedin.

Brunton, W (2003) The origins of deinstitutionalisation in New Zealand. *Health and History* 5, 75–103.

Conradson, D (2003) Spaces of care in the city: the place of a community drop-in centre. *Social & Cultural Geography* 4, 507–25.

Crossman, R (1969) Ely hospital, Cardiff. *Hansard* HC 780, cc1808–20.

Curtis, S (2004) *Health and inequality: geographical perspectives*. Sage, London.

Dean, H (Ed) (1999) *Begging questions: street-level economic activity and social policy failure*. Policy Press, Bristol.

Dean, KG & James HD (1981) Social factors and admission to psychiatric hospital. *Transactions of the Institute of British Geographers* 6, 39–52.

Dear, MJ and Taylor, M (1982) *Not on our street: community attitudes to mental health care*. Routledge, London.

Dear, MJ & Wolch, J (1987) *Landscapes of despair: from deinstitutionalization to homelessness.* Princeton University Press, Princeton, NJ.

Dear, MJ, Gaber, L, Takahashi, L & Wilton, R (1999) Seeing people differently: the socio-spatial construction of disability. *Environment and Planning D: Society & Space* 15, 455–80.

DeVerteuil, G, Hinds, A, Lix, L, Walker, J, Robinson, R, & Roos, LL (2007) Mental health and the city: intra-urban mobility among individuals with schizophrenia. *Health & Place* 13, 310–23.

DH (2012) *Transforming care: a national response to Winterbourne View Hospital.* Department of Health, London.

DHSS (1981) *Care in the community: a consultative document on moving resources for care in England.* HMSO, London.

Digby, A (1985) *Madness, morality and medicine: a study of the York Retreat, 1796–1914.* Cambridge University Press, Cambridge.

ECCL (2008) *Report of the ad hoc expert group on the transition from institutional to community-based care.* European Commission, Brussels.

Evans, J (2011) Exploring the (bio)political dimensions of voluntarism and care in the city: the case of a 'low barrier' emergency shelter. *Health & Place* 17, 24–32.

Finnane, M (1981) *Insanity and the insane in post-famine Ireland.* Barnes and Noble, Totowa NJ.

Fogerty, W (1867) On the planning of lunatic asylums. *The Irish Builder* 9, 39–40.

Foucault, M (1965) *Madness and civilisation: a history of insanity in the age of reason.* Pantheon Books, New York.

Giggs, JA (1973) The distribution of schizophrenics in Nottingham. *Transactions of the Institute of British Geographers* 59, 55–75.

Gleeson, B & Kearns, RA (2001) Remoralising landscapes of care. *Environment and Planning D: Society & Space* 19, 61–80.

Goffman, E (1959) *On the characteristics of total institutions.* Penguin, London.

Goodley, D, Hughes, B & Davis, L (Eds) (2012) *Disability and social theory: new developments and directions.* Palgrave Macmillan, London.

Greally, H (2008) *Bird's nest soup.* Cork University Press, Cork.

Hall, GB & Joseph, AE (1988) Group home location and host neighborhood attributes: an ecological analysis. *The Professional Geographer* 40, 297–306.

Joseph, AE (1979) The referral system as a modifier of distance decay effects in the utilization of mental health care services. *The Canadian Geographer* 23, 159–69.

Joseph, AE & Kearns, RA (1996) Deinstitutionalization meets restructuring: the closure of a psychiatric hospital in New Zealand. *Health & Place* 2, 179–89.

Joseph, AE, Kearns, RA & Moon, G (2012) Re-imagining psychiatric asylum spaces through residential redevelopment: strategic forgetting and selective remembrance. *Housing Studies* 28, 135–53.

Kamundia, E (2013) Choice, support and inclusion: implementing article 19 of the CRPD in Kenya. *African Yearbook on Disability Rights* 1, 49–72.

Kearns, RA & Moon, G (2002) From medical to health geography: novelty, place and theory after a decade of change. *Progress in Human Geography* 26, 605–25.

Kearns, RA, Joseph, AE & Moon, G (2010) Memorialisation and remembrance: on strategic forgetting and the metamorphosis of psychiatric asylums into sites for tertiary educational provision. *Social & Cultural Geography* 11, 731–49.

Kearns, RA, Joseph, AE & Moon, G (2012) Traces of the New Zealand psychiatric hospital: unpacking the place of stigma. *New Zealand Geographer* 68, 175–86.

MDAC (2003) *Caged beds: inhuman and degrading treatment or punishment in four EU accession countries.* MDAC, Hungary.

MindFreedom Kenya (2008) *Report on mental health in Kenya.* MindFreedom Kenya, Nairobi.

Moon, G, Kearns, R & Joseph, AE (2006) Selling the private asylum: therapeutic landscapes and the (re)valorization of confinement in the era of community care. *Transactions of the Institute of British Geographers* 31, 131–49.

Moon, G, Kearns, RA & Joseph, AE (2015) *The afterlives of the psychiatric asylum: recycling concepts, sites and memories*, Routledge, London.

Parr, H (2000) Interpreting the 'hidden social geographies' of mental health: ethnographies of inclusion and exclusion in semi-institutional places. *Health & Place* 6, 225–37.

Parr, H (2008) *Mental health and social space: towards inclusionary geographies*. Blackwell, Oxford.

Parr, H & Philo, C (1996) *A forbidding fortress of locks, bars and padded cells: the locational history of mental health care in Nottingham*. Historical Geography Research Group, Glasgow, UK.

Parr, H, Philo, C & Burns, N (2003) 'That awful place was home': reflections on the contested meanings of Craig Dunain asylum. *Scottish Geographical Journal* 119, 341–60.

Parr, H, Philo, C & Burns, N (2004) Social geographies of rural mental health: experiencing inclusions and exclusions. *Transactions of the Institute of British Geographers* 29(4), 401–19.

Philo, C (1987) 'Fit localities for an asylum': the historical geography of the 'mad-business' in England viewed through the pages of *The Asylum Journal. Journal of Historical Geography* 13, 398–415.

Philo, C (2004) *The geographical history of institutional provision for the insane from medieval times to the 1860s in England and Wales*. Edwin Mellen Press, Lewiston.

Porter, R (1992) Madness and its institutions. In: Wear, A (Ed) *Medicine in society*. Cambridge University Press, Cambridge, 277–301.

Porter, R & Wright, D (Eds) (2003) *The confinement of the insane: international perspectives, 1800–1965*. Cambridge University Press, Cambridge.

Powell, E (1961) *Water tower speech*, viewed 2 February 2016, http://studymore.org.uk/xpowell.htm

Power, A, Lord, J & DeFranco, A (2013) *Active citizenship and disability: achieving the personalisation of support*. Cambridge University Press, New York.

Radford, JP & Park, CP (1993) 'A convenient means of riddance': institutionalisation of people diagnosed as 'mentally deficient' in Ontario, 1876-1934. *Health and Canadian Society* 1, 369–92.

Rothman, DJ (1971) *The discovery of the asylum: social order and disorder in the New Republic*. Little, Brown and Co, Boston.

Saris, AJ (1996) Mad kings, proper houses, and an asylum in rural Ireland. *American Anthropologist* 98, 539–54.

Scheper-Hughes, N (1979) *Saints, scholars, and schizophrenics: mental illness in rural Ireland*. University of California Press, Berkeley, CA.

Scull, A (1979) *Museums of madness: the social organization of insanity in nineteenth-. century England*. St. Martin's Press, New York.

Sibley, D (1995) *Geographies of exclusion*, Routledge, London.

Smith, CJ (1976) Distance and the location of community mental health facilities: a divergent viewpoint. *Economic Geography* 52, 181–91.

Smith, CJ and Giggs, JA (Eds) (1988) *Location and stigma: contemporary perspectives on mental health and mental health care*. Routledge, London.

Townsend, P (1962) *The last refuge: a survey of residential institutions and homes for the aged in England and Wales*. Routledge & Kegan Paul, London.

Williston, WB (1971) *A report to the Honourable A.B.R. Lawrence, Minister of Health on present arrangements for the care and supervision of mentally retarded persons in Ontario*. Ontario Department of Health, Toronto.

Wilton, R (1998) Disability, identity and exclusion: community opposition as boundary maintenance. *Geoforum* 29, 173–85.

Wolpert, E & Wolpert, J (1974) From asylum to ghetto. *Antipode* 6, 63–76.

Wolpert, J, Dear, M & Crawford, R (1975) Satellite mental health facilities. *Annals of the Association of American Geographers* 5, 24–35.

Part III

Producing Health

Chapter 8

Ecological Approaches to Public Health

Introduction

Mortality and morbidity differences between neighbourhoods, regions and countries have been observed for decades in many countries. In the United Kingdom, Sally Macintyre (1999) notes that Edwin Chadwick's 1842 report to the Poor Law Commission documented social and spatial differences in mortality between three 'social orders'. The affluent 'gentry' did best in Bath and Rutland (both of which are rural towns) and the least affluent 'labourers and artisans' did best in Rutland, with both doing the worst in Liverpool (by 1842 a fast expanding urban centre in the North West of England). Chadwick's report was therefore one of the first to document that there existed differences in ages of death in England between places and by social position (see Box 11.1, Chapter 11). Such social and spatial inequalities in mortality and morbidity are still routinely observed today, and up until the late 1990s were still widening in many high-income countries such as the United Kingdom (Dorling 1997; Shaw et al. 1999), United States (Singh and Siahpush 2006) and New Zealand (Pearce and Dorling 2006) and across continents such as the regions of Europe (Richardson et al. 2014). Today there still exists a large geographical divide in life expectancy. Men and women living in the most affluent areas of the United Kingdom have a life expectancy at birth of 79.1 years and 83.0 years, respectively, but for their counterparts in the most deprived areas it is 71.2 and 77.1, a geographical 'gap' of 7.9 and 5.9 years (ONS 2015). There has also been very little change in this geographical pattern over the last decade, indicating how little progress has been made in reducing these spatial inequalities (ONS 2015). What this suggests is that 'place' matters for health, mortality and life expectancy.

In this chapter we introduce the question of how geography is important in understanding the production and maintenance of health inequalities and outline early contextual and compositional explanations for the emergence of geographical inequalities in health. We question whether these explanations are still useful today and suggest that by

Health Geographies: A Critical Introduction, First Edition. Tim Brown, Gavin J. Andrews, Steven Cummins, Beth Greenhough, Daniel Lewis, and Andrew Power.
© 2018 John Wiley & Sons Ltd. Published 2018 by John Wiley & Sons Ltd.

having a deeper appreciation of the social and physical environmental characteristics of 'place' we can better capture and understand the specific causal mechanisms that might affect health. This is illustrated by using the example of obesity and its associated health behaviours, diet and physical activity. We finish by reflecting critically on how 'place' is represented in much public health literature and suggest that a more dynamic, relational conception of place may help advance our understanding of contextual effects on health.

Placing the Geography of Health Inequalities

Throughout the long history of public health, different aspects of place have been considered important as potential 'causes' of disease and this thinking has its roots in the more holistic Hippocratic approach to medicine (Meade and Earickson 2002; see Chapter 3). In its earliest origins, ways of thinking about public health were essentially ecological, relating environmental factors to the development of poor health and disease (Diez-Roux 1998). During the twentieth century interest in environmental factors, mainly associated with environmental quality and sanitation, dwindled with the advent of the epidemiological transition from communicable to non-communicable 'diseases of affluence' in high-income nations combined with advances in scientific thinking within the biological and life sciences which led to the search for new 'causal' risk factors. This search resulted in a move away from the ecological and placed an increasing emphasis on, and interest in, individual biological and behavioural characteristics, leading to a more 'individualistic' approach to preventing disease.

   During the last decade of the twentieth century this more individualistic approach began to be the subject of sustained critique as it was seen to increasingly neglect the social and environmental conditions in which individuals live as factors that might lead to declines in population health – the so-called 'causes of the causes' (Link and Phelan 1995). As a result, since the beginning of the 1990s, there has been a theoretical and empirical resurgence in interest in the role of ecological factors in shaping population health. This 'new' ecological approach embraces the biological, behavioural and socio-environmental factors that impact on socio-spatial inequalities in health behaviours and outcomes. Renewed interest in this area has been stimulated by a realisation within the health sciences (disciplines such as epidemiology and public health) that the increasing individualisation of approaches to thinking about disease causation and the distribution of causally relevant risks to health was, in part, inadequate when confronted by large and increasing socio-spatial inequalities in health. As the epidemiologist Ana Diez-Roux writes:

> the individualisation of risk has perpetuated the idea that risk is individually determined rather than socially determined… lifestyles and behaviours are regarded as matters of free individual choice and dissociated from the social contexts that shape and constrain them. (1998, p. 216)

This realisation prompted a call for a refocusing of effort in public health research by paying greater attention to the social, structural and environmental determinants of health as a way of explaining the socio-spatial patterning of health (see Kaplan 1996; Schwartz 1994; Susser 1994). The ecological approach has, at its core, the idea that place or contextual factors are fundamentally important in determining the social and spatial patterning of the health of individuals. In epidemiology and public health this was seen as a relatively new way of thinking that chimed with wider contemporary debates about the 'new public health', which included a call for a better understanding of the social and economic factors that shape health. However, geographers and sociologists have long argued that place is important in explaining the social and spatial patterning of health because it both *constitutes* and *contains* social relationships and physical environmental resources (e.g. Jones and Moon 1993; Kearns 1993; Kearns and Joseph 1993; Macintyre et al. 1993). In the sections that follow, we explore how geographers have engaged with place as it relates to explanations of the geographical patterns of health inequalities.

Compositional and contextual explanations

Underpinning much of the 'new' thinking in this field was the important distinction between compositional and contextual explanations for spatial variations in a variety of health outcomes and behaviours. A compositional explanation for the spatial patterning of health would be that places have different types of people residing there and that the differences in the characteristics of individuals between these places would account for the observed area difference in health. For example, it might be argued that poorer people die earlier than richer people so it is no surprise that areas with relatively larger numbers of poorer people have higher mortality rates and a lower life expectancy. Poorer people would die earlier and have poorer health than richer people wherever they lived, suggesting that geographical differences in health are purely the result of the geographical patterning of where poorer and richer people live. Thus compositional explanations locate the reasons for geographical differences at the individual level. Compositional factors might, for example, include individual social and economic characteristics such as age, sex, ethnicity, poverty or social class (Sloggett and Joshi 1994, 1998).

A contextual explanation suggests that there are features of the social and physical environment that directly and indirectly influence the health of residents of that environment, or even other individuals who might be exposed as a result of working, going to school or spending leisure time in that environment. It is these contextual differences between places that are hypothesised to drive the socio-spatial patterning of health in addition to, or in an interaction with, the characteristics of individuals themselves. Therefore, contextual explanations suggest that people may live longer, healthier lives if they live in non-polluted areas, with access to the resources, opportunities and amenities that promote healthy living and mitigate individual-level risk factors that might be harmful to health. Such features might include access to parks and green space (to promote physical activity and mental wellbeing), increased exposure to poor quality food environments (such as fast-food outlets which promote the consumption of a poor diet) or the design of active transport infrastructure (to promote active travel such as walking and cycling). As Sally Macintyre et al. (1993) outline:

> Rather than treating the characteristics of areas as the sum of individual characteristics of their residents, and instead of taking for granted what we all know about different sorts of places, this approach would seek to examine, systematically, those characteristics of areas that might influence the physical or mental health of residents. (1993, p. 220)

Macintyre and her colleagues were among the first to outline a framework for which aspects of the physical and social environment might promote or damage health. The authors initially outlined five broad areas in which they believed contextual or place characteristics might influence the development of health and disease (see Box 8.1).

Box 8.1   Key Concepts: Contextual Explanations for Health Inequalities

Sally Macintyre and colleagues (1993) identified a number of features of the social and physical environment of an area that they argued helped to explain the observable patterns of health inequalities. These were:

1. physical features of the environment shared by all residents of that locality (e.g. air and water quality, geology, latitude);
2. the availability of healthy and unhealthy environments at home, at work and at play (e.g. housing provision, secure employment, safe recreation);
3. services provided, privately or publically, to support people in their daily lives (e.g. education, public transport, policing, churches, community groups);
4. socio-cultural features of neighbourhoods (e.g. the past and current socio-political climate, norms and values, community integration and support); and
5. the reputation of a neighbourhood (e.g. perceptions of an area by residents, outsiders and statutory bodies influencing migration patterns and self-esteem and morale of residents).

This framework suggested that there should be a focus on understanding which features of the local environment might inhibit health and using that information to develop interventions that may ameliorate them. However, initial research in this area focused on trying to unpick which was more important – context or composition. An early paper by Andrew Sloggett and Heather Joshi (1994) challenged the idea that 'place' matters at all by undertaking a longitudinal study of mortality in over 300,000 people in England. They suggested that any effect of neighbourhood deprivation on premature mortality could be almost entirely explained by controlling for a measure of individual-level disadvantage. In the researchers' own words, the 'evidence *does not* confirm any social miasma whereby the shorter life expectancy of disadvantaged people is further reduced if they live in close proximity to other disadvantaged people' (1994, p. 1473. Emphasis added).

This paper was followed by work by other researchers that was similar in approach but which extended investigations of the effects of area deprivation to a wider range of outcomes including health behaviours (Duncan et al. 1993), psychiatric morbidity (Duncan et al. 1995) and longstanding illness (Macintyre 1999). Many of these early studies, using the approach taken by Sloggett and Joshi, tended to find that any area or neighbourhood effects of deprivation were strongly attenuated or disappeared entirely after controlling for measures of individual deprivation which suggested that compositional factors might explain geographical variations in health, giving credence to compositional explanations. However, in the late 1990s, with the advent of an improved analytical technique called multi-level modelling, which allowed for a more robust approach to identifying the existence of area effects, it became apparent that in many studies there in fact existed a residual effect of 'area', usually operationalised as neighbourhood of residence (see Box 8.2). These residual neighbourhood effects were observed for a wide range of important health outcomes such as blood pressure, obesity, smoking and cardiovascular disease, even after a wide range of individual compositional factors had been taken into account (Davey Smith et al. 1998).

Box 8.2   Key Themes: Place Effects on Health

The published scientific literature on place effects on health is remarkably inconsistent in its use of terminology. Early work tended to use the phrases 'area' and 'ecological' effects but these were soon superseded by the terms 'place', 'neighbourhood' and 'context' – the first being favoured by geographers and the last two by epidemiologists and sociologists, particularly in the United States. These terms often conveyed an idea of place as rooted and bounded in particular administrative geographies and scales, with the term 'neighbourhood effects' being particularly popular in the field. More recently, the term 'environmental' has also been added to the lexicon, primarily in relation to studies that focus on obesity and its related health behaviours, and is becoming increasingly popular both in the wider scientific and policy literature. This conception tends to refer generally to everything outside of the individual, but still has 'place' at its heart. This linguistic plurality is probably due to the varied disciplinary interests in the field, ranging from epidemiology and clinical medicine to sociology, geography and the nutritional and exercise sciences. Nonetheless the overall theoretical conception is the same.

These findings were not just confined to the United Kingdom. Important early work in the United States found that measures of neighbourhood disadvantage (operationalised as poverty area status) predicted mortality from a range of causes (Haan et al. 1987; Waitzman and Smith 1998) and cardiovascular disease prevalence and related behaviours (Diez-Roux et al. 1997) even after allowing for a large number of other individual characteristics and attributes that might explain these relationships. Reviews of the science in the late 1990s and early 2000s confirmed this earlier work and tended to support the general conclusion that area or neighbourhood effects exist and that living in a deprived or disadvantaged neighbourhood is generally associated with poorer health (Pickett and Pearl 2001; Riva et al. 2007). However, the strength of these associations varies greatly across studies and this suggests that even though contextual effects are likely to exist they were probably not as important as individual level risk factors in contributing to poor health (Pickett and Pearl 2001; Riva et al. 2007; Diez-Roux and Mair 2010). An important point made by some researchers at this time was that any identified neighbourhood effects were not necessarily universal. Interactions were observed between characteristics of areas and individual factors such as age, gender, ethnicity and social class, suggesting that health effects of area and neighbourhood factors varied by these individual characteristics. Thus, rather than supporting the existence of a universal area effect, a picture began to emerge of contextual effects being detected for some health outcomes, in some people and in some types of places (Macintyre et al. 2002).

Context or composition: A useful dichotomy?

As the discussion on compositional and contextual explanations outlines, it is important to understand the differences between these models when exploring social and spatial inequalities in health. However, much of the early understanding in the field ignored the possible interactions between the characteristics of people and the characteristics of places in the production of health, despite empirical work that demonstrated that such interactions might exist.

Thinking in the field was instead driven by the demonstration of the 'independent' effect of each (Macintyre et al. 2002). However, this approach fails to acknowledge that in fact context and composition do not necessarily exert independent effects but may act synergistically through a process termed deprivation amplification. Deprivation amplification (Macintyre 2007) is a process whereby individual-level disadvantage is compounded by area- or neighbourhood-level disadvantage. For example, if a person is on a low income and has limited education it is likely that this individual will be 'sorted' into a type of place with poorer quality housing or fewer community resources that may be less conducive to maintaining good health, further amplifying individual level risk. If you have a high income and are well educated you may be able to choose to live in a more advantaged neighbourhood with access to a wider range and higher quality set of resources such as parks and green spaces, food shopping opportunities and facilities for physical activity. It might also be true that within these areas there may be greater or fewer opportunities for employment, education and training which in turn may then partly determine your ability to be employed or well-educated and trained. Thus, the underlying social and spatial processes that determine individual level risk may also be partly a product of the environment to which you are exposed. The implication then is that those suffering from personal disadvantage tend to have the worst access to resources that might promote health, a phenomenon akin to the well-known inverse care law which states that access to medical care tends to vary inversely with population need (Tudor Hart 1971).

Thus, early work in the field has tried to establish the independent contribution of contextual and compositional factors on health. As Steven Cummins and colleagues (2007) have demonstrated, this has had the unintended consequence of constructing places and people as mutually exclusive and competing explanations for social and spatial inequalities in health. In an earlier paper, Sally Macintyre and colleagues (2002) identify three problems with this approach. First, the distinction between context and composition may be more conceptually fuzzy than it first appears. The characteristics of individuals are plausibly shaped by the contextual characteristics to which they are exposed; for example, occupational social class might be a product of the choices available in the local labour market. Second, certain individual characteristics such as health behaviours like smoking status, diet or physical activity may be in fact intervening variables on the causal pathways to the outcome of interest and are therefore not 'confounders' in any analysis, obscuring the existence of neighbourhood effects. Third, and relatedly, there appears to be a lack of clear theorising about the mechanisms that might link neighbourhood of residence to health outcomes or behaviours and that might in turn form the basis of a better understanding of what relevant data to collect. The underlying implied area effect conceptual models are therefore constructed as being simple and unproblematic, with composition and context proposed as obvious explanatory distinctions. The end result of all of this is that context is therefore treated as the 'residual category' that contains the sum of all other (non-individual) environmental influences on health which are to be explained away after accounting for these individual-level factors. Thus, neighbourhoods and areas have the status of a 'black box' (Macintyre et al. 2002) – a mysterious spatial container of all the unspecified and unknown contextual influences on health and health behaviours.

Unpacking the 'black box' of place

The majority of the work outlined above has tended to utilise off-the-shelf measures of neighbourhood disadvantage, usually derived from routine secondary data sources such as the census, in order to investigate the existence of area effects. However, there are important limitations in the interpretation and understanding of such data, and the use of the administratively defined 'geographies' that go with it. A central concern is that neighbourhood measures of deprivation were often created by aggregating data derived from the social and economic characteristics of individual residents, which raises the question of how far theoretically independent exposures created from the same data can be meaningfully separated conceptually and empirically. Taking such an approach may result in erroneous findings if area measures calculated from aggregating individual data are poor proxies for 'true' causally relevant neighbourhood factors. More fundamentally, as alluded to previously, it does not allow elucidation of *how* neighbourhood effects might actually work. Such an approach does not allow the unpacking of the 'black box' of place in order to identify the specific contextual features of neighbourhoods that may be the most relevant to a specific health outcome or behaviour and to unpick the causal mechanisms by which such neighbourhood effects might operate (Diez-Roux and Mair 2010). Without understanding which neighbourhood factors matter the most for which health outcomes, it would be difficult to improve causal inference and virtually impossible to develop and test policies and interventions that might plausibly improve health.

The call for a greater emphasis on identifying and understanding the precise neighbourhood factors and contextual mechanisms that might affect health has helped stimulate the development of more sophisticated approaches to conceptualising and measuring the area- or neighbourhood-level factors thought to be most relevant for the specific health outcomes under consideration. For the first time, many authors began *a priori* to articulate explicit conceptual models that identified the relevant plausible factors to explore and the specific causal pathways through which they might operate and then test them empirically. One early example was developed by Ana Diez-Roux (2003) who created a simple conceptual model of the possible pathways by which neighbourhood environments might impact on cardiovascular disease risk (see Figure 8.1).

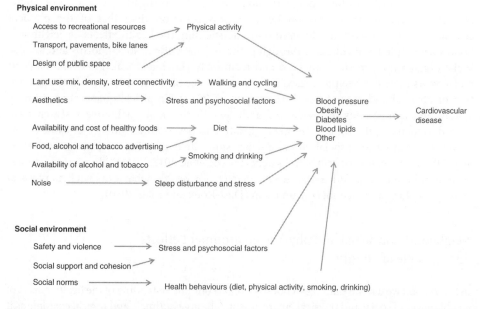

Figure 8.1   Conceptual model of the possible neighbourhood pathways for cardiovascular disease risk. Source: Adapted from Diez-Roux, 2003.

As reflected in Figure 8.1, the exploration and understanding of neighbourhood factors can be seen to have coalesced into two broad domains of interest that may be relevant to health: features of the physical environment and features of the social environment. These are briefly described in the next two sections.

Neighbourhood physical environment

Risks to health of the neighbourhood physical environment have been theorised to encompass a wide range of environmental hazards as well as features of the built environment that might plausibly be good or bad for health. These environmental risks include: longstanding and well-known health-damaging influences such as air pollution and noise but also less well understood features including elements of urban design such as streets, buildings and land use; transportation, public open and green space and access to health-promoting and health-damaging local resources such as grocery stores, supermarkets and fast-food outlets; and facilities for physical activity, leisure and recreation. A rapidly growing body of work has sought to assess the effects of these possible factors on a variety of health outcomes and behaviours. These studies have found neighbourhood effects for a range of outcomes including physical activity (Davison and Lawson 2006), diet (Caspi et al. 2012), obesity (Black and Macinko 2008), cardiovascular disease (Diez-Roux 2003; Chaix 2009) and psychological health, such as depression and anxiety and positive mental wellbeing (Clark et al. 2007).

Neighbourhood social environment

Elements of the neighbourhood social environment that might positively or negatively affect health include a wide range of features related to the social life of the neighbourhood. These elements include the level of social capital and cohesion and the degree of social connectedness, social support and social relationships between residents. They also include local social norms, objective and perceived levels of safety and the presence of crime, violence and disorder within a neighbourhood. Research investigating the effects of neighbourhood social environments on health is less common than that of the physical environment. Much work has focused on understanding the health effects of neighbourhood social capital and cohesion through pathways that enforce social norms and involve social organisation, trust, mutual aid and reciprocity (Lochner et al. 1999), although in recent years there has been increased interest in the role of crime and safety in the promotion of physical and mental health (Lorenc et al. 2012). Empirical quantitative primary studies and comprehensive reviews of both quantitative and qualitative research have tended to focus on the impact on mental health and have found evidence of associations between neighbourhood social capital and cohesion with depression, anxiety and stress (De Silva 2005), crime, fear of crime and safety (Lorenc et al. 2012, 2013). More recent studies have found a mix of positive and negative effects for health behaviours such as physical activity, smoking and alcohol consumption (Diez-Roux and Mair 2010).

Neighbourhood social and physical environment effects: The example of obesity

In this section we use the example of obesity to chart our understanding of the health effects of neighbourhood social and physical environment. Obesity is a timely and topical example as it is now a major concern for governments worldwide and has major impacts on health. Research suggests that excess body weight is directly associated with a range of serious health problems including hypertension, type 2 diabetes and osteoarthritis and is indirectly associated with an increased risk of death through its role as a major risk factor for a range of chronic diseases such as cardiovascular disease and some cancers (Finucane et al. 2011; *cf.* Chapter 2). For example, in England, the rapid increase in the prevalence of overweight and obesity has resulted in the proportion of adults with a body mass index (BMI) classified as 'healthy' decreasing from 41.0 per cent to 32.1 per cent among men and from 49.5 per cent to 40.6 per cent among women between 1993 and 2012. There has also been a marked increase in the proportion of adults classified as obese, rising from 13.2 per cent to 24.4 per cent among men and from 16.4 per cent to 25.1 per cent among women (HSCIC 2014). Globally, although they vary by nation, gender and age, obesity rates have risen substantially over the last three decades with countries such as Tonga and American Samoa having prevalence of overweight and obesity of 86.1 per cent and 84.0 per cent respectively (Ng et al. 2014).

The underlying cause for the recent and rapid increase in the population prevalence of obesity is thought to be environmental, with changes in the food and physical activity environment acting as the primary drivers of weight gain (Egger and Swinburn 1997). This 'ecological' approach to understanding obesity proposes that environmental influences are the root cause of disruption in individual energy balance with decreases in energy intake falling more slowly than energy expenditure over time, thus causing weight gain. Egger and Swinburn argued that the environment to which we are all exposed is becoming increasingly 'obesogenic' and that overweight and obesity is therefore a normal response to an increasingly pathogenic environment. The authors later developed a conceptual model that categorised environmental influences from the macro (of the wider population) to the micro (closer to the individual) and suggested that three environmental domains (similar to those described earlier in the chapter) were important: the physical environment, the economic environment and the socio-cultural environment (Swinburn et al. 1999). Table 8.1 reproduces this original list of possible influences.

The ANGELO (analysis grid for environments leading to obesity) framework is a comprehensive list of possible ecological influences and includes access to food prices and marketing, agricultural policy, taxes, access to fast-food and grocery stores, changing transport modes and the status of leisure activity and recreation. This framework has been used as a starting point to guide much contemporary theoretical and empirical work in the field. It is notable that it is theoretically much more expansive than the neighbourhood effects work discussed earlier in the chapter as it expressly considers the aspects of the macro-level environment that operate at the national or international level.

This next part of the chapter briefly reviews the major environmental risk factors thought to influence obesity. Much of this work uses, implicitly or explicitly, a multi-level ecological model as it allows the assessment of independent environmental influences on obesity at differing spatial scales such as school, neighbourhood, city or nation. Features of the social and physical environment that are hypothesised to promote obesity are chiefly thought to operate through influencing the main behaviours related to obesity: diet, physical activity and sedentary behaviour. Reviews have found a wide variety of potential social and physical environmental influences that have been loosely organised into aspects of the food environment, the physical activity environment and the social environment.

Food environment

Studies have found that dietary patterns and obesity rates vary between neighbourhoods, with living in a low-income or deprived neighbourhood independently associated with poor diet and obesity. These associations have been consistently reported in a variety of

Table 8.1 The analysis grid for environments leading to obesity (ANGELO) framework.

	Physical environment		Economic environment		Socio-cultural environment	
	Food	Activity	Food	Activity	Food	Activity
Macro	Food laws and regulation	Labour saving devices	Food taxes and subsidies	Cost of labour versus automation	Traditional cuisine	Attitudes to recreation
	Food technology	Cycleways and walkways	Cost of food technology	Investment in parks and recreational facilities	Migrant cuisines	National sports
	Low fat foods	Fitness industry policies	Marketing costs	Costs of petrol and cars	Consumer demand	Participating versus watching culture
	Food industry policies	Transport system			Food status	Gadget status
Micro	Food in house	Local recreation facilities	Food prices	Costs of cycleways	Family eating patterns	Peers' activities
	Choices at school or work cafeterias	Second cars	Family income	Gym or club fees	Peer attitudes	Family recreation
	Food in local shops	Safe streets	Other household expenses	Owning equipment	Pressure from food advertising	School attitude to sports
			Subsidised canteens	Subsidised local events		

Source: Adapted from Swinburn et al. 1999.

countries such as the United Kingdom, Netherlands, Belgium, Australia, the United States and Canada (Cummins and Macintyre 2006). As outlined earlier, a process of 'deprivation amplification' may be in operation by which exposure to poor-quality food environments amplifies the individual risk factors for obesity. Environmental influences on diet are primarily considered to involve two pathways: physical and economic access to foods for home consumption from supermarkets and grocery stores, and exposure to prepared food for home and out-of-home consumption from fast food outlets, takeaways and restaurants. Early work suggested that accessibility to supermarkets and grocery stores was poorer in more deprived neighbourhoods with residents having access to fewer supermarkets and larger numbers of convenience stores. Better access to large supermarkets was also shown to be associated with higher diet quality (Gordon-Larsen et al. 2009), as supermarkets tend to offer a wider choice of healthy food at a lower cost than other types of stores, particularly small independent grocers and convenience stores (Cummins and Macintyre 2006). In the United States disadvantages in food access were often demonstrated to have a racial dimension as residents of predominantly African American and Latino neighbourhoods tended to have poorer access compared to their white counterparts. Grocery stores in the former neighbourhoods are also less likely to stock healthy foods (such as fruit and vegetables) or healthier versions of standard foods (Sloane et al. 2003). Caitlin Caspi and colleagues (2012) recently examined the state of the science in a systematic review and found that even though consistent associations with neighbourhood disadvantage and supermarket accessibility and the price and availability of food have been found, more recent work has found inconsistent associations with dietary outcomes.

Foods purchased from fast-food outlets and takeaway restaurants have become an increasingly important part of an individual's diet. The consumption of fast food is associated with weight gain and portion sizes are often larger than those of home-prepared foods (Pereira et al. 2005). Research has found that fast-food outlets are more prevalent in relatively deprived compared to relatively affluent neighbourhoods and that this may act as a mechanism to explain the greater prevalence of obesity amongst residents of more disadvantaged neighbourhoods (Fleischhacker et al. 2010; Macdonald et al. 2007; Pearce et al. 2007). In some studies, fast-food outlets were found to be up to 2.5 times more common in more deprived neighbourhoods (Reidpath et al. 2002). However, only recently have geographical differences in exposure to fast food been linked directly to dietary outcomes and obesity, and the evidence base remains underdeveloped. In another systematic review, Sheila Fleischhacker and colleagues (2010) note that only six of the ten existing studies have found a positive association between access to fast-food outlets and obesity. Further, Thomas Burgoine and colleagues (2014) found that increased exposure to fast-food outlets was associated with increased consumption of fast food at home, in the workplace and during the commute to work, with the strongest associations observed in the workplace. However, the magnitude of these associations with diet remains small in most cases.

Physical activity environment

The influence of neighbourhood deprivation on physical activity has been found to be consistent across the world's richest nations (Jones et al. 2007) with those living in more deprived neighbourhoods having lower levels of physical activity. Within the ANGELO framework, physical environmental factors chiefly consist of aspects of urban built form plausibly associated with sports participation and routine physical activity such as walking and cycling. These might include access to amenities such as parks and green spaces, sports facilities, infrastructure that supports active travel, access to destinations, land use and how 'walkable' a neighbourhood might be. Since 2005, research in this area has proliferated and has generally supported the hypothesis that deprived and ethnic minority neighbourhoods are disadvantaged in access to recreation facilities, have poor neighbourhood aesthetics, are less walkable and have poorer active transportation (Sallis et al. 2012). In particular, studies of the built environment, physical activity and obesity have tended to focus on how well these environments support active modes of travel, either for leisure or commuting purposes. Residents of less 'walkable', less safe and less physically 'connected' neighbour-hoods tend to rely more on motorised private transport (Frank et al. 2007) and are therefore less physically active. Recent reviews tend to suggest that there is consistent evidence that greater population density, a greater land-use mix, presence of pavements and sidewalks and proximity to destinations – all key components of neighbourhood walkability – are linked to walking for leisure and transportation (Saelens and Handy 2008). Access to green spaces, such as parks and public open spaces, has also been found to be a potential predictor of physical activity and BMI among residents. Parks and green spaces are hypothesised to contribute to increased physical activity by providing opportunities for leisure and recreation and improving neighbourhood aesthetic quality which encourages people to walk for recreation, thus reducing obesity. Studies show that some significant positive asso-ciations exist between parks and green spaces and physical activity (Kaczynski and Henderson 2007), although overall the evidence remains relatively inconsistent and depends heavily on factors related to quality and amenity (Lachowycz and Jones 2011).

Social environment and obesity

The social environment in which an individual is embedded may also be important for the development of obesity, although this is relatively less well studied. Cultural factors such as the social norms associated with a community or group can determine physical activity and dietary habits by influencing how much and what type of food is eaten and culturally appro-priate, how much physical activity is undertaken or what activities are favoured or deemed appropriate, or even simply how likely people are to drive rather than walk to their destina-tion (Rozin 2005). Emerging aspects of the social environment that have been investigated include the role of social networks in the spread of obesity which implicitly invoke a theory of 'social contagion' (Brown 2013). Recent work has demonstrated that having close rela-tionships with obese individuals (such as friends, spouses or other family members) can increase an individual's risk of obesity (Christakis and Fowler 2007). This study suggested that a person's chance of becoming obese increases if they have a close friend (by 57 per cent), an adult sibling (by 40 per cent) or a spouse (by 37 per cent) who is also obese and that social rather than spatial ties are important (no effects have been found for having a neighbour who is obese).

Neighbourhood crime, fear of crime and safety have also come under scrutiny as they are important determinants of residents' use of space and are a particular concern in urban environments. Perceptions that the neighbourhood is unsafe or has high levels of crime can reduce social trust and increase social isolation. This leads to residents of a neighbourhood, especially more vulnerable groups such as children and the elderly, being less likely to use their local environment for routine physical activity such as walking and cycling as well as playing and recreation. One classic study discovered that an increase in murders in a neigh-bourhood in Boston prevented parents from letting their children play outside (Lopez and Hynes 2006). In the run-up to the London 2012 Olympics the increase in policing and security led to improvements in perceptions of personal safety, allowing residents of East London to feel more able to use parks and public open space at night, although this was seen as only temporary as security was reduced after the Games had finished (Thompson et al. 2015). This chimes with reviews that suggest that improvements in personal safety are seen as crucial if physical activity interventions are to be successful (Lorenc et al. 2008).

Thinking Critically about Neighbourhood and Contextual Effects on Health

The previous sections of this chapter have outlined why and how context might matter for the health of individuals; however, the theoretical approaches and conceptual models employed to investigate neighbourhood effects have been critiqued. As we have discussed in Chapter 2 and Chapter 3, both the epistemological underpinnings of research in this field and its framing of some bodies as pathological have been brought into question. Others' critiques have argued that this research has failed to deal effectively with the political structures that help to determine the spatial patterning of health inequalities (see Krieger 2011; Shrecker and Bambra 2015). Outside of these critiques, other concerns have been raised that are perhaps driven more by questions of explanatory value than epistemology and what might be referred to as the politics of identity. Central to these critiques is that the research in the field has mainly been driven by trying to distinguish between contextual and composition effects. It has been argued that rather than focus on separating out context and composition, researchers should devote more effort to understanding the processes and interactions that occur between people and the places to which they are exposed (Cummins et al. 2007). This 'relational' perspective also allows a reassessment of how core geographical concepts of location and scale have been uncritically employed within neighbourhood and contextual effects research. A central tenet of geographical thinking, which is often absent in the epidemiologically driven work in the wider field, is the idea that places make people and people make place. This thinking suggests a tight interrelationship between individuals and their contexts. An illustration of the utility of this can be found when considering research that explores the role of 'neighbourhood ethnic density' on health (Acevedo-Garcia and Osypuk 2008). This work explores whether membership of a particular ethnic minority group has an effect on health over and above the ethnicity of the individual themselves. The degree of concentration of a minority group in an area affects health differently. A moderate concentration has been found to be protective for mental wellbeing and high concentrations are found to have negative effects; these effects vary depending on the ethnic group to which the individual belongs (Bratter and Eschbach 2005). This work demonstrated the difficulty in disentangling contextual and compositional explanations; is ethnic concentration a compositional issue associated with individual characteristics of that group, or a contextual issue through group-level processes such as culturally enforced behaviours, or the concentration of specific types of services salient for that group such as traditional foods or culturally specific forms of leisure and recreation (Cummins et al. 2007).

In addition to processes, relatively little is known about how individuals interact and respond to their environment in their everyday life. Much research also assumes that individuals who are most exposed to environmental risks (usually defined as residents of disadvantaged neighbourhoods) respond to environmental cues in a uniform way and does not investigate what shape these responses take or whether they vary. In research conducted for her thesis, Claire Thompson (2013) investigated the food-shopping routines of residents of a deprived neighbourhood and investigated whether they responded differently to the same environmental cues. She discovered that that there existed a diversity of food-shopping routines and that these routines were strongly mediated by the level of individual agency a person possessed. This work suggests that a better understanding of how individuals interact with their environment could potentially lead to a more nuanced understanding of environmental effects on different people and allow the optimisation of environmental interventions.

Taking a relational perspective also prompts a reassessment of another under-theorised area in the field – defining the relevant spatial contexts. A recurring problem is the definition and operationalisation of the 'neighbourhood'. Neighbourhoods are often defined in many different ways and the relevance for each definition might depend on the processes that might be hypothesised to be operating. Stephen Matthews and colleagues' (2005) geo-ethnographies of family life show that the maintenance of family life is not necessarily synonymous with spatial proximity. The majority of environmental resources utilised were external to the neighbourhood and varied in terms of the number of times they were accessed. Similarly, studies utilising global positioning systems (GPS) demonstrate (somewhat unsurprisingly) that many activities relevant to health take place outside of one's immediate neighbourhood. To this end, Daniel Rodriguez and colleagues (2005) demonstrated that less than half of the physical activity undertaken by study participants took place inside their local residential environment. A focus on the residential neighbourhood also neglects the potential role of other types of 'context' including the workplace and school; in reality neighbourhood effects are really only a subset of a much larger set of contexts (Diex-Roux and Mair 2010).

This idea that the 'local' neighbourhood scale is the 'only' meaningful unit of interest in investigating neighbourhood effects and the development of environmental interventions has been referred to as the 'local trap' (Born and Purcell 2006; Purcell 2006). Although the origin of the 'local trap' lies in development planning and studies of urban democracy, the concept can be usefully extended to contextual effects on health by questioning whether the 'local' is always the appropriate scale for analysis or for the assessment of contextual exposures. As a result it has been proposed that, with the advent of ubiquitous location-based technologies that allow the monitoring of people's movement through space, it is now possible to trace an individual's course through multiple contexts at home, work, school or neighbourhood that might differ in terms of their health-promoting or health-damaging features (Cummins et al. 2007). This 'activity-space' approach can greatly enhance the measurement of exposure to environmental risks and more accurately quantify contextual effects on health (Perchoux et al. 2013). As an example, in a recent study of the fast-food environment and diet, Thomas Burgoine and colleagues (2014) found that cumulative exposure to unhealthy food environments at work, in the neighbourhood and on the commute predicted poor diet, but that workplace environments were the most important, indicating the importance of considering multiple contexts across time and space.

Conclusion

This chapter has charted the development of thinking about ecological approaches in the promotion of population health. It opens up a space for geographers to think about how their perspective allows for a deeper understanding of the production and maintenance of health and health inequalities. It focuses primarily on how neighbourhood and contextual effects on health have been articulated and how, more explicitly, geographical thinking has exposed their theoretical and empirical limitations. Advances in the field are currently being driven by the use of experimental studies of the health effects of environmental interventions and the emergence of more sophisticated theoretical models driven by geographical theory, complexity science and systems thinking. These approaches are not considered here but are the subject of Chapters 9 and 10. As Ana Diez-Roux and Christina Mair (2010) note, fundamentally work on the contextual effects on health highlights the potential impact on health and health inequalities of policies and processes often thought to be unrelated to health such as urban planning and design, transportation and retail food system development – central concerns of human geographers from all parts of the discipline. Geographers have a central role in promoting the idea that individual health is a product of interactions with multiple health-damaging and health-promoting contexts, across time and space, and at multiple scales. Such an approach is crucial if geographers are to help the field better understand the role of place in the promotion of health and the reduction of health inequalities.

Questions for Review

1. What is the difference between context and composition, and can you give some examples of contextual and compositional influences on health?
2. What are the different environmental risk factors that might influence physical activity? Can you describe how you might 'change' the environment to promote physical activity?
3. How is 'place' conceived in many of the research studies? Can you critically assess the limitations of this theoretical approach and make some suggestions about how these theories might be improved?

Suggested Reading

Cummins, S, Curtis, S, Diez-Roux, AV & Macintyre, S (2007) Understanding and representing 'place' in health research: a relational approach. *Social Science & Medicine* 65, 1825–38.
Diez-Roux, AV & Mair, C (2010) Neighborhoods and health. *Annals of the New York Academy of Sciences* 1186, 125–45.
Macintyre, S, Ellaway, A & Cummins, S (2002) Place effects on health: how can we conceptualise, operationalise and measure them? *Social Science & Medicine* 55, 125–39.
Macintyre, S, Maciver, S & Sooman, A (1993) Area, class and health: should we be focusing on places or people? *Journal of Social Policy* 22, 213–34.

References

Acevedo-Garcia, D & Osypuk, TL (2008) Invited commentary: residential segregation and health—the complexity of modeling separate social contexts. *American Journal of Epidemiology* 168, 1255–8.
Black, JL & Macinko, J (2008) Neighborhoods and obesity. *Nutrition Reviews* 66, 2–20.

Born, B & Purcell, M (2006) Avoiding the local trap: scale and food systems in planning research. *Journal of Planning Education and Research* 26, 195–207.

Bratter, JL & Eschbach, K (2005) Race/ethnic differences in nonspecific psychological distress: evidence from the national health interview Survey. *Social Science Quarterly* 86, 620–44.

Brown, T (2013) Differences by degree: fatness, contagion and pre-emption. *Health: An Interdisciplinary Journal for the Social Study of Health, Illness and Medicine* 18, 117–29.

Burgoine, T, Forouhi, NG, Griffin, SJ, Wareham, NJ & Monsivais, P (2014) Associations between exposure to takeaway food outlets, takeaway food consumption, and body weight in Cambridgeshire, UK: population based, cross sectional study. *British Medical Journal* 348, g1464.

Caspi, CE, Sorensen, G, Subramanian, SV & Kawachi, I (2012) The local food environment and diet: a systematic review. *Health & Place* 18, 1172–87.

Chaix, B (2009) Geographic life environments and coronary heart disease: a literature review, theoretical contributions, methodological updates, and a research agenda. *Annual Review of Public Health* 30, 81–105.

Christakis, NA & Fowler, JH (2007) The spread of obesity in a large social network over 32 years. *New England Journal of Medicine* 357, 370–9.

Clark, C, Myron, R, Stansfeld, S & Candy, B (2007) A systematic review of the evidence on the effect of the built and physical environment on mental health. *Journal of Public Mental Health* 6, 14–27.

Cummins, S (2007) Commentary: investigating neighbourhood effects on health—avoiding the "local trap". *International Journal of Epidemiology* 36, 355–7.

Cummins, S & Macintyre, S (2006) Food environments and obesity – neighbourhood or nation? *International Journal of Epidemiology* 35, 100–4.

Cummins, S, Curtis, S, Diez-Roux, AV & Macintyre, S (2007) Understanding and representing 'place' in health research: a relational approach. *Social Science & Medicine* 65, 1825–38.

Davison, K & Lawson, CT (2006) Do attributes in the physical environment influence children's physical activity? A review of the literature. *International Journal of Behavioral Nutrition and Physical Activity* 3, 19.

De Silva, MJ (2005) Social capital and mental illness: a systematic review. *Journal of Epidemiology & Community Health* 59, 619–27.

Diez-Roux, AV (1998) Bringing context back into epidemiology: variables and fallacies in multilevel analysis. *American Journal of Public Health* 88, 216–22.

Diez-Roux, AV (2003) Residential environments and cardiovascular risk. *Journal of Urban Health: Bulletin of the New York Academy of Medicine* 80, 569–89.

Diez-Roux, AV & Mair, C (2010) Neighborhoods and health. *Annals of the New York Academy of Sciences* 1186, 125–45.

Diez Roux AV, Nieto FJ, Muntaner C, Tyroler HA, Comstock GW, Shahar E, Cooper LS, Watson RL, Szklo M. Neighborhood environments and coronary heart disease: a multilevel analysis. *American Journal of Epidemiology* 1997, 48–63

Dorling, D (1997) *Death in Britain: how local mortality rates have changed: 1950s–1990s.* Joseph Rowntree Foundation, York.

Duncan, C, Jones, K & Moon, G (1993) Do places matter? A multi-level analysis of regional variations in health-related behaviour in Britain. *Social Science & Medicine* 37, 725–33.

Duncan, C, Jones, K & Moon, G (1995) Psychiatric morbidity: a multilevel approach to regional variations in the UK. *Journal of Epidemiology & Community Health* 49, 290–5.

Egger, G & Swinburn, B (1997) An "ecological" approach to the obesity pandemic. *British Medical Journal* 315, 477–80.

Finucane, MM, Stevens, GA, Cowan, MJ, Danaei, G, Lin, JK et al (2011) National, regional, and global trends in body-mass index since 1980: systematic analysis of health examination surveys and epidemiological studies with 960 country-years and 9·1 million participants. *The Lancet* 377, 557–67.

Fleischhacker, SE, Evenson, KR, Rodriguez, DA & Ammerman, AS (2010) A systematic review of fast food access studies. *Obesity Reviews* 12, e460–e471.

Frank, LD, Saelens, BE, Powell, KE & Chapman, JE (2007) Stepping towards causation: do built environments or neighborhood and travel preferences explain physical activity, driving, and obesity? *Social Science & Medicine* 65, 1898–1914.

Gordon-Larsen, P, Boone-Heinonen, J, Sidney, S, Sternfeld, B, Jacobs, DR & Lewis, CE (2009) Active commuting and cardiovascular disease risk. *Archives of Internal Medicine* 169, 1216–23.

Haan, M, Kaplan, G & Camacho, T (1987) Poverty and health: prospective evidence from the Alameda County Study. *American Journal of Epidemiology* 125, 989–98.

HSCIC (2014) *Statistics on obesity, physical activity and diet – England, 2014,* viewed on 12 February 2016, http://www.hscic.gov.uk/catalogue/PUB13648.

Jones, A, Bentham, G, Hillsdon, M & Panter, J (2007) *Tackling obesities: future choices – obesogenic environments – evidence review government office for science,* viewed 12 February 2016, https://www.gov.uk/government/uploads/system/uploads/attachment_data/file/295681/07-735-obesogenic-environments-review.pdf.

Jones, K & Moon, G (1993) Medical geography: taking space seriously. *Progress in Human Geography* 17, 515–24.

Kaczynski, AT & Henderson, KA (2007) Environmental correlates of physical activity: a review of evidence about parks and recreation. *Leisure Sciences* 29, 315–54.

Kaplan, G (1996) People and places: contrasting perspectives on the association between social class and health. *International Journal of Health Services: Planning, Administration, Evaluation* 26, 507–19.

Kearns, RA (1993) Place and health: towards a reformed medical Geography. *The Professional Geographer* 45, 139–47.

Kearns, RA & Joseph, AE (1993) Space in its place: developing the link in medical geography. *Social Science & Medicine* 37, 711–17.

Krieger, N (2011) *Epidemiology and the people's health: theory and context.* Oxford University Press, New York.

Lachowycz, K & Jones, AP (2011) Greenspace and obesity: a systematic review of the evidence. *Obesity Reviews* 12, e183–e189.

Link, BG & Phelan, J (1995) Social conditions as fundamental causes of disease. *Journal of Health and Social Behavior* 35, 80–94.

Lochner, K, Kawachi, I & Kennedy, BP (1999) Social capital: a guide to its measurement. *Health & Place* 5, 259–70.

Lopez, RP & Hynes, PH (2006) Obesity, physical activity, and the urban environment: public health research needs. *Environmental Health* 5, 25.

Lorenc, T, Brunton, G, Oliver, S, Oliver, K & Oakley, A (2008) Attitudes to walking and cycling among children, young people and parents: a systematic review. *Journal of Epidemiology & Community Health* 62, 852–7.

Lorenc, T, Clayton, S, Neary, D, Whitehead, M, Petticrew, M et al. (2012) Crime, fear of crime, environment, and mental health and wellbeing: mapping review of theories and causal pathways. *Health & Place* 18, 757–65.

Lorenc, T, Petticrew, M, Whitehead, M, Neary, D, Clayton, S et al. (2013) Environmental interventions to reduce fear of crime: systematic review of effectiveness. *Systematic Reviews* 2, 30.

Macdonald, L, Cummins, S & Macintyre, S (2007) Neighbourhood fast food environment and area deprivation—substitution or concentration? *Appetite* 49, 251–4.

Macintyre, S (1999) Geographical inequalities in mortality, morbidity and health-related behaviour in England. In: Gordon, D, Shaw, M, Dorling, D & Davey-Smith, G (Eds) *Inequalities in health: the evidence presented to the independent inquiry into inequalities in health.* The Policy Press, Bristol.

Macintyre, S (2007) Deprivation amplification revisited; or, is it always true that poorer places have poorer access to resources for healthy diets and physical activity? *International Journal of Behavioral Nutrition and Physical Activity* 4, 32.

Macintyre, S, Ellaway, A & Cummins, S (2002) Place effects on health: how can we conceptualise, operationalise and measure them? *Social Science & Medicine* 55, 125–39.

Macintyre, S, Maciver, S & Sooman, A (1993) Area, class and health: should we be focusing on places or people? *Journal of Social Policy* 22, 213–34.

Matthews, SA, Detwiler, JE & Burton, LM (2005) Geo-ethnography: coupling geographic information analysis techniques with ethnographic methods in urban research. *Cartographica: The International Journal for Geographic Information and Geovisualization* 40, 75–90.

Meade, M & Earickson, R (2002) *Medical geography*. 2nd edition. The Guilford Press, New York.

Ng, M, Fleming, T, Robinson, M, Thomson, B, Graetz, N et al. (2014) Global, regional, and national prevalence of overweight and obesity in children and adults during 1980–2013: a systematic analysis for the global burden of disease study 2013. *The Lancet* 384, 766–81.

Office For National Statistics (2015) *Life expectancy at birth and at age 65 by local areas in England and Wales, 2012 to 2014*, viewed 12 February 2016, http://www.ons.gov.uk/ons/rel/subnational-health4/life-expectancy-at-birth-and-at-age-65-by-local-areas-in-england-and-wales/2012-14/stb-life-2012-14.html.

Pearce, J & Dorling, D (2006) Increasing geographical inequalities in health in New Zealand, 1980–2001. *International Journal of Epidemiology* 35, 597–603.

Pearce, J, Blakely, T, Witten, K & Bartie, P (2007) Neighborhood deprivation and access to fast-food retailing. *American Journal of Preventive Medicine* 32, 375–82.

Perchoux, C, Chaix, B, Cummins, S & Kestens, Y (2013) Conceptualization and measurement of environmental exposure in epidemiology: accounting for activity space related to daily mobility. *Health & Place* 21, 86–93.

Pereira, MA, Kartashov, AI, Ebbeling, CB, Van Horn, L, Slattery, ML et al. (2005) Fast-food habits, weight gain, and insulin resistance (the CARDIA study): 15-year prospective analysis. *The Lancet* 365, 36–42.

Pickett, KE & Pearl, M (2001) Multilevel analyses of neighbourhood socioeconomic context and health outcomes: a critical review. *Journal of Epidemiology & Community Health* 55, 111–22.

Purcell, M (2006) Urban democracy and the local trap. *Urban Studies* 43, 1921–41.

Reidpath, DD, Burns, C, Garrard, J, Mahoney, M & Townsend, M (2002) An ecological study of the relationship between social and environmental determinants of obesity. *Health & Place* 8, 141–5.

Richardson, EA, Pearce, J, Mitchell, R, Shortt, NK & Tunstall, H (2014) Have regional inequalities in life expectancy widened within the European Union between 1991 and 2008? *European Journal of Public Health* 24, 357–63.

Riva, M, Gauvin, L & Barnett, TA (2007) Toward the next generation of research into small area effects on health: a synthesis of multilevel investigations published since July 1998. *Journal of Epidemiology & Community Health* 61, 853–61.

Rodriguez, DA, Brown, AL & Troped, PJ (2005) Portable global positioning units to complement accelerometry-based physical activity monitors. *Medicine & Science in Sports & Exercise* 37, S572–S581.

Rozin, P (2005) The meaning of food in our lives: a cross-cultural perspective on eating and well-being. *Journal of Nutrition Education and Behavior* 37, S107–S112.

Saelens, B & Handy, S (2008) Built environment correlates of walking. *Medicine & Science in Sports & Exercise* 40, S550–S566.

Sallis, JF, Floyd, MF, Rodriguez, DA & Saelens, BE (2012) Role of built environments in physical activity, obesity, and cardiovascular disease. *Circulation* 125, 729–37.

Schrecker, PT & Bambra, C (2015) *How politics makes us sick: neoliberal epidemics.* Palgrave Macmillan, London.

Schwartz, S (1994) The fallacy of the ecological fallacy: the potential misuse of a concept and the consequences. *American Journal of Public Health* 84, 819–24.

Shaw, M, Dorling, D & Gordon, D (1999) *The widening gap: health inequalities and policy in Britain.* The Policy Press, Bristol.

Singh, GK & Siahpush, M (2006) Widening socioeconomic inequalities in US life expectancy, 1980–2000. *International Journal of Epidemiology* 35, 969–79.

Sloane, DC, Diamant, AL, Lewis, LB, Yancey, AK, Flynn, G et al. (2003) Improving the nutritional resource environment for healthy living through community-based participatory research. *Journal of General Internal Medicine* 18, 568–75.

Sloggett, A & Joshi, H (1994) Higher mortality in deprived areas: community or personal disadvantage? *BMJ* 309, 1470–4.

Sloggett, A & Joshi, H (1998) Indicators of deprivation in people and places: longitudinal perspectives. *Environment and Planning A* 30, 1055–76.

Smith, GD, Hart, C, Watt, G, Hole, D & Hawthorne, V (1998) Individual social class, area-based deprivation, cardiovascular disease risk factors, and mortality: the Renfrew and Paisley study. *Journal of Epidemiology & Community Health* 52, 399–405.

Susser, M (1994) The logic in ecological: I. The logic of analysis. *American Journal of Public Health* 84, 825–9.

Swinburn, B, Egger, G & Raza, F (1999) Dissecting obesogenic environments: the development and application of a framework for identifying and prioritizing environmental interventions for obesity. *Preventive Medicine* 29, 563–570.

Thompson, C, Cummins, S, Brown, T & Kyle, R (2013) Understanding interactions with the food environment: an exploration of supermarket food shopping routines in deprived neighbourhoods. *Health & Place* 19, 116–23.

Thompson, C, Lewis, DJ, Greenhalgh, T, Smith, NR, Fahy, AE & Cummins, S (2015) "Everyone was looking at you smiling": East London residents' experiences of the 2012 Olympics and its legacy on the social determinants of health. *Health & Place* 36, 18–24.

Tudor Hart, J (1971) The inverse care law. *The Lancet* 297, 405–12.

Waitzman, NJ & Smith, KR (1998) Phantom of the area: poverty-area residence and mortality in the United States. *American Journal of Public Health* 88, 973–6.

Chapter 9

Capturing Complexity

Introduction

This chapter is not about complexity *per se*; as Steven Manson (2003) recognises, complexity is not a self-evident property of reality, rather it exists in the theory and models of reality that we as social scientists construct. Complexity exists because there are things that we do not fully understand and cannot fully explain. Femke Reitsma (2003) draws a distinction between complicated systems which, despite the number of moving parts they have, can ultimately be completely and accurately described, and complex systems in which the whole cannot be fully understood through simple reduction. Reitsma (2003) goes on to suggest that if any system, no matter how complicated, can be explained in a reductionist manner, then 'complicated' is synonymous with 'simple'. Complex systems are beyond complicated, and yet a number of geographers and health geographers suggest that they offer great utility for geographical research on health (Manson 2001).

Whilst complex system approaches engender a great many perspectives relevant to health, our focus in this chapter is on new developments in understanding the interdependence of individuals and their environments. This is a topic area that seeks to revitalise the promise of neighbourhood effects on health discussed in Chapter 8, once held up to be the missing piece of the puzzle in accounting for variation in health behaviours and outcomes left unexplained by individual-level factors. As literature reviews speak of mixed or equivocal evidence and debate the uncertainties in capturing the true, causally relevant neighbourhood, we argue that a move to considering complexity in geographical studies of population health is essential. Adopting complexity as a new orthodoxy, alongside existing approaches, in understanding health and place is important for two key reasons: first, it imposes a theoretical rigour on the design of analysis in terms of the processes and mechanisms understood to be operating across space; second, it moves health geography research beyond the static, aggregate statistics of ecological studies and will help to more fully realise on-going incursions into explaining how dynamics – processes of change over time – impact upon health.

Health Geographies: A Critical Introduction, First Edition. Tim Brown, Gavin J. Andrews, Steven Cummins, Beth Greenhough, Daniel Lewis, and Andrew Power.
© 2018 John Wiley & Sons Ltd. Published 2018 by John Wiley & Sons Ltd.

Tensions in Ecological Health Research

Two geographers, Steven Manson (2001, 2003) and David O'Sullivan (2004, 2006), have been particularly helpful in framing complexity science in the context of studying space and place. Key to their insight is that complexity is a perspective on scientific understanding: on the one hand, complexity science itself makes few restrictive assumptions about how the world is (Manson and O'Sullivan 2006); on the other, the investigator decides what exists and what does not in any given model (O'Sullivan 2004). In this vein, O'Sullivan (2004) makes it clear that the critical break in complexity science is not any claimed move away from reduction, but rather the process of reduction and then reassembly; reduction is, he claims, unavoidable. Despite this cautionary note, O'Sullivan (2004) suggests that there is a strong resonance and affinity between complexity science and geography because of the integrating, interdisciplinary nature of both disciplines.

Anthony Gatrell (2005) adopts this notion of complexity science as an integrating theme in the only paper of its kind to position complexity science within health geography (*cf.* Curtis and Riva 2010a, 2010b). The reconstituted health geography discussed in Chapter 3 is key to Gatrell, who feels complexity can effectively support the 'braided river' used metaphorically by Robin Kearns and Graham Moon (2002) to represent the growing connections between health geography and other fields of study. Furthermore, Gatrell positions complexity science as a possible way of dissolving the binaries (i.e. medical/socio-cultural; structure/agency) that had hitherto persisted in medical geography; complexity science is for Gatrell a way to harness the 'fuzzy boundaries' of health geography and move from debates about structure or agency towards relating these concepts as both irreducible and persistent across micro- and macro-scales. Throughout Gatrell's (2005) paper there exist a number of examples of how complexity can be factored into the geographies of human health, and of health care and health policy. However, the most recent, and perhaps the most considered framing of health and place as a complex system has developed from the study of 'neighbourhood effects': how the contextual and compositional nature of where you live, or the places you regularly go, can influence your health outcomes and health behaviours (see Chapter 8).

Jamie Pearce and colleagues (2012) succinctly pose the core challenge of neighbourhood effects research: how do we analyse something that consists of a complex series of influences that operate at multiple scales and affect some groups in some places (see Box 9.1)? As they suggest, it is a 'live' question as to whether interventions that aim to improve health should be made at the level of people or place. Indeed, the modelling of neighbourhood effects as ecological – concerned with both the individual and their environment – has led sociologists such as Robert Sampson (2003) to suggest that interventions will only be effective if they target modifiable behaviours or environments at multiple scales in such a way that community-level prevention complements individual-specific approaches.

It is now commonplace in public health literature, including that produced by health geographers, to see authors identifying factors at multiple levels – biological, individual, family, household, neighbourhood, region, country and so on – as being complicit in influencing health and disease (*cf.* Cummins et al. 2007; Fagg et al. 2006; Oppong and Harold 2010). Sandro Galea and colleagues (2010) suggest that the predominant reason for this approach is the identification of the range of modifiable causes of ill health, which can be used to intervene in and improve individual and population health. Despite this, they state that research to date has generally been designed to isolate the single causes that make a difference to the health of individuals and populations and tends to have followed a model

Box 9.1   Key Themes: The 'Glasgow Effect'

Glasgow is notable as having the worst life expectancy of anywhere in the UK; even when compared to similar cities such as Liverpool or Manchester it fares badly. So remarkable is this difference that the term 'the Glasgow effect' has been coined; this effect remains largely unexplained despite a number of hypotheses. There is a considerable body of work that aims to describe and explain it; in particular Dr Linsay Gray and Professor Alastair Leyland at the University of Glasgow have been active in trying to understand the health problems faced by Glasgow residents and why they might be more pronounced than in other places in Scotland, the United Kingdom and Western Europe.

Gray and Leyland's work points to the fact that explanations for Glasgow's poor health and shorter life expectancy are attributable not to a single causal factor but to a range of negative health behaviours, including higher than average rates of alcohol consumption, smoking and poor dietary quality. In addition to these individual behaviours, Glasgow contains neighbourhoods that rank amongst the most deprived in Scotland and demonstrate some of the largest health inequalities in the United Kingdom. To this end, Gray (2007, p. 14) has suggested that 'concerted action across the range of health issues is required' and that the 'health deficit experienced in the Glasgow area is a consequence of the socio-economic characteristics of the place and its people'.

The phrase 'Glasgow effect' expresses a frustration that the health disparities seen in Glasgow cannot be easily explained using the common tools of quantitative health geography. However, seeing the 'Glasgow effect' in terms of complexity may suggest that it is in fact an artefact of the modelling process; in a sense, the multiple disadvantages faced by the Glasgow population may be 'more than the sum of their parts' with respect to the resultant effects on health and wellbeing.

of cause and causality that favours the 'counterfactual' approach. In essence, the counterfactual approach aims to generate evidence for the effectiveness of an intervention, or the impact of a particular behaviour or context, by comparing a group of people who are exposed to that intervention, behaviour or context with another equivalent group that has not been similarly exposed (see Chapter 5 for a discussion of the growing importance of evidence-based approaches to health).

The generally accepted *best* approach to inferring causality in health research is the randomised controlled trial, in which participants are (in its simplest form) randomly assigned to groups representing either intervention (exposure) or control (no exposure; the counterfactual). However, as in many historical and contemporary examples, it is often not possible to use a random design in population health research because of feasibility and ethical considerations (see Galea et al. 2010). Following on from this, Ana Diez-Roux (2011) describes many of the conventional approaches to health research as reductivist in nature. Isolating single causal factors requires that reality be abstracted, with measureable and quantifiable components of reality (data) selected according to the governing hypothesis of the research. These data comprise a model that is testable according to the research question(s) set and in its simplest form is understood in terms of: an outcome of interest, usually a health outcome or behaviour; an exposure of interest, usually a modifiable factor hypothesised to impact health that varies across the population of interest; and a set of confounding factors that aim to mitigate the likelihood that changes in the outcome result from any factors other than the exposure. Whilst methods have been developed that allow for factors at multiple levels to be controlled for, there is nonetheless growing concern that an on-going focus on isolating the causal effect of a single exposure through a strictly reductive approach is outmoded.

One of the most important areas of research undertaken by health geographers that demonstrates the presence of multiple competing and complementary factors across a diverse range of scales is obesity (see also Chapter 8). Although spatial, demographic and socio-economic patterns in obesity prevalence can be demonstrated – by urbanicity, ethnicity, age, sex, affluence and so on – no single factor that fully accounts for the increasing global burden of obesity can be identified. This can be seen in the United Kingdom's obesity strategy, which has sought to map out the factors that influence obesity in the population. Dianna Smith and Steven Cummins (2009) provide a detailed overview of the 'obesogenic city', describing how built, social and political environments in cities have been hypothesised to contribute causally to obesity rates. This provides a good insight into explicitly geographical contributions to the obesity debate (see Chapter 2 for other geographical perspectives); however, these ecological factors only represent a fraction of the wider unfolding perspective on obesity. This is well illustrated by the 'Foresight' report (Government Office for Science 2007), which identifies a dense network of possible interactions and challenges the popular narrative that individuals alone should take responsibility for their food consumption and physical activity, instead describing a complex system of contributory factors based on the evidence of independent scientific enquiry (see Figure 9.1).

Ana Diez-Roux (2011) takes this discussion further by applying the multiple-cause, multiple-scale hypothesis to all studies of health inequalities. Early in the neighbourhood effects literature, Sally Macintyre, Anne Ellaway and Steven Cummins (2002) discredited the idea that places could be broken into a neat binary of independent compositional and contextual effects on health, arguing that these effects were in fact mutually and inextricably reinforcing aspects of place. Diez-Roux develops this perspective, suggesting that in addition to seeing factors across many levels as mutually constituent in understanding multi-scale impacts on health, we also need a more balanced appreciation of the backcloth of processes from which the spatial patterning of inequality materialises. Diez-Roux (2011) highlights processes of: residential segregation; the differential location of health services; and, selection effects based on individual preferences that lead to a sorting of population into particular neighbourhoods. Moreover, she views these processes as dynamic, not only in terms of how a neighbourhood can change over time, but also in terms of how different processes at different scales can interact with one another and exacerbate the impact of health inequalities.

Towards Realistic Complexity in Ecological Health Research

Realistic complexity is a useful catch-all to highlight how criticisms of, and suggestions for improvements to, neighbourhood effects on health tend to function. Craig Duncan, Kelvyn Jones and Graham Moon (1998) make use of the term 'realistically complex' in their early discussions of multi-level models to reflect how the then-emerging method allowed for many levels of analysis and hence constituted a significant advance in the quantitative analysis of the geographies of health. However, David O'Sullivan (2004) is cautious about

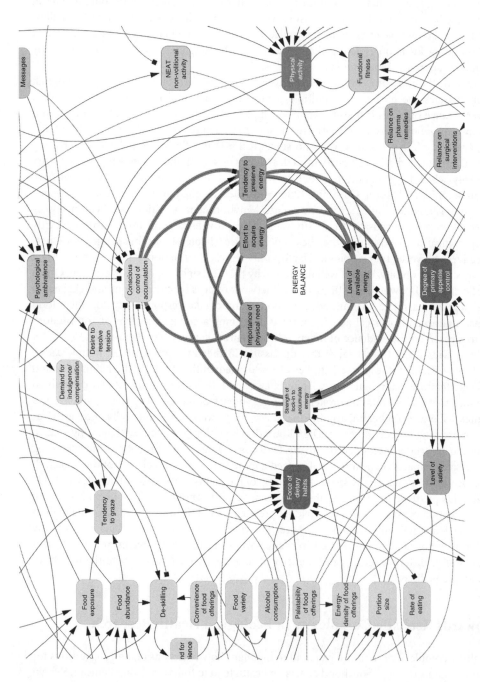

Figure 9.1 Extract of Foresight Obesity System Map. Source: Government Office for Science, 2007. Reproduced under the terms of the Open Government License v3.0.

asserting the validity of models of complex systems, expressing concern that there will often be no way of knowing whether knowledge derived from a model led to the 'right' decisions being taken. The standard attitude to models that O'Sullivan presents is that 'a valid model is one that is useful' (2004, p. 290), which is inherently limited in critical scope. Whilst similarly limited, the idea of practical adequacy is perhaps a good starting point for thinking about realistic complexity: 'To be practically adequate, knowledge must generate expectations about the world and about the results of our actions which are actually realized' (Sayer 1992, p. 69. Cited in O'Sullivan 2004, p. 290).

The underlying criticism of current approaches to a model-based understanding of neighbourhood effects is that they are overly simplistic; the idea behind realistic complexity, or practical adequacy, is to be pragmatic about what a model needs in order to advance our understanding of social phenomena. This approach helps to explain how research has developed from unsophisticated models that associate, for example, material deprivation with headline health outcomes like life expectancy, where practical interventions are difficult to envision, to complicated attempts to capture the 'active ingredients' driving particular health behaviours. Recently, progress in this domain has involved, to varying degrees, conceptual improvements, better measurement and data collection, and statistical or mathematical innovations.

The items covered here make up a partial view of proposals to advance research in neighbourhoods and health; however, they provide an illumination of how investigators are driving for realistic complexity through incremental improvements to contemporary models that fulfil a sense of practical adequacy. As highlighted in the text so far, criticisms tend to coalesce around the idea that models of the environment in ecological research on health are overly reductive. The straightforward response is thus to make models more complicated in the hope that in doing so a better representation is made of the processes and mechanisms that shape reality. However, as has been previously noted, there exists a distinction between models that are merely complicated and those that are genuinely complex. Complicated models may be time consuming and fiddly, but they will ultimately be tractable with traditional statistical tools such as regression analysis or analysis of variance approaches; complex models are ultimately not tractable within this framework. Academics including Gatrell, O'Sullivan, Diez-Rouz and Galea seem convinced that a range of problems in human geography, health geography and public health more broadly are genuinely complex. As such, health geographers will need a working understanding of complexity science and complex systems in order to engage with these new disciplinary perspectives, and for this purpose we need to evaluate what is meant by complexity. The next section seeks to define complexity and offers examples to aid understanding. Sometimes, as Gatrell notes, complexity is a case of 'old wine in new bottles'; in others, however, as O'Sullivan (2004) suggests, complexity is 'hard to pin down'.

Introducing complex systems

The first meaningful step we have to take in thinking about complexity is to begin to view neighbourhoods and individuals not conventionally, as discrete and independent entities, but as interdependent systems. Mike Batty (2013), drawing on contemporary work in complexity science, states that systems in general are hierarchically constructed from the bottom up. Individuals are described in terms of the relationships they have with other individuals or groups of individuals. In turn, the functioning of these relationships forms the building blocks for all kinds of social, cultural and economic sub-systems; Batty describes these flows of 'materials, people and information' ultimately as networks of 'work and play'. To understand how these various networks of work and play 'act', 'interact' and 'transact' with each another is to understand the system itself. This understanding is what O'Sullivan (2004) is getting at when he talks about 'reassembly' as being the key to complexity science.

Batty (2013) articulates systems as being inherently 'modular'; a system of interest, such as an urban neighbourhood, is composed of sub-systems performing specific functions relevant not only to the functioning of the larger system but also to the functioning of other sub-systems. This exemplifies the interdependent nature of a complex system; if one sub-system is subject to change, this has implications not just for the system as a whole but also for other connected and interacting subsystems. Batty therefore sees one of the key insights of complexity science as developing the tools to 'unpick' systems and 'reveal' the networked patterns of flows and relationships that define a given system. This view of complex systems is naturally compatible with calls for 'relational' understandings of place within human geography research (Cummins et al. 2007; see Chapter 8).

Keeping this in mind, we can think about an urban neighbourhood as being a system of interest to environment and health research. Figure 9.2 gives a crude rendering of how a systems approach expands the existing perspective within health geography. Much research that exists on the neighbourhood adopts a conventional view in which the neighbourhood is a simple container of data, drawn at a particular scale and subject to strict geographical boundaries. Useful work has been done using this conventional approach; recently, however, it has been suggested that this effect might be being underestimated owing to the simplicity of the chosen model of neighbourhood (Cummins et al. 2007; Chapter 8). Progressive approaches to characterising an urban neighbourhood might attempt to increase the realism of the model of neighbourhood by adding new data layers that define neighbourhoods not in terms of their material deprivation but in terms of particular environments – the food environment, the alcohol environment, green and civic spaces,

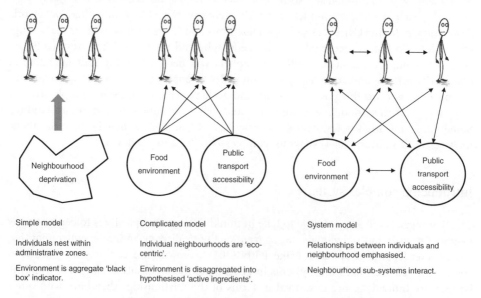

Figure 9.2   Simple, complicated and complex systems models illustrated.

transport infrastructure and so on. If we add in these elements, what we have is still a conventional view of neighbourhood, albeit a complicated one.

Undertaking research on a complex system is still, as O'Sullivan (2004) stresses, reductive; it means identifying a system of interest and considering the relevant sub-systems and interconnections hypothesised to act on particular health outcomes or health behaviours. A criticism of the 'complicated' models in environment and health research might hold that it has largely been the environment that has been complicated and not the interaction between individuals and their environment. This leads to a sense that neighbourhoods and health research is disembodied and lacking in an express accounting of individual agency in favour of generalised landscapes of exposure (see Chapter 2). This is something that a complex systems approach needs to develop; for those interested, a good framework for doing so exists in Nancy Krieger's 'ecosocial theory' which intends to explain the multi-scale causation of disease and behaviour (Krieger 2001). Krieger's framework (see Box 9.2) applies many of the ideas behind complexity that are discussed in the following text, but does so with a particular focus on embodiment. In the following section, we go further into considering what makes a system complex, picking up features of complex systems that complexity scientists have proposed as being integral features, and outlining how they contribute to our understanding of complexity.

Features of complex systems

In the description and analysis of complex systems, a number of features, or properties of systems, that are specific to complexity re-occur. These properties have come to be part of the language of complexity, and observing their presence in a system of interest has become a strong indicator of complex processes. In this section, we will examine the following important properties: openness; dynamics; emergence; non-linearity; scaling; feedback, path dependency and lock-in; self-organisation; and lack of central control.

Openness

Saroj Jayasinghe (2011) suggests that taking the perspective that a given system is 'open' is a founding principle of research on systems. An open system approach accepts that a defined system of interest could be influenced by other external sub-systems not specifically modelled. By comparison, closed systems only allow interactions within a defined system. As it is unlikely that we would ever be able to describe a system that comprehensively and accurately represents all interactions between sub-systems, openness is a pragmatic response to the requirements of modelling realistic complexity. A closed systems approach might be appropriate if we can assume that the system of interest is sufficiently well-defined as to be independent from external influences. However, in the case of environment and health research it is unlikely that we could reach a state of systemic independence within the boundaries of what we could tractably analyse. This can be evidenced in the Foresight system map of obesity shown earlier – an evaluation of the obesogenic environment necessitates an open system approach as it is not feasible to capture all hypothesised contributory elements within a single model.

Dynamics

The term 'dynamic' encapsulates two important aspects of complex systems: first, that systems change over time; and second, that these changes can be subject to lags and feedback effects. A system that changes over time, and in an interdependent way, often produces

Box 9.2   Key Thinkers: Nancy Krieger

Health geography requires that we bring together biology and society in order to describe and explain health inequalities. For Nancy Krieger this requires an understanding of 'how we literally incorporate, biologically, the world around us' (2001, p. 668). Krieger sets up this premise as one of embodiment, the intent being to reveal 'who and what is responsible for population patterns of health, disease, and well-being, as manifested in present, past and changing social inequalities in health' (2001, p. 668). Such an approach is reminiscent of the humanistic and welfarist traditions of human geography present in early work by David Harvey (1973) and David M. Smith (1977), who famously asked 'who gets what, where, and how?'

Krieger (2001) points out that ecosocial theory is not a theory of everything but part of a toolkit for guiding specific inquiry and action, particular in light of a contemporary understanding of (ill)health and its causes as dynamic and multi-dimensional. Key to the ecosocial theory is the alloying of a social production of disease perspective to biological and ecological analysis, leading to four key constructs:

1. *embodiment*: the representation or expression of exposure to the material and social world over the life course as incorporated biologically. Krieger suggests that 'no aspect of our biology can be understood absent [to] knowledge of history and individual and societal ways of living' (2001, p. 672).
2. *pathways of embodiment* indicate the impacts to embodiment brought about by the structure of society through the processes of social development and the evolutionary trajectory of our biology.
3. *cumulative interplay between exposure, susceptibility and resistance* takes the pathways of embodiment and considers the multiple levels and domains at which aspects of society or biology might be complicit in health across time and space.
4. *accountability and agency* relates to how the knowledge and behaviours around embodiment, both within institutions and households and of individuals, enable and constrain health at different scales and levels.

Krieger (2001) suggests that taking these constructs together allows for the creation of new knowledge about population health, biological expressions of social relations and the social construction of disease, and hence to a new basis for action and intervention.

behaviours or outcomes that are non-linear. Change in a system or sub-system is often described in terms of the growth or decline of a particular function, observable by variations in the amount or magnitude of interaction occurring. Unexpected behaviours or outcomes can occur in a complex system because the interaction of two dynamic sub-systems may not be immediately predictable. Mike Batty (2009) discusses cities as being subject to slow and fast dynamics: slow dynamics represent changes that take a long time (years, decades); and fast dynamics represent changes occurring frequently (hourly, daily). These two perspectives, slow and fast, have direct application to studies of the environment and health articulated through 'selection' effects and mobility.

Slow dynamics that relate to the residential migration of individuals over time and between residential neighbourhoods may reflect the preferences of those individuals.

This is endogeneity, and we may find it difficult or impossible to assert how causality works in this context. For instance, people may move to a walkable neighbourhood because they have a preference for walking; in this situation it may be difficult to ascribe changes in walking behaviour to a neighbourhood effect as opposed to confounding brought about by individual preferences. Generally speaking, we do not have a good understanding of how complicit health is in residential migration; however, recent cross-sectional work by Helena Tunstall and colleagues (2014) in the United Kingdom has challenged the generalisation that residential migration is selective for good health.

Health research has recently made much more progress on the role of fast dynamics, expressed in terms of the everyday mobility of individuals. Shifting focus from the residential neighbourhood to the daily activity space, the area or set of locations visited by an individual in the course of a normal day, has resulted in (it is claimed) a better measure of daily environmental exposure. For example, Thomas Burgoine and colleagues (2014) suggest using measures that capture individual residential and work neighbourhoods, as well as the commuting route, for exposure to takeaway food outlets in Cambridgeshire, United Kingdom. They demonstrate that the combined exposure of all these environments is a better predictor of fast-food consumption than any single exposure on its own.

However, these approaches are still rooted within the 'complicated' model approach, and the examples given are cross-sectional rather than longitudinal, which means statements about causation cannot be made. These examples are progressive in their outlook; they certainly contribute to a richer picture of health inequalities, they are more conceptually nuanced than earlier work and they use measures of exposure that are more focused on the specific mechanisms hypothesised to affect health. In this sense, they offer potential for a better understanding of the associations between environment and health. However, they are still parsimonious in their weighing of factors relevant to understanding the behaviours of, and relationships between, multiple factors across multiple levels over time. They are still fundamentally models of single causes. Engaging a complex systems approach could further help us understand the dynamics of interactions between the environment and flows of people, with implications for how and where we stage public health interventions.

Emergence

Emergence describes the process by which complex organisations or behaviours develop from smaller or simpler individuals or systems which on their own do not exhibit such organisation or behaviour. Douglas Luke and Katherine Stamatakis (2012) describe how the systematic vaccination of people through a national vaccine programme is a complex system that demonstrates emergence. 'Herd immunity' is an emergent property of systematic vaccination which offers protection to members of a population who are unvaccinated, provided that a large enough number of people are vaccinated. This is because the transmission of contagious diseases relies on interaction between infected and susceptible persons; if population immunity is high enough and the population is 'well mixed', the chances of this happening are reduced. Any vaccinated individual on their own offers no additional protection to unvaccinated persons from contagious diseases; however, understood as an interacting system of vaccinated and unvaccinated persons, a level of protection is assured.

In the context of neighbourhoods and health, there is potential to see neighbourhood trajectories as the emergent properties of the neighbourhood system. Brian Robson, Kitty Lymperopoulou and Alasdair Rae (2008) explored the different functional types of deprived neighbourhoods in the United Kingdom based upon residential migration into and out of them; they reasoned that the origins of movers into a deprived neighbourhood and the destinations of leavers would give some insight into the overall trajectory of that place. They argue that understanding the trajectory of neighbourhoods is crucial to tackling inequalities and improving conditions for all across a range of social determinants of health. A neighbourhood's trajectory emerges from the dynamic set of flows and interactions complicit in migration and neighbourhood change; one such trajectory that has been the source of substantial enquiry is 'gentrification'. Gentrification has received attention in urban geography through simulation studies based on the principles of complex systems. Both David O'Sullivan (2002) and Paul Torrens and Atsushi Nara (2007) tackle the problem using models that explore the transition of neighbourhoods from areas with relatively low value property markets to higher value ones. Whilst such work is exploratory, it is clear that from relatively simple rules regarding the interaction of current residents and new residents in a neighbourhood, models can demonstrate emergent changes in property markets and in the socio-economic profile of a neighbourhood. Health geography could develop such an approach to ask how health behaviours change with respect to processes of change in a neighbourhood system.

Non-linearity

As suggested earlier, non-linearity can be a property of a dynamic system and is the statistical representation of the oft-used maxim, 'the whole is more than the sum of its parts'. A linear system *is* the sum of its parts; if you change two sub-systems in a linear system, producing a change due to one sub-system of 1 and a change due to the other sub-system of 2, then the total effect on the system as a whole is 3. This is not true of non-linear systems, in which changing two sub-systems produces a result greater than the sum of the two sub-systems. Tony Gatrell (2005) emphasises this, suggesting that the implication of non-linear systems is that small changes in sub-systems can lead to substantially larger changes in the system as a whole.

Disease epidemics often exhibit non-linearity in the spread of a disease. Influenza is an infectious disease that spreads from person to person via airborne droplets. The passing of the influenza virus from person to person can work like a chain reaction; each newly infected person passes on the infection to several susceptible individuals, amplifying the speed of the spread unless interventions to mitigate the spread are taken. In the urban context, look back to Box 9.2 on the 'Glasgow effect'. Conventional modelling approaches have been unable to completely explain this phenomenon; however, it is possible that Glasgow's worse health is the product of small differences in individual and environmental variables producing large differences in health outcomes – in this sense, worse health in Glasgow could simply be a property of non-linear system dynamics.

Scale and scaling

Understanding scale and scaling is important to complex systems, but it can be difficult as any system of interest invokes scale in two ways: spatial scale and temporal scale. Spatial scale generally refers to the spatial extent of a system that is embedded in space (such as a neighbourhood system), but it can also relate to a more generic extent in systems that are not specifically embedded in space (such as networked flows of data or money). Temporal scale is similarly the window of time for which a system of interest is modelled: the temporal extent. These two scales thus define the spatio-temporal dimensions of a system and constrain its dynamics.

Spatial scale is an important consideration because, within a system, the impact of a change in a sub-system may be experienced differently by individuals according to the scale at which that change is modelled to have taken place. Writing in the journal *Nature*, Jonathan Patz and colleagues (2005) consider the range of impacts that regional climate change will likely have on human health, in which it is clear that effects will be multi-scale. Amongst other scenarios, they discuss the regional effects of heatwaves on respiratory and cardiovascular disease, the specific local effects of urban heat islands and extreme heat on excess morbidity and mortality, and the possibility of crop failures which could have effects ranging from the local to the global on food security and malnutrition. The impacts of climate change will be felt across a range of scales and similarly there is no one scale at which to target interventions to mitigate the effects of climate change – global cooperation and political impetus is needed, but buy-in is required at all levels, from individual practices, through municipal policies, national enforcement and supra-national agreement.

Temporal scale relates to how far backwards or forwards in time a model is allowed to go; in practical terms, this might speak to how a system is described and interpreted. Similarly, it might factor in the size of the 'time steps' at which the system is modelled to operate – often models do not deal with time continuously but move in steps of hours, days, years, even decades, depending upon the research question. Quantitative analyses of the Ebola outbreak in West Africa involved making a choice as to the spatio-temporal frame of analysis. Gerardo Chowell and colleagues (2015) used weekly counts of reported Ebola at three spatial scales: regional, national and subnational. In their analysis, they found that whilst Ebola demonstrated roughly exponential growth in the number of cases at the national level, local epidemics displayed slower than expected growth, potentially resulting from the effect of interventions aimed to mitigate the spread of the disease.

Scaling extends the idea of scale to a process of transformation of a system over space and time. Scaling is inherent in Chowell and colleagues' model of the growth of Ebola as it relates to the changing number of weekly cases caused by the process of contagion through interaction. Mike Batty (2013) suggests that scaling is a 'basic signature' of complexity and that simple processes are intrinsic to activity (action, interaction, transaction) at all scales. Scaling tells us about the ordering of a particular system and the effects of change over time; focusing on cities, Batty (2013) tells us that as spatial scale increases (i.e. cities get larger) they also '"tend" to get wealthier, greener and denser' (p. 8). Lazaros Gallos and colleagues (2012) have looked at the spread of obesity in the United States from the perspective of complexity and scaling. They note that there is a spatial component to obesity; in the United States neighbouring counties seem to cluster together in terms of their mutual obesity rates. Comparison of how population growth and growth in obesity rate scale over space suggests that the two are markedly different. Thus, Gallos et al. suggest that the dynamics of obesity are 'anomalous' when compared to the dynamics of population growth – according to their model an increase in obesity prevalence in a given place can spread significantly further than we might expect given population change. Thus, they state that the clustering of obesity observed is likely to be the result of collective behaviour – behaviour occurring at a level higher than that of the individual – and hence obesity cannot be viewed as simply the 'consequence of fluctuations of individual habits' (p. 5).

Feedback, path dependency and lock-in

Feedback describes the way in which interactions in a dynamic system can have effects on individuals or sub-systems which then either directly or indirectly impact the original individual or sub-system. Anthony Gatrell (2005) suggests a simple example of this: air pollution caused by vehicle exhausts leads to increased incidence of asthma and subsequently leads to policy interventions aimed at reducing vehicle exhaust emissions. This is conceived of as 'negative' feedback as it reduces the effect of the original change over time; by contrast, positive feedback is a growth-reinforcing feedback. An example of positive feedback might be the growth and sprawl of American suburbs in light of the growth in availability of the automobile (Frumkin 2002).

Situations such as US urban sprawl, in exhibiting positive feedback, can be said to be path-dependent systems in which the future states of these systems depend on previous states and not just the present state. David O'Sullivan (2004) summarises the notion of path dependency simply – 'history matters' – explaining that positive feedback and path dependency can lead to lock-in, in which particular processes or behaviours become normalised to the point where actually challenging the status quo could lead to significant instability in the system of interest. In our example of US urban sprawl, the positive feedback driven by automobile production led to more sprawl and an urban structure that locked in car use. We can see now that the automobile-led design of US cities has had some significant impacts on population health, but that challenging this orthodoxy is extremely difficult (Speck 2013).

Self-organisation and lack of central control

Self-organisation goes back to the notion of what a complex system is and describes the process whereby order and hierarchy arise at higher levels from the interactions of individuals or sub-systems at lower levels. Mike Batty (2013) notes that city systems are problematic in this sense, as cities, like urban neighbourhoods, exhibit emergent properties that arise spontaneously from the bottom up but at the same time are subject to explicit top-down processes, either directly intended to instil a particular kind of order or to act in some way as constraints against the emergence of particular behaviours or types of order. David O'Sullivan (2004) suggests that the idea that complex systems organise themselves is central to the study of complex systems but cautions that a single exact definition of self-organisation is not available. He also notes that the presumed tendency for systems to evolve from disordered to ordered states via self-organisation has an implicit tension as it suggests that initial conditions in a system converge to broadly similar outcomes, while dynamics, feedback and non-linearity might lead us to suggest that this is unlikely to be the case, creating instead a range of divergent outcomes.

Coupled with the ideas of self-organisation and emergence is the condition that a system has a lack of central control, and similarly, as Sarah Curtis and Mylène Riva (2010a) describe, 'components with limited "knowledge" of each other' (p. 216). Curtis and Riva thus suggest that geography is a function of the fact that interactions are more likely to take place in proximate parts of the system, both in terms of geographical position and social position. In a spatial sense, this is known as Tobler's First Law of Geography (Tobler 1970), which states that everything is related, but near things are more related than distant things. In a social sense, interactions are a product of social networks, often themselves embedded in space (but not necessarily so), in which the likelihood of different groups interacting is a function of the presence of ties between individuals and groups. 'Social complexity' is the term used by sociologists such as Manuel DeLanda (2006) to consider the role that scale plays in understanding society from within the individual through to the global.

Consolidation

These, and other terms, provide a basis for engaging with complex systems. They have become part of the language of complexity and have themselves taken on a level of syntactic complexity that renders them increasingly difficult to define. Despite their ubiquity and relevance to ongoing research they remain largely descriptive in terms of what they can tell us about a system of interest. In research on the environment and health, they will not only have to be integrated into a growing disciplinary lexicon if they are to move the field forward, but they will also have to underscore their descriptive possibilities with the promise of relevance to policy and polity. In the next section, we consider the multiple roles that complex systems approaches could play in the design of analysis in environment and health research, and the importance of seeing system models of the environment as an extension rather than a supersession of existing research effort.

Implications of Complexity for Health Geography Research

If health geography is to benefit from the integration of ideas around complexity and complex systems, it is not good enough simply to talk about complexity; rather we must look to practical applications. Steven Manson (2001) distinguishes three types of complexity – algorithmic, deterministic and aggregate – of which aggregate complexity is most instructive to health geographers. Aggregate complexity describes how we have chosen to construct the neighbourhood in this chapter, as a 'system of linked components… [which] attempts to access the holism and synergy resulting from the interaction of system components' (Manson 2001, p. 409). David O'Sullivan (2004) puts it a bit more plainly in stating that aggregate complexity is about '*relationships* between entities' (p. 284. Emphasis in original). O'Sullivan observes that 'each entity has different relations to others and, therefore, that *where* an entity is in the system has significance for the unfolding behaviour of entities individually, and of the system collectively' (2004, p. 284). Understanding systems of aggregate complexity to people like David O'Sullivan, Steven Manson and Mike Batty means not simply breaking down and reducing the system but also reassembling it in order to understand how it works. Further, as O'Sullivan notes, aggregate complexity is particularly interesting to geographers as 'it implies that the local spatial configuration of interactions affects outcomes at the whole system level' (2004, p. 284).

Douglas Luke and Katherine Stamatakis (2012) stress that complex systems abound in many of the domains of interest to health geography; as such they call for the greater use of complexity science in the design and analysis of studies. They justify this by critiquing one of the most predominant methods of primary data collection in health geography, the sample survey, with a wonderful quotation: 'the survey is a sociological meatgrinder, tearing the individual from his [sic] social context' (Barton 1968. Cited in Luke and Stamakis 2012, p. 359). Essentially, in an effort to control that which is being studied through randomised survey-based designs, and to thus produce 'good' estimates of intervention effects, we are actually washing away our ability to learn something about spatial behaviour. This, Luke and Stamakis suggest, renders the external validity of studies moot, and hinders attempts to concurrently investigate aspects of context such as the neighbourhood.

For a long time, randomised controlled trials (RCTs) have been the gold standard for assessing cause and effect relationships in health. Where RCTs are not possible, quasi-experimental designs are used in such a way as to best fit the controlled aspect of the RCT. Recently, there has been increased interest in the use of 'natural experiments', which are 'events, interventions, or policies which are not under the control of researchers, but which are amenable to research which uses the variation in exposure they generate to analyse their impact' (Medical Research Council 2009, p. 4; see Chapter 10). A natural experiment might involve looking at the social effects of new infrastructure such as parks or transport – you cannot randomise who uses the park or transport infrastructure, but you can still treat it as an experiment, looking at how behaviour changes before and after the new infrastructure is built for users and non-users, and evaluating whether this produces a positive social or political outcome. On the topic of RCTs, Luke and Stamakis suggest that if our objective is a better understanding of behaviour, then randomisation removes the essential contextual factors that influence behaviour – an aspect that would have been criticised as 'contamination' in a conventional research design. Similarly, in both RCTs and quasi-experiments (such as natural experiments), they argue that existing studies only prove or disprove the existence of a hypothesised effect, without necessarily explicating the mechanism(s) at work.

RCTs will probably continue to serve a purpose in public health and epidemiology, particularly in clinical areas such as the development of drugs or treatment approaches. However, such experimental designs may not be well suited to questions about context and the multiple scales and multiple factors that affect population health. The focus of health geographers needs to shift and start practically integrating ideas from researchers like Nancy Krieger (see Box 9.2) and Steven Cummins and colleagues (see Chapter 8) in order to better quantify the effect of neighbourhoods on health.

Conclusion

Complex systems approaches offer health geographers tools to better understand 'process' – the underlying causal mechanisms that explain why things happen – which Ana Diez-Roux (2015) suggests satisfies a frustration with the limitations of conventional research design. However, she also notes that the current crop of research that supports complex systems approaches does not yet, despite its potential, deliver meaningful insights. Importantly, Diez-Roux draws attention to the inescapable nature of complex systems approaches as 'essentially made-up worlds', reliant less on observational data and more on the simulation of reality in a computer. The point that Diez-Roux is ultimately making is that there lies a distinction between 'causal inference based on observations (as in traditional epidemiology) and causal inference based on simulation modeling' (2015, p. 101). Arriving at causal explanations using the tools of complexity will ultimately only relate to the artificial causality that exists within our virtual world, thus this causality will be a plausible simulacrum for real-world causality but not necessarily true evidence of causality. David O'Sullivan (2004) offers similar words of caution when working with 'computational laboratories', wherein understanding the adequacy of a given model in relation to the real world is crucial. O'Sullivan challenges the process of using virtual worlds to guide decisions in the real world, suggesting that we are 'badly equipped philosophically and practically to use models of complex systems critically and responsibly' (p. 290).

As such, in conclusion we find ourselves back at the beginning. Research, whether quantitative or qualitative, relies on models of reality. All models are reductive and what we propose in this chapter is that researchers strive for realistic complexity (practical adequacy) and try to frame the world as a system of interacting parts. The famous American psychologist Abraham Maslow is credited with stating, 'I suppose it is tempting, if the only tool you have is a hammer, to treat everything as if it were a nail' (1966). Thinking critically about health geography ultimately invites a consideration of the tools at your disposal in light of whether a nail is in fact a nail. In the context of research into neighbourhoods and health, where there has been recent conceptual debate over the role that complex systems approaches could play, we suggest that an approach that builds on the existing work that asserted the complicity of environmental context in explaining population health is merited. We feel that although moving to a complex systems framing of neighbourhood effects on health would constitute a 'paradigm shift', in so much as we support a revision of the basic assumptions that underpin how such research is conducted, we would seek to cast the shift as an evolution. It is not strictly necessary, or progressive, to think of changes in academia in terms of large fractures in the status quo; such depictions are alienating and devalue much that has gone before or is on-going. As such, we feel that complex systems approaches, as an evolution of, and a complement to, existing research in health are one cogent way that progress can be made as part of a process of developing critical health geographies.

Questions for Review

1. What distinguishes a complex systems approach from a conventional approach to quantitative health geography?
2. What are the key features of a complex systems approach?
3. How might we design research using complex systems?

Suggested Reading

Diez-Roux, A (2011) Complex systems thinking and current impasses in health disparities research. *American Journal of Public Health* 101, 1627–34.
Luke, D & Stamatakis, K (2012) Systems science methods in public health: dynamics, networks, and agents. *Annual Review of Public Health* 33, 357–76.
O'Sullivan, D (2004) Complexity science and human geography. *Transactions of the Institute of British Geographers* 29, 282–95.

References

Barton, A (1968) Bringing society back in: survey research and macro-methodology. *The American Behavioural Scientist* 12, 1–9.
Batty, M (2009) Urban modelling. In: Thrift, N & Kitchin, R (Eds) *International encyclopedia of human geography. Volume 12.* Elsevier, Oxford, 51–8.
Batty, M (2013) *The new science of cities.* MIT Press, Cambridge, MA.
Burgoine, T, Forouhi, N, Griffin, S, Wareham, N & Monsivais, P (2014) Associations between exposure to takeaway food outlets, takeaway food consumption, and body weight in Cambridgeshire, UK: population based, cross sectional study. *BMJ* 348, g1464.
Chowell, G, Viboud, C, Hyman, J & Simonsen, L (2015) The Western Africa Ebola virus disease epidemic exhibits both global exponential and local polynomial growth rates. *PLOS Current Outbreaks*, January 21.
Cummins, S, Curtis, S, Diez-Roux, A & Macintyre, S (2007) Understanding and representing 'place' in health research: a relational approach. *Social Science & Medicine* 65, 1825–38.
Curtis, S & Riva, M (2010a) Health geographies I: complexity theory and human health. *Progress in Human Geography* 34, 215–23.
Curtis, S & Riva, M (2010b) Health geographies II: complexity and health care systems and policy. *Progress in Human Geography* 34, 513–20.

DeLanda, M (2006) *A new philosophy of society: assemblage theory and social complexity*. Continuum, London.

Diez-Roux, A (2011) Complex systems thinking and current impasses in health disparities research. *American Journal of Public Health* 101, 1627–34.

Diez-Roux, A (2015) The virtual epidemiologist – promise and peril. *American Journal of Epidemiology* 181, 100–2.

Duncan, C, Jones, K & Moon, G (1998) Context, composition and heterogeneity: using multilevel models in health research. *Social Science & Medicine* 46, 97–117.

Fagg, J, Curtis, S, Stansfeld, S & Congdon, P (2006) Psychological distress among adolescents, and its relationship to individual, family and area characteristics in East London. *Social Science & Medicine* 63, 636–48.

Frumkin, H (2002) Urban sprawl and public health. *Public Health Reports* 117, 201–17.

Galea, S, Riddle, M & Kaplan, G (2010) Causal thinking and complex system approaches in epidemiology. *International Journal of Epidemiology* 39, 97–106.

Gallos, L, Barttfeld, P, Havlin, S, Sigman, M & Makse, H (2012) Collective behavior in the spatial spreading of obesity. *Nature Scientific Reports* 2, 454.

Gatrell, A (2005) Complexity theory and geographies of health: a critical assessment. *Social Science & Medicine* 60, 2661–71.

Government Office for Science (2007) *Foresight. Tackling obesities: future choices – project report. Second edition*, viewed 12 September 2015, https://www.gov.uk/government/collections/tackling-obesities-future-choices

Gray, L (2007) *Comparisons of health related behaviours and health measures between Glasgow and the rest of Scotland. Glasgow Centre for Population Health. Briefing Paper 7*, viewed 10 September 2015, http://www.gcph.co.uk/assets/0000/0384/GCPH_briefing_paper_FS_7_web.pdf Last

Harvey, D (1973) *Social justice and the city*. Edward Arnold, London.

Jayasinghe, S (2011) Conceptualising population health: from mechanistic thinking to complexity science. *Emerging Themes in Epidemiology* 8, 2.

Kearns, R & Moon, G (2002) From medical to health geography: novelty, place and theory after a decade of change. *Progress in Human Geography* 26, 605–25.

Krieger, N (2001) Theories for social epidemiology in the 21st century: an ecosocial perspective. *International Journal of Epidemiology* 30, 668–77.

Luke, D & Stamatakis, K (2012) Systems science methods in public health: dynamics, networks, and agents. *Annual Review of Public Health* 33, 357–76.

Macintyre, S, Ellaway, A & Cummins, S (2002) Place effects on health: how can we conceptualise, operationalise and measure them? *Social Science & Medicine* 55, 125–39.

Manson, S (2001) Simplifying complexity: a review of complexity theory. *Geoforum* 32, 405–14.

Manson, S (2003) Epistemological possibilities and imperatives of complexity: a reply to Reitsma. *Geoforum* 34, 17–20.

Manson, S & O'Sullivan, D (2006) Complexity theory in the study of space and place. *Environment and Planning A* 38, 677–92.

Maslow, A (1966) *The psychology of science: a reconnaissance*. Harper, New York.

Medical Research Council (2009) *Using natural experiments to evaluate population health interventions: guidance for producers and users of evidence*, viewed 7 October 2015, https://www.mrc.ac.uk/documents/pdf/natural-experiments-guidance/

Oppong, J & Harold, A (2010) Disease, ecology, and environment. In: Brown, T, McLafferty, S & Moon, G (Eds) *A companion to health and medical geography*. Wiley-Blackwell, London, 81–95.

O'Sullivan, D (2002) Towards micro-scale spatial modelling of gentrification. *Journal of Geographical Systems* 4, 251–74.

O'Sullivan, D (2004) Complexity science and human geography. *Transactions of the Institute of British Geographers* 29, 282–95.

O'Sullivan, D (2006) Space, place, and complexity science. *Environment and Planning A* 38, 611–7.

Patz, J, Campbell-Lendrum, D, Holloway, T & Foley, J (2005) Impact of regional climate change on human health. *Nature* 438, 310–7.

Pearce, J, Barnett, R & Moon, G (2012) Sociospatial inequalities in health-related behaviours: pathways linking place and smoking. *Progress in Human Geography* 36, 3–24.

Reitsma, F (2003) A response to simplifying complexity. *Geoforum* 34, 13–6.

Robson, B, Lymperopoulou, K & Rae, A (2008) People on the move: exploring the functional roles of deprived neighbourhoods. *Environment and Planning A* 40, 2693–714.

Sampson, R (2003) The neighborhood context of well-being. *Perspectives in Biology and Medicine* 46, S53–64.

Sayer, A (1992) *Method in social science: a realist approach. Second edition.* Routledge, London.

Smith, D & Cummins, S (2009) Obese cities: how our environment shapes overweight. *Geography Compass* 3, 518–35.

Smith, DM (1977) *Human geography: a welfare approach.* Edward Arnold, London.

Speck, J (2013) *Walkable city: how downtown can save America, one step at a time.* Macmillan, New York.

Tobler, W (1970) A computer movie simulating urban growth in the Detroit region. *Economic Geography* 46, 234–40.

Torrens, P & Nara, A (2007) Modeling gentrification dynamics: a hybrid approach. *Computers, Environment and Urban Systems* 31, 337–61.

Tunstall, H, Pearce, J, Shortt, N & Mitchell, R (2014) Residential mobility and the association between physical environment disadvantage and general and mental health. *Journal of Public Health* 37, 563–72.

Chapter 10

Interventions for Population Health

Introduction

As we have outlined in earlier chapters, the existence of longstanding geographical inequalities in health and life chances has led to a resurgence of interest in the idea that where you live matters for health independently of personal characteristics. Over the last 25 years, investigations of such area effects on health have become increasingly common as a result of a revitalisation of interest in understanding the social determinants of health (Diez-Roux 2007). Contextual factors, as independent risk factors, have been observed for a wide range of health outcomes and behaviours, including cardiovascular disease, psychological wellbeing, smoking, diet and physical activity (Cummins et al. 2007; Riva et al. 2007). This suggests that modification of features of the local environment may have the potential to improve an individual's health and may also reduce social and environmental inequalities in health.

This environmental approach to improving public health has inevitably led researchers and policymakers to consider those interventions and policies that might go some way to reducing these environmental risks. One of the attractions of modifying features of the local environment to promote health gain is that changes can often be made locally, using processes already established within municipal government structures across a wide variety of policy sectors such as planning, health and social care, economic and community development and the environment. This often makes contextual interventions inherently appealing as they fit well with the broader socio-ecological model of health discussed in Chapter 8 and with the notion of complexity discussed in Chapter 9 (Bronfrenbrenner 1977). Such an approach is also particularly appropriate if improvements to population health, rather than individual strategies to promote behaviour change, are the goal. A policy focus on the environmental determinants of health through the use of area-based or explicitly contextual interventions might involve trying to improve the spatial distribution of and access to health-promoting amenities and resources and reducing exposure to environmental risks

Health Geographies: A Critical Introduction, First Edition. Tim Brown, Gavin J. Andrews, Steven Cummins, Beth Greenhough, Daniel Lewis, and Andrew Power.
© 2018 John Wiley & Sons Ltd. Published 2018 by John Wiley & Sons Ltd.

via mechanisms such as urban regeneration, economic development, master-planning and zoning regulations (Macintyre 2007). It is upon these interventions that this chapter focuses.

Improving Health or Reducing Inequalities?

There is a need to distinguish between what appear to be two competing goals when thinking about improving public health (Woodward and Kawachi 2000). First, do we want to improve health? Second, do we want to reduce health inequalities? This dilemma is important as some interventions may not improve health *and* reduce health inequalities at the same time; they may in fact increase both at one and the same time. In order to be able to address these questions we need to be clear on what is meant by health inequalities as this will drive how we interpret the impact of related health interventions. As Vani Kulkarni and S.V. Subramanian (2010) suggest, the subject of health inequalities is a contentious one and it is a topic that has occupied considerable attention within debates in the health sciences, including health geography (Curtis and Rees Jones 1998; Smith and Easterlow 2005). At issue is whether we regard health inequalities (or in a North American context health disparities) as simply expressions of variations or differences in population health or rather as differences in health arising as a consequence of 'a group's social advantage and disadvantage over the life course, and [therefore as] unfair and unjust' (Kulkarni and Subramanian 2010, p. 376).

Thinking in terms of health inequalities or health disparities demands that we not only consider the question of interventions in *value-neutral* terms, but as a *value-loaded* phenomenon. Nancy Krieger and Anne-Emmanuelle Birn (1998), in an essay commemorating the 150th anniversary of public health in the United States, are very clear on this point. As they argue, '[s]ocial justice is the foundation of public health… It is an assertion that reminds us that public health is indeed a public matter, that societal patterns of disease and death, of health and well-being, of bodily integrity and disintegration, intimately reflect the workings of the body politic for good and for ill' (1998, p. 1603). With this in mind, interventions that are put in place to promote health should also work to reduce health inequalities; the two should not in our view be separate goals. However, as we shall go on to discuss in more detail, achieving this goal is not straightforward. For example, area-based initiatives are often used to target low-income households or specific groups of concern, such as children living in poverty, lone-parent households or teenage mothers (see Box 10.1). Although this approach focuses attention and resources on disadvantaged groups and places, focusing resources on them does not always mean that the most disadvantaged individuals are being reached, as not all people who live in deprived neighbourhoods are disadvantaged. In fact, such an approach may even increase health inequalities within the targeted area if more advantaged groups benefit more from the intervention.

This may appear counterintuitive; however, in the British context we might question, for example, whether the introduction of the National Health Service in 1948 reduced health inequalities. There is little question that a universal health care system such as this improved the health of the population as a whole, but the findings of the 'Black Report', which was published in the late 1970s, raised questions about its capacity to reduce inequalities in health. As is by now well known, the Report, which was ignored by the incumbent Conservative government under the leadership of Margaret Thatcher, provided detailed evidence of the extent to which poor health and early death were unequally distributed among the British population (Townsend et al. 1992; Macintyre 1997). The Report did not

---

Box 10.1   Key Concepts: Area-based Interventions

Area-based interventions (ABIs) have been popular since the 1960s with the aim of improving conditions in the most deprived areas and narrowing the gaps between these areas (Smith 1999). Exemplars include Heath Action Zones and the New Deal for Communities in the 1990s in the United Kingdom, and Moving to Opportunity in the 1990s in the United States. The UK New Deal for Communities programme (NDC) in particular, was an innovative, substantial and sustained example of community-based and community-guided approaches. NDC Partnerships worked across five policy areas – worklessness, crime, education and skills, health and housing and the physical environment – and used a community-led 'joined-up' approach to the identification of local needs and the creation of local policy solutions. In total there were 39 NDC areas with a combined budget of £2 billion that ran from 1999 to 2011.

Table 10.1   Standardised mortality rates for men aged 15–64.

Cause of mortality	Social class*					
	I	II	IIIN	IIIM	IV	V
Cancer of trachea, bronchus and lung	53	68	84	118	123	143
Bronchitis, emphysema and asthma	36	51	82	113	128	188
Acute myocardial infarction	88	92	115	107	108	108
Chronic ischaemic heart disease	87	86	108	106	111	12

Source: Blane 1985. Reproduced with permission of John Wiley & Sons.

* Social class is categorised using occupational classes: I (professional, etc., occupations); II (managerial and technical occupations); III (skilled occupations: N – non-manual; M – manual); IV (partly skilled occupations); and V (unskilled occupations).

place the blame for these inequalities in health on the NHS; however, it did demonstrate that even in the face of improvements in overall health, the issue of inequality in health remained a considerable problem (for example, see Table 10.1). For the authors of the Black Report, the explanation for these inequalities relates to what we now refer to as the social determinants of health (see Chapter 8).

Equally, we might explain at least part of this inequality through reference to what Julian Tudor Hart called the inverse care law (see Tudor Hart 1971); that is, inequalities reflect the idea that those who are most in need of health care are least likely to receive it and, conversely, those with least need of health care tend to use health services more (and more effectively). Thinking about this in relation to area-based interventions, it is possible that advantaged groups may find it easier to benefit from them because they have better personal resources such as time, finance, education and skills (Marmot 2010). More disadvantaged groups might do worse as they are harder to reach, find it more difficult or are less motivated to change behaviour, perceive less benefit from improvements in lifestyle changes and better access to services, may be poorly educated and have less time and money to invest in their own self-care. There is also a possibility that targeting interventions at only the most disadvantaged groups undermines the services being provided to them (e.g. in terms of their quality) and potentially results in the stigmatisation of those receiving the services

(Marmot 2010). Moreover, questions may also be raised about specifically targeted services being funded through general taxation. It is here that debates regarding the promotion of health and reduction of health inequalities are rendered political and value-laden decisions are often made with regards to what it is that interventions aim to achieve (Schrecker and Bambra 2015).

Thus, the twin goals of public health may sometimes conflict and result in complex ethical and political questions being raised when designing environmental interventions. One partial solution to the dilemma is to consider the concept of proportionate universalism, which refers to the idea that although interventions should be universal, for example encompassing whole neighbourhoods, cities or regions or populations, they can be delivered with a scale and intensity that is proportionate to the level of social or environmental need (Marmot 2010). For example, home visiting, which is a universal service offered to all families in the United Kingdom aimed at improving health in the early years (0–5), can be tailored or intensified based on a family's need or circumstances. This approach can allow for improvements in public health *and* reductions in health inequalities as it recognises the continuum of need across a population and addresses the possible disadvantage of a purely universal approach. However, proportionate universalism requires a judgement as to the weighting and allocation of resource by 'need', which is fraught with challenges. It requires an assessment of need and an understanding of the likely impact of the allocation of any additional resource on inequalities in the particular outcome of interest. Evidence to support such decision-making may often be partial or even absent, thus the on-going generation of evidence through evaluation of the impacts of social and environmental interventions is often required.

Environmental Interventions and Population Health

In the previous section, we set out some of the ethical questions that need to be raised when addressing health and health inequalities through area-based interventions. As noted, the intervention strategies put in place are inevitably shaped by the social and political context within which they emerge. As critical geographers, we should always be alert to this fact. In this section, we highlight in more detail the kinds of interventions that have been implemented and consider both their strengths and their limitations, and whether area-based or environmental interventions can improve population health.

Targeting poverty and health

As stated above, in recent years large-scale policies and programmes that tackle entrenched social deprivation through improvements in living conditions have become an increasing feature of the policy landscape. Such interventions have often taken the form of large-scale urban regeneration and neighbourhood renewal programmes which tend to focus on the wider social and environmental determinants of physical and mental health, and hence are well positioned to tackle health inequalities (Thomson 2008). In the last 30 years alone, spending on such schemes in the United Kingdom has reached in excess of £11 billion (Thomson et al. 2006). Many of these schemes involve the targeting of places that are considered to be in the greatest social and economic need, emphasising a focus on 'place poverty' rather than 'people poverty' (Powell et al. 2001). Internationally, as well as in the United Kingdom, these area-based initiatives often target low-income or minority neighbourhoods or areas suffering from high levels of social or material deprivation and commonly comprise investment in the key socio-economic determinants of health, for example employment, housing, education, income and welfare (O'Dwyer et al. 2007; Thomson 2008).

There may also be wider benefits from urban renewal programmes in the form of additional infrastructural improvements to the built environment such as better transport links, provision or upgrading of retail space, parks and public areas and general aesthetic improvement through the provision of street lighting, furniture and pedestrianisation schemes, all of which might have direct and indirect effects on health and wellbeing. For example, the provision of street lighting might reduce the incidence of crime which in turn might reduce stress and improve psychological wellbeing (Lorenc et al. 2012). In the past, area-based regeneration initiatives were rarely designed specifically to target health and health inequalities, although 'health gain' was often routinely cited as a justification for investment. More recently, however, links between wider non-health focused social and infrastructural programmes and the fundamental social and environmental determinants of health have been made more explicit, leading to clearer and more direct policy links between area-based strategies across a range of policy areas and population health (Thomson 2008). For example, action to reduce transport-related carbon emissions led by transport planners now routinely includes the promotion of more active (and thus less environmentally damaging) modes of transport which in turn may have a direct impact on physical activity.

Area-based social, economic and environmental programmes that tackle disadvantage to improve health are popular amongst policymakers because they are assumed to efficiently target deprived people; to provide opportunities for local involvement in identifying problems and solutions and recognise that structural and environmental factors matter and have a real effect (Lupton 2003; Stafford et al. 2008). In terms of tackling health inequalities, area-based initiatives are also thought to: (i) improve the health of the most disadvantaged in absolute terms; (ii) narrow health inequalities between deprived and more affluent neighbourhoods by improving the health of residents of the worst-off places at a faster rate than residents of the most advantaged; or, (iii), tackle the health gradient across whole populations (Graham 2004). As Mai Stafford and colleagues recognised from their analysis of the New Deal for Communities programme (see Box 10.1), even though the aggregate health status of residents of poor areas may improve relative to the rest of the population, health inequalities may widen within areas (for the reasons noted previously) if there is differential uptake of interventions locally by differing social and economic groups (Stafford et al. 2008). More specifically, they concluded that there were changes in inequalities in health but that those people with the lowest educational attainment and the poorest health experienced the smallest improvements, moreover that '[h]ealth and socioeconomic inequalities among residents in [intervention] areas were no smaller at follow-up than inequalities in comparator areas' (Stafford et al. 2008, p. 303), despite some £1.71 billion being spent on 6,900 projects.

More than policies for poverty

More recently area-based interventions have not just focused on tackling neighbourhood deprivation but have also had population health improvement as a central goal. Early area-based initiatives such as Sure Start and Health Action Zones in the United Kingdom and

Head Start in the United States were explicitly focused on improving the health and life chances of vulnerable groups and communities (Belsky et al. 2006; see Box 10.1). One more recent example of an explicitly area-based approach that tackles the environmental determinants of health is the Healthy Communities Challenge Fund (HCCF) in England. The HCCF was set up in 2008, towards the end of New Labour's period of governance in the United Kingdom, to encourage the development of healthier lifestyles through improving opportunities to consume a healthy diet and increase physical activity in nine towns across England. These nine so-called 'Healthy Towns', which included large cities such as Manchester, Portsmouth and Sheffield and small towns such as Dudley and Tewkesbury, as well as the London Borough of Tower Hamlets, each received a maximum of £5 million over the life of the programme and were a key part of health policy thinking at the time. The HCCF was established to pilot and test a series of social and environmental interventions aimed at tackling the 'obesogenic' environment in England as part of the wider Change4Life national health promotion movement (Department of Health 2009).

The recent history of area-based interventions suggests that as appreciation of the importance of the social and environmental determinants of health has increased, area-based programmes have themselves evolved. We can see that area-based public policy approaches have moved from being primarily vehicles for delivering economic uplift and having health as an associated or secondary benefit to programmes that have been expressly designed with health improvement as a central policy goal from the outset.

Can area-based interventions improve population health?

Despite compelling evidence for the importance of social and environmental factors in the production of poor health and health inequalities there remains limited evidence for the effectiveness of interventions aimed at modifying these risk factors (Macintyre et al. 2001). In this context the challenge to public health policymakers in many high-income nations when delivering environmental interventions is to provide better evidence of their effectiveness both in the improvement of public health and the reduction of health inequalities (see Chapter 5 for a discussion of evidence-based health policy). In the United Kingdom, despite billions of pounds having been invested in area-based programmes over the past 35 years we have very little knowledge about the public health effects of such initiatives. Referring to this issue, a hearing of the UK Government Health Select Committee in 2009 noted that:

> Governments have spent large sums of money on social experiments to reduce health inequalities, but we do not know whether these experiments have worked, or whether the money has been well spent. Time and again we have heard that policies to tackle health inequalities have been introduced without sufficient thought being given to designing them in a way which enables them to be properly evaluated. (UK House of Commons Health Select Committee 2009)

This is a salutary lesson that suggests that despite large-scale investment in the development and delivery of social and environmental interventions to improve health we still do not know whether they work to improve health and to reduce health inequalities.

Retaining our current focus on the United Kingdom, health reviews of the evidence generated from national evaluations of area-based urban regeneration interventions established between 1980 and 2004 have synthesised the published evidence for direct and indirect effects on both health and the socio-economic determinants of health (Thomson et al. 2006). The authors identified 35 published reports, of which 18 reported impacts on health or socio-economic factors. Overall there were positive impacts on employment, educational attainment and household income. Impacts on health were also reported, with some evidence for a very modest improvement in mortality rates. What is notable is that many of these evaluations were not directly comparable but instead reported impacts on a wide variety of outcomes including self-reported health, mortality, employment, educational attainment, income and housing quality, making it difficult to draw any firm conclusions about the impacts of area-based initiatives. Most importantly, there was a paucity of evidence on direct impacts on health, with only three evaluations measuring the impact on health outcomes over time in order to assess sustainability of any positive or negative effects. Where such prospective evaluations were available the evidence was very mixed with both positive and negative impacts on health reported (Thomson et al. 2006).

If we look again at the evaluation of the health and socio-economic impacts of the New Deal for Communities (NDC) programme in the United Kingdom discussed earlier, it is apparent that similarly modest improvements in a variety of health-related outcomes were reported, for example in psychological wellbeing, limiting long-term illness, fruit and vegetable consumption and smoking cessation (Stafford et al. 2008). Importantly, even though overall effects were small, they were differentially distributed by socio-economic and demographic characteristics, particularly education (for long-term limiting illness and smoking cessation), with women in particular appearing to become more physically active. However, even though the health of residents in NDC areas improved across a variety of domains, there was also a similar level of improvement in individual health in non-NDC comparison areas. It is difficult, therefore, to infer that the NDC programme had any substantive, causal effect on health. Yet as Hilary Thomson, one of the authors on the review of urban regeneration programmes, has argued elsewhere, this should not necessarily lead to the abandonment of area-based approaches; as she notes, 'investment to alleviate socioeconomic deprivation can be justified on grounds of social justice' (Thomson 2008, p. 935). Rather, she argues that we need to explore the nature of the evidence that it is possible to provide. In order to consider further this tension in the arguments for and against area-based health interventions we turn in the following section to two initiatives implemented in the United Kingdom: Sure Start and Health Action Zones.

Sure Start and Health Action Zones: A tale of two initiatives

The area-based programmes previously described were not set up with health improvement as a primary focus but rather prioritised tackling area deprivation through initiatives that promoted local social and economic development. However, in the United Kingdom there have been two large government projects with health improvement as their primary aim: Sure Start and Health Action Zones (HAZ). These programmes were designed to be explicitly area-based and were specifically targeted at deprived areas; they were defined using official indices of multiple deprivation (HAZ) plus indicators relating to low birth weight and teenage pregnancy (Sure Start). Sure Start was announced as a flagship policy of the New Labour government in 1998 and despite changes to the programme over time continues today, albeit under considerable financial pressure and in reduced form following the election of austerity governments in 2010 (Conservative–Liberal Coalition) and 2015 (Conservative). Health Action Zones also began in 1998 with an initial four years of funding and were then mainstreamed into local health budgets for a further three years before being discontinued in 2005. HAZs in particular were described as being 'trailblazing' area-based social policies with the express purpose of tackling health inequalities (Powell and Moon 2001). Both of these programmes have also been subject to robust evaluations of their impacts.

Sure Start was modelled on Head Start in the United States and was developed in order to improve the health and wellbeing of young children in deprived neighbourhoods with the express aim of intervening in the early years in order to break the cycle of poverty and social exclusion and thus increase social mobility (Melhuish and Hall 2007). Sure Start has evolved over time since its original conception; now a national programme, Sure Start programmes were initially area-based, with residents of the 20 per cent most deprived areas in England as selected targets for Sure Start initiatives (Melhuish et al. 2008). In total, over 524 initiatives were in place by 2004 (before the national programme was rolled out in 2005) and the Sure Start programme allowed a high degree of local autonomy, with priority setting developed in conjunction with local residents. In addition to covering core services (e.g. community health care and family health and child development), Sure Start also provided services that were aimed to meet local needs, such as skills training for parents, personal development courses and practical advice and support such as debt counselling and language or literacy training.

Initial evaluations of the original area-based Sure Start programmes found small and limited effects on family functioning, with some indication of improvements in parenting skills and less chaos at home (Belsky et al. 2006). In line with the challenges associated with area-based programmes in improving health, these outcomes were found to have varied by relative social deprivation with more advantaged families benefiting more from Sure Start programmes. Conversely, outcomes for relatively more vulnerable and disadvantaged residents (e.g. teenage mothers) were found to have worsened (Belsky et al. 2006). Interestingly, purely health-led Sure Start programmes appeared to be the most effective, with greater improvements in outcomes (Belsky et al. 2006). Later evaluations of fully implemented Sure Start programmes found that children had better social development, more positive social behaviour and greater independence, and families had less negative parenting, provided a better home learning environment and used more services (Melhuish et al. 2008). In contrast with the earlier evaluations, the later evaluations did not find any evidence of any adverse effects on the most disadvantaged groups within Sure Start areas, with reported positive impacts evenly distributed across population sub-groups. This indicated that increased duration of exposure to Sure Start programmes had a beneficial effect and that the direct effects of programmes may have taken longer to appear in some groups compared to others.

In comparison to Sure Start programmes which had (and still have, but to a much lesser degree) sustained government support, the experience of Health Action Zones was very different. HAZs were the first area-based intervention instituted by the New Labour government in the United Kingdom and were announced just 8 weeks after it was elected to power in 1997 (Powell and Moon 2001). HAZs were multi-agency partnerships explicitly set up to focus on area-based initiatives to tackle health inequalities and were, initially at least, very high profile both nationally and internationally (Benzeval and Judge 2005). HAZs were set up in 26 areas of England in two waves between 1998 and 1999 and were originally scheduled to have a life of seven years but in fact ceased meaningful operation in early 2003, although they were mainstreamed into local public health budgets (Judge and Bauld 2006). The strategic objectives of HAZs included improving health and reducing health inequalities, empowering local communities and reshaping health and social care, with improving access to services as a key goal and developing effective partnerships. In terms of specific programmes they were broad, tackling a range of goals; in terms of intervention delivery they were hugely heterogeneous with over 750 separate activities identified in the first wave of the programme (Judge 1999). The highly heterogeneous nature of the programme also made it difficult to summarise. Interventions ranged from the provision of smoking cessation services aimed at individuals to including local people in the planning and delivery of local health and social services.

In terms of health improvement and the reduction of health inequalities, the delivery of a broad range of activities aimed at a wide range of health behaviours and outcomes and concentrated in specific areas appeared to have little measurable impact over the truncated lifespan of HAZs (Judge and Bauld 2006). The 'policy failure' of HAZs was attributed, in part, to changes in government policies and the over-ambitious expectations of local and national policymakers. Despite the lack of a direct impact on health, successes of the HAZ programme included the establishment and mainstreaming of partnership working by a variety of local agencies, together with awareness and knowledge of the health inequalities agenda (Sullivan et al. 2004; Judge and Bauld 2006). Partnership approaches are now commonplace in health prevention initiatives, but at the time this was considered a new way of thinking about public health that recognised the importance of the social determinants of health.

'Natural Experiments': Generating Better Quality Evidence

The examples of Sure Start and HAZs suggest that area-based programmes and policies, although politically popular (especially amongst political parties aligned with broadly social democrat principles) and, as Hilary Thomson argues, justifiable on the grounds of their broad commitment to issues of social justice, have been demonstrated to have mixed effects on health as well as on the social determinants of health. Assessment of the overall success of such programmes is clearly very difficult and raises a series of questions about how best to assess the effectiveness of area-based interventions, especially within a policy environment that increasingly demands evidence-based health policy. A key issue here is that although evaluations of area-based interventions – initiatives that tackle health indirectly by focusing on social deprivation or directly by focusing on changing health behaviours – have been widely undertaken internationally, much of the work is fraught with methodological difficulties (Petticrew et al. 2005). Evaluations are often found in the non-peer reviewed grey literature, do not directly assess the health impact of area-based programmes, or focus on 'audit' oriented outcomes that document what money has been spent on and the process of interventions rather than their impacts (Thomson 2008).

Evaluations of the majority of area-based interventions that tackle the environmental risk factors for poor health are inherently 'natural experiments', experiments where the evaluator has very little control over the nature and delivery of the intervention. It is often the case that not one single intervention or a single health outcome is being evaluated. In fact, area-based interventions are themselves often inherently complex and multi-factorial and are being implemented on complex and diverse populations. Thus, the nature and content of such interventions can lead to many methodological challenges, for example: attribution of causality (what aspect of the environmental intervention may causally relate to which outcome); definitions of the populations being exposed (not all local residents will be equally affected or participate in the overall intervention or programme); and, adequately capturing the context of an area that has already probably been subject to multiple interventions throughout its history. The question we ask here is: what is required to generate better evidence of the effectiveness of area-based interventions? In order to understand the challenges in assessing the effectiveness of environmental interventions we use the example of the Philadelphia Food Environment Study, a quasi-experimental evaluation of a natural experiment to improve the food environment in order to promote better diet and diet-related health in Philadelphia.

Learning from natural experiments: Philadelphia, Glasgow and Leeds

The underlying cause for the recent and rapid increase in the population prevalence of obesity is thought to be environmental (Egger and Swinburn 1997; see Chapter 8). This suggests that population-level approaches to obesity prevention should include environmental interventions to reduce energy intake and improve diet quality as part of a wider population-level strategy (Swinburn et al. 1999). Residing in ethnic minority and low-income neighbourhoods, with poor access to healthy foods, has been shown to be an important risk factor for diet (Cummins and Macintyre 2006; Black and Macinko 2008). Food environment interventions are thus thought to hold potential as effective strategies for creating population-level improvements in diet (and hence prevalence of overweight and obesity and diseases such as Type 2 diabetes). On this basis, structural interventions to improve the food environment have formed a major component of recent policy initiatives, particularly in the United States and the United Kingdom. One example is The Pennsylvania Fresh Food Financing Initiative, a public–private initiative aimed at encouraging the development of food supermarkets in underserved areas by providing grants and loans to defray the infrastructure costs of developing new grocery stores (see Box 10.2).

Similar interventions have been deployed in British cities (e.g. Glasgow and Leeds) through so-called 'regeneration partnerships' in deprived areas where food stores have been developed in conjunction with a major food retailer as part of wider area investment and neighbourhood renewal. These interventions are based on the idea that encouraging supermarkets and grocery stores to open in disadvantaged neighbourhoods will translate into improvements in individual diet and diet-related health through improvements in local food access and affordability. However, despite these environmental interventions being delivered at great cost, evidence for their effectiveness is almost entirely absent.

In Pennsylvania, controlled quasi-experimental evaluations of the FFFI (Cummins et al. 2014; Dubowitz et al. 2015) found no positive impact on aspects of diet or diet-related poor health such as fruit and vegetable intake or obesity, nor a knock-on negative effect on the existing retail offer due to increased competition, although there were improvements in residents' perceptions of food accessibility. In Glasgow, while there was an increase in fruit and vegetable consumption in the intervention area of around a third of a portion per day, a similar increase was observed in the control area, making the attribution of change to the supermarket, rather than any wider secular change, difficult (Cummins et al. 2005); these finding were contrary to earlier work undertaken in Leeds (Wrigley et al. 2003). In Glasgow, contrary to the expectations of local shopkeepers, the development appeared to have little negative knock-on effect on structural aspects of the existing local food retail economy in the intervention area (Cummins et al. 2008b), a concern that was frequently raised at consultation stage by local stakeholders when the development was going through the process of obtaining planning permission.

Box 10.2   Key Themes: The Pennsylvania Fresh Food Financing Initiative

The Pennsylvania Fresh Food Financing Initiative (FFFI) was a statewide financing programme designed to attract supermarkets and grocery stores to underserved urban and rural communities; it ran from 2004 to 2010. The objectives of the programme were: to stimulate investment of private capital in low-wealth communities; to remove financing obstacles and lower operating barriers for supermarkets in poor communities; to reduce the high incidence of diet-related diseases by providing healthy food; to create living wage jobs; and to prepare and retain a qualified workforce.

The FFFI was developed as a public–private partnership between the Commonwealth of Pennsylvania, The Reinvestment Fund, The Food Trust and the Urban Affairs Coalition and was seeded by the State with a $30 million grant, which resulted in a further $145 million of leveraged investment. The funds were then used to provide loans and grants for predevelopment, acquisition, equipment and construction costs, as well as for start-up costs such as employee recruitment and training.

The FFFI attracted 206 applications from across Pennsylvania, with 88 projects financed by 2010. In total, more than $73.2 million in loans and $12.1 million in grants were approved. Projects approved for financing were expected to bring 5,023 jobs and 1.67 million square feet of commercial space. Projects ranged in size from large, full-service supermarkets in urban neighbourhoods to small grocery stores in rural areas. This programme has been viewed as a success by non-profit and policy organisations, with 88 new or expanded fresh food retail projects developed, improving access to healthy food for an estimated 500,000 children and adults (Karpyn et al. 2010).

Despite the limitations of these studies and their failure to demonstrate a positive impact of food environment interventions on diet, they do raise methodological and conceptual issues involved in the design and evaluation of environmental interventions (Petticrew et al. 2005, 2007). Based on the studies reported above, four broad methodological and conceptual issues emerged: (i) the need for adequate control groups; (ii) triangulation of quantitative and qualitative data; (iii) lack of control over the intervention; and (iv) the need for a strong underlying 'theory of change' model. These are considered in turn below.

The need for adequate control groups in monitoring impacts

In any assessment of the impact of an environmental intervention, there needs to be consideration of the counterfactual; that is, what would have happened in the absence of the intervention. In Leeds a positive relationship between increased provision of access to and increased consumption of healthy food was found; however, there was no control group (i.e. a similar study conducted in a similar area where no intervention had taken place for comparison). When comparing the findings with Glasgow, without a control area, it is likely that there would have been attribution of the small change in diet observed in the intervention area to the new supermarket; yet, if similar positive improvements were also observed in the control area this would tell us that positive impacts were the result of other changes occurring over time and were not directly a result of the intervention itself.

Controlled evaluations of 'natural' area-based interventions such as these are therefore crucial, but difficult to achieve in practice. A key complicating factor is the challenge of finding control and intervention areas where people and place characteristics do not differ at baseline in important ways that may be related to the health outcomes of interest (Petticrew et al. 2005). 'Natural experiments' can be contrasted with the gold-standard randomised controlled trial, which is often employed in the evaluation of effectiveness of new clinical interventions such as drugs, health technology and clinical techniques where known and unknown confounding factors are distributed at random. In order to engender confidence amongst the health care agencies and regulators who constitute the end-users of evaluations of area-based interventions, evaluations need to adequately address baseline differences by matching areas as far as is possible. This is further complicated by the fact that it is unlikely that perfect matching can ever occur (the real world is a complex, messy place) and area-based differences may not be easily identified, adjusted for or even observed (Petticrew et al. 2005). Thus, a defining feature of evaluations of area-based interventions is the difficulty in establishing causality and, as such, studies have been used as indicative (showing likely trends) rather than conclusive (proving cause and effect) in the production of evidence of effectiveness (Macintyre 2003). Such a pragmatic approach to evaluation also reflects Thomson's request for a 'dose of realism' (Thomson 2008).

Triangulating quantitative and qualitative assessments of impacts and exposures

Many evaluations of the health impacts of environmental interventions consider only quantitative evaluation, however qualitative data are also important for robust evaluation because 'not everything that is important can be quantified' (Mindell et al. 2001). The Glasgow study used both conventional observational quantitative epidemiological techniques and more social science-informed qualitative data collection, which was carried out post intervention (after the building of the supermarket). A repeated retail survey was also carried out to collect information of the impact of the store in the local retail economy. This involved baseline survey work to 'map' the retail structure and then repeat surveys at 6-monthly intervals to assess change. This is particularly noteworthy as qualitative data are rarely used longitudinally (i.e. over time) to monitor the impacts of environmental interventions. Existing secondary sources (e.g. data from local authority surveys and trade bodies) were used, but 'ground-truthing' these data by direct observation techniques – ensuring that the secondary data were actually a true representation of what was really on the ground – in both areas identified errors, omissions and changes from these secondary sources.

In the case of the Glasgow study, analysis of qualitative data suggested that the new store did not have a significant impact on diet, which was corroborated by similar findings from the quantitative arm of the study. It also allowed the investigation of the impact of the store on local people's perceptions of the quality and range of food available to them, and to explore attitudinal and other barriers to use of the superstore. There were, however, also challenges. Defining the affected population (who should be surveyed) was difficult. A new supermarket is not just used by the local population, and conversely local people may use other retailers. This problem of defining who is exposed also raises contamination problems, as some area-based interventions cannot be limited to those who reside in that specific area. This highlights the need for multi-method approaches where qualitative material can help to explore process and mechanisms and help explain further the findings generated from quantitative data.

Lack of control over the intervention

As noted previously, the majority of area-based interventions can be viewed as 'natural experiments': interventions where the researcher has very little control over the content, timing and implementation of the intervention. In the Philadelphia study, the economic recession delayed the supermarket company's store development plans. In the Glasgow study, the supermarket was built in the original control area, resulting in a pragmatic decision to switch intervention and control areas, a difficulty probably not often encountered in true 'experiments'. Timing was another problem, as delays in the planning process inevitably led to delays in the opening of the new superstores in both Glasgow and Philadelphia. Political, economic and budgetary considerations (as exemplified by the experience of HAZs) can interfere with the successful evaluation of interventions. Timetables are not always followed, which in turn has implications for research. In evaluating area-based interventions, if possible, flexibility should be built into evaluation protocols to allow for unforeseen changes in design and timing.

The need for a robust underlying 'theory of change'

On the basis of existing theory about the environmental determinants of diet, and past observational research, we would have realistically expected to observe some small changes in diet in the community where the stores were built. However, the qualitative elements of the Glasgow evaluation revealed flaws in the underlying conceptual model, or theory of change, about how the intervention might work. Interviews with local residents in the intervention area raised questions of boundary and ownership of neighbourhood food resources; that is, what constituted local and appropriate food access for different individuals (Cummins et al. 2008a, 2008b). Although the new provision was acknowledged to have improved the range, choice and quality of food locally, there were also concerns over the temptation to spend beyond household economic means. Even the construction of what 'local' meant for food shopping differed amongst respondents. In one case, a respondent reported their 'local' shopping as several miles from their current address as this was where the respondent had grown up and lived for many years (Cummins et al. 2008a). For this individual, although the neighbourhood food resource was physically distant it was socially proximate and thus any change in local provision had little impact on food shopping behaviour and thus diet. Such findings demonstrate the importance of incorporating qualitative work in evaluation designs to assess the impact of environmental interventions as these can help refine conceptual models and underlying theories about how the causal pathways from interventions to outcomes are thought to operate.

If we are to take seriously the role of contextual factors in the production and maintenance of health inequalities then, logically and morally, we must also think seriously about the utility of environmental interventions that may help ameliorate them. Evaluations of the effectiveness of area-based or environmental interventions have not always been seen as an important area of enquiry for health geographers due to their applied nature, and have therefore primarily been undertaken more by applied health and social researchers. However, critical geographical thinking can help us better understand how interventions might (or might not) work in the real world and also allow us to supply better evidence for whether environmental factors are truly causally associated with health outcomes and behaviours.

Conclusion

On one level, this chapter has documented the somewhat disappointing track record, in terms of health impact, of environmental interventions. The limited nature of the evidence of their impact on health and the social determinants of health ensures that definitive conclusions about effectiveness cannot realistically be drawn (as is the case in many areas of the social sciences). However, this should not necessarily persuade the reader that such interventions do not work. In order to populate the evidence base, evaluations of area-based 'natural experiments' are likely to provide the best and most realistic opportunities, at least in the short term, to estimate the potential impacts of environmental interventions on health and health inequalities.

The examples in Glasgow and Philadelphia demonstrate how an opportunity to undertake an evaluation of a naturally occurring area-based intervention to improve the food environment, and thus diet, allowed reflection on the difficulties of generating evidence for the effectiveness of area-based programmes that aim to improve health and reduce health inequalities. Effective evaluation needs to be realistic and pragmatic with a clear definition of control and experimental conditions and the populations exposed to the intervention, together with the flexibility to deal with the practical difficulties of evaluating area programmes that are inherently complex and dynamic and often change in response to external influences beyond the evaluator's control. It is crucial to have a clear and rigorous *a priori* specification of the underlying conceptual causal models (or theory of change) and pathways that drive area-based interventions; this could be aided by the incorporation of qualitative approaches in testing and refining these models.

Complaints from researchers, practitioners and policymakers about the scarcity and quality of the available evidence for the effectiveness of environmental interventions should provide sufficient justification for ensuring that the evaluations of area-based interventions are routinely undertaken. Only then will useful evidence be generated which can be translated into designing and implementing effective environmental interventions to improve population health.

Questions for Review

1. How might the twin goals of improving health and reducing health inequalities sometimes conflict? What type of policy approach might be a solution to this conflict?
2. What is a theory of change? Can you outline a theory of change for an environmental intervention that might improve diet?
3. What is a natural experiment? How might natural experiments be useful for researchers who are interested in the environmental determinants of health?

Suggested Reading

Petticrew, M & Roberts, H (2003) Evidence, hierarchies, and typologies: horses for courses. *Journal of Epidemiology & Community Health* 57, 527–9.

Petticrew, M, Cummins, S, Ferrell, C, Findlay, A, Higgins, C et al. (2005) Natural experiments: an underused tool for public health? *Public Health* 119, 751–7.

Rychetnik, L, Frommer, M, Hawe, P & Shiell, A (2002) Criteria for evaluating evidence on public health interventions. *Journal of Epidemiology & Community Health* 56, 119–27.

Woodward, A & Kawachi, I (2000) Why reduce health inequalities? *Journal of Epidemiology & Community Health* 54, 923–9.

References

Belsky, J, Melhuish, E, Barnes, J, Leyland AH, Romaniuk, H (2006) Effects of sure start local programmes on children and families: early findings from a quasi-experimental, cross sectional
study. *BMJ* 332, 1476–80.

Benzeval, M & Judge, K (2005) The legacy of health inequalities. In: Barnes, M, Bauld, L, Benzeval, M,
Judge, K, Mackenzie, M & Sullivan, H (Eds) *Health Action Zones: partnerships for health.*
Routledge, Abingdon, 1–16.

Black, JL & Macinko, J (2008) Neighborhoods and obesity. *Nutrition Reviews* 66, 2–20.

Blane, D. (1985) An assessment of The Black Report's explanations of health inequalities. *Sociology of
Health and Illness* 7, 423—45.

Bronfenbrenner, U (1977) Toward an experimental ecology of human development. *American
Psychologist* 32, 513–31.

Cummins, S (2005) Large scale food retailing as an intervention for diet and health: quasi-experimental
evaluation of a natural experiment. *Journal of Epidemiology & Community Health* 59, 1035–40.

Cummins, S & Macintyre, S (2006) Food environments and obesity – neighbourhood or nation?
International Journal of Epidemiology 35, 100–4.

Cummins, S, Curtis, S, Diez-Roux, AV & Macintyre, S (2007) Understanding and representing "place"
in health research: a relational approach. *Social Science & Medicine* 65, 1825–38.

Cummins, S, Findlay, A, Higgins, C, Petticrew, M, Sparks, L et al. (2008a) Reducing inequalities in
health and diet: findings from a study on the impact of a food retail development'. *Environment
and Planning A* 40, 402–22.

Cummins, S, Findlay, A, Petticrew, M & Sparks, L (2008b) Retail-led regeneration and store-switching
behaviour. *Journal of Retailing and Consumer Services* 15, 288–95.

Cummins, S, Flint, E & Matthews, SA (2014) New neighborhood grocery store increased awareness
of food access but did not alter dietary habits or obesity. *Health Affairs* 33, 283–91.

Curtis, S & Rees Jones, I (1998) Is there a place for geography in the analysis of health inequality?
Sociology of Health & Illness 20, 645–72.

Department of Health (2009) Change4Life, viewed 21 December 2016, http://www.nhs.uk/
change4life/Pages/overview-policy-background.aspx?filter=OverviewAndPolicyBackground

Diez-Roux, A-V (2007) Neighborhoods and health: where are we and where do we go from here?
Revue d'Épidémiologie et de Santé Publique 55, 13–21.

Dubowitz, T, Ghosh-Dastidar, MA, Cohen, D, Beckman, R, Steiner, ED et al. (2015) Diet and perceptions change with supermarket introduction in a food desert, but not because of supermarket
use. *Health Affairs* 34, 1858–68.

Egger, G & Swinburn, B (1997) An "ecological" approach to the obesity pandemic. *BMJ* 315,
477–80.

Graham, H (2004) Tackling inequalities in health in England: remedying health disadvantages,
narrowing health gaps or reducing health gradients? *Journal of Social Policy* 33, 115–31.

House of Commons Health Select Committee (2009) Health Inequalities, viewed 21 December 2016,
http://www.publications.parliament.uk/pa/cm200809/cmselect/cmhealth/286/28612.htm

Judge K (1999) Health Action Zones: Learning to make a difference. Report submitted to the
Department of Health, viewed 21 December 2016, http://www.pssru.ac.uk/pdf/dp1546.pdf

Judge, K & Bauld, L (2006) Learning from policy failure? Health action zones in England. *The
European Journal of Public Health* 16, 341–3.

Karpyn A, Manon M, Treuhaft S, Giang T, Harries C, McCoubrey K (2010) Policy solutions to the
grocery gap. *Health Affairs* 29, 473–80.

Krieger, N & Birn, A-E (1998) A vision of social justice as the foundation of public health: commemorating 150 years of the spirit of 1848. *American Journal of Public Health* 88, 1603–6.

Kulkarni, V.S. & Subramanian, S.V. (2010) Social perspectives on health inequalities. In: Brown, T, McLafferty, S & Moon, G (Eds) *A companion to health and medical geography*. Wiley-Blackwell, Oxford, 375–98.

Lorenc, T, Clayton, S, Neary, D, Whitehead, M, Petticrew, M et al. (2012) Crime, fear of crime, environment, and mental health and wellbeing: mapping review of theories and causal pathways. *Health & Place* 18, 757–65.

Lupton, R (2003) *Neighbourhood effects: can we measure them and does it matter? CASE/73. Centre for Analysis of Social Exclusion*. London School of Economics and Political Science, London.

Macintyre, S (1997) The Black Report and beyond: what are the issues? *Social Science & Medicine* 44, 723–45.

Macintyre, S (2003) Evidence based policy making. *BMJ* 326, 5–6.

Macintyre, S (2007) Deprivation amplification revisited; or, is it always true that poorer places have poorer access to resources for healthy diets and physical activity? *International Journal of Behavioral Nutrition and Physical Activity* 4, 32.

Macintyre, S, Chalmers, I, Horton, R, Smith, R (2001) Using evidence to inform health policy: case study. *BMJ* 322, 222–5.

Marmot, M (2010) *Fair society, healthy lives: the Marmot review; strategic review of health inequalities in England post-2010*. The Marmot Review, London.

Melhuish, E & Hall, D. (2007) The policy background to Sure Start. In: Belsky, J, Barnes, J & Melhuish, E (Eds.) *The national evaluation of Sure Start: does area-based early intervention work?* Bristol, Policy Press, 3–21.

Melhuish, E, Belsky, J, Leyland, AH & Barnes, J (2008) Effects of fully-established sure start local programmes on 3-year-old children and their families living in England: a quasi-experimental observational study. *The Lancet* 372, 1641–7.

Mindell, J, Hansell, A, Morrison, D, Douglas, M & Joffe, M (2001) What do we need for robust, quantitative health impact assessment? *Journal of Public Health* 23, 173–8.

O'Dwyer, LA, Baum, F, Kavanagh, A & Macdougall, C (2007) Do area-based interventions to reduce health inequalities work? A systematic review of evidence. *Critical Public Health* 17, 317–35.

Petticrew, M, Cummins, S, Ferrell, C, Findlay, A, Higgins, C et al. (2005) Natural experiments: an underused tool for public health? *Public Health* 119, 751–7.

Petticrew, M, Cummins, S, Sparks, L & Findlay, A (2007) Validating health impact assessment: prediction is difficult (especially about the future). *Environmental Impact Assessment Review* 27, 101–7.

Powell, M & Moon, G (2001) Health Action Zones: the "third way" of a new area-based policy? *Health and Social Care in the Community* 9, 43–50.

Powell, M, Boyne, G & Ashworth, R (2001) Towards a geography of people poverty and place poverty. *Policy & Politics* 29, 243–58.

Riva, M, Gauvin, L & Barnett, TA (2007) Toward the next generation of research into small area effects on health: a synthesis of multilevel investigations published since July 1998. *Journal of Epidemiology & Community Health* 61, 853–61.

Schrecker, T & Bambra, C (2015) *How politics makes us sick: neoliberal epidemics*. Palgrave Macmillan, Basingstoke.

Smith, G (1999) *Area-based initiatives: the rationale and options for area targeting. CASE/25. Centre for Analysis of Social Exclusion*. London School of Economics and Political Science, London.

Smith, SJ & Easterlow, D (2005) The strange geography of health inequalities. *Transactions of the Institute of British Geographers* 30, 173–90.

Stafford, M, Nazroo, J, Popay, JM & Whitehead, M (2008) Tackling inequalities in health: evaluating the new deal for communities initiative. *Journal of Epidemiology & Community Health* 62, 298–304.

Sullivan, H, Judge, K & Sewel, K (2004) "In the eye of the beholder": perceptions of local impact in English Health Action Zones. *Social Science & Medicine* 59, 1603–12.

Swinburn, B, Egger, G & Raza, F (1999) Dissecting obesogenic environments: the development and application of a framework for identifying and prioritizing environmental interventions for obesity. *Preventive Medicine* 29, 563–70.

Thomson, H (2008) A dose of realism for healthy urban policy: lessons from area-based initiatives in the UK. *Journal of Epidemiology & Community Health* 62, 932–6.

Thomson, H, Atkinson, R, Petticrew, M, Kearns, A (2006) Do urban regeneration programmes improve public health and reduce health inequalities? A synthesis of the evidence from UK policy and practice (1980–2004). *Journal of Epidemiology & Community Health* 60, 108–15.

Townsend, P (1992) *Poverty in the United Kingdom: a survey of household resources and standards of living.* University of California Press, Berkeley.

Tudor Hart, J (1971) The inverse care law. *The Lancet* 297, 405–12.

Woodward, A & Kawachi, I (2000) Why reduce health inequalities? *Journal of Epidemiology & Community Health* 54, 923–9.

Wrigley, N (2002) "Food deserts" in British cities: policy context and research priorities. *Urban Studies* 39, 2029–40.

Wrigley, N, Warm, D & Margetts, B (2003) Deprivation, diet, and food-retail access: findings from the Leeds 'food deserts' study. *Environment and Planning A*, 35, 151–88.

Part IV

Emerging Geographies of Health and Biomedicine

Chapter 11

Epidemics and Biosecurity

Introduction

An epidemic is a disease that spreads rapidly and extensively by infection, affecting many individuals in an area or population at the same time (like the 2014–2016 outbreak of Ebola in West Africa). If the epidemic becomes more widespread (clustered in time but not in space), as is, for example, the current global human immunodeficiency virus/acquired immune deficiency syndrome (HIV/AIDS) outbreak, it becomes a pandemic. In contrast, if a disease remains prevalent in but restricted to a particular region, community or group of people, it is referred to as endemic. For example, malaria is presently endemic in a broad band around the equator, in areas of the Americas, many parts of Asia and much of Africa; it is in sub-Saharan Africa where 85 to 90 per cent of malaria fatalities occur. Epidemics are not always fatal (consider annual outbreaks of the common cold virus, for example), but even non-fatal outbreaks can have a significant impact in terms of lost time in work due to sickness. However, it is the 'big killers' – epidemics with a high mortality rate – which tend to stand out both historically and in terms of being objects of social and political concern. Consequently, it is these high-mortality epidemics that form the focus of this chapter.

The chapter begins by exploring different infectious agents and how their distinctive characteristics impact the probability that any particular disease outbreak will reach epidemic or pandemic proportions. In the sections that follow, we examine the epidemiology of emerging infectious disease, outlining the key factors seen to be shaping where outbreaks occur and how they spread. We then consider the different strategies used to respond to epidemic outbreaks and how these are refined through advances in scientific research before turning to the relationship between infectious disease and what we refer to as its securitisation. Throughout we also explore how the ways in which infectious diseases emerge, and the ways governments and international organisations respond, echo many of the key themes of this volume. Specifically, we examine the impact of globalisation and

Health Geographies: A Critical Introduction, First Edition. Tim Brown, Gavin J. Andrews, Steven Cummins, Beth Greenhough, Daniel Lewis, and Andrew Power.
© 2018 John Wiley & Sons Ltd. Published 2018 by John Wiley & Sons Ltd.

inequality on disease ecology, the operation of biopolitics in tackling epidemics, the role of neoliberal policies in limiting access to vaccines and antivirals, and inequalities in who bears the greatest blame for, and impact of, epidemic outbreaks.

What Causes Epidemic Disease?

Table 11.1 lists the world's most deadly outbreaks, many of which, like the fourteenth century 'Black Death' or the 'Spanish flu' epidemic of 1918, constitute key moments in human history. It is notable that since 1918 only one disease –HIV/AIDS – has exceeded the death toll of the Spanish flu. The reasons for this might be found in the specific combination of the distinct nature of HIV/AIDS as opposed to other infectious diseases, geographical factors affecting the epidemiology of infectious diseases, scientific advances that have shaped our ability to respond to epidemic outbreaks and social, political and cultural factors that can influence both disease emergence and government responses to outbreaks.

When looking at epidemics it is important to appreciate the range of infectious agents as this can shape the way diseases are understood and managed. As we noted in Chapter 2, disease is an embodied phenomenon – materiality matters – and this is as true for infectious agents as it is for diseased human bodies. There are different kinds of infectious agents, including viruses (e.g. H5N1 'avian flu'), bacteria (e.g. whooping cough, anthrax, botulism), protozoa (e.g. African sleeping sickness, malaria) and multi-cellular parasites (e.g. tapeworms, onchocerciasis (which causes river blindness), Guinea worms). These can further be divided into two categories: *anthroponoses*, microbes that have adapted to use humans as their primary and usually only host; and *zoonoses* for which non-human species are the natural reservoir (e.g. Ebola, avian influenza, rabies). These are then further classified into those agents that are directly transmitted from host to host (*anthroponoses*, e.g. tuberculosis (TB), HIV/AIDS and measles, and *zoonoses*, e.g. rabies) and those that are indirectly transmitted via vectors such as ticks or mosquitoes (*anthroponoses*, e.g. malaria and dengue fever, and *zoonoses*, e.g. Lyme disease). The nature of epidemic agents shapes the kinds of treatments and tactics we can use to try and control them. For example, antibiotics such as penicillin can be effective to treat diseases caused by some bacteria but are ineffective against viral infections.

Table 11.1   Comparison of history's worst epidemics by number of deaths. Data taken from *National Geographic* (2014) and WHO (http://apps.who.int).

Epidemic	Estimated number of deaths
Black Death (bubonic plague) 1346–1350	50,000,000
HIV/AIDS 1960–date	35,000,000
Spanish flu 1918–1920	20,000,000
Sixth cholera pandemic 1899–1923	1,500,000
Swine flu 2009	284,000
Great plague of London (bubonic plague) 1665–1666	100,000
Ebola epidemic, West Africa 2014–2016	11,325
Haiti cholera epidemic 2010–date	9,200
Congo measles epidemic 2011–2013	5,045
Severe acute respiratory syndrome (SARS) 2002–2003	774

The nature of the infectious agent is one of a number of factors that shape whether or not it could be the source of the next major epidemic outbreak. Epidemiologist Christophe Fraser (cited in Young 2015) suggests that there are four key factors that shape how severe an epidemic will be: (i) how easily the disease is transmitted; (ii) how easy it is to develop a vaccine or treatment; (iii) the length of time the patient is asymptomatically infectious (i.e. infectious to others while showing no signs of the disease themselves); and, (iv) the severity of the disease or knowing that a high proportion of people who contract it will die. To be the source of a major epidemic outbreak a disease would need to have all four of these elements. Table 11.2 lists several recent outbreaks and how they measure up against these criteria. As we can see, each disease listed is missing one of the four elements needed to make it the next pandemic. For example, Ebola, while having high mortality and no vaccine available at the time of outbreak, is not easily transmitted as it is spread through bodily fluids and requires direct contact with an infected individual. Furthermore, those infected with Ebola are not infectious until they show symptoms, making it easier for them to be quarantined and isolated to prevent infection spreading. Severe acute respiratory syndrome (SARS), in contrast, is airborne and very easily transmitted. However, as symptoms appeared before people became infectious, those infected could be easily quarantined to prevent spread. HIV/AIDS is distinctive in the long period in which people remain asymptomatic but infectious, but it is not easily transmitted. The possibility for carriers to be infectious while asymptomatic partly explains why HIV/AIDS remains one of the world's biggest killers, claiming an estimated 35 million lives so far and with a further 36.7 million people living with HIV, the majority (around 25 million) in Sub-Saharan Africa (WHO 2016, unpaginated). H1N1 (swine flu) is easily transmitted, people are infectious before symptoms show and when it first emerged in 2009 no vaccine was available. However, it was no more lethal than normal flu. None of these viruses therefore qualifies to reach the scale of devastation caused by the 1918 Spanish flu or the Black Death (bubonic plague).

However, Table 11.2 needs to be placed in context. Each of the factors listed is conditioned by when and where the outbreak occurs. For example, the impact of a virus is greatly reduced if there is a treatment or vaccine available. As scientific knowledge of a disease grows, it arguably becomes less deadly as we are better able to treat it. For example, in 1996, Brazil made anti-retrovirals (ARVs) available to all registered HIV/AIDS patients and obliged the public health system to dispense them, leading to a dramatic (35 per cent) reduction in AIDS deaths (see Chapter 12). In addition, the living and working conditions of those at risk of disease can greatly expedite or reduce the rate of infection. The sections 'Disease Ecology' and 'Tackling Epidemics' therefore serve, first to outline changing environmental conditions and how these have contributed to the emergence of infectious

Table 11.2 Several recent diseases mapped against Fraser's four key criteria for a major epidemic outbreak. Data taken from Young (2015).

Disease	Ease of transmission	No vaccine available at time of outbreak	Infectious while asymptomatic	High mortality
Ebola		×		×
SARS	×	×		×
HIV		×	×	×
H1N1	×	×	×	

disease and, second, to explore developments in medical science, epidemiology and public health policy that aim to guard against the risk of epidemic outbreak and to manage outbreaks when they occur.

Disease Ecology

Medical geographers have played a key role in both contemporary and historical mapping of outbreaks of infectious disease and in understanding disease ecology – the complex interactions between pathogenic agents, their human and non-human hosts and vectors and the wider environment (see Meade and Emch 2010). Recent work in this field has focused on what has been termed the emergence and re-emergence of infectious diseases. There was a period in the mid twentieth century when it was widely assumed that infectious disease outbreaks were becoming a thing of the past. The global eradication of smallpox, as declared by the WHO in 1980, marked a high point in the history of the world's battle against epidemic disease and is described by the WHO as 'the first disease to have been fought on a global scale' (WHO 2010, unpaginated). However, this optimism was short-lived and the last decades of the twentieth century saw increasing concern over the threat to global health and security posed by both the re-emergence of known diseases such as cholera and TB and the emergence of new pandemic diseases such as HIV/AIDS and SARS.

Geographers such as Peter Haggett, Andrew Cliff and Matthew Smallman-Rayner (see Haggett 1994; Cliff et al. 2009), as well as medical geographers such as Jonathan Mayer (2000), Michael Emch and Elisabeth Root (2010), have sought to examine how changes in the dynamic equilibrium between population, society and environment can result in the emergence or re-emergence of infectious diseases. The latter, in particular, identify a number of key geographical dimensions to disease ecology, including ecological change, evolutionary change, human behaviour change, demographic change, political conflict, public health infrastructure collapse, hypermobility and globalisation and social and political processes. We briefly explore each of these aspects in turn (with the exception of social and political processes, which will be addressed separately in the section 'Governing Epidemics: Biopolitics, Securitisation and Global Threat'), drawing on how each contributes to the two-step process of disease emergence: first, introducing diseases into new populations, and second, facilitating their establishment and spread within those populations.

Ecological change

Ecological change is a key means through which previously unaffected populations are exposed to disease agents. For example, reforestation and the creation of new farmland can create new opportunities for humans to come into contact with wild animals who may be the source of zoonoses. The most often used example of this process is the emergence of Lyme disease in New England, United States, in the 1960s and 1970s. The abandonment of farmland led to a growth in new woodland areas, creating an ideal environment for the deer populations that host the *Ixodes* ticks that are the vectors for the disease. In addition, the expansion of suburban estates into the borders of these wooded areas and a rise in the use of these woodlands for leisure brought humans into contact with both the deer and the ticks. Further examples can be seen in areas subject to irrigation and the construction of dams, which create the ideal stable, slow-moving water bodies that serve as habitats for the snails that host schistosomes – the parasitic worms which cause bilharzia – and which have been linked to outbreaks of this disease in Eygpt following the construction of the Aswan high dam in the 1960s and in Senegal and South East Asia in the 1980s, following a shift towards more intensive farming methods.

Climate change has a notable impact on the geographical range of pathogens, vectors (which transmit the disease between hosts) and reservoirs (the 'natural' or preferred host of a particular pathogen). For example, in a recent report, the WHO (2003) suggested 'globally, temperature increases of 2–3 °C would increase the number of people who, in climatic terms, are at risk of malaria by around 3–5%, i.e. several hundred million due to the expansion of the habitat for the mosquitoes that host the malaria parasite. Further, the seasonal duration of malaria would increase in many currently endemic areas'.

Evolutionary change

Bacteria, viruses and parasites are continually evolving in response to environmental conditions. One possible source of emerging diseases is the mutation of pathogens that already exist into a new, more virulent form. This is most frequently observed in the case of influenza, the classic case being the emergence of the Spanish flu virus strain in 1918, source of a worldwide pandemic estimated to have killed between 20 and 40 million people. Recent research suggests that the four-fold increase seen in infectious disease outbreaks since the 1980s can largely be accounted for by an increase in zoonoses (microbes that use a non-human host for part of their lifecycle) and vector-borne diseases (Smith et al. 2014).

Evolutionary pressures include the selective pressures of human interventions such as the use of antibiotics and antivirals, the overuse of which has been linked to the emergence of new resistant strains such as meticillin-resistant *Staphylococcus aureus* (MRSA) and multidrug-resistant tuberculosis (MDR-TB). The World Health Organization's (2014) report on antimicrobial resistance (AMR) identifies this as a serious worldwide threat to public health. In the United Kingdom a current public health campaign is targeted at reducing the use of antibiotics, especially in cases (such as people presenting to physicians with respiratory symptoms) where the agent of disease (viral or bacterial) is unknown, in order to reduce AMR caused (many argue) by excessive and non-compliant use (e.g. people not finishing the course) of antibiotics. Others link the rise of drug-resistant strains of infectious diseases to the overuse of antibiotics in industrial farming, both prophylactically (as a precaution against disease) and as a means of stimulating animal growth.

Demographic change

Migration has long been recognised as a means by which pathogens are introduced into new, non-immune populations. This is seen in historical examples such as the impact of the smallpox virus which arrived in Mexico with the Spanish colonists in 1520, decimating the local Aztec population. Linked to migration, and in particular migration from rural to urban areas, is the process of urbanisation. Urbanisation is a double-edged sword when it comes to epidemic disease. In some cases, urbanisation can be associated with better sanitation and improved access to health care services, reducing opportunities for disease transmission and facilitating treatment to reduce mortality. On the other hand, high population densities and the challenges of ensuring good sanitation for a rapidly grow-ing urban population – as seen for example in cities in the West during the nineteenth century and in contemporary rapidly urbanising cites in Africa, East Asia and Latin America (Konteh 2009) – pose particular challenges in the management of disease, espe-cially when there are insufficient resources available to tackle them.

Today (2016) 54 per cent of the world's population live in urban areas. Analysis by the United Nations (2014) suggests that 66 per cent of the world's population will be urban by 2050, with 37 per cent of this rise accounted for by just three countries: India, China and Nigeria. Much of this growth takes place in informal settlements, generally referred to as slums or shanty towns and what Robert Snyder and colleagues (2014) refer to as the 'elephant in the room' in discussions of the 2014–2016 Ebola outbreak. Informal settlements are unplanned and often characterised by poor sanitation and lack of access to clean water, creating ideal conditions for outbreaks of cholera and typhoid. High-density, multiple-occupancy housing and over-crowded public transport systems also facilitate the transmission of TB in cities such as Mumbai, where it kills around 20 people per day and accounts for 8.5 per cent of all deaths (Praja 2014). A further consideration is the highly mobile nature of slum populations who often lack secure employment and are forced to 'migrate, clandestinely and often illegally, to new cities and countries', thereby subverting screening measures and presenting 'an immi-nent threat to other informal communities and the rest of the world' (Snyder et al. 2014, unpaginated).

The challenges of urbanisation are compounded by population growth. Alfred Crosby (2003, p. xiii) notes how the rapid growth in both the human population (three times greater now than in 1918) and in the populations of animals with which we exchange flu (among other) viruses, such as pigs and aquatic birds, creates many more opportunities for viruses to spread. China, for example, has seen an exponential growth in meat consump-tion (more than six-fold between 1980 and 2007) and now accounts for 31 per cent of world meat production, concentrated largely in pigs and poultry (FAO 2009), which are well-known hosts for strains of influenza. To feed this growing demand there has been an expansion of industrialised agriculture and intensive farming methods, which critics sug-gest creates ideal conditions (overcrowding, poor animal welfare) for incubating new and emerging viral strains (Wallace 2009).

Human behaviour can also impact the dissemination of infectious disease, most readily seen in the transmission of sexually transmitted diseases (STDs). For example, the overall decline in new HIV cases in the United States has been linked to needle exchange programmes for intravenous drug users and education programmes warning against risky sexual practices (although see Chapter 2 for a more critical discussion of the relationships between public health policy, urban infrastructure and HIV).

Hypermobility and globalisation

As noted previously, travel exposes non-immune populations to new pathogens, a process now greatly expedited by the rapid decrease in travel times facilitated by international air travel. Crosby (2003, p. xiii), in the preface to a new edition of his seminal work on the 1918

Spanish flu outbreak – *America's Forgotten Pandemic* – draws a striking comparison between the routes for viral transmission then and now:

> In 1918, the fastest way to cross the oceans was by steamship. In 2003, thousands of us daily and tens of millions of us annually make such trips in aircraft at speeds not far short that of sound, carrying with us in our lungs and bowels, on our hands and in our hair, micro-organisms of all kinds, including pathogens. We are all, so-to-speak, sitting in the waiting room of an enormous clinic, elbow to elbow with the sick of the world.

We might term this hypermobility.

S. Harris Ali and Roger Keil (2007) further refine this analysis, noting that while the potential for the high population densities and poor sanitation found in urban areas to facilitate viral transmission has always been there, globalisation has exacerbated such tendencies, as the flows (intensities), number of connections (extensities) and speed of connections (velocities) between cities increase. This global interconnectivity means in turn that the impact propensities, or capacity for small local events (or outbreaks) to be magnified through global networks, also increase: '2.1 billion airline passengers travelled in 2006; an outbreak or epidemic in any one part of the world is only a few hours away from becoming an imminent threat somewhere else' (WHO 2007, p. x). Passengers can now move between global cities before any symptoms of an infection become apparent, unwittingly spreading the disease. This was starkly illustrated by the 2003 outbreak of SARS. Originating in China, the disease spread to Hong Kong and from there rapidly to Toronto, Singapore, San Francisco, Manila and several other countries via air travel (see Ali and Keil 2007). Here we can see – as noted previously – that the materiality of the virus is important, in terms of its incubation period and mortality, but this is nuanced by contextual factors, including the speed of air travel which is now shorter than the incubation period (the time before symptoms appear) of many influenza strains. Furthermore, it is not only humans that can transport diseases. Dengue fever is thought to have been introduced to cities in the Americas by mosquitoes that hatched from eggs laid in the pools of water gathered in imported, used car tyres (Emch and Root 2010).

Tackling Epidemics

Throughout history human authorities have attempted to manage outbreaks of epidemic disease, predominantly through practices of isolation, quarantine and social distancing. However, contemporary approaches to preparing for and tackling epidemics have arguably been shaped by: (i) the increasing application of mapping and other surveillance tools to understand epidemiology; (ii) scientific advances in microbiology and the development of vaccines and treatments for infectious disease; and (iii) the rise of public and more recently global health as an area of governance and political action. Studying the ways in which human societies respond to outbreaks is an important task for health geographers as it provides insight into the ways in which public health measures, science and technology serve to condition both the ways in which we perceive epidemics (making them visible and thereby governable; see Box 11.2) and our capacities to respond to epidemic outbreaks. Inequalities in the ways in which outbreaks are governed, the technologies available and the capacity of those affected to recover from an outbreak also generate global disparities between populations in terms of their vulnerability to epidemic threats and their capacities to respond to and recover from an epidemic outbreak.

Isolation, quarantine and social distancing

Isolation refers to the separation of someone who has been infected with a communicable disease in a place where they cannot either directly or indirectly infect others while they remain infectious. For example, in the United Kingdom, health care workers infected with Ebola during the recent outbreak were isolated in the country's only high-level isolation unit which is housed in the Royal Free Hospital, London. Obviously this unit is used for exceptional cases; other more pragmatic approaches to isolation are used for less severe diseases, depending on the nature of transmission. Another traditional approach to managing infectious disease outbreaks is the practice of quarantining infected individuals, which involves restricting the travel and activities of a seemingly healthy person who is likely to have been exposed to a communicable disease, for a time equal to the incubation period of that disease, in order to establish if they are infected and if so to prevent them from infecting others. Quarantine can be voluntary or legally enforced and may take place in specially designated zones or facilities or at an individual's home (see Chapter 14).

Although they are effective and long-established methods for controlling the spread of disease, both isolation and quarantine have notable social and economic impacts. Isolation, for example, can be traumatic for the friends and family of an infected individual. It also impacts the health workers who must effectively isolate themselves (through protective clothing, masks and so on) from infected individuals, in ways that are perhaps at odds with the kind of personal, affective relations usually seen to constitute good care (see Chapter 6). Health care workers supporting the efforts to contain Ebola during the 2014–2016 outbreak in West Africa reported feeling exhausted, dehydrated and overwhelmed by the smell of chlorine as well as socially distant from those people they were caring for. Moreover, when isolation and quarantine practices are combined with the practice of social distancing – whereby opportunities for interaction are limited by restricting access to sites and activities that involve large gatherings of people (e.g. schools, shops and public transport) – there are potentially severe impacts on essential services, communities and the economy. For example, during Toronto's SARS outbreak of 2002, Canada's gross domestic product fell by $3–6 billion (US) and growth decreased by 1 per cent. In Sierra Leone during the recent Ebola epidemic (2014–2016) charities, including UNICEF, worked with the Ministry of Education, Science and Technology to provide education over the radio in order to try to ensure that learning continued despite widespread school closures (UNICEF 2014).

These are not the only public health measures that are used to contain infectious diseases; public information campaigns are often implemented before, during and sometimes after an outbreak to encourage good hygiene practices in order to reduce the (future) spread of infectious disease. Like isolation, quarantine and social distancing, such campaigns are longstanding and involve fairly benign messages such as hand washing and covering your mouth and nose when you sneeze (see Figure 11.1). They can also be targeted to address particular cultural practices that are identified as promoting the spread of disease. For example, during the recent (2014–2016) Ebola outbreak, health authorities including the WHO identified traditional burial practices in West Africa, which may involve viewing, washing and touching the body, as posing a risk of transmission because the body remains contagious for several days after death. In response public health campaigns promoted 'safe burial practices', where those in charge of preparing bodies for burial were informed that they should wear protective clothing and bodies were wrapped in body bags to prevent the contamination of mourners. Although designed to promote health, such campaigns are often questioned because of the representations of diseased bodies and places that they help

CATCH IT

Germs spread easily. Always carry tissues and use them to catch your cough or sneeze.

BIN IT

Germs can live for several hours on tissues. Dispose of your tissue as soon as possible.

KILL IT

Hands can transfer germs to every surface you touch. Clean your hands as soon as you can.

Figure 11.1   Catch it, Bin it, Kill it – respiratory and hand hygiene campaign in the United Kingdom (2008–2009). Reproduced under the terms of the Open Government License v3. Source: http://www.dh.gov.uk/en/Publicationsandstatistics/Publications/PublicationsPolicyAndGuidance/ DH_080839

to construct (see Chapter 2) or because they are seen to interfere with important social and cultural practices; for example, interference in the burial practices described above resulted in hostility and even violence in parts of West Africa (see Calain and Poncin 2015).

Epidemiology, surveillance and public health

Whereas isolation, quarantine and social distancing form one response to outbreaks of infectious diseases, epidemiological surveillance reflects another. The study of epidemic outbreaks, the populations they affect and their frequency, distribution and determinants, is generally regarded as the object of epidemiology. Epidemiology plays a key role in the governance of health and disease at local, national and increasingly (through the actions of the WHO and other international organisations) global scales (see Chapter 14). Epidemiology also has strong ties to medical geography, drawing on geographical techniques in order to survey and represent the spread of disease. This is perhaps best illustrated by one of the central stories (or some would argue myths, see McLeod 2000) of the emergence of medical geography or perhaps more appropriately medical cartography (see Koch 2005, 2009): John Snow's infamous dot maps and their use in the control of cholera in mid-Victorian London (see Box 11.1). Alongside disease mapping, the emergence of vital statistics also played a key role in enabling the governance of infectious disease.

The origin of the relationship between the collection of vital statistics and public health is generally traced to nineteenth century figures such as Louis René Villermé in France and William Farr in England. The former, Villermé, produced one of the first systematic investigations of the relationship between mortality rates, social status and place in his studies of Paris arrondissements in the 1820s. As Nancy Krieger (1992) notes, Villermé established an almost perfect fit between those areas with the lowest proportion of poor households and those with the lowest mortality rates, and vice versa. Studies such as Villermé's helped to shape the development of sanitary statistics, which highlighted the considerable toll that life in the urban slums of the nineteenth century had on the poor in the industrialising nations of France, England, Germany and the United States. In England, William Farr took up Villermé's mantle in the statistical work that he conducted for the Office of the Registrar General, established in 1837. Farr's statistical work, as well as that of many others who regularly shared their statistical insights at institutions such as the London Statistical Society, was the evidence base upon which the nineteenth century public health movement was built (see Hamlin 1998; see Box 11.1).

Box 11.1   Key Concepts: Miasma and Germ Theories

Sir Edwin Chadwick 1800–1890 was a UK social reformer known for his work seeking to promote sanitary reform and public health. In 1842 he published the *Report on the Sanitary Condition of the Labouring Population of Great Britain*, which was a government inquiry that helped to demonstrate the link between high rates of infectious disease and child mortality and grossly unsanitary conditions and polluted drinking water. His work shows starkly the impact of the industrial urban environment on human health. Housing segregation led to social segregation, which was also reflected in a growing health divide, not only between urban and rural dwellers but between rich and poor. This is often demonstrated through a table adapted from this inquiry showing the average age at death by social status and UK district (see Table 11.3).

Table 11.3   Average life expectancy by social status and UK district according to Chadwick's 1842 report.

Average life expectancy	Professional trades	Tradesmen	Labourers
Rutland	52	41	38
Leeds	44	27	19
Liverpool	35	22	15
Manchester	38	20	17
Bolton	34	23	18

Note the disparity in average age of death between the professional trades of the rural district of Rutland and the labourers (working classes) of urban Liverpool and Manchester. The main causes of death at this time were fevers (caused by infectious diseases such as respiratory TB, scarlet fever, typhoid and cholera), industrial accidents and malnutrition, although it should be noted that the average age of death would also reflect high levels of infant mortality.

Explanations for the high rates of mortality from infectious diseases varied during this period. Chadwick was a subscriber to the miasma (derived from the ancient Greek word for 'pollution') theory of disease, which maintained that infectious disease was caused by 'vapours' or bad air contaminated by small particles of dead and decaying matter and noticeable by its foul smell. Such a theory would have made sense to Chadwick, as outbreaks of disease tended to be concentrated in noxious smelling and poorly sanitised districts. In response, Chadwick pioneered the sanitary reform movement which campaigned for the rebuilding and redesign of cities on sanitary lines and the creation of local boards for public health. The movement led to the 1848 UK Public Health Act and the establishment of a ministry for public health in England and Wales (Hamlin and Sheard 1998).

British physician John Snow (1813–1858) was a dissenter to the then commonly accepted miasma theory of disease transmission promoted by Chadwick and his disciples. Snow is often held to be one of the 'fathers' of both modern epidemiology and spatial analysis for his pioneering work on the transmission of cholera in Victorian London. Through an intervention in Soho in 1854, in which he had a pump handle removed from a public well during a cholera outbreak, Snow demonstrated that water and sanitation played a key role in cholera transmission (McLeod 2000). In Snow's 'grand experiment', residents of Victorian South London were unwittingly divided into two groups by virtue of the service areas of two water companies: one supplied water contaminated with the sewage of London, including the waste of cholera patients, and the other took uncontaminated water upstream of London. There was little to distinguish between the two populations, aside from the source of water provision; however, the group exposed to the contaminated water presented strong evidence that cholera was a waterborne disease as they contracted cholera in greater numbers than their counterparts. Over time, Snow's compelling evidence, along with evidence generated by numerous other scientists, supported the common uptake of the germ theory of disease, in which diseases are recognised to be caused by bacteria, viruses and other organisms.

Where sanitary statistics played a crucial role in shaping the response of public health to infectious diseases during its so-called 'golden era' of the mid to late nineteenth century, its contemporary version comes in the form of the international disease surveillance networks that have been implemented by institutions such as the World Health Organization (see Weir and Mykhalovskiy 2010). Surveillance programmes such as the Global Influenza Surveillance and Response (GISAR) network act as early warning systems against epidemic and potentially pandemic diseases; in this instance, tracking the spread and evolution of the influenza virus, as well as updating diagnostic tests and identifying whether the strains respond to existing vaccines and antiviral drugs. Therefore, as Ali and Keil (2007, p. 1211) note, 'although the forces of globalization may have facilitated the diffusion of infectious disease in certain ways, they may also increase the potential for an effective and coordinated international response in other ways'. Although its track record is patchy and it has been severely criticised for its failure to respond effectively to the SARS epidemic and the recent Ebola outbreak, the WHO perhaps more than any other international organisation plays this role because of the surveillance networks it has developed (and inherited) since being established in 1948 (see Chapter 14).

Microbiology, vaccines and antimicrobials

As we note earlier in the book, science and medicine have for a very long time grappled with the problem of infectious disease, through the study of pathogenic agents and through the development of vaccines and antimicrobials to treat infectious disease. The development of new treatments is shaped by its own distinctive health geography, specifically where new treatments are developed, who they are developed for and who has access to them. In this section we briefly outline the key developments in vaccines and antimicrobials to provide a context for more critical discussions about access to these technologies in the next section.

Instances of inoculation (exposing a healthy person to a small amount of a pathogen in order to trigger an immune response) have been traced to China as early as 1000 CE; however, the modern history of vaccination begins with Edward Jenner's successful use of cowpox material to immunise human patients against smallpox in 1796. This was followed in 1885 by Louis Pasteur's rabies vaccine. The late nineteenth and early twentieth centuries saw the rise of germ theory (the belief that disease is caused by micro-organisms) and the development of the field of bacteriology (replacing the earlier miasma theory) (see Worboys 2000). A large number of new vaccines and antitoxins emerged through the 1930s, including vaccines against cholera, tetanus, tuberculosis and plague. Developments in virology through the mid twentieth century, including techniques for culturing and studying viruses *in vitro* (in the laboratory), led to further developments, including vaccines for polio and measles, mumps and rubella and the first antiviral medications in the 1950s and 1960s, as well as more effective vaccines. This period marked the heyday for the discovery of new classes of antibiotic drug and also saw a rise in the number of institutions and companies able to develop and manufacture vaccines as well as advances in effective treatments for secondary complications (e.g. antibiotics for chest infections). That said, we focus here on the contemporary development and use of vaccines, antibiotics and antivirals.

While the public health systems of many countries routinely promote the vaccination of their populations against new epidemic diseases, in the face of an outbreak or an epidemic it is unlikely that a vaccine will be immediately available. The development of vaccines can pose many practical challenges as, for example, in the recent 2014–2016 Ebola outbreak in West Africa. Like influenza, Ebola is a rapidly evolving and mutating virus, meaning any vaccine has to be able to protect against multiple strains. Furthermore, before the recent outbreak, the fact that Ebola only occurred in remote rural villages posed a challenge for researchers who needed access to the virus in order to study it. In an account of the challenges of trying to conduct research on Ebola, Nancy Sullivan and colleagues (2003, p. 9733) suggest that progress has been hampered by 'the difficulty in obtaining samples and studying the disease in the relatively remote areas in which the outbreaks occur'. They also note the restrictions placed on this kind of work due to fears about the highly pathogenic nature of the virus meaning 'a high degree of biohazard containment is required for laboratory studies and clinical analysis'.

In addition to vaccines, responses to epidemics also see a focus on attempts to develop new treatments. As noted above, during earlier outbreaks most treatments given were focused on the relief of symptoms, which provided the patient as much comfort as possible while they either pulled through or did not. For example, in the Spanish flu pandemic it was often the secondary infections that followed the virus – such as pneumonia – that were the actual cause of death. Considerable advances were made following Alexander Fleming's discovery of penicillin (the first antibiotic) in 1929, and through the 1940s large-scale fermentation processes necessary to engineer the drug for mass production were developed. The dramatic impact of antibiotics is reflected in contemporary fears about their declining effectiveness as a result of the rise of AMR. Today antibiotics play a key role in treating the secondary infections that develop (and often prove to be the actual cause of death) in patients whose immune responses are inhibited or lowered by viral infections such as influenza or HIV/AIDS. However, recent decades have seen the development of new treatments including the anti-retroviral drugs used to treat persons living with HIV/AIDs and the antiviral drugs developed to treat influenza. These drugs work by preventing or slowing down the replication of the virus in the body and therefore in some cases can also be used prophylactically to prevent an infection developing during the first two or three days of illness.

Collectively, vaccines and antimicrobials provide a key resource for tackling epidemic outbreaks, but one which (as we shall see below and in Chapter 12) is not equally accessible to all.

Governing Epidemics: Biopolitics, Securitisation and Global Threat

As noted in the previous section, one of the key impacts of increased disease monitoring and surveillance has been to render disease and its impact on populations visible and in some cases even to predict the likely outbreak of disease. This process is essential to tackling epidemics, rendering infectious disease outbreaks governable. It is no coincidence that increased surveillance is accompanied by the attempt to systematically govern public health and guard against epidemic disease outbreaks. The French philosopher Michel Foucault uses the term biopolitics (see Box 11.2) to describe this process whereby governments begin to view and try to manage populations as biological objects. This in turn links to broader questions about how epidemics and pandemics are seen as biosecurity issues and are responded to in ways that reflect national strategies to secure the health of particular populations. As biosecurity often involves making decisions about which populations to protect and which should be excluded as a threat, critics suggest that the governance of epidemics often serves to exacerbate – as opposed to redress – the inequalities between rich and poor, Global North and Global South, produced under neoliberalism (Sparke and Anguelov 2012, p. 726).

Inspired by Marxist theory, this work sees health inequalities as a form of structural violence, whereby the dominant capitalist mode of production and neoliberal government policies create an unequal society in which the poorest and most marginalised populations bear the highest burden of infectious diseases (among other burdens) while having the fewest resources (medicines, income, shelter and so on) with which to try and tackle them. Thus, in contrast with direct physical violence, structural violence is exercised through the distribution of the costs and benefits of economic growth. As capitalist enterprise, motivated

Box 11.2   Key Thinkers: Michel Foucault and Biopower

The French philosopher Michel Foucault is a key figure for contemporary health geographers, particularly noted for his development of three concepts – biopower, anatamopolitics and biopolitics – which capture the various ways in which the biological dimensions of human existence emerged as core concerns in modern society. Biopower broadly encapsulates the idea that from the eighteenth century people were increasingly treated as biological beings rather than as political subjects, informed by the modern, scientific approach to the management of disease that was replacing the belief that disease was God-given. Anatamopolitics and biopolitics refer to particular axes of this new form of power. Anatomopolitics sees the individual human body as the object of political strategies that seek to make human bodies useful and docile (discussed in Chapter 2), to instil in individuals a sense that the care of the self was the responsibility of the self, and fuelling the growth in private medicine and the emergence of personal health care industry. In contrast, biopolitics operates at the level of the population, focusing on the ways in which the state and charitable organisations began to seek to manage and survey disease, especially in those populations seen as less able to manage themselves. This was co-current with a growth in the use of scientific methods of surveillance, such as early nineteenth century statistics societies, who began to compile and map data of health and illness within populations in order to create national and global perspectives on health. These two spheres are closely related, through, for example, the way the state sought to mobilise parents to take responsibility for the health of their children through participation in vaccination programmes or through schemes to promote hygienic practices within the population. Biopolitics offers a key way of conceptualising national and international strategies for governing epidemic space. Stephan Elbe (2010), for example, draws on the Foucauldian concept of biopolitics to frame his analysis of the re-shaping of HIV/AIDS as a security issue. Elbe argues that the massive international intervention signalled by the establishment of the Global Fund to Fight AIDS, Tuberculosis and Malaria (see http://www.theglobalfund.org/en/history/) and the United States President's Emergency Plan for AIDS Relief (PEPFAR) suggests that HIV/AIDS, and more broadly the health of populations, were afforded the highest governmental priority.

by maximising profits, is constantly driven to find ways of reducing the costs of production, it habitually seeks out areas where the costs of both raw materials and/or labour power are lowest. Often these are areas with high levels of unemployment (and therefore a large population of people willing to work long hours for low wages) and low levels of regulations (compliance with which can impact on costs and profits, either through the costs of implementing safety procedures and equipment, or through measures to protect the rights of workers, such as holiday pay, sick pay and minimum wages). The workers are the ones subject to violence – low pay and poor working conditions – which can both generate myriad health problems (such as industrial accidents and respiratory and other diseases caused by manufacturing processes and materials) and make workers vulnerable to infectious disease.

Matt Sparke and Dimitar Anguelov (2012) use this framework to suggest four key forms of inequality: (i) inequality for blame for the outbreak; (ii) inequalities in risk management;

(iii) inequalities in access to medicines; and (iv) inequalities as a factor in determining when and where outbreaks occur. In the next sections we address each of these in turn, reflecting how they also contribute to broader biopolitical strategies, that is, strategies for governing the health of the population.

Inequalities in blame: The social construction of disease

First, we might look at the way in which narratives of epidemics are socially constructed or shaped by the beliefs and values of those who produce them, generating stories of who is seen as the source of the infection and who becomes the target for intervention strategies. Priscilla Wald (2008) discusses how stories of disease emergence divide populations into insiders (who need to be protected from infection) and outsiders (often seen as the sources of disease). Susan Craddock's (2000) analysis of smallpox in nineteenth century San Francisco, discussed in detail in Chapter 2, highlights the ways in which the disease, despite being European in origin, came to be closely associated with the immigrant Chinese population. In a more contemporary example, Paul Farmer (2006) talks about 'geographies of blame' with reference to HIV/AIDS and shows how while outbreak narratives from America accused Haitians of bringing HIV to the United States, subsequent epidemiological analysis revealed that it was Americans who brought the disease to Haiti through sex tourism. Sparke and Anguelov (2012) describe how, in the case of H1N1 (swine flu), the outbreak narrative focused on the case of a five-year old boy from Mexico, which led in the US media to the construction of H1N1 as a 'Mexican' disease, a social construction that arguably played on existing strong anti-immigrant feelings towards Mexicans. A similar scapegoating is readily apparent in the coverage of the 2014–2016 Ebola outbreak. Writing for the left-wing pan-African journal *Pambazuka News*, Amira Ali (2014, unpaginated) notes how 'the African Ebola patient is classically "othered" and portrayed as a villain and perpetrator, while the American Ebola patient is depicted as a victim'.

Social constructions of disease influence the application of seemingly objective scientific criteria in deciding who is to be monitored and excluded through quarantine during an outbreak. In Craddock's example of smallpox in nineteenth century San Francisco, Chinatown became the focus of highly invasive sanitisation measures, including disinfecting people's homes and burning their belongings. Following the recent 2014–2016 Ebola outbreak in West Africa, countries including the United Kingdom, United States, Canada, France and the Czech Republic introduced temperature checks and health questionnaires for travellers arriving from Ebola-affected regions. This is despite considerations that for other epidemic outbreaks such as influenza, which has a similar incubation period, 'in general, providing information to domestic and international travellers (risks to avoid, symptoms to look for, when to seek care) is a better use of health resources than formal screening' and that 'entry screening of travellers at international borders will incur considerable expense with a disproportionately small impact on international spread' (Knobler et al. 2005, p. 151).

Inequalities in risk management and securitisation

One of the ways in which outbreak narratives are increasingly constructed is through discourses of securitisation – the discursive processes through which a disease threat (amongst other threats) is raised above the normal response of politics. Securitisation is a product of what Ben Anderson (2010) calls anticipatory action or how, in response to uncertain and unknowable future threats, governments use models, imagined scenarios and role-play exercises to render more tangible multiple possible futures. These models then provide the basis for contingency planning in order to try to secure particular forms and ways of life. Andrew Lakoff (2008, p. 421) suggests that this emphasis on 'preparedness' constitutes a marked biopolitical shift in the last 30 years, drawing comparisons between the United States' responses to the 1976 swine flu campaign and the 2005 avian flu threat. In 1976 the focus was on securing the health of the national population, using what Lakoff terms the 'classical methods of public health' and based on surveillance and statistical models derived from historical incidences of disease outbreak. In 2005 the scale and focus of the disease threat had become global, including international surveillance and response counter-measures, and drawing on knowledge gleaned from imagined future scenarios.

There has been a growing concern evidenced on both a national and international scale with biosecurity, the need to protect valued things – principally the economy, the environment and human and animal populations – from diseases, pests and bioterrorism. This concern is fuelled by two factors. First, there is the impact of hypermobility and globalisation, leading to an acknowledgement that 'in the context of infectious diseases, there is nowhere in the world from which we are remote and no one from whom we are disconnected' (Institute of Medicine 1992. Cited by Feldbaum and Lee 2004, p. 22). In short, we are all potentially vulnerable (see Brown 2011). Second, Bruce Braun (2007) suggests that developments in molecular biology allow us to trace the molecular geographies that transmit viruses between, for example, birds and humans but they also highlight the unpredictability and waywardness of molecular life. The result is the rather belated recognition by policy-makers in the Global North of shifting patterns in health and disease and in particular the appearance of emerging and re-emerging infectious diseases – emerging ones such as HIV/AIDS, variant Creutzfeldt–Jakob disease (vCJD), SARS and Ebola, and re-emerging ones like cholera, malaria and TB – as serious threats to health and life outside of the Global South (Ingram 2005). It is not simply that these diseases have *emerged* or *re-emerged*, but that their appearance has 'shaken the notion of Western *security*' (Bankoff 2001, p. 21. Emphasis added). The fear that such diseases might cause economic, social and political instability within already 'unstable' regions has helped to raise the geopolitical profile of such global health issues, justifying ever more stringent biosecurity measures.

The WHO surveillance mandate discussed previously places particular emphasis on countries that 'lack the capacity to respond to an epidemic themselves'. Implicit in this last statement is a need to tackle the disease 'over there' before it reaches 'over here'. This is reflected in the ways in which the WHO's surveillance activities are 'tied in turn to paid response teams administered by the WHO, which arrive in "hot spots" within 24 hours to do on-the-spot investigations, confirm diagnoses, help with patient management and ultimately contain any outbreak' (Braun 2007, p. 20). This defensive rhetoric is even more explicit in the pandemic response strategies of individual nations. Consider, for example, this statement from the UK House of Lords report on intergovernmental organisations (IGOs) and disease control:

> We believe that it is an integral part of Britain's own defences against the spread of pandemic outbreaks of disease that warning and preventive systems in developing countries be strengthened and that, where necessary, the resources and skills to effect this are provided. (Intergovernmental Organisations Committee, *First Report*, 7 July 2008, UK House of Lords 2008, para 56)

This form of targeting is also evident within cities. Colin McFarlane (2008, p. 431), for example, describes how contemporary sanitary interventions within Mumbai are shaped by a desire to create clean and safe environments, where the elite can retreat to gated enclaves while slum sanitation policies aiming to demolish the external threat are justified by 'attempts to blame the poor themselves for a lack of sanitation'. As Anderson (2010, p. 791) observes, 'to protect, save and care for certain forms of life is to potentially abandon, dispossess and destroy others'. The result of these securitisation strategies is a stark divide between those (predominantly wealthy, elite populations in the Global North) who are seen as needing to be secured, and those who need to be secured against (poorer, marginalised populations, predominantly from the Global South).

Further inequalities emerge when we consider which diseases are seen to pose the highest global risk and in particular a tendency to focus on 'a disease that *might* effect the wealthy rather than other diseases that *already* effect the poor' (Sparke and Anguelov 2012, p. 730). As Michael Emch and Elisabeth Root (2010) note, there is a stark contrast between the activism and media attention surrounding HIV/AIDS and the concern over the so-called 'neglected diseases' for which there is little media and public health attention as well as a lack of incentive for the development of new drugs and treatments (see Chapter 12). Sparke and Anguelov (2012, p. 729) question why there has been a global outcry about the risk posed by H1N1 (2009) and more recently by Ebola (2014–2016) when these are dwarfed by 'global mortality and morbidity due to malnutrition, diarrhoea and deaths of infants and mothers during childbirth'.

Inequalities in access to medicines

This leads to a third set of inequalities, concerned with the ability to access the resources and manufacturing capacity needed to develop vaccines and antivirals. Despite global advances in vaccine production capacity, health services and knowledge of viral aetiology and surveillance, there remain huge disparities between relatively 'rich' and 'poor' nations in terms of their capacity to prepare for a pandemic. Many countries in the Global South lack the financial resources to purchase vaccine supplies and the public infrastructure to deliver them. They are also faced with competing public health priorities such as on-going outbreaks of malaria or HIV/AIDS (Tangcharoensathien 2007). These challenges were readily apparent in the recent Ebola (2014–2016) epidemic in West Africa. To date (December 2016) there has been no vaccine approved for Ebola, in part some would suggest because there has been (until the most recent outbreak) little incentive to develop one. In a particularly damning statement, WHO Director-General Margaret Chan suggested that, '[b]ecause Ebola has historically been confined to poor African nations. The R&D incentive is virtually non-existent. A profit-driven industry does not invest in products for markets that cannot pay' (Chan 2014. Cited in Cooper 2014 unpaginated; see also Chapter 12).

Like many drugs today, most vaccines and antivirals are developed commercially and, due to the high costs involved, remain under patent protection for 10 to 20 years so that manufacturers can recoup the substantial costs of drug development. Consequently during an epidemic there are conflicts of interest between governments and international organisations, like the WHO, who wish to procure large amounts of medication at as low a cost as possible, and drug companies who, in order to protect commercial interests, argue that they need to retain control over the production of the drugs and keep costs high. The significance of this is demonstrated by the case of the antiviral treatment oseltamivir (commercially known as Tamiflu). In 2005, in the wake of growing concern about a possible avian flu (H5N1) pandemic, the WHO launched a series of guidelines on pandemic preparedness, including the need to secure supplies of antiviral drugs. However, they also noted a disparity between those countries who could afford to purchase supplies of Tamiflu and those who could not:

> wealthy countries are presently the best prepared; countries where H5N1 is endemic [in birds] – and where a pandemic virus is most likely to emerge – lag far behind … *A November 2004 WHO consultation reached the stark conclusion that, on present trends, the majority of developing countries would have no access to a vaccine during the first wave of a pandemic and possibly throughout its duration.* (WHO 2005, p. 2. Emphasis added)

One notable response to these inequalities was the action taken in January 2007 by the Indonesian government, who suspended the shipment of samples from Indonesian flu patients to WHO surveillance laboratories on the grounds that (i) they would be unlikely to be able to afford access to the treatments developed using those samples, and (ii) to develop their own (Sedyaningsih et al. 2008). Indonesia came under criticism for taking action in a way that limited the WHO's ability to monitor and respond effectively to the global health threat posed by H5N1 (avian flu), but they also forced WHO reforms that emphasise the need to share the benefits of discoveries made using donated viral samples in ways which try to ensure access for all (see Elbe 2010; Sparke and Anguelov 2012, p. 729).

Inequalities determining epidemic occurrence

The factors that underpin the re-emergence of infectious disease have become a subject of concern for political ecologists (see Chapter 2) who investigate the specific combinations of political and environmental factors that shape health and disease within populations, paying particular attention to the ways they are shaped by, and reproduce, existing patterns of global inequality. Sparke and Anguelov (2012, p. 727) suggest that while more recent studies of the social determinants of health (see Chapter 8) have recognised the role of inequality in determining who is most vulnerable within defined populations, they are less able to register the impact of broader global inequalities: 'by only focusing on the proximate mechanics linking individual bodies to population statistics such accounts risk obscuring the more global and more complex socio-economic dynamics unleashed by market-led globalisation'.

These writers raise some interesting questions about the ways in which political factors, and in particular global capitalism and neoliberal policy, shape disease ecology. For example, the problems posed by slums, Snyder and colleagues (2014) argue, point to the wider structural and socio-economic causes of epidemics, as the demands of capitalist industry for cheap labour and services fuel the growth of slums but provide little of the economic security or investment necessary to either incentivise or fund improvements. Similarly, August H. Nimtz (2014) argues that the recent Ebola outbreak in West Africa was a product of a long history of colonial exploitation. This history is coupled with weak and corrupted contemporary governments subject to the neoliberal demands of international lending agencies such as the International Monetary Fund, who in turn impose conditions that restrict investment in health care and education, again contributing to an environment within which disease can flourish. Each of these examples reflects how capitalism leads to structural violence and this in turn can both fuel disease outbreaks and limit the capacity of affected populations to respond to them.

Such problems are not limited to the so-called 'Global South'. As Ali and Keil (2007, p. 1218) note, the neoliberal conditions prevailing in cities in the world's richest nations create ideal environments for diseases to thrive. Hospitals in major urban centres, such as those in Toronto during the 2003 SARS outbreak, provided perfect breeding ground for disease, at least in part because of the pressures placed on them by the way in which contemporary capitalism is organised. A focus on profits above people leads to problems with overcrowding, high staff turnover and falling standards (of, for example, cleanliness), combined with high traffic and plenty of immune-compromised subjects vulnerable to contagion.

The pressures of neoliberal economic policy, urbanisation and globalisation are also seen as facilitating the emergence of new epidemics within domesticated animal populations. Outbreaks of new, highly pathogenic strains of influenza (characterised by severe disease in humans, rapid contagion and high mortality) through antigenic drift (mutations that significantly alter the antigens of the influenza strain) have been linked to industrialised farming practices in South-Eastern China (the so-called 'epicentre of influenza') characterised by high densities of humans and animals in close proximity: 'Factory farming practices provide what seems to be an amenable environment for the evolution of a variety of virulent influenzas, including pandemic strains' (Wallace 2009, p. 924). This creates multiple opportunities for genetic re-assortment, recombination and mutation between diverse human and animal viral strains, leading to the rapid emergence of new viral genotypes.

For the WHO, however, large-scale industrial farms are preferable as these are more easily biosecured:

> The logistics of recommended control measures are most straightforward when applied to large commercial farms, where birds are housed indoors, usually under strictly controlled sanitary conditions, in large numbers. Control is far more difficult under poultry production systems in which most birds are raised in small backyard flocks scattered throughout rural or periurban areas. (WHO 2006, unpaginated)

These assumptions effectively mean that the response to avian flu, which imposes mass culling to control outbreaks and new sanitary regimes in farming, has had a disproportionate impact on particular (and perhaps less economically 'valued') groups within the population. Steve Hinchliffe and Nick Bingham (2008) describe how the bird culling policy in Egypt following the detection of avian flu in 2005–2006 was accompanied by a decision by the Egyptian government to encourage a shift in poultry farming away from 'primitive' methods and towards to large-scale industrial chicken farms. In this way, biosecurity becomes a rationale for a wide-scale modernisation of agricultural practices. The labour and infrastructure required to implement intensive biosecurity measures is expensive, precluding small-scale animal husbandry and 'rooftop poultry'. This in turn has implications for women in low-income areas for whom rooftop flocks formed a way of life and a vital source of protein (and who probably would not be able to afford factory chickens). One of the questions we may wish to ask, as geographers, is whose interests do these new biosecurity measures serve?

Conclusion

The spread and impact of epidemic disease are shaped by a number of key factors. The first, is the materiality of the disease, which determines how it is transmitted, which humans and animals serve as its hosts, how effectively it moves between hosts and its consequent impact on human (and animal) morbidity and mortality. Second is disease ecology, which is concerned with the ways in which changes in physical environment (evolutionary and ecological change) and human environment (globalisation, urbanisation, population growth and the collapse or absence of public health infrastructure) facilitate the emergence and re-emergence of infectious disease. We also noted how capitalist interests and neoliberal policies promoting intensive industrial farming systems could contribute to the emergence of new disease ecologies. The third factor consists of the approaches taken to tackle epidemic outbreaks, including 'classic' public health measures such as isolation, quarantine and social distancing, public health campaigns and surveillance, as well as scientific developments leading to better understanding of disease agents and new vaccines and antimicrobial treatments.

In addition, we need to take into account broader social and political processes and how these generate inequality, seen in the forms of structural violence that emerge from neoliberal economic policies and capitalist enterprise, creating populations vulnerable to infectious disease and lacking (both individually and collectively) the capacity to respond effectively when outbreaks do occur (e.g. lacking the resources to stockpile expensive new vaccines). We should also consider the ways in which narratives of outbreaks are socially constructed, reflecting the beliefs, values and prejudices of those who produce them, leading to some groups being unjustly blamed as the source of an outbreak and creating divides between insiders (who become the objects to be protected by biosecurity measures) and outsiders (who are to be secured against). These biosecurity measures reflect wider biopolitical strategies aimed at securing national and global public health.

Questions for Review

1. Comparing 1918 and today, what do you consider to be the key differences in the approach taken by nation states responding to epidemic threats?
2. With reference to a recent epidemic, what examples can you find of biopolitics in action?
3. Which do you consider to be most important to explaining inequalities in the way epidemics are governed, social construction or structural violence?

Suggested Reading

Ali, SH & Keil, R (2007) Contagious cities. *Geography Compass* 1, 1207–26.
Braun, B (2007) Biopolitics and the molecularization of life. *Cultural Geographies* 14, 6–28.
Emch, M & Root, ED (2010) Emerging and re-emerging diseases. In: Brown, T, McLafferty, S & Moon, G (Eds) *A companion to health and medical geography*. Wiley-Blackwell, Oxford, 154–72.
Hinchliffe, S & Bingham, N (2008) Mapping the multiplicities of biosecurity. In: Keil, R & Ali, SH (Eds) *Networked disease: emerging infections in the global city*. Blackwell, Oxford, 214–28.
Sparke, M & Anguelov, D (2012) H1N1, globalization and the epidemiology of inequality. *Health & Place* 18, 726–36.

References

Ali, A (2014) Ebola's villain and victim. *Pambazuka News*, viewed 5 November 2014, http://pambazuka.org/en/category/features/93238
Ali, SH & Keil, R (2007) Contagious cities. *Geography Compass* 1, 1207–26.
Anderson, B (2010) Preemption, precaution, preparedness: anticipatory action and future geographies. *Progress in Human Geography* 34, 777–98.

Bankoff, G (2001) Rendering the world unsafe: 'vulnerability' as western discourse. *Disasters* 25, 19–35.

Braun, B (2007) Biopolitics and the molecularization of life. *Cultural Geographies* 14, 6–28.

Brown, T (2011) 'Vulnerability is universal': considering the place of 'security' and 'vulnerability' within contemporary global health discourse. *Social Science & Medicine* 72, 319–26.

Calain, P & Poncin, M (2015) Reaching out to Ebola victims: coercion, persuasion or an appeal for self-sacrifice? *Social Science & Medicine* 147, 126–33.

Cliff, AD, Smallman-Raynor, MR, Haggett, P, Stroup, DF & Thacker, SB (2009) *Emerging infectious diseases: a geographical analysis.* Oxford University Press, Oxford.

Cooper, C (2014) *WHO chief: Ebola vaccine was never developed 'because it only affected poor African countries',* viewed 5 November 2014, http://www.independent.co.uk/life-style/health-and-families/health-news/who-chief-Ebola-vaccine-was-never-developed-because-it-only-affected-poor-african-countries-9836952.html

Craddock, S (2000) *City of plagues.* University of Minnesota Press, Minneapolis, MN.

Crosby, AW (2003) *America's forgotten pandemic: the influenza of 1918.* Second Edition. Cambridge University Press, Cambridge.

Elbe, S (2010) *Security and global health: toward the medicalization of insecurity.* Polity, Cambridge.

Emch, M & Root, ED (2010) Emerging and re-emerging diseases. In: Brown, T, McLafferty, S & Moon, G (Eds) *A companion to health and medical geography.* Wiley-Blackwell, Oxford, 154–72.

FAO (2009) *The state of food and agriculture,* viewed 3 November 2014, http://www.fao.org/docrep/012/i0680e/i0680e.pdf.

Farmer, P (2006) *AIDS and accusation: Haiti and the geography of blame.* University of California Press, Berkeley, CA.

Feldbaum, H & Lee, K (2004) Public health and security. In: Ingram, A (Ed) *Health, foreign policy & security.* The Nuffield Trust, London, 19–28.

Haggett, P (1994) Geographical aspects of the emergence of infectious diseases. *Geografiska Annaler. Series B, Human Geography* 76, 91–104.

Hamlin, C (1998) *Public health and social justice in the age of Chadwick: Britain, 1800–1854.* Cambridge University Press, Cambridge.

Hamlin, C & Sheard, S (1998) Revolutions in public health 1848 and 1998. *BMJ* 317, 587–91.

Hinchliffe, S & Bingham, N (2008) Mapping the multiplicities of biosecurity. In: Keil, R & Ali, SH (Eds) *Networked disease: emerging infections in the global city.* Blackwell, Oxford, 214–28.

Ingram, A (2005) The new geopolitics of disease: between global health and global security. *Geopolitics* 10, 522–45.

Knobler, SL, Mack, A, Mahmoud, A & Leomon, SM (2005) *The threat of pandemic influenza: are we ready? Workshop summary.* National Academies Press, Washington, DC.

Koch, T (2005) *Cartographies of disease: maps, mapping, and medicine.* Esri Press, Redlands, CA.

Koch, T (2009) Social epidemiology as medical geography: back to the future. *GeoJournal* 74, 99–106.

Konteh, F (2009) Urban sanitation and health in the developing world: reminiscing the nineteenth century industrial nations. *Health & Place* 15, 69–78.

Krieger, N (1992). The making of public health data: paradigms, politics, and policy. *Journal of Public health Policy* 13, 412–27.

Lakoff, A (2008) The generic biothreat or how we became unprepared. *Cultural Anthropology* 23, 399–428.

Mayer, JD (2000) Geography, ecology and emerging infectious diseases. *Social Science & Medicine* 50, 937–52.

McFarlane, C (2008) Governing the contaminated city: infrastructure and sanitation in colonial and post-colonial Bombay. *International Journal of Urban and Regional Research* 32, 415–35.

McLeod, KS (2000) Our sense of Snow: the myth of John Snow in medical geography. *Social Science & Medicine* 50, 923–35.

Meade, MS & Emch, M (2010) *Medical geography,* 3rd edition. The Guilford Press, London.

National Geographic (2014) *Graphic: as Ebola's death toll rises, remembering history's worst epidemics*, viewed 7 April 2016, http://news.nationalgeographic.com/news/2014/10/141025-ebola-epidemic-perspective-history-pandemic/

Nimtz, AH (2014) Ebola in Africa: a product of history, not a natural phenomenon. *Pambazuka News*, viewed 5 November 2015, http://pambazuka.org/en/category/features/93235

Praja (2014) *Causes of death in Mumbai 2008-14*, viewed 9 July 2014, http://www.Praja.org

Sedyaningsih, ER, Isfandari, S, Soendoro, T & Supari, SF (2008) Towards mutual trust, transparency and equity in virus sharing mechanism: the avian influenza case of Indonesia. *Annals Academy Medicine Singapore* 37, 482–8.

Smith, KF, Goldberg, M, Rosenthal, S, Carlson, L, Chen, J et al. (2014) Global rise in human infectious disease outbreaks. *Journal of the Royal Society: Interface* 11, 1742–5662.

Snyder, RE, Marlow, MA & Riley, LW (2014) Ebola in urban slums: the elephant in the room. *The Lancet Global Health* 2, e685.

Sparke, M & Anguelov, D (2012) H1N1, globalization and the epidemiology of inequality. *Health & Place* 18, 726–36.

Sullivan, N, Yang, Z-Y & Nable, GJ (2003) Ebola virus pathogenesis: implications for vaccines and therapies. *Journal of Virology* 77, 9733–7.

Tangcharoensathien, V (2007) *Developing countries perspective: increasing the access of developing countries to H5N1 and other potentially pandemic vaccines, WHO*. WHO, Geneva.

UK House of Lords (2008) *House of Lords Select Committee on intergovernmental organisations report – diseases know no frontiers: how effective are intergovernmental organisations in controlling their spread?*, viewed 24 November 2014, https://www.gov.uk/government/uploads/system/uploads/attachment_data/file/238696/7475.pdf

UNICEF (2014) In Sierra Leone, getting back to school – on the airwaves, viewed 5 November 2015, http://www.unicef.org/infobycountry/sierraleone_76352.html.

United Nations, Department of Economic and Social Affairs, Population Division (2014) *World urbanization prospects: the 2014 revision, highlights* (ST/ESA/SER.A/352), viewed 7 April 2016, http://esa.un.org/unpd/wup/Publications/Files/WUP2014-Highlights.pdf

Wald, P (2008) *Contagious: cultures, carriers and the outbreak narrative*. Duke University Press, Durham, NC.

Wallace, RG (2009) Breeding influenza: the political virology of offshore farming. *Antipode* 41, 916–51.

Weir, L & Mykhalovskiy, E (2010) *Global public health vigilance: creating a world on alert*. Routledge. London.

WHO (2003) *Climate change and human health – risks and responses*, viewed 7 September 2014, www.who.int/globalchange/climate/summary/en/index5.html.

WHO (2005) *Responding to the avian influenza pandemic threat: recommended strategic actions*, viewed 6 November 2014, http://www.who.int/csr/resources/publications/influenza/WHO_CDS_CSR_GIP_05_8-EN.pdf

WHO (2006) *Avian influenza ("bird flu") – Fact sheet*, viewed 6 November 2014, http://apps.who.int/csr/disease/avian_influenza/avianinfluenza_factsheetJan2006/en/index.html

WHO (2007) *The world health report 2007: a safer future: global public health security in the 21st century*. WHO, Geneva.

WHO (2010) *The smallpox eradication programme - SEP (1966–1980)*, viewed 3 November 2014, http://www.who.int/features/2010/smallpox/en/

WHO (2014) *Antimicrobial resistance: global report on surveillance 2014*, viewed 7 September 2014, http://www.who.int/drugresistance/documents/surveillancereport/en/

WHO (2016) *HIV/AIDS: fact sheet 360*, viewed 14 December 2016, http://www.who.int/mediacentre/factsheets/fs360/en/

Worboys, M (2000) *Spreading germs: disease theories and medical practice in Britain, 1865-1900*. Cambridge University Press, Cambridge.

Young, E (2015) The next plague: how many mutations are we away from disaster? *New Scientist* 6th May.

Chapter 12

Pharmaceuticalisation and Medical Research

Introduction

This chapter focuses on the growing influence of the pharmaceutical industry in shaping global health outcomes. Nikolas Rose (2007) has suggested that the ways in which western societies approach the challenges of poor health and disease are becoming increasingly molecularised and pharmaceuticalised. As has been discussed elsewhere by geographers such as Chris Philo (2000), the French philosopher and social theorist Michel Foucault described the way in which in the nineteenth century clinicians began to look inside the body for the causes and effects of disease and a new kind of medical gaze emerged which saw the body as the object to be treated through surgical interventions. Rose suggests that this gaze now operates on a molecular level and health care and medical agencies increasingly look to cellular processes and genetics (often as opposed to environmental factors; see Chapter 8) to explain disease. This 'molecular gaze' has implications for how we treat disease, including placing a much greater emphasis on pharmaceutical fixes or drugs.

Owing to a combination of neoliberal development policies, which aim to reduce public spending and promote private sector investment in the research and development of new products, and the high costs of drug development – estimated at between 2.6 billion (Tufts Center 2014) and 1.3–1.7 billion US dollars (Collier 2009) – much of the work in developing new drugs has been undertaken in the private sector. This sector has seen massive growth in the latter part of the twentieth century, with the total market value of the biotechnology sector globally now exceeding 1 trillion US dollars (Ernst and Young 2015). For a new drug to be viable, commercial companies argue that they have to recover its development costs (and those associated with all the failed drugs) through sales. This means there is little incentive to develop drugs for which there is no significant market, either due to the rarity of the condition or disease that they treat or to the lack of resources (money to finance drug treatment) amongst the affected population. In the United States a special status – Orphan

Health Geographies: A Critical Introduction, First Edition. Tim Brown, Gavin J. Andrews, Steven Cummins, Beth Greenhough, Daniel Lewis, and Andrew Power.
© 2018 John Wiley & Sons Ltd. Published 2018 by John Wiley & Sons Ltd.

Drug status – has been created where companies are given funding and tax incentives for drugs that are likely to have a small American market (less than 200,000 patients). The high costs of drug development also provide a rationale for the patent protection (around 20 years in the United States and United Kingdom) granted to those credited with inventing a new drug or treatment. During this period the patent holder has exclusive rights to produce and market the new drug in all countries that are signatories of the 1994 worldwide general agreement on Trade-Related aspects of Intellectual Property Rights (TRIPS) (WTO 2015).

This is where the processes of drug development become a key emerging issue for health geographers and other social scientists concerned with social justice, who can ask important questions about who benefits from the processes of drug development both in terms of the profits generated by the industry and access to the new medicines produced. Equally, geographers can also question who bears the costs of testing and trialling new drugs, noting the traces of long colonial histories in which marginalised populations are exploited as resources for biomedical research, serving as sources of knowledge about natural remedies, bodily commodities (extracted from genes and tissue samples) and clinical trial subjects. Such questions highlight how the pharmaceutical industry operates over a global scale. This chapter focuses on three key aspects of the drug development process (see Box 12.1, Table 12.1): bioprospecting, clinical trials and marketing. We explore how the work of health geographers and allied social scientists is providing insights into the ways in which pharmaceuticalisation is shaping the forms of health care provided, who bears the costs of developing those products and who has access to them once they are approved. It addresses the importance of regulation as both a means of incentivising private sector drug development (through the protection of intellectual property) and of seeking to redress inequalities in who bears the costs and receives the benefits of new drugs and treatments.

Bioprospecting: Sourcing New Active Compounds

While the majority of this volume considers the public in their position as consumers of health, the next two sections offer a slightly different perspective – considering how human populations act also as resources for biomedical research, ranging from supplying expertise in traditional medicines, to acting as sources of genetic material for research to volunteering to participate in clinical trials. This position creates some interesting tensions whereby the concerns over who supplies the 'raw' material of biomedical research intersect with more traditional health geography concerns over who benefits from that research in terms of access to medicines. In this section we consider the inequalities in terms of who benefits both from the profits derived from bioprospecting and the medicines produced. Here again we can also note the influence of neoliberalism and capitalist modes of production in shaping the operation of pharmaceutical research and development, as well as the global scale across which such inequalities are manifest.

Humans have always found substances in nature to relieve their suffering and cure their ills. In Africa, it is estimated that 80 per cent of the population relies on traditional remedies extracted from plants to treat illnesses (WHO 2003). An estimated two-thirds of the drugs sold in pharmacies owe their existence to natural biodiversity, including many familiar substances such as morphine, quinine and digitalis. These traditional plant remedies can serve as a useful starting point for the development of new drugs, an activity known as bioprospecting. While bioprospecting is only one of four possible routes to sourcing new compounds from which to develop new drugs (see Box 12.1), the 1990s witnessed a resurgence of public and private interest in the potential of plant-based sources for new

Table 12.1 Key phases of the drug development process.

Laboratory tests	When an active compound is first identified it undergoes: extensive laboratory tests including *in vitro* (test-tube) analysis; tests of the drug on tissue cultures; computer simulations and so on.
Ethical approval sought for animal trials	
Animal tests	Animal trials are used to establish: (i) exactly what the effects of the drug are, and (ii) how toxic it is at different doses.
Ethical approval for human trials	
Phase I human trials: establish whether the drug has any negative effects, how quickly it enters and leaves the body and what effects it has on target cells or proteins.	These usually: • involve a very small number of healthy subjects; • are carried out in dedicated facilities. In parallel with the Phase I trials, manufacturing processes are developed and a suitable drug product is formulated.
Phase II human trials are used to establish how safe and effective the drug is for the intended use.	These are usually: • controlled (some patients receive the drug under trial, others a placebo or existing treatment – for serious conditions where a treatment exists it is considered unethical to give a placebo); • randomised (assignment of patients to control or experimental arms of a trial is random but groups are matched in terms of physical characteristics, e.g. age, weight); • double blind – neither the patient nor the trial team knows who is on the experimental drug and who on the placebo.
Phase III human trials are much more extensive evaluations of the long-term safety and effectiveness of the drug on a wider selection of patients.	They are usually carried out in hospitals or GP surgeries and involve up to a few hundred patients. • They involve several thousand volunteers, maybe in a range of centres/locations and take between 1 and 4 years to complete. • They are also randomised, controlled and double blind. • They are usually carried out in hospitals or GP surgeries. For Novartis (2013) some of these trials, referred to as mega-trials, involve more than 10,000 patients across over 40 countries.
If the drug proves as (or more) safe and effective as an existing treatment then the company can apply for a new drug license – this usually takes just over a year to be approved.	

pharmaceutical products after a steady decline in such research since the mid twentieth century (Greene 2004; Parry 2006).

One of the best places to seek out these novel biological materials was in the biodiversity-rich areas of the Global South, and the resurgence of bioprospecting coincided with a growing awareness of global threats to biodiversity. However, the high cost of drug development

---

Box 12.1   Key Themes: The Drug Development Process

There are four key strategies for developing or finding new pharmaceutical products.

1. Bioprospecting: exploring natural sources (plants, animals and micro-organisms) for new active compounds that have useful clinical or other applications (e.g. anti-freezing properties).
2. Pharmaceutical companies develop artificial or synthesised molecules that are then tested for their potential therapeutic benefits. These synthesised molecules currently make up the bulk of the compound libraries held by pharmaceutical companies, alongside a smaller proportion of naturally occurring compounds, and are now the first port of call for the development of new drugs.
3. The creation of 'me too' drugs, which are effectively drugs that are very similar to an existing product with only minor differences in chemical structure and effects to allow a claim that this is a new or novel treatment.
4. Researchers may find new uses for existing drugs, for example the use of the pain-killer aspirin as a prophylactic treatment for heart disease.

In the case of either naturally found (bioprospected) or synthesised compounds, extracts are tested *in vitro* to determine whether they are biologically active (proof of concept). To ensure the safety of administering a new drug candidate to healthy volunteers and patients, extensive toxicological and safety pharmacological profiles are determined in both laboratory tests and animals. Drug development then moves into the human trial phases. Table 12.1 outlines the key phases of clinical trials. Once this first series of trials is complete, the results from all preclinical and clinical studies are collected and analysed together with the quality data and the description of the manufacturing process and submitted in an appropriate form to the regulatory authorities for review. If the regulators agree that the data prove the quality, efficacy and safety of the drug, a marketing authorisation is granted. From then on, the new drug can be made commercially available to patients. Once the drug is on the market, companies continue to look at potential side effects and the drug's impact in particular groups (e.g. children), in what are sometimes known as Phase IV trials. At each stage, the screening process is extremely thorough. Generally, a single molecule is retained out of 10,000 compounds analysed. Alongside the scientific tests are a number of marketing decisions. Whether to develop a drug for one purpose or another may be as much a financial decision (which products are most likely to command a significant profit that will recover the costs of their development) as a scientific one.

---

has led to a pharmaceutical market dominated by multinational pharmaceutical companies, mainly based in the Global North (see Figure 12.1) and focused (until recently) largely on the diseases of those who could afford to pay for the drugs developed. We explore this in greater depth in the following sections. Somewhat ironically, this meant that many of the local communities whose traditional healers and plant resources provided the knowledge and material to bioprospecting expeditions benefited neither from the profits made nor the treatments developed through bioprospecting activity. For health

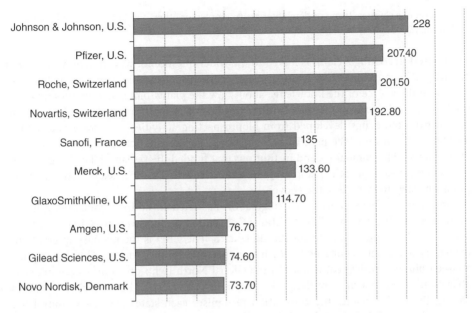

Figure 12.1   Top 10 biotech and pharmaceutical companies worldwide 2013, based on market value (in billion US dollars). Reproduced with kind permission of Statista. Source: http://www. statista.com/statistics/272716/global-top-biotech-and-pharmaceutical-companies-based-on-market-value/

geographers, this poses important questions about which diseases should be targeted by research and development into new medicines, who (if anyone) should be allowed to derive profits from those medicines and who should have access to or be able to afford those medicines once produced.

Bioprospecting has a distinctive mythological rhetoric, evoking images of 'the miracle drugs that presumably lie undiscovered in the depths of the tropical forest' (Greene 2004, p. 213). For the geographer Bronwyn Parry this mythology harks back to earlier colonial histories of collecting and the Enlightenment period of European history, when educated colonials were involved in the process of expanding biological knowledge through the collection and cataloguing of biological materials. Through the processes of collecting and cataloguing, these western scientists were also laying particular kinds of claim to those biological materials, transforming them from indigenous specimens to objects of western scientific knowledge and ownership. The question of who might be able to stake a claim in plants collected in the Global South and industrialised in the Global North is central to the way in which social scientists like Cori Hayden approach the study of bioprospecting practices (in Hayden's case in Mexico). As she argues:

> Central to the politics of bioprospecting is the question of who shall be able to stake a claim in knowledge or plants collected in the south and industrialised in the north … we might in this vein pose prospecting's central dilemma as a question of the capacity of knowledge and artefacts to represent interests: How do scientists, rural Mexicans, national governments, and

corporations claim, activate or deny interests (their own or others') in knowledge and nature? (Hayden 2003, p. 21)

The interest in staking a claim is linked to the wider question of who should benefit from bioprospecting and how? Claims to 'own' either the plants and biological examples, or to have been the source of the knowledge about how the plants/biological samples might be used medicinally, form the basis of different kinds of property rights or entitlements to benefit from the drugs developed from bioprospecting activities. So, who has a right to profit from the drugs developed? The scientists who isolated the active compound from the plant sample? The companies and institutions that funded the research? The local governments of the areas where the plant samples were collected? The local healers who identified promising specimens? All of the above?

One way in which international regulation has tried to address concerns over bioprospecting is through the United Nations Convention on Biodiversity (CBD), ratified as part of the 1992 Earth Summit in Rio de Janeiro. The CBD is the primary international regulatory agreement concerned with bioprospecting. In an effort to address inequities between pharmaceutical companies in the Global North (who previously were under no obligation to return a share of the profits to source countries) and biodiversity-rich countries in the Global South, the convention recognises each state's sovereign control over access to biological resources found in its national territory:

> article 8j of the convention suggests that bioprospecting efforts that draw on traditional uses of biological resources and result in successful commercial ventures should entail protection for and benefit sharing with the indigenous or local populations whose knowledge contributes to biologically engineered products. (Greene 2004, p. 213)

This provides poorer nation-states with considerable leverage in negotiating terms for the extraction of biological resources from their territories – resources that were previously considered part of a universal public domain or common heritage of humankind. The possible income from a share in the profits of new drugs was also seen as an incentive to conserve biodiversity. In this way, it was argued, everyone would win. Western researchers and pharmaceutical companies could continue to engage in bioprospecting, while local populations would receive a share in any profits, incentivising them to conserve biodiversity rather than, for example, exploit those resources as farmland or fuel.

As a consequence of the CBD, bioprospecting became increasingly negotiated through benefit-sharing agreements:

> The term benefit sharing involves a balance between access to genetic resources and fair and equitable sharing of the benefits of their use through wide variety of monetary and non-monetary mechanisms, ranging from profit sharing or equitable stakes in the bioprospecting business, and also technology transfer, training and collaborative research. (Government of Costa Rica 1998)

However, a number of problems emerged with benefit-sharing agreements. First, as Ruth Chadwick (1999, p. 443) notes in the case of population-based bioprospecting, '[w]e need to determine what is understood by the word "benefit," ... Does it mean financial and health gains (for example, free medicines from Hoffmann La Roche) or does it also include more intangible benefits such as prestige to the country?' In the case of bioprospecting it can involve license fees to undertake collecting activity, the provision of resources or training to help develop the country's biological research capacity or a share of the royalties from any product produced. Second, the high-profile debates about bioprospecting and biopiracy have meant that bioprospecting agreements often inspire unrealistic expectations about the profits and benefits to be gained amongst source communities. Parry (2004) also points out that this has led some indigenous groups and local government agencies in the Global South to 'overcharge' bioprospectors and put them off. Third is the question of who any benefits should go to. We might have a fairly good idea of who represents a biotechnology company, but it is much harder to pin down who should represent a nation's medical knowledge or biodiversity. As Greene (2004, p. 222–3) notes:

> there is a common assumption on all sides of the debate that indigenous collectives must possess a centralized structure of representative authority comparable to that of consolidated nation-states with which external actors can negotiate. Establishing who are the legitimate representatives of indigenous collectives is, however, often a matter of internal and external debate.

Joshua Rosenthal (1998, p. 15; see also Parry 2004) notes that laborious Prior Informed Consent (PIC) procedures can also raise the costs of a project to the point where it becomes unfeasible, providing a disincentive to companies who are seeking to reduce the time it takes to get a new drug on the market, not increase it.

The issues around patenting drugs developed from bioprospecting have led some to suggest that bioprospecting might better be thought of as biopiracy. Indian activist and academic Vanda Shiva (1999) argues that even when individuals or groups are compensated or receive shares or money for their knowledge and plant genetic resources, what is lost is not just the plant genetic resources or knowledge but an entire system or way of life relating to that knowledge and a culture of how that knowledge is produced and consumed and what health geographers might think of as a form of complementary or alternative medicine (see Chapter 4). Furthermore, anthropologist Hayden (2003) notes how often scientific firms bypass bioprospecting legislation and procedures by shopping for readily available herb and medical products in local markets.

Despite a growing number of bioprospecting agreements being put in place through the 1990s many supplying countries and communities have yet to receive any substantial economic returns from the exploitation of their collected materials. It could be argued that this is simply because no products have been developed from the materials but this seems unlikely given that this latest era of bioprospecting has been taking place for 20 years and that 25 per cent of all prescription drugs in recent decades have been derived from natural products. An alternative explanation would be that these collected biological materials have, of course, formed the basis of many commercial products during that period; it is just that this has not been established or factually acknowledged, not necessarily because those behind benefit-sharing agreements were not well-intentioned but because the complex process of drug development makes monitoring and compensating for the use of the source materials for particular active compounds particularly difficult (Parry 2004, pp. 254–5).

A final point to note is that it is not just plant genetic and biological material that is of interest to bioprospectors. Human cells, tissue, genetic material and medical records can also be valuable resources for medical research. Famous examples include the immortal cell lines, derived from cervical cancer cells taken from a patient, Henrietta Lacks, in 1951 (HeLa), and from John Moore's spleen (extracted 1979). John Moore's case is particularly noted because he failed in his attempt to sue the physician (Dr Golde) who obtained a US patent on the cell line derived from his spleen and therefore was not able to benefit from a share in the substantial revenue generated through Dr Golde's commercial arrangements with two biotech firms. Attempts by the US National Institute of Health in 1991 to gain patent protections for a cell line developed from the DNA of a Hagahai (semi-nomadic hunter–horticulturalists living in the fringe highlands of Madang Province in Papua New Guinea) donor sparked controversy over whether the Hagahai donor's consent (and the consent of the community that shares his DNA) had, or should have, been obtained before the resulting cell line was patented. Equally controversial were attempts by the Icelandic government in 1998 to create a new Act of Parliament licensing a private firm, deCODE Genetics, to use data from national medical records in their gene discovery research in exchange for an annual license fee (see Chadwick 1999; Greenhough 2006).

Clinical Trials

A second way in which the public serve as resources for biomedical research is in their role as clinical trial subjects. Again there are important intersections between medical research and the provision of medical care to be noted here: first, in the ways in which neoliberalism – seen in the rolling back of welfare state health services (see Chapter 6) and the structural violence of capitalism (see Chapter 11) – creates vulnerable, marginalised populations who are arguably open to exploitation by those seeking to outsource the testing of new drugs and pharmaceuticals; and, second, in the social injustices and inequalities evident in a system where the communities who serve as test bed for the development of new pharmaceutical products are in no way guaranteed to be able to access or benefit from those products in the long term.

As can be seen in Box 12.1, once an active compound has been identified and undergone *in vitro* (laboratory) and *in vivo* (animal) testing, trials may begin with human volunteers. In the past, the sources of volunteers for clinical trials varied widely. During the eighteenth and nineteenth centuries, colonial subjects often formed the objects of medical and public health experiments (Harrison 2005). However, the twentieth century was marked by a period of increasing regulation in response to concerns over medical experimentation. Two key incidents stand out. The first was the Tuskegee Study of Untreated Syphilis in the Negro Male, in Tuskegee, Alabama (USA). Conducted between 1932 and 1972, the study recruited 399 poor and mostly illiterate African American sharecroppers who were denied treatment for syphilis (plus a 201-strong control group without syphilis). This study became notorious because it was conducted without due care to its subjects and led to major changes in how patients are protected in clinical studies (CDC 2016). The second instance was the use of prisoners of war for medical experiments by the Nazis during World War II, which formed the basis for current key regulations pertaining to clinical trials, including the Nuremberg Code (1946) and the World Medical Association's Helsinki Declaration (1964). A key principle of these ethical regulations is the need for informed consent:

> In any research on human beings, each potential subject must be adequately informed of the aims, methods, sources of funding, any possible conflicts of interest, institutional affiliations of the researcher, the anticipated benefits and potential risks of the study and the discomfort it may entail. The subject should be informed of the right to abstain from participation in the study or to withdraw consent to participate at any time without reprisal. After ensuring that the subject has understood the information, the physician should then obtain the subject's freely-given informed consent, preferably in writing. If the consent cannot be obtained in writing, the non-written consent must be formally documented and witnessed. (Helsinki Declaration, World Medical Association, 1964, Article 22)

However, as was the case with bioprospecting, this emphasis on informed consent does little to address emerging inequalities between the populations who are the recipients of new drugs developed and those on whom the drugs are tested, especially in light of new trends towards offshoring clinical trials, discussed in the following paragraphs.

The demand for clinical trials has grown significantly in recent decades. Estimates suggest that between 1995 and 1999 the number of human subjects involved in clinical trials grew from 4,000 to 400,000 (Petryna 2006, p. 47). There are a number of reasons for this. The first is a growth in the number of patented compounds in need of testing (driven partly by competition between large pharmaceutical firms). Second, concerns over safety have led to regulatory demands for larger numbers of patients to be included in clinical trials. Third, as drug efficacy and safety are assessed statistically, larger populations in some cases can help make a drug that looked ineffective appear statistically significant or disguise the impact of adverse reactions: 10 severe adverse drug reactions (ADRs) in 10,000 looks better than 10 in 1,000. Finally, the pool of available subjects in western countries such as the United States is shrinking due to 'treatment saturation', whereby volunteers are already taking so many medications that the trials produce too many drug–drug interactions, making the study results less clear (Petryna 2006).

Simultaneously, it has become easier to 'offshore' clinical trials to Europe and the Global South due to several key factors. First, the International Conference on Harmonisation (ICH) was initiated in 1990 as an agreement between the United States, Europe and Japan. It sought to create international standards for assessing the quality and safety of clinical trials including guidelines on good clinical practice and the implementation of institutional review boards (IRBs) to ethically review research proposals (see the ICH website – http:// www.ich.org/home.html). This eased the acceptance of trial data from foreign investigation sites by the US Food and Drug Administration (FDA) among others. In short, it made western regulators more likely to approve the results of clinical trials conducted elsewhere.

Second, there has been a marked growth in, and globalisation of, contract research organisations (CROs) which run clinical trials on behalf of pharmaceutical firms as well as offering advice on applying for approvals (to run trials across a range of international contexts) and marketing. The expertise of CROs lies in knowing the most efficient and cost-effective ways of carrying out clinical trials and their ability to identify 'good populations' for trials, especially Phase II and III trials. They look at unemployment levels, disease profiles, morbidity and mortality, per patient costs and potential for future marketing of the drug. They also look at the host country's regulatory environment and health care provision. Some even have their own internal ethical review boards.

CROs are rapidly expanding into areas such as Eastern Europe, Latin America, the Middle East and Africa. According to Adriana Petryna (2006), CROs see Eastern Europe as a good site for recruiting for clinical trials due to: the collapse of basic health care, meaning quick recruitment and enrolment of volunteers; the centralised post-soviet health care system which is conducive to running efficient trials; high literacy, leading to more meaningful 'informed consent'; and 'treatment naivety' (due to a lack of basic health care there is a widespread absence of the treatment for both common and uncommon diseases that would 'interfere' with the trial results). An example of this expansion into Eastern Europe comes from Poland, where Petryna (2006) notes that pharmaceutical companies invest almost half a billion dollars in clinical research in the country each year.

Outsourcing to Eastern Europe raises a number of key issues. Notable amongst these is the increasing dependence of governments in Eastern Europe on clinical trials as a source of both foreign direct investment (FDI) and medical care, filling the gaps created by post-soviet welfare decline (Petryna 2007), echoing trends of declining state provision for health care noted elsewhere in this volume (see Chapters 5 and 6). National health and regulatory experts often have high stakes in attracting and retaining clinical trial investments and play a key role in promoting trials to the public. Concerns are also emerging about the quality of care clinical trials provide. CROs will often manipulate the study requirements in order to achieve better or more valid results, for example by using cheaper modes of pain monitoring which reduce costs but also may mean that adverse side effects are inadequately reported.

India too has become a key site for outsourcing clinical trials. Again there are a number of factors underlying this growth. First, it costs less. Studies suggest that Phase I trials are 50 per cent cheaper than those carried out in the United States, and Phase II and III are 60 per cent cheaper. Second, the country has a vast, largely 'treatment naive' population, which has many common diseases but also increasingly the 'diseases of affluence' (those common among affluent western populations such as cancer, heart disease and type 2 diabetes) which are of most interest to western pharmaceutical firms. Third, there are high enrolment rates and good patient compliance and retention rates. Fourth, India has a well-developed drug industry, well-equipped hospitals and western-trained, English-speaking doctors to conduct trials (Sharma 2004). As a result, the clinical trial industry in India has developed rapidly, although not entirely without contention (see Box 12.3).

From a Marxist perspective, the CRO industry is a further example of the inequalities produced under neoliberalism. Many of the areas from which clinical trial participants are recruited are already victims of industrial restructuring and what Marxists would call 'structural economic violence' (see also Chapter 11), while others (especially former Soviet States) are dealing with the health care gap left by the withdrawal of the welfare state. Kaushik Sunder Rajan (2010) describes a trial conducted by Wellquest in the mill districts of Mumbai. Detailing the decline in the textile industry, Rajan describes a vicious circle in which the former millworkers were driven to the streets to work as street hawkers and then subsequently off the streets (and in some cases out of their homes) because of the impact of middle class gentrifiers on the districts. With this contextual information in place, Rajan questions how the workers are supposed to make a fair and autonomous decision to participate in a trial (the basis of informed consent), especially given the enticement of the financial compensation offered to trial participants. Furthermore, as Rajan (2010, p. 387) argues, these people will probably never benefit from the drugs they test:

> In the Indian context … there is no guarantee that an experimental drug tested on a local population will necessarily be marketed there after approval – let alone be made available at affordable cost. The Indian state has made no moves to ensure this, for example, through mechanisms such as compulsory licensing regulations. The likely outcome is therefore a situation where Indian populations are used purely as experimental subjects, without the implicit social contract of eventual therapeutic access.

The phrase 'social contract' here refers to the belief that people take part in clinical trials for the good of their community, even if there is no direct benefit to themselves (compare with the definition of this term in the introduction to this volume). Yet, as noted above in the case of Poland, for many people clinical trials are an increasingly important way of accessing medical care. Petryna (2006, pp. 41–2) argues, 'clinical trials have become social good in themselves'; put differently, they are an important way of accessing health care in the context of declining or absent state provision.

This raises further issues. First, the benefits of clinical trials are unevenly distributed. CROs can change locations and have generally no commitment to provide long-term care.

Second, many trials involve the use of placebos where a control group is given a non-active substitute for the compound being tested so only half the group receive an active treatment. Finally, there are concerns around what happens when a trial ends. For example, Petryna (2007) reports a case in Brazil in 2005 where a hospital was running a trial of a treatment for a rare genetic disorder. The patients recruited had never received treatment before and because the director of genetics at the hospital was keen to secure the study he agreed (without his colleagues' knowledge) to the company's requirement that they could withdraw supplies of the drug at any time. The company informally agreed to provide the drug for two years. The drug worked well, but in the third year the company suddenly withdrew the study drug. There was no more treatment and within four years the advanced stage patients would probably die. In cases where clinical trials offer a form of 'alternative public health', the consequences of treatment withdrawal can be fatal.

Constituting Pharmaceutical Markets

In this section we return to focus on patients once again as consumers of medical products, exploring how the needs and demands of patients, as well as their role as a potential market for pharmaceutical products, intersect with the regulation of medical research and development. Interesting for health geographers here is the relationship between the neoliberal vision of the patient as an active consumer of health care choices and development of the demand for pharmaceutical products. In this section, we also consider the ways in which regulation tries to address some of the inequalities and social injustices noted in previous sections between those who bear some of the costs of the drug development process and those who eventually benefit from the drugs developed. Two different areas of the pharmaceutical market are explored. The first is concerned with the need for the pharmaceutical industry to create a demand for their products amongst wealthy populations (who include both those in the Global North and elites and rising middle classes in the Global South) and states who can afford to pay. The second turns to look at strategies being developed to try to incentivise a marketised pharmaceutical industry to produce drugs and new treatments for diseases that affect populations who have limited or no ability to pay for treatment.

Generating demand in a treatment–saturated market

So far we have focused on the exploitation of populations in the Global South and Eastern Europe, but Rajan (2010) suggests that western consumers are also being exploited by an industry that sees health as a market to be expanded. He argues that pharmaceutical companies need to generate 'surplus health' by creating ever more conditions that need pharmaceutical intervention or by expanding the length of time and dose of pharmaceutical needed for a treatment. Rajan (2010, p. 386) argues that the same therapeutic saturation that drives the outsourcing of clinical trials also represents a 'saturated market' for drug producers. As a result,

> rising therapeutic consumption can either be achieved by increasing the number of people who take a particular drug most effectively achieved by 'off-label use', i.e. prescribing drugs for treatments other than those for which the drug was initially approved—or by increasing the timespan of the prescription, justified by reframing diseases as chronic states rather than events.

Further, Joseph Dumit (2012) suggests that currently the average American is consuming between 9 and 13 prescription-only drugs a year, many of these being employed to manage the side effects of initial drug treatments.

There has also been a growth in the consumption of 'lifestyle drugs' targeting conditions such as hair loss, weight loss or impotency, and the use of clinical drugs in a 'lifestyle way', for example using contraceptive pills to postpone a period when going on holiday. By turning lifestyle conditions into biomedical ones, pharmaceutical companies can both gain approval for their new drug – in the United States, for example, the Food and Drug Administration (FDA) will only approve a drug if it is targeting an established disease – and get national health systems (such as the NHS in the United Kingdom) or private medical insurers to pay for them. Lifestyle drugs represent a new and valuable market: within three months of receiving the approval for sildenafil (Viagra), Pfizer's profits jumped 38 per cent (Fox and Ward 2008). They also constitute a shift in the way the public is targeted by these drug manufacturers, moving from being seen as patients to consumers.

Rather than targeting only medical practitioners, pharmaceutical companies now target patients/consumer directly. In the United States this is done through commercial adverts in the media; in the United Kingdom and other countries, where direct-to-consumer (DTC) advertising is banned, pharmaceutical companies access 'consumers' through the internet, often supporting self-help groups for particular medical conditions. These sites are key places for promoting particular conditions and biomedical understandings of them. For example, Kalman Applbaum (2006, p. 104) cites a marketing manager of an American pharmaceutical company working in Tokyo:

> The best way to reach patients today is not via advertising but the Web. The Web basically circumvents DTC [direct-to-consumer] rules, so there is no need to be concerned over these. People go to the company website and take a quiz to see whether they might have depression. If yes, they go to the doctor and ask for medication. [Our company] doesn't push anyone. I believe it is crass to advertise antidepressants … If someone has a problem and [Product Z] is a solution to that problem, then they ought to buy it … [Such a] system moves us towards patient choice and [Product Z] wins in such a case because [Product Z] is a brand name and consumer will be inclined to take it up on that account.

Here, we see biopolitics (see Chapter 11), with its emphasis on individuals taking responsibility for their health, creating a market of 'educated patients' or biological citizens keen to explore what the pharmaceutical companies have to offer.

The creation of drugs for many more disorders often sees the 'discovery' of the biomedical disorder and the development of the drug going hand in hand. One of the most significant areas to be affected by the shift towards pharmaceuticalisation is physiological disorders. Rose (2007) describes how the focus on visualising and mapping molecular processes in the brain gave us both a new definition of what counts as a 'normal brain' (defined biologically) and new ways of understanding mental disorders. For example, schizophrenia becomes the over-activity of dopamine neurons. This in turn creates a new market for pharmaceuticals that can equally claim to operate at a molecular level. For example, the popularity of Prozac lies not in the fact that it was more effective than previous anti-depressants, but because it claimed to work on a molecular level – a molecule designed to interrupt another molecule.

Thus these molecularised and pharmaceuticalised understandings increasingly frame the way medical professionals and their patients understand disease. For example, attention deficit hyperactivity disorder (ADHD) was recognised as a medical condition at around the same time that Ritalin came onto the market; it is now difficult to talk about one without imagining the other. Rose (2007) suggests that today mental disorders serve as vital opportunities for the development of new drugs and constitute emerging markets for pharmaceutical companies: between 1990 and 2000 the psychiatric market increased in value by over 200 per cent in South America, 137 per cent in Pakistan, 50 per cent in Japan, 126 per cent in Europe and 638 per cent in the United States (Rose 2007, p. 209). The case of Japan is a particularly striking example. Applbaum (2006) describes the process by which American pharmaceutical companies tried to launch selective serotonin re-uptake inhibitors (SSRIs) in Japan, noting how at the same time they also had to 'educate' Japanese society and medicine about mental health, and in particular about new biomedical understandings of what mental disease is and how it should be treated (see Box 12.2).

The state may also play a role in promoting a particular 'pharmaceutical' approach to solving public health problems; it can increase access to drugs but in doing so also implicitly endorses the dominant perception that these are pharmaceutical problems with pharmaceutical solutions. A very well known example of this is found in the form of Brazil's HIV/AIDS drug policies. In 1996, under pressure from activists and public opinion, Brazil became the first nation in the Global South to make anti-retrovirals (ARVs) available to all registered HIV/AIDS patients and obliged the public health system to dispense them. This led to a

---

Box 12.2   Key Themes: Creating a Pharmaceutical Market

For many years Japan was seen as an unattractive and inaccessible market to pharmaceutical companies due to: slow testing and registration procedures; the only relatively recent acceptance of mental illness, which had been highly stigmatised; few mental health experts; a provider-driven health care system in which the state – rather than patient/consumer demand – controls which drugs are supplied; pricing policies that tend to squeeze the profit margins for companies introducing new drugs; and a clinical trial scheme that focuses on minimising side effects as opposed to evaluating drug efficacy. However, recent changes, including a growth in prescriptions for depression, the introduction of the ICH guidelines which help speed up approval procedures (including replacing Phase III trials with bridging trials) as well as growing competition within the global pharmaceutical market, led researchers to reconsider Japan.

Selective serotonin re-uptake inhibitors (SSRIs) such as Prozac are a new class of anti-depressants currently being launched round the world. Key to the strategies for marketing these drugs in Japan was a process of educating Japanese medical professionals and the public about mental health. Foreign pharmaceutical firms, along with Pharmaceuticals Research and Manufacturers of America (PRMA), spearheaded a campaign to de-stigmatise mental health and raise awareness of how widespread depression, anxiety and other disorders are, supported by both local practitioners and the media. Pharmaceutical companies employed public relations specialists to organise conferences – particularly for young general practitioners – and either commissioned reports from specialists at leading universities or reproduced short excerpts from professional journals for pamphlets which were then distributed to practitioners in hospitals nationwide. Applbaum notes that, in a study quoted to him by an industry expert, it was estimated that today in Japan 'psychiatrists obtain approximately 70% of their information regarding medications from brochures distributed by sales representatives of drug companies' (2006, p. 105).

dramatic (35 per cent) reduction in AIDS-related deaths and economic gains from a fall in hospital admissions and the use of emergency services. Brazil's HIV/AIDS programme is an example of the pharmaceuticalisation of public health. A few months before the 1996 statement on free treatments, the government had signed Brazil up to international patent protection agreements, leading to an increase in pharmaceutical imports and Brazil becoming one of the ten biggest pharmaceutical markets in the world. Brazil's AIDS/HIV medicines access policy created a captive and viable market for pharmaceutical companies but its own pharmaceutical industry also benefitted from being able to manufacture generic varieties of early drugs that were not under patent protection. Later, when generic treatments began to lose their efficacy, Brazil's capacity to manufacture its own drugs – and the threat of compulsory licensing (see next section) – allowed it to negotiate substantial price discounts on imported HIV/AIDS medicines. In 2007 Brazil successfully negotiated a 30 per cent reduction in the price of a new AIDS treatment, Kaletra (BBC 2007). Earlier that year it had broken a patent law by importing a cheaper generic version of the drug Efavirenz from India; see Box 12.3 for some of the history of India's role in developing cheaper generic versions of drugs.

Box 12.3   Key Themes: India's Clinical Trial and Patent Regulations

India has played an interesting role in the global pharmaceutical and clinical trials markets, marked by an increasing tendency to align with western models of pharmaceutical development and production. Before 2005, the Indian clinical trial regulations were set up to protect Indian citizens from exploitation and banned Phase I trials of drugs developed outside India. Furthermore, Phase II and III trials were only permitted after similar studies had been conducted elsewhere. In January 2005 these restrictions were relaxed, arguably in order to support a growing clinical trials industry. Critics are concerned that the drug controller of India (FDA equivalent) is poorly equipped to deal with the likely influx of clinical trial applications once the rules were relaxed; that a growing clinical trials industry will take advantage of the poor and vulnerable in Indian society; and, finally, that poor Indians will very likely be taking the risks of clinical trials for drugs they will never be able to afford or have access to (Sharma 2004).

Alongside these changes, amendments to the Indian Patent Act in March 2005 gave foreign companies the assurance that data collected in trials of their drugs in India will not be used by local companies to manufacture and market cheap generic versions. The Act included new laws giving full patent protection to drugs, conforming to World Trade Organization (WTO) obligations to observe international laws from 2005. The move was controversial as India has a long tradition of producing generic alternatives of patented pharmaceuticals. In the past, India had a reputation for using a legal loophole to permit the reverse-engineering of drugs under patent protection in order to produce cheap generic versions. This practice made India a key supplier of new drugs (such as ARVs) to impoverished states and communities in the Global South. Again, critics are concerned that India's new tighter patent laws will restrict the production of these cheaper versions of new and emerging drug treatments, with implications for the provision of affordable new medicines for patients across the Global South. Human rights organisations like the Affordable Medicines Treatment campaign (a grass roots organisation of lawyers and HIV/AIDS activists) argued that India had played a key role in improving the accessibility and availability of HIV/AIDS drugs.

In many ways the case of Brazil's HIV/AIDS drug policy can be seen as a success story; however, critics draw attention to two areas of concern. The first is the role of the pharmaceutical companies in creating the demand for novel ARVs and the latest emerging treatments. Petryna (2007) notes how a researcher in the University Hospital in Brazil was concerned by the way in which CROs were influencing the course of medical research and public health in Brazil. Clinical trials became a way of 'launching' a new drug in Brazilian hospitals and bringing it to the attention of powerful patient activist groups that could then lobby the government to fund the treatments (often still under patent protection and therefore expensive), capitalising on patient resistance and biological citizenship to marketised ends. In some cases, these new drugs might be 'me too drugs', constituting only minor modifications of existing drug compounds, which, although more expensive, often do not offer significant improvements in effectiveness. Second, there are broader concerns that investment was being focused on drugs, perhaps at the expense of other areas of medical care such as the provision of clinics and treatment centres for more marginalised elements of the HIV/AIDS affected population (Biehl 2006, p. 229).

Addressing the 'Global Drug Gap'

In contrast to the efforts made to promote pharmaceutical solutions to key personal and public health problems are the equally significant concerns over how to promote the development of pharmaceutical products and vaccines for diseases where there is little or no market. These could be diseases that only affect a very small proportion of the population (such as those targeted by orphan drug policies in the United States). More often concerns are raised over broader global inequalities or the so-called 'global drug gap' (Reich 2000; see also Craddock 2007 on vaccines), a term that captures the divide between the greatest global disease burden, arguably borne by those in the Global South (including the double burden of both epidemic disease and diseases of affluence), and the drug development capacity that arguably remains focused on the markets of the Global North. Strenuous criticism directed at the pharmaceutical sector has seen in recent decades a concerted effort to address these concerns, notably through public–private partnerships (PPPs) between states, international organisations, non-governmental organisations (NGOs) and charities, including the Bill and Melinda Gates Foundation.

There are a number of strategies to address the global drug gap. First, with respect to already existing drugs, one option is to use the market. Governments can purchase the new drugs, as Brazil's government did, representing a large potential market for pharmaceutical companies. Purchasing contracts play a key role in incentivising companies to develop new vaccines and treatments. Companies could also support this strategy by offering tiered pricing – making drugs available at lower cost in countries less able to afford them. However, this will only work if companies can protect their rich-country markets from parallel imports. Furthermore, we might question a government's decisions to invest heavily in prophylactic vaccine programmes when there are so many other pressing health concerns. In the case of swine flu, both the WHO and national governments (such as the United Kingdom) came under criticism for allowing the pharmaceutical sector undue influence over their policy. In the United Kingdom, this influence led to a substantial investment of public health resources in an advance purchase of the GSK vaccine Pandemrix during the 2009 swine flu outbreak in anticipation of a pandemic that 'never materialised' (Borland 2010, unpaginated; see also Hine 2010; Sparke 2012).

A second option is the use of compulsory licensing. In response to concerns over patent protection and high costs for new drugs posing challenges for ensuring access to medicines, especially amongst those in poorer countries, flexibilities and exceptions are built into the TRIPS agreement. A patent owner could abuse their rights, for example by failing to supply the product on the market. To deal with that possibility, the agreement says that governments can issue 'compulsory licences', allowing a competitor to produce the product or use the process under licence under conditions where this is viewed necessary, such as an epidemic outbreak where the patent holder is unable to produce a drug in sufficient quantities and/or at a cost affordable to those who need it. Compulsory licensing would allow a national government to either manufacture the new drugs within their country under certain conditions or, where they lack manufacturing capacity, purchase new drugs from countries where the price is low. However, attempts to use compulsory licensing have met with strong opposition from both the US government and the pharmaceutical sector.

A third approach is to rely on the third sector, including expanding the donation programmes already run by many pharmaceutical companies. A well-known example is Merck's donation programme of Mectizan for river blindness, which has provided 530 million treatments since the programme's inception in 1987 (Hwang 2012).

Beyond these, slightly different strategies can be employed to encourage companies to focus their research and development on diseases common in the Global South. First, products can be subsidised through, for example, the World Health Organization's Special Programme for Research and Training in Tropical Diseases (TDR). Second, PPPs can be created with a focus on specific diseases or products such as the Medicines for Malaria Venture (which was initiated within the TDR programme) or the Global Fund to Fight AIDS, Tuberculosis and Malaria. Critics, however, suggest that much of the philanthropic (e.g. Gates Foundation) and international (e.g. Global Fund) funding is directed towards the 'big three' diseases – malaria, HIV/AIDS and tuberculosis (TB) – at the expense of other diseases such as river blindness (onchocerciasis) which, while less deadly, have a severe impact on quality of life. Third, promoting patent protection and signing up to TRIPS in nations in the Global South could create incentives for private-sector research on drug therapies for diseases common in those countries, much as it does in the Global North. This rationale underpinned the somewhat controversial decision by India's lower house of parliament in 2003–2004 to approve a bill to reform the country's patent laws, bringing them closer to international standards (see Box 12.3).

There has arguably been much progress in recent years towards addressing the global drug gap, seen both in the actions of organisations like the Global Fund and in more recent programmes to target the so-called 'neglected' diseases, namely those other than malaria, HIV/AIDS and TB. However, questions still remain about the nature and sustainability of such interventions, and how best to reconcile a capitalist model of drug development with the concerns of inequality and social justice.

Conclusion

Health geographers are expanding their research remit to consider how the public are not only the recipients and consumers of health, but also serve as resources for biomedical research. Populations can serve as sources of traditional plant remedies and ethnobotanical knowledge that can form the basis for developing new drugs (bioprospecting); as the sources of medical data, genetic material and tissue samples used in research; and as clinical trial subjects. Increasingly these resources are found in the biodiversity-rich areas and marginalised populations of the Global South and, in the case of clinical trials, Eastern Europe. However, there is no guarantee that these populations will benefit from either the profits generated by drug development or the medicines produced. Critics argue that the exploitation of these populations often capitalises on and exacerbates the inequalities generated through the structural violence imposed by a neoliberal economic policy and the decline or absence of a welfare state.

Neoliberal, marketised approaches to pharmaceutical research and development also lead to an industry focused on producing medicines and treatments targeted at diseases, patients and places which can afford to pay for them, found predominantly in the Global North. However, the greatest disease burden is felt in less economically well-resourced and marginalised populations in the Global South. This is known as the global drug gap. There are a number of regulatory strategies available to try and address inequalities between those who provide the resources for medical research and those who benefit from them, including international agreements such as the Convention on Biological Diversity as well as more market-focused mechanisms such as compulsory licensing. Public–private partnerships, international organisations and charities also play a key role. Critical social scientists have also pointed to the strategies used by the pharmaceutical sector to generate new markets amongst wealthy populations in the Global North, as well as emerging markets such as Japan and Brazil, notably increasing the range of lifestyle and psychological disorders now diagnosed as chemical problems in need of pharmaceutical solutions. Rose terms this process pharmaceuticalisation.

Questions for Review

1. Do you think benefit-sharing agreements are effective in addressing concerns about bioprospecting?
2. Do you agree that clinical trials can be a 'social good'?
3. Explore the websites of some of the key agencies seeking to address diseases in the Global South, such as PEPFAR, the Global Fund or the Bill and Melinda Gates Foundation. Think about which diseases they tackle, how they approach them and which countries they focus on. What diseases, places or aspects of health care (e.g. nursing provision) are excluded?
4. Do you think direct-to-consumer (DTC) advertising of medicines should be permitted?

Suggested Reading

Craddock, S (2007) Market incentives, human lives, and AIDS vaccines. *Social Science & Medicine* 64, 1042–56.

Fox, NJ & Ward, KJ (2008) Pharma in the bedroom … and the kitchen … The pharmaceuticalisation of daily life. *Sociology of Health & Illness* 30, 856–68.

Parry, B (2006) New spaces of biological commodification: the dynamics of trade in genetic resources and 'bioinformation'. *Interdisciplinary Science Review* 31, 19–31.

Petryna, A (2007) Clinical trials offshored: on private sector science and public health. *BioSocieties* 2, 21–4.

Petryna, A, Lakoff, A & Kleinman, A (2006) *Global pharmaceuticals: ethics, markets, practices*. Duke, London.

The following films also highlight some of the issues raised in the chapter:

The Constant Gardener (2005)

Dallas Buyers Club (2013)

References

Applbaum, K (2006) Educating for global mental health: the adoption of SSRI's in Japan. In: Petryna, A, Lakoff, A & Kleinman, A (Eds) *Global pharmaceuticals: ethics, markets, practices*. Duke, London, 85–110.

BBC (2007) *Brazil gets cut-price AIDS drug*, viewed 30 March 2015, http://news.bbc.co.uk/1/hi/world/americas/6272044.stm

Biehl, J (2006) Pharmaceutical governance. In: Petryna, A, Lakoff, A & Kleinman, A (Eds) *Global pharmaceuticals: ethics, markets, practices*. Duke, London, 206–39.

Boreland, S (2010) *Ministers 'wasted millions on stockpile of swine flu drugs for epidemic that never arrived'*, viewed 8 December 2016, http://www.dailymail.co.uk/news/article-1291099/British-taxpayers-spent-1-2bn-swine-flu-pandemic-was.html

CDC (2016) U.S. Public Health Service Syphilis Study at Tuskegee, viewed 21 March 2016, http://www.cdc.gov/tuskegee/timeline.htm

Chadwick, R (1999) The Icelandic database – do modern times need modern sagas? *BMJ* 319, 441–4.

Collier, R (2009) Drug development cost estimates hard to swallow. *CMAJ* 180, 279–80.

Craddock, S (2007) Market incentives, human lives, and AIDS vaccines. *Social Science & Medicine* 64, 1042–56.

Dumit, J (2012) *Drugs for life*. Duke University Press, Durham.

Ernst and Young (2015) *Beyond borders: Biotechnology industry report 2015*, viewed 14 December 2016, https://www.ey.com/Publication/vwLUAssets/EY-beyond-borders-2015/$FILE/EY-beyond-borders-2015.pdf

Fox, NJ & Ward, KJ (2008) Pharma in the bedroom …and the kitchen…The pharmaceuticalisation of daily life. *Sociology of Health & Illness* 30, 856–68.

Government of Costa Rica (1998) *Benefit sharing: experience of Costa Rica*, viewed 7 March 2015, http://www.ots.ac.cr/rdmcnfs/datasets/biblioteca/pdfs/nbina-1927.pdf

Greene, S (2004) Indigenous people incorporated? Culture as politics, culture and property in pharmaceutical bioprospecting. *Current Anthropology* 45, 211–37.

Greenhough, B (2006) Decontextualised? Dissociated? Detached? Mapping the networks of bioinformatics exchange. *Environment and Planning A* 38, 445–63.

Harrison, M (2005) Science and the British empire. *Isis* 96, 56–63.

Hayden, C (2003) *When nature goes public*. Princeton University Press, Oxford.

Hine, D (2010) *The 2009 Influenza Pandemic An independent review of the UK response to the 2009 influenza pandemic views*, viewed 8 December 2016, https://www.gov.uk/government/uploads/system/uploads/attachment_data/file/61252/the2009influenzapandemic-review.pdf

Hwang, JJ (2012) *Is Merck's corporate social responsibility good for the global health?* viewed 8 December 2016, https://gps.ucsd.edu/_files/faculty/gourevitch/gourevitch_cs_hwang_jungjoo.pdf

Novartis (2013) *Drug development*, viewed 15 September 2013, http://www.nibr.novartis.com/OurScience/drug_development.shtml

Parry, B (2004) *Trading the genome*. Columbia, New York.

Parry, B (2006) New spaces of biological commodification: the dynamics of trade in genetic resources and 'bioinformation'. *Interdisciplinary Science Review* 31, 19–31.

Petryna, A (2006) Globalizing human subjects research. In: Petryna, A, Lakoff, A & Kleinman, A (Eds) *Global pharmaceuticals: ethics, markets, practices*. Duke, London, 33–60.

Petryna, A (2007) Clinical trials offshored: on private sector science and public health. *BioSocieties* 2, 21–4.

Philo, P (2000) The Birth of the Clinic: an unknown work of medical geography. *Area* 32, 11–19.

Rajan, K (2010) Experimental values: Indian clinical trials and surplus health. In: Good, BJ, Fischer, MMJ, Willen, SS & DelVecchio Good, M-J (Eds) *A reader in medical anthropology: theoretical trajectories, emergent realities*. Wiley-Blackwell, Oxford, 377–88.

Reich, M (2000) The global drug gap. *Science* 287, 1979–81.

Rose, N (2007) *The politics of life itself: biomedicine, power, and subjectivity in the twenty-first century*. Princeton University Press, Oxford.

Rosenthal, J (1998) *The International Cooperative Biodiversity Groups (ICBG) Program*, viewed 15 April 2016, https://www.cbd.int/doc/case-studies/abs/cs-abs-icbg.pdf

Sharma, D (2004) India pressed to relax rules on clinical trials. *The Lancet* 363, 1528–9.

Shiva, V (1999) *Biopiracy: the plunder of nature and knowledge*. South End Press, Boston, MA.

Sparke, M & Anguelov, D (2012) H1N1, globalization and the epidemiology of inequality. *Health & Place* 18, 726–36.

Tufts Center (2014) *Cost to develop and win marketing approval for a new drug is $2.6 billion*, viewed 31 March 2014, http://csdd.tufts.edu/news/complete_story/pr_tufts_csdd_2014_cost_study

WHO (2003) *Traditional medicine*, viewed 31 March 2015, http://www.who.int/mediacentre/factsheets/2003/fs134/en/

World Medical Association (2013) Declaration of Helsinki, viewed 15 April 2016, http://www.wma.net/en/30publications/10policies/b3/

WTO (2015) *Intellectual property: protection and enforcement*, viewed 7 March 2015, https://www.wto.org/english/thewto_e/whatis_e/tif_e/agrm7_e.htm

Chapter 13

Health and Medical Tourism

Introduction

Health tourism and medical tourism are in some regards contentious terms. In the United Kingdom, for example, health tourism is associated with the supposed pull factor of the nation's National Health Service. For those on the right of the nation's political spectrum, and no doubt for some placed elsewhere within it, 'health tourism' renders visible the image of overseas migrants flocking to the nation to make use of free access to health care services, facilitated by the same process of globalisation that allows the ready movement of both diseases (see Chapter 11) and drugs (see Chapter 12). Prior to the emergence of affordable anti-retroviral treatment for HIV/AIDS in sub-Saharan African countries, right-leaning newspapers which dominate the British media landscape regularly opined on the arrival of large numbers of HIV-positive black African migrants seeking free treatment. Even the left-leaning New Labour government in the mid 2000s raised its concerns over the issue, the then Minister of Health, John Hutton, stating that although he was unaware of the exact figures, there was 'no doubt in my mind and I think in the mind of any other person who has dealings on this subject in the NHS that there is a significant amount of abuse going on', that is, by overseas migrants (including refugees and asylum seekers) (cited in BMJ 2008). In this sense the social construction of medical tourists echoes negative images of populations and places associated with infectious disease (see Chapters 4 and 11).

Yet, as we shall go on to discuss, health and medical tourism does not only involve the one-way movement of migrants from the world's poorest and most resource-deprived nations to the world's richest in search of health care that they would otherwise not receive. Although it might be argued that this is a perfectly legitimate response to the inequalities in access to health care resources discussed in Chapter 12, our purpose here is not to dwell on this specific issue but to explore the full extent of these two closely interrelated phenomena, health and medical tourism and globalisation. As we go on to discuss, travel relating to

Health Geographies: A Critical Introduction, First Edition. Tim Brown, Gavin J. Andrews, Steven Cummins, Beth Greenhough, Daniel Lewis, and Andrew Power.
© 2018 John Wiley & Sons Ltd. Published 2018 by John Wiley & Sons Ltd.

the promotion of health as well as the receipt of medical care has existed for centuries. To an extent, this is accounted for by the therapeutic landscapes concept (see Chapter 4). As scholars such as Wilbert Gesler have demonstrated, the taking of waters at spas and springs (for example, Bath Spa in Britain) was popular amongst the Romans and the reputation of such places as sites of healing was maintained into the eighteenth and nineteenth centuries. In more recent times, geographers such as John Connell, Meghann Ormond and Valorie Crooks, as well as other social science and humanities scholars, have extended our understanding of health and medical tourism considerably and the aim of this chapter is to consider the full breadth of this scholarly engagement and how critical health geographers might participate in it.

Early Forms of Health and Medical Tourism

From ancient times people have sought out healing places in pursuit of spiritual and physical wellbeing, with some sites such as Bath in the United Kingdom and Lourdes in France having reputations for healing that stretch back centuries (see Chapter 4). However, the origins of modern western medical travel are found in the eighteenth century when, faced with increasing pollution, poor sanitation and the noise and bustle of the city, those who could afford to (largely the upper and later upper-middle classes) sought to escape to the countryside or further afield. Many of these journeys were undertaken explicitly for the promotion of health and wellbeing and were behind the rapid popularity and growth of spa towns such as Bath and Buxton in the United Kingdom. These spa towns embodied many of the characteristics of therapeutic landscapes discussed earlier in this book, including 'natural characteristics such as magnificent scenery, water, and trees' as well as human constructions such as 'healing temples or spa baths; contributions to sense of place such as feelings of warmth, identity, rootedness, or authenticity; symbolic features such as healing myths; the incorporation of familiar, daily routines into the treatment process' (Kearns and Gesler 1998, p. 8).

As John Connell (2006) notes, some of the earliest forms of local tourism were effectively health tourism, as the wealthy, upper classes and nobility travelled to the spa towns to 'take the waters' and recuperate from the rigours of the 'London Season'. Such travel was not limited to the United Kingdom. In territories associated with European colonialism, for example the British Raj in India, colonial administration retreated to the so-called 'hill stations' to recover from the heat and what was, for them at least, the 'unhealthy' tropical environment (see Box 13.1). In the latter half of the twentieth century the introduction of holidays for the masses became associated with a rise in sea bathing and outdoor pursuits, and the countryside and coast became a resource for health and relaxation for a much broader section of the population in the West. Moreover, within the United Kingdom, United States and across continental Europe, one of the key aims of the national parks movement was to open up a healthy outdoor lifestyle to a broader range of people. Throughout the twentieth century some sites and tourist areas have, then, actively promoted themselves as 'health' destinations, for example Hot Springs in South Dakota (Geores 1998). Others came to embody popular ideals of 'health' retreats, such as the Indian ashrams popularised by British pop band the Beatles during the 1960s. Today, health spas and retreats remain a popular holiday option, but contemporary medical travel has also expanded rapidly towards what is often referred to as medical tourism.

Box 13.1   Key Themes: Indian Hill Stations

As Kennedy (1996, p. 1) notes, hill stations were established by British colonists in India in the early nineteenth century as 'sanitaria within the subcontinent where European invalids could recover from the heat and disease of the tropics' by retreating to the cooler climates found at higher elevations. The belief that Europeans, in order to preserve both their physical and moral health, needed to escape to the hills reflects the tropical thinking – or association of tropical landscapes and climates with disease and immorality (see Chapter 2) – that was prevalent at the time. Geographers too, in their later studies of hill stations, reflect the assumptions made about the relationship between climate, race and health: 'the lowlands everywhere from western India around to northern China and southern Japan are so hot, humid, and uncomfortable for some part of the year that the white man suffers acutely when continuing to reside there' (Spencer and Thomas 1948, p. 638). This occurred partly, as Spencer and Thomas go on to explain, due to diseases associated with heat and humidity, and partly due to 'willful failure to live rightly in an unsatisfactory climatic environment' (ibid.). Hill stations were effectively a form of therapeutic landscape (see Chapter 4) where the climate was found to be more salubrious and conducive to European health.

While at some points in the year the colonial administration effectively operated from these 'summer capitals', notably Simla, their principal purpose was one of health and relaxation. Over time amenities expanded to include clubs, gardens, swimming pools and golf courses, and hill stations evolved to become shrines to memories of home, planted and landscaped in a British style. The stations served as spaces of security at times of civil unrest, with relatively high populations of women and children compared to other colonial settlements. While the role of hill stations as a retreat for European elites ended following the decline of the Raj and Indian independence, they remain popular destinations for domestic tourists, notably the Indian middle classes, popularised by their use as settings in the Hindi film industry.

As Connell (2006) notes, the term medical tourism (MT) is widely accepted to signal a shift in the nature of the health care encounter. Whereas health tourism focuses on providing an atmosphere conducive to health, medical tourism is most often used to refer to travel in order to receive a direct medical intervention, most commonly surgery. There is a change in scope also, with the largely short-term benefits of an increased sense of wellbeing and relaxation associated with health tourism being replaced with much longer term, and in many cases permanent, effects. However, within the academic community this definition and the appropriateness of the term 'medical tourism' have proved in themselves topics of considerable debate and disagreement. Connell (2013, p. 2) suggests that despite the growing body of academic work exploring medical tourism 'at least four basic issues remain unresolved: what is MT, who are the medical tourists (MTS), how many of them are there and what impact do they have?' In the rest of this chapter, we address each of these elements in turn, touching on many of the key themes of this volume including the impact of neoliberal policies and cuts to public health services, the globalisation of medical care and inequalities in access to medical tourism benefits.

Defining Medical Tourism

While the terms medical tourism, medical travel and health tourism are often conflated, there is widespread consensus that medical tourism is distinguished from other forms of health travel by a number of key elements. First, the object of travel is the pursuit of a direct non-emergency medical, dental or surgical intervention, which is usually paid for out-of-pocket. Second, there is an expectation that as well as receiving medical treatment medical tourists will at the same time be holidaymakers, staying in hotel-style accommodation and possibly participating in typical tourist activities such as sightseeing during a recuperation period. Third, there is a sense that this travel is often long-distance; many writers exclude cross-border travel or more localised movements. For some authors, intent is a key factor in determining whether or not a particular individual is a medical tourist; that is, the individual must travel with the explicit objective of obtaining medical care. Others place an emphasis on who bears the costs, insisting that medical tourists are only those who meet their expenses out-of-pocket (Crooks et al. 2010). However, as Connell (2013; see also Turner 2007; Ormond 2014) notes, this effectively excludes a considerable number of patients who are sent abroad by governments, employers, health care agencies or insurers. For example, many Japanese companies send employees to Singapore and Thailand for annual health checks as the costs are lower than providing the same service in Japan, while the National Health Service in England has sent patients to France and Spain for procedures in order to try to cope with a backlog of cases.

Others make a distinction based on the gravity of the procedure. Essential surgery is seen as closer to the definition of medical tourism than less invasive elective procedures such as cosmetic surgery or dentistry, where the medical procedure may not form the main motivation for travel or may even have been taken up opportunistically during (as opposed to prior to) a vacation. In this way, medical tourism is distinguished from wellness tourism (usually used to refer to spiritual retreats or spa breaks, even though some of these do now provide minor, usually cosmetic-style treatments), from health tourism for preventative medicine (such as diet and fitness assessments) and from the cross-border trade in health services that forms the focus for trade specialists and economists. It also tends to exclude more exceptional kinds of medical travel such as transplant tourism, reproductive tourism and suicide tourism whose controversial and quasi-legal if not illegal nature argues for separate treatment. However, these divisions are increasingly hard to sustain in the face of an increasingly complex picture whereby brokers offer a range of services from '"wellness packages", spa retreats, Ayurvedic medicine and traditional Chinese medicine to cosmetic surgery, orthopedic procedures, cataract surgery, dental care, cardiac surgery, organ and bone marrow transplants, and stem cell injections' (Turner 2007, p. 308). The conflation of these services in the marketplace makes it difficult for consumers and academic analysts alike to separate them out.

There are also problems with the phrase 'medical tourism' and what it implies. For Leigh Turner (2007) and John Connell (2013) the term medical tourism, with its connotations of pleasurable and enjoyable activity, is a poor descriptor of some of the more painful and complex medical procedures or of the experience of travelling with serious medical conditions. It also arguably fails to reflect the circumstances of those driven by financial desperation and the unaffordability of care in their home countries (see the next section, 'Who are Medical Tourists?'). These concerns have led these authors, among others, to prefer the term *medical travel*.

Who are Medical Tourists?

Connell (2013) suggests we might think of medical tourists in terms of a number of different categories, which have been mapped out in Table 13.1. While these categories are neither exhaustive nor mutually exclusive they provide a useful framework and serve to highlight the diverse forms that medical tourism can take. The first group, *elite medical tourists*, represent a long tradition of those who have the resources to travel internationally in search of the most skilled medical practitioners, the highest standards of care and cutting edge treatments through the private sector. This group forms the core client base for established centres of medical excellence such as Harley Street in London, United Kingdom. Interestingly, this group, which often includes elite patients travelling from countries in the Global South, challenges the assumption that most medical tourism consists of consumers from the Global North seeking health care in the Global South. Tilman Ehrbeck and colleagues (2008) suggest that they constitute around 40 per cent of inpatient medical travellers and travel predominantly from Latin America (38 per cent), the Middle East (35 per cent), Europe (16 per cent) and Canada (7 per cent) to the United States.

However, it is the participation of the second group, the *global middle class*, in medical travel that has attracted the most attention from the academic and commercial gaze (Connell 2013). The rise in this group of medical travellers is attributed to a number of 'push' and 'pull' factors. Push factors include high health care costs and/or lack of adequate health insurance, long waiting lists (especially for non-essential surgeries such as knee replacements and for fertility treatment), and in those countries where public sector provision is available, an increasing discontent with the quality and availability of provision. The ageing population in many countries in the Global North puts an added pressure on health care resources, exacerbating problems with access and service availability.

We might also consider the ways in which biological citizenship places an imperative on patients to accumulate medical knowledge and take responsibility for their health: 'In place of the passive patient who leaves healthcare decisions and responsibility to the medical authorities, citizens are being disciplined to become more active and engaged healthcare consumers for the sake not only of themselves but also of their families and of national health systems' (Bell et al. 2015, pp. 285–6). Patients may also travel to seek treatments that are either unavailable or restricted in their home country, for example organ transplantation and fertility treatments, experimental procedures such as stem cell treatments or procedures that are restricted on cultural or religious grounds such as gender reassignment, abortion,

Table 13.1   A typology of medical tourists. Source: Derived using data from Connell 2013.

Patient type	Form of medical tourism
Elite patients from a range of regions	Travelling to locations such as London and New York for exclusive and costly treatment
Global middle class	Travelling for cosmetic surgery or cheaper necessary services not covered by insurance – this group is the focus of both the commercial sector and much academic analysis
Diaspora patients	Wide variety of social and economic status
Cross-border patients	Seeking culturally sensitive, cheaper, quicker or more reliable care
Desperate patients	Seeking last resort care or care unavailable in their home country

euthanasia and fertility treatment for single women or gay couples (Ormond 2014). For these patients medical tourism offers a renewed sense of hope when they feel they have been failed by the medical services available in their home country (Snyder et al. 2014). Finally, Connell (2013) and Ruth Holliday and colleagues (2015) both note how cosmetic surgery, in particular, reflects a sense of both entitlement and desire to achieve 'the perfect body', driven by the neoliberal imperative towards 'self-realisation' extended from the realm of the elite to lower and middle-class office workers.

Pull factors include increases in the relative wealth of the post-war baby boom generation, combined with increased spending power as a result of reduced transport costs and favourable economic exchange rates. These price differences are especially an incentive for people seeking elective procedures such as cosmetic surgery, tattoo removal and dental work not covered by health insurance or state welfare systems. Interestingly, however, in Ehrbeck and colleague's report (2008) these elective treatments comprised only 4 per cent of the (inpatient-focused) sample, which was dominated by those seeking medically necessary procedures (56 per cent). Other factors may also include a need for anonymity (e.g. for sex change operations) or exclusivity (e.g. for celebrity clients) (Connell 2006).

While in the past one of the key challenges has been convincing global middle-class patients in high-income countries that lower cost does not necessarily mean lower quality (Connell 2006), globalisation has now led to an increase in foreign travel and exposure to global media networks as well as internet marketing campaigns that help to make what would once have seemed an alien environment more familiar. This has been accompanied by a growing appreciation of the increased availability of cutting-edge techniques and technologies across middle-income countries such as India. There has also been a rapid increase in medical travel brokers who negotiate between hospitals and patients and often also make travel arrangements, making it easier for patients to arrange medical treatment abroad (Turner 2007; Connell 2013). Meghann Ormond (2014) argues that researchers need to look at the spaces in between host and destination countries, for example the partnerships formed between medical tourism providers and airlines, especially in South-East Asia, or the role of the internet in promoting medical tourism, with many of the key providers having a strong web presence (e.g. Bumrungrad International Hospital) as well as intermediaries such as MedRetreat. Both these brokers and the top medical tourism providers offer, 'services such as translators and airport pickups, to ease patient worries...' and 'reassure patients by giving them access to physicians ahead of time. Many medical travellers know more about their doctors overseas than they do about their doctors back home' (Ehrbeck et al. 2008, p. 9). Further assurances are provided by international agreements such as the General Agreement on Trade in Services (GATS – compare to TRIPS and the ICH discussed in Chapter 12) and international accreditation schemes such as the US-based Joint Commission International (http://www.jointcommissioninternational.org). However, Ehrbeck and colleagues (2008) also note that the market is volatile, especially in the face of geopolitical events such as the September 2001 terrorist attacks in the United States, which saw a dramatic decrease from 44 to 8 per cent of medical travellers from one country in the Middle East by 2003, largely due to the difficulties they faced in obtaining US visas.

The third group, *diaspora patients*, constitutes a significant proportion of medical travellers, although this group is less frequently the object of academic attention. Here motivations are believed to be not only economic but also shaped by the desire to be treated within a more familiar health care system, for example Mexican medical travellers returning to Mexico for treatment from the United States or the return of the more widespread Indian and Middle Eastern diaspora populations to their home nations for treatment. In India, for example,

22 per cent of medical travellers were non-resident or second-generation Indians and a further 19 per cent came from neighbouring Bangladesh, Nepal and Sri Lanka (Connell 2013, p. 4).

Some would dispute whether the fourth group, *cross-border patients*, should be classed as medical travellers at all, given that they are seeking health care in a familiar (as opposed to 'exotic' or foreign) location close to home. However, as Meghann Ormond (2014) suggests, these 'backyard' settings are likely to be more common than more distant 'playgrounds' as destinations for health and medical travellers. Furthermore, she argues, there are clear examples of how cross-border care can work: 'Flexible Austrian insurance reimbursement clauses embrace the notion of a single EU market, and Austrian dentists are establishing practices alongside their Hungarian counterparts on the Hungarian side of the shared border to offer Austrian "cross-border shoppers" high-quality, low-cost dental care' (Ormond 2014, p. 430 citing Michalkó et al. 2012).

There is also considerable dispute over whether the last group, *desperate patients*, should be included in broader definitions of medical travel. While they share some characteristics with other kinds of medical travellers, in particular elite medical travellers, there are also often further mitigating circumstances that shape their experiences. This is especially the case when they seek treatments that may be illegal in their home country and in some cases also in the destination country. This group includes reproductive tourists and surrogacy tourists, transplant tourists, stem cell tourists and suicide tourists.

Bronwyn Parry's (2015) work on reproductive tourism highlights how differences between the United States and other countries in the regulation of the sale of human gametes (sperm), especially pertaining to the ability for US donors to remain anonymous, become unique selling points for these products. However, Jenny Gunnarsson Payne (2015) notes that for many participants in this market 'choice' is actually highly constrained. Her analysis of the experiences of reproductive tourists in Europe noted that the availability of donor gametes, far from being an international market, is constituted primarily of prospective donors from former Eastern Bloc countries enticed by the opportunity to enter a growing market in reproductive services. Parry's example of US anonymous donation also reflects how reproductive tourism or 'procreation vacation' raises diverse ethical questions around individual and state responses to liberty, rights and autonomy. Such questions arguably become even more fraught in the case of international surrogacy, where parents in one country employ a woman in another country, for example India, to carry a child to term for either medical or (some claim) lifestyle reasons. Here, there are increasing concerns about the complications in obtaining citizenship for children born abroad using surrogate mothers and donor gametes (see also Schneider 2015), highlighted in a recent case where Australian parents apparently refused to claim one of a pair of twins (the twin diagnosed with Down's syndrome) gestated by a surrogate in Thailand (CNN 2014).

Nancy Scheper-Hughes' (2000, 2005) shocking analyses of the global organ trade remains perhaps one of the most extensive investigations into this field. Kidneys remain the most frequently transplanted organs and a combination of improved prognosis, the globalisation of organ transplantation, aging western populations and the expansion of the categories of patient deemed eligible for organ transplant has placed increasing pressure on legal supplies and cadaveric donations. One way in which this shortage is being addressed is through the (in many countries illegal) trade in human kidneys – so-called 'transplant tourism' – whereby wealthy individuals in one country (which has tighter regulations and an organ gap) travel to another to 'buy' transplant services. To facilitate this trade there has emerged a new class of organ brokers (a black market parody of the medical tourism

---

Box 13.2   Key Themes: Organ Trafficking and the Positive Side of the Organ Trade?

While some authors highlight the negative impacts of transplant tourism, Scheper-Hughes (2000) and Sallie Yea (2015) note how selling a kidney has become widely accepted and naturalised in places such as Manila in the Philippines. In some slums and shanty towns kidney donation is almost seen as a right. Even though it prevents people from subsequently taking part in traditional heavy work, in these areas with limited economic opportunities, prospective donors feel entitled to the opportunity to earn an income by becoming a donor. In some areas there is even a waiting list of prospective donors angry they have not been selected. Elsewhere kidney selling has become a form of economic niche, with generations stepping forward to contribute to the family income. For example, Cohen (2005) notes how in some parts of India the income from selling kidneys has become one strategy whereby poor families afford a dowry in order to arrange a marriage for an 'extra' daughter. Furthermore, on a wider scale the trade in illegal transplant surgery can often support public medical facilities in places such as South Africa, where illegal transplants provide the funding that can help to keep medical facilities open, again echoing some of the impacts of more conventional forms of medical tourism.

---

brokers described above), ranging from sophisticated businessmen, travel agents and insurance brokers to local kidney hunters and the criminal underworld. While the commerce in human organs is illegal according to the official codes of virtually all nations where organ transplantation is practised, nowhere are the renegade surgeons (who are well known to their professional colleagues), organ brokers or kidney buyers (or sellers) pursued by the law, let alone prosecuted (Scheper-Hughes 2005, p. 156). The result is a growing trade in organs from 'living donors'. In today's organ market, a kidney purchased from a Filipino costs as little as US$1,200, one from a Moldovan peasant US$2,700 and one from a Turkish worker up to US$8,000, while a kidney purchased from a housewife in Lima, Peru, can command up to US$15,000 in a private clinic. Where some scholars point to more positive portrayals of medical tourism (see Box 13.2), Scheper-Hughes highlights how the inequalities within the organ trade map onto existing inequalities in wealth and power:

> In general, the circulation of kidneys follows the established routes of capital from South to North, from poorer to more affluent bodies, from black and brown bodies to white ones, and from females to males, or from poor males to more affluent males. (Scheper-Hughes 2000, p. 193)

In another context, Tamra Lysaght and Douglas Sipp (2015) suggest that labelling patients who travel to access cutting-edge treatments such as stem cell therapy 'medical tourists' fails to capture the extent to which they are at high risk of exploitation. While blood-forming (haematopoietic) stem cells are used routinely in the treatment of very specific types of blood and immune system disorders, their use for treatment of other disorders including macular degeneration, spinal cord injuries and heart attack remains in the early stages of clinical trial. Despite this, a growing number of commercial organisations are offering these treatments to patients through direct-to-consumer (DTC) marketing over the internet for a wide range of conditions including 'cardiovascular diseases, Down's syndrome, liver disease, Parkinson's disease, HIV/AIDS, Alzheimer's disease, cerebral palsy, autism and multiple sclerosis'

(Lysaght and Sipp 2015, p. 211). South Korea remains the only country to authorise stem cell treatments on the open market; they are generally made available in other locations only when regulatory authorities are unwilling or unable to control their use. Medical tourism to these destinations has become increasingly common, but there remain considerable concerns over both the nature of treatments offered – many of which do not actually use stem cells and in the worst cases may be nothing more than saline solution – and the way in which the label 'tourism' focuses attention on the patients rather than the providers and their regulation. Lysaght and Sipp also point out the effort made by leading medical tourism providers to distance themselves from these treatments, noting, for example, that Bumrungrad International Hospital explicitly states on its website that it will not offer stem cell treatments that fail to meet regulatory requirements or standards of care. Lysaght and Sipp therefore suggest that the label 'medical tourism' is one that many stem cell providers have yet to earn and should only be applied to legitimate registered organisations able to offer assurances of the quality, nature (i.e. actually containing stem cells) and efficacy of their treatments.

Where do they Travel and in what Numbers?

While the assumption is that most patients are travelling from the Global North to the Global South, in practice (as noted previously) the picture is a complex mix of different kinds of medical travellers with varying motivations travelling in multiple directions. This is captured to an extent in Figure 13.1, a map that Ehrbeck and colleagues (2008) produced in their capacity as employees of McKinsey and Company, a global management consultancy. Here, key movements reflect some of the trends outlined in previous sections. Note, for example, the high proportion of patients from Africa travelling to the United States – arguably, to access treatments unavailable in their home country, and the large proportion of patients travelling from North America and Europe to Asia – arguably, in search of low-cost treatments.

As the map reveals, most medical tourists are from North America, Western Europe and the Middle East. European patients favour India, Thailand and Malaysia, although there are also emerging medical tourism sectors in countries without a strong history of western tourism, including former Eastern Bloc nations such as Belarus, Latvia, Lithuania and Hungary as well as countries in the Caribbean such as Costa Rica (Connell 2006). Patients from the Middle East travel to India and Singapore. A significant proportion of Indian patients come from the Indian diaspora. Some areas specialise in particular medical procedures. Cuba, for example, specialises in skin diseases, Thailand specialises in sex change operations and more recently plastic surgery, and Eastern European countries focus on providing dental care and plastic surgery. Other countries, such as India, capitalise on their links with the West, importing western medical approaches and protocols.

Our understandings of medical tourism are further confounded by the lack of accurate data on medical tourist movements. This is compounded by the fact that many of the data are provided by medical tourist enterprises themselves or even by governments with a strong economic interest in promoting medical tourism, both of whom have a tendency to skew the data in their own interests with little oversight or independent adjudication (although this is changing, see 'What are the Impacts of Medical Tourism?'). There are also problems, as noted previously, with isolating medical tourism from other forms of health travel, seen in, for example, the conflation of medical travellers with other foreign patients

Medical travelers by point of origin

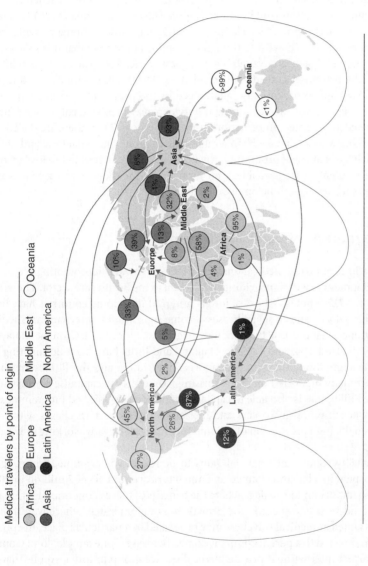

Source: Interviews with providers and patient-level data; McKinsey analysis

Figure 13.1 Exhibit from "Mapping the market for medical travel", May 2008, McKinsey Quarterly, www.mckinsey.com. Copyright ©2008 McKinsey & Company. All rights reserved. Reprinted by permission McKinsey & Company.

who may be receiving care as the result of an accident while abroad or who are expatriates resident in the country of treatment (Connell 2013).

One of the most often cited sources for data on the extent of medical travel is the 2008 report produced by Ehrbeck and colleagues for McKinsey and Company, which estimates that worldwide the medical travel industry serves around 60,000 to 85,000 patients a year (although this importantly excluded outpatients, who may make up a considerable portion of medical travellers). More recent estimates suggest this figure has now reached around 6 million (Youngman 2015); Bumrungrad International Hospital in Thailand (2014), one of the leading medical tourism providers, claims to treat 520,000 international patients from over 190 different countries each year (although it is important to note that this figure *does* include outpatients). The lack of accurate data suggests a need for further research, but research in the field also poses considerable challenges. There is the difficulty of tracking down patients, for whom confidentiality (guaranteed by the provider) is often a key issue. Commercial and public sector medical tourism providers are often reticent to share information due to the need to protect information from competitors. Then there are the ethical challenges of working with a perceived 'vulnerable' patient group and what Ormond (2014) refers to as the 'delicate' nature of promoting private medical care in middle- to low-income countries. These challenges are arguably even more acute for those wishing to research illegal procedures such as work done on organ trafficking.

What are the Impacts of Medical Tourism?

For many destination countries, medical tourism is seen as a means of promoting economic growth and development as well as providing investment in the health care sector. Therefore, as Ormond (2014, p. 428) notes, 'a host of lower- and middle income countries have been aggressively promoted as – and in several cases become significant – international medical tourism destinations over the last two decades (e.g. Costa Rica, Cuba, India, Malaysia, Mexico, South Africa and Thailand)'. While Thailand and India have been dominating the industry for quite some time, Malaysia, Singapore, South Korea and the Philippines have put in place government-supported medical tourism programmes to capitalise on this growing industry. The Philippines is also able to capitalise on its long-established programmes for training English-speaking health workers and the familiarity of western clients with their medical staff given the high proportion of Filipino medical staff already working in UK and US hospitals.

There are arguably significant financial gains to be made. For example, Bumrungrad International Hospital in Thailand claimed an annual turnover of US$ 477 million in 2013. However, it is also important to consider where the benefits of these economic gains are felt. An important trend in this respect is the growth in conglomerates, whereby, although medical services aimed at medical travellers may be located in a particular place, the profits may actually be redirected to a parent company somewhere else. For example, John Connell notes how 'the largest international private medical service group in India, Apollo, had 37 hospitals in India in 2004, partnerships in hospitals in Kuwait, Sri Lanka and Nigeria, and plans for others in Dubai, Bangladesh, Pakistan, Tanzania, Ghana, Singapore, Philippines, London and Chicago' (Connell 2006, p. 1099).

A second potential gain for host countries is the investment fuelled by medical tourism developments, including not only work to raise local hospitals and clinics to international standards but also the associated development of tourist infrastructure such as hotels and entertainment facilities. Each of these developments provides employment opportunities for local people; some suggest that it reverses the 'brain drain' of highly qualified medical personnel leaving to seek higher-earning opportunities abroad. Critics, though, question the extent to which local people will benefit from these improvements in private sector medical services, which remain largely inaccessible to the poorer sections of society. As Meghann Ormond notes, although some countries such as Malaysia have targeted local middle-class patients as well as foreign patient-consumers, the majority see 'medical tourism as a spectacular opportunity for outsourcing and offshoring' and 'are intent on developing low-cost, high-volume medical enclaves meant solely for foreign patient-consumers' (Ormond 2014, p. 429). At worst, a medical tourism strategy can channel limited state funds away from domestic health care and welfare provision and into the private sector. Furthermore, inequalities in wealth between foreign patients and local people create opportunities for other, more unsavory, markets to emerge. Kaushik Sunder Rajan (2010) has argued that poverty in areas such as Mumbai, India, often the legacy of dis-investment following previous layers of capitalist enterprise (see Chapter 11 on structural violence), leaves the local population vulnerable to exploitation by brokers searching for clinical trial subjects, surrogates or organ donors (see also Scheper-Hughes 2000).

For the patients there may also be substantial benefits, notably reduced costs. A procedure such as heart valve replacement that may have cost over US$100,000 in the United States can be found for US$38,000 in Latin America and only US$12,000 in Asia (Ehrbeck et al. 2008, p. 5). Table 13.2 provides further cost comparisons for a series of medical procedures in the United States, Germany and India in 2012.

Yet there are risks too. Leigh Turner (2015) suggests that the profit-driven nature of the medical tourism sector puts patients at risk of being encouraged to opt for procedures that may be unnecessary, which may not meet leading international standards of health care provision (leading to a greater risk of complications and infection), and about which they may be poorly informed. Furthermore, once the procedure is completed there are concerns about the provision (and cost to the public sector) of post-operative care in the home country and legal redress should things go wrong. Such issues are complicated by the international nature of medical travel. Ironically, the very advantages exploited by some medical tourists to access procedures illegal in their home country become barriers when seeking legal redress for medical harm. More recently, an incident where a British medical tourist returning from India proved to be the source of a deadly meticillin-resistant *Staphylococcus aureus* (MRSA) outbreak in UK hospitals raised concern that returning medical tourists themselves constitute a potential biosecurity risk to their home countries and medical systems (Crooks et al. 2013).

The presence of, and concerns over, these more controversial forms of medical travel also reflect some of the challenges of regulating medical travel. First, there is a lack of available

Table 13.2 Costs (US$) of a series of medical procedures in the United States, Germany and India in 2012. Data taken from http://www.washingtonpost.com/wp-srv/special/business/high-cost-of-medical-procedures-in-the-us/, viewed 15 April 2016.

Procedure	United States	Germany	India
CT scan, head	510	272	43
Cataract surgery	3,748	2,514	885
Hip replacement	38,017	11,418	4,308

information about, and regulation of, the quality of care provided by foreign hospitals and health care services and concerns about the ability of patients to make an informed evaluation of the information that is supplied (Crooks et al. 2013). A key challenge for regulators remains the lack of accurate and comparable information on medical tourism providers, incorporating key objective indicators such as mortality, avoidable error and acquired infection rates. Second, there are concerns over the lack of legal redress for medical patients who suffer from malpractice. Third, there are also concerns over the regulation of private insurance providers who may make use of the services of foreign (as opposed to domestic) health care providers. This last issue is less of a concern for those countries like the United Kingdom that have public medical systems, but there are concerns about the standardisation of reimbursement rates across Europe, for example. Glenn Cohen (2015) suggests that what is needed are 'channeling regimes' in order to direct patients to those providers who have robust accreditation and who will consent to international jurisdiction or provide insurance in cases of medical malpractice. One possible route forward are initiatives such as the recent EU directives on blood (2002/98/EC), cell and tissue (2004/23/EC), advanced therapy medicinal products (2001/83/EC) and organ transplantation (2010/53/EC), which provide oversight on issues such as quality and safety; however, it remains most likely that international normative frameworks will be established not through state agency but through self-regulation from within the medical tourism industry, driven by the demands of health care insurance providers and industry professional benchmarks (Schneider 2015).

While the drive to standardise regulation seen within the medical tourism industry through, for example, Joint Commission International (JCI) accreditation, is often couched in positive terms, others bemoan the westernisation of medical services as a new form of cultural imperialism. Ruth Holliday and colleagues (2013), for example, talk about medical non-places, where the distinctiveness supplied by local cultures or traditions and expertise is lost in favour of the reproduction of a sterile, western-style environment. However, such critiques perhaps underestimate the new medical tourism hybrids, which, as noted previously, make these trends so hard to capture and define. Alongside the more widespread adoption of western medical technologies we also see a growing market in complementary and alternative treatments, including preventative health and wellbeing related tourism packages from a wide range of providers. Consequently, as Turner (2007) observes, there is a shift from an industry focused on a few major hospitals such as Bumrungrad International and Bangkok International to government agencies, private hospital associations, airlines, hotel chains, investors and probate equity funds and medical brokerages, offering everything from spa retreats and traditional Chinese medicine to cardiac surgery, organ transplants and stem cell therapies.

Medical Tourism and Health Geography

While medical tourism can be seen as emerging from a long tradition of health-related travel, it remains a relatively new area of both development and research. Industry reports focus on weighing up the economic costs and benefits. Academics take a more critical perspective, highlighting how a combination of global disparities in income, restricted access to public sector health care and/or the high costs of private sector health care in many countries and the impact of globalisation on both the availability of medical procedures abroad and the perceptions of potential patients, has opened up the possibility of medical travel to a much wider group of people. The result is a shift in perception, whereby patients/

consumers go from seeing the Global South as a site of health risk (see Chapter 3) to perceiving it as a source of cut-price, excellent health care. What is absent from these accounts is the perspective from provider countries themselves (Ormond 2014) who may well share many of the concerns of Global North countries with respect to the impacts of medical tourism (Crooks and Snyder 2014).

Furthermore, geographers such as John Connell (2013, p. 6) argue that medical tourism needs to be placed within a wider story around neoliberal global health restructuring, as a function of 'the growing privatisation and commodification of health care, where the ability to pay has become the key to obtaining medical care'. The result is a redistribution of care as patients shift from being participants in national health care systems to patient-consumers in a global market. Those who can afford to use this opportunity seek out the best possible care at the best possible price, motivated not only by medical need but by the increased medicalisation of all aspects of life and health and the pursuit of the neoliberal ideal of the perfect, healthy body (Holliday et al. 2015). Those who cannot afford to do this remain unable to access even basic health care services, the state-of-the-art medical facilities made available to lucrative foreign clients remaining beyond the financial reach of many of the local population in key medical tourism destinations such as India and Thailand.

Medical tourism or medical travel remains an under-researched area but health geographers among others have begun to play a key role in understanding why medical tourists travel (Cameron et al. 2014), the economic and social impacts of medical tourism (Connell 2006, 2013; Ormond 2014), the role of brokers, how medical tourism interacts with the wider tourism industry, the ethical and legal issues raised by medical tourism (Crooks et al. 2013) and where medical tourism fits within the wider picture of global health restructuring (Connell 2013).

Conclusion

While the definition of exactly what constitutes medical tourism remains contested, there is a broad consensus that it consists of international travel in pursuit of a direct non-emergency medical, dental or surgical intervention, usually paid for out-of-pocket, while staying in hotel-style accommodation and possibly participating in typical tourist activities such as sightseeing during a recuperation period. The decision of many of these people to take their health into their own hands reflects broader trends towards the responsibilisation of people for their own health.

There are a number of different kinds of medical tourist, usefully divided into five broad groups: elite patients, the global middle class, diaspora patients, cross-border patients and desperate patients. The motivations for travel differ between these different groups, ranging from the search for the best possible service and standards (elite patients), more affordable medical care (global middle class and cross-border patients), a more familiar health care system (diaspora patients), to seeking services that may be illegal or inaccessible in their country of origin (desperate patients). Research to date has mainly focused on the global middle class, although it has been suggested that the majority of medical travellers are actually cross-border patients. There is a lack of accurate data on both the numbers and movements of medical tourists, and many of the data that are available are supplied by companies and governments who have a vested interest in promoting medical tourism. The majority of medical tourists are from North America, Western Europe and the Middle East, and popular destinations include India, Thailand, Singapore and Malaysia, although there are also emerging medical tourism sectors in the Baltic States and Eastern Europe.

For many destination countries, medical tourism is seen as a means of promoting economic growth and development, as well as providing investment in the health care sector. In this way it is reflective of broader neoliberal approaches to health care provision. Critics, however, question whether the benefits brought by medical tourism are accessible to all, reflecting wider patterns of global inequality. For patients there are clear cost savings to be made, but they also face the risks inherent in seeking care from a foreign provider, including a lack of independent monitoring and reliable information and the difficulties in obtaining legal redress if things go wrong.

Questions for Review

1. What kind of images does the phrase 'medical tourism' evoke for you? (Perhaps try Googling medical tourism images and see how destinations promote themselves.)
2. Do you agree that the term 'medical travel' is preferable to 'medical tourism'?
3. Why do countries like Thailand seek to promote medical tourism?

Suggested Reading

Cameron, K, Crooks, VA, Chouinard, V, Snyder, J, Johnston, R et al. (2014) Motivation, justification, normalization: talk strategies used by Canadian medical tourists regarding their choices to go abroad for hip and knee surgeries. *Social Science & Medicine* 106, 93–100.
Connell, J (2006) Medical tourism: sea, sun, sand and surgery. *Tourism Management* 27, 1093–100.
Connell, J (2013) Contemporary medical tourism: conceptualisation, culture and commodification. *Tourism Management* 34, 1–13.
Ormond, M (2014) Medical tourism. In: Lew, AA, Hall, CM & Williams, AM (Eds) *The Wiley-Blackwell Companion to tourism.* Wiley-Blackwell, Oxford, 425–34.
Parry, B, Greenhough, B, Brown, T & Dyck, I (2015) *Bodies across borders: the global circulation of body parts, medical tourists and professionals.* Ashgate, Farnham.
Turner, L (2007) First world health care at third world prices: globalization, bioethics and medical tourism. *BioSocieties* 2, 303–25.

References

Bell, D, Holliday, R, Ormond, M & Mainil, T (2015) Transnational health care, cross-border perspectives. *Social Science & Medicine* 124, 284–9.
BMJ (2008) Refused asylum seekers are entitled to free NHS care, says BMA. *BMJ* 337, a1552.
Bumrungrad International Hospital (2014) *Bumrungrad factsheet,* viewed 10 October 2014, https://www.bumrungrad.com/en/about-us/bumrungrad-factsheet
Cameron, K, Crooks, VA, Chouinard, V, Snyder, J, Johnston, R et al. (2014) Motivation, justification, normalization: talk strategies used by Canadian medical tourists regarding their choices to go abroad for hip and knee surgeries. *Social Science & Medicine* 106, 93–100.
Cohen, L (2005) Operability, bioavailability and exception. In: Ong, A & Collier, S (Eds) *Global assemblages: technology, politics, and ethics as anthropological problems.* Blackwell, Oxford, 79–90.
Cohen, G (2015) Medical tourism for services legal in the home and destination country: legal and ethical issues. In: Parry, B, Greenhough, B, Brown, T & Dyck, I (Eds) *Bodies across borders: the global circulation of body parts, medical tourists and professionals.* Ashgate, Farnham, 173–90.

Connell, J (2006) Medical tourism: sea, sun, sand and surgery. *Tourism Management* 27, 1093–100.

Connell, J (2013) Contemporary medical tourism: conceptualisation, culture and commodification. *Tourism Management* 34, 1–13.

CNN (2014) *Surrogate mom vows to take care of ill twin 'abandoned' by parents*, viewed 15 April 2106, http://edition.cnn.com/2014/08/04/world/asia/thailand-australia-surrogacy/

Crooks, VA & Snyder, J (2014) Need to broaden the scope of recent Canadian dialogues about medical tourism. *Canadian Medical Association Journal*. eLetter published September 8, 2014.

Crooks, VA, Kingsbury, P, Snyder, J & Johnston, R (2010) What is known about the patient's experience of medical tourism? A scoping review. *BMC Health Services Research* 10, 266–78.

Crooks, VA, Turner, L, Cohen, IG, Bristeir, J, Snyder, J et al. (2013) Ethical and legal implications of the risks of medical tourism for patients: a qualitative study of Canadian health and safety representatives' perspectives. *BMJ Open* 3, e002302.

Ehrbeck, T, Guevara, C & Mango, PD (2008) Mapping the market for medical travel. *The McKinsey Quarterly* May 1–11.

Geores, ME (1998) Surviving on metaphor: how "Health = Hot springs" created and sustained a town. In: Kearns, RA & Gesler, WM (Eds) *Putting health into place: landscape, identity, and well-being*. Syracuse University Press, Syracuse, NY, 36–52.

Gunnarsson Payne, J (2015) Reproduction in transition: cross-border egg donation, biodesirability and new reproductive subjectivities on the European fertility Market. *Gender, Place and Culture* 22, 107–22.

Holliday, R, Hardy, K, Bell, D, Hunter, E, Jones, M et al. (2013) Beauty and the beach. In: Botterill, D, Pennings, G & Mainil, T (Eds) *Medical tourism and transnational health care*. Palgrave Macmillan, Basingstoke, 83–97.

Holliday, R, Bell, D, Hardy, K & Hunter, E (2015) Beautiful face, beautiful place: relational geographies and gender in cosmetic surgery tourism websites. *Gender, Place and Culture* 22, 90–106.

Kearns, RA & Gesler, WM (1998) Introduction. In: Kearns, RA & Gesler, WM (Eds) *Putting health into place: landscape, identity, and well-being*. Syracuse University Press, Syracuse, NY, 1–16.

Kennedy, D (1996) *The magic mountains: hill stations and the British Raj*. University of California Press, Berkeley, CA.

Lysaght, T & Sipp, D (2015) Dislodging the direct-to-consumer marketing of stem cell-based interventions from medical tourism. In: Parry, B, Greenhough, B, Brown, T & Dyck, I (Eds) *Bodies across borders: the global circulation of body parts, medical tourists and professionals*. Ashgate, Farnham, 211–22.

Michalkó, G Tamara R & Mátyás, H (2012) Spatial differences in Hungarian medical tourism supply based on service providers' online presence. *Hungarian Geographical Bulletin* 61, 31–47.

Ormond, M (2014) Medical tourism. In: Lew, AA, Hall, CM & Williams, AM (Eds) *The Wiley-Blackwell Companion to tourism*. Wiley-Blackwell, Oxford, 425–34.

Parry, B (2015) A bull market? Devices of qualification and singularisation in the international marketing of US sperm. In: Parry, B, Greenhough, B, Brown, T & Dyck, I (Eds) *Bodies across borders: the global circulation of body parts, medical tourists and professionals*. Ashgate, Farnham, 53–72.

Parry, B, Greenhough, B, Brown, T & Dyck, I (2015) *Bodies across borders: the global circulation of body parts, medical tourists and professionals*. Ashgate, Farnham.

Rajan, K. (2010) Experimental values: Indian clinical trials and surplus health. In: Good, BJ, Fischer, MMJ, Willen, SS & DelVecchio Good, M-J (Eds) *A reader in medical anthropology: theoretical trajectories, emergent realities*, Wiley-Blackwell, Oxford, 377–88.

Scheper-Hughes, N (2000) The global traffic in human organs. *Current Anthropology* 41, 191–211.

Scheper-Hughes, N (2005) The last commodity: post-human ethics and the global traffic in 'fresh' organs. In: Ong, A & Collier, S (Eds) *Global assemblages: technology, politics, and ethics as anthropological problems*. Blackwell, Oxford, 145–67.

Schneider, I (2015) Race to the bottom or race to the top? Governing medical tourism in a globalised world. In: Parry, B, Greenhough, B, Brown, T & Dyck, I (Eds) *Bodies across borders: the global circulation of body parts, medical tourists and professionals*. Ashgate, Farnham, 191–210.

Snyder, J, Adams, K, Crooks, VA, Whitehurst, D et al. (2014) 'I knew what was going to happen if I did nothing. And so I was going to do something': faith, hope, and trust in Canadian multiple sclerosis patients' decisions to seek experimental treatment abroad *BMC Health Services Research* 14, 445.

Spencer, JE & Thomas, WL (1948) The hill stations and summer resorts of the Orient. *Geographical Review* 38, 637–51.

Turner, L (2007) First world health care at third world prices: globalization, bioethics and medical tourism. *BioSocieties* 2, 303–25.

Turner, L (2015) Bioethics, transnational healthcare and the global marketplace in health services. In: Parry, B, Greenhough, B, Brown, T & Dyck, I (2015) *Bodies across borders: the global circulation of body parts, medical tourists and professionals*. Ashgate, Farnham, 95–114.

Yea, S (2015) Masculinity under the knife: Filipino men, trafficking and the black organ market in Manila, the Philippines. *Gender, Place and Culture* 22, 123–142.

Youngman, I (2015) *Medical tourism research: facts and figures 2015*, viewed 7 September 2015, http://www.imtj.com/resources/medical-tourism-research-facts-and-figures-2015/

Chapter 14

Global Health Geographies

Introduction

As historians Theodore Brown, Marcos Cueto and Elizabeth Fee (2006) have outlined, the growing preference for the term 'global health' to describe what was once more commonly referred to as 'international health' or 'world health' can be traced to the 1990s. Although the prefix 'global' has much longer roots than this (e.g. Brown and colleagues suggest that it was used by the World Health Organization in their malaria eradication programme of the 1950s), there has been an exponential growth in its use since this time (see also Sparke 2009). Geographers have begun to add to this academic discourse, with a growing number of journal articles and edited collections that scope the field and its relevance to geography (e.g. Brown and Moon 2012; Brown et al. 2012; Herrick 2014), as well as others which consider global health in light of such issues as climate change (Curtis and Oven 2012; Papworth et al. 2015), political economy and inequality (e.g. Sparke 2009; Day et al. 2008; Pearce and Dorling 2009) and international security (e.g. Ingram 2005, 2008; Brown 2011). Despite this, health geographers more generally have thus far been quite reticent in their engagement with global health.

In order for geographers to position themselves more effectively in the field of global health it is important to develop a broader understanding of it. To this end, we focus in this chapter on two broad questions: first, what are the circumstances in which a concern for global, rather than international, health arose? This is an important question and one that demands we consider the genealogy of global health. Here, we use the term 'genealogy' not simply with reference to its association with the tracing of a lineage or history. There is almost inevitably a suggestion of this when one mentions 'doing a genealogy'. In contrast, we aim to achieve two things – on the one hand, we examine global health's emergence as a specific field of enquiry, one that produces a particular form of knowledge about the present and, on the other, we open up discussion about the further possibilities for

Health Geographies: A Critical Introduction, First Edition. Tim Brown, Gavin J. Andrews, Steven Cummins, Beth Greenhough, Daniel Lewis, and Andrew Power.
© 2018 John Wiley & Sons Ltd. Published 2018 by John Wiley & Sons Ltd.

geographical engagement in global health. This transformative element of genealogy relates to our second question: what might critical geographies of global health look like?

From International Dialogue to Overseas Intervention

While the term 'global health' has been widely used only relatively recently, it is generally accepted that international health – described as the concern for health in countries other than one's own (Koplan et al. 2009, p. 1994) – came into focus in the mid nineteenth century. This emergence coincided with epidemics of infectious diseases such as plague, smallpox, typhus, yellow fever and especially cholera (see Chapter 11). Rapid and largely unplanned urbanisation during this period had helped create urban environments within which such diseases could thrive. Moreover, the intensive and extensive movement of people and things associated with international commerce and colonial, and more broadly imperial, endeavour had increased the *scale* and *scope* of epidemics, and improvements in transport, initially in shipping but later in the railways, considerably enhanced their *velocity* (Cliff et al. 1998; Budd et al. 2009). Although all of the diseases mentioned above were considered a threat to life and health during the early part of the nineteenth century, it was the 'havoc and panic' caused by successive waves of cholera after 1830 that brought major European trading nations and other imperial powers such as Russia, Turkey and later the United States into international dialogue and diplomacy (Birn 2009).

Indeed, it was the experience of the third major epidemic of 'Asiatic cholera', so called because its origins lay in the endemic regions of India, which resulted in the convening of the first International Sanitary Conference in Paris, 1851. In total there were 14 of these sanitary conferences between 1851 and 1938 (10 in the nineteenth century); often lasting several months at a time, the conferences involved leading physicians and diplomats and provided an opportunity for delegates to share their experiences of epidemic disease as well as to consider the effectiveness of public health measures put in place to contain their spread. The detail of these conferences is well covered in the historical literature (see Howard-Jones 1975; Stern and Markel 2004), as is their limited success in bringing about international agreement on disease control measures. For example, it is widely acknowledged that the demands of imperial trading nations such as Britain and France were such that international public health concerns were set against commercial and imperial interests. This was so even in the face of cholera, which was the focus of eight of the 10 conferences in the nineteenth century. As an illustration, in the 1880s the British blocked attempts to impose additional restrictions on ships carrying passengers or crew potentially infected with cholera through the Suez Canal to Europe.

This instance illustrates the tension that was at the heart of these emerging international discussions. There was general international agreement that traditional public health responses to epidemics of plague, smallpox and yellow fever were unworkable and needed to be amended. Even in the face of pandemic cholera, which caused considerable anxiety because of the nature of its symptoms and the speed with which its victims succumbed, quarantine regulations or the imposition of *cordons sanitaires* were considered an 'intolerable hindrance' (Howard-Jones 1950, p. 1034). Despite this, there was also an acknowledgement that something had to be done. It is the nature of this response that is of most importance to our genealogy of global health and it is this element that will be of most interest to critical health geographers. As Anne-Emanuelle Birn (2009) notes, the zealous commitment to maintaining trade liberalisation shaped a contradictory position on the increased threat of epidemics such as cholera. It was not simply that countries such as Britain, France and later the United States appeared to prioritise trade over public health, it is also apparent that they often sought to shift the responsibility for the emerging epidemics onto others. A single example will suffice here: the annual *Hajj* to Mecca.

That the *Hajj* played a role in the diffusion of cholera from India is not in question; the first recorded outbreak of the disease in India in 1817 was followed by outbreaks in the Hijaz (a former kingdom in Arabia containing the holy cities of Medina and Mecca) in 1821 and again in 1831, the latter associated with the deaths of 20,000 pilgrims (Peters 1994). However, it was the pandemic of 1865, which resulted in 15,000 deaths amongst the 90,000 pilgrims in the Hijaz and over 200,000 worldwide that brought the role of the *Hajj* into focus. It is at this juncture that questions of broader interest to geographers arise, questions not limited to the spatial diffusion of the epidemic. In particular, analyses of the International Sanitary Conferences and the response of the European delegations on the role of the *Hajj* reveal a desire to act across international borders and to construct 'buffer zones' against the threat of epidemic disease. As Valeska Huber (2006) reveals, this was evident from the outset with delegates at the 1851 conference in Paris seeking to encourage countries to the east of Europe, specifically Russia, to protect the region in the same way that Austria had when it erected a physical barrier against the 'Oriental plague' in the previous century.

After the 1865 epidemic, it was the Ottoman Empire that was targeted as a potential buffer zone. As Huber (2006) argues, double standards were in operation here. On the one hand, European delegates were quite explicit in their belief that existing quarantine regulations and *cordons sanitaires* were not only ineffective but were impossible to implement. Yet, on the other, the strategy agreed upon by the European delegates relied on exactly this kind of response and the only difference was that the measures imposed were targeted at the *Hajj* and were implemented beyond the borders of Europe. For example, a 15–20 day quarantine period was established for any ship suspected of carrying passengers with cholera after the 1866 sanitary conference in Constantinople. While certain vessels were exempt from such quarantine measures, notably European troopships, the reality for pilgrims travelling from Mecca following the *Hajj* was that they experienced vastly longer stays in what Patrick Zylberman (2006, p. 25) describes as a 'militarized zone'. Importantly, this zone was located outside of Europe in the Red Sea region, with quarantine camps established in places such as al-Tûr in the Sinai peninsula; in 1885 there were approximately 200 guards securing the borders of these camps, and by 1890 this number had risen to 450, with pilgrim ships also being secured by military guards.

Such measures were refined as communication systems became more sophisticated and as transport networks became more advanced. By the time of the 1892 International Sanitary Conference in Venice, delegates were able to agree upon, and subsequently implement, a surveillance system that used telegram communications with ships travelling through the Suez Canal to determine their relative risk. Those ships that carried doctors and appropriate disinfection equipment were allowed to pass unimpeded; those that did not (or contained pilgrims heading for Mecca) were subject to inspection and observation (Huber 2006). We shall develop this point further in subsequent sections; however, what this example reveals is that at the heart of this emerging internationalism was a re-conceptualisation of public health in a 'world without borders'. While many profited from this new world, a semi-permeable membrane was constructed – one that allowed freedom of movement to some but was 'impenetrable to others' (Huber 2006, p. 474).

Emerging Global Biopolitics

The idea that a permanent international health agency should be established was first discussed at the International Sanitary Conference in Vienna, 1874. The main purpose of such an institution was to protect nations (primarily those in Europe and the Americas) from contamination by others (Bashford 2006a). This concern is reflected in the plethora of intergovernmental agencies that emerged prior to the establishing of the World Health Organization in 1948. For example, the International Sanitary Office of the American Republics, established in 1902 and later renamed the Pan American Sanitary Bureau and now known as the Pan American Health Organization (PAHO), was originally set up to protect commerce from yellow fever epidemics that spread along the trade routes between South and North America (Fee and Brown 2002; Cueto 2007; Markel 2014). Also, the *Office Internationale d'Hygiène Publique* (OIHP), established in 1907 and based in Paris, functioned as a modern-day disease surveillance centre – gathering and reporting the latest national morbidity, mortality and epidemiological data, with a particular emphasis placed on infectious diseases such as cholera, plague and yellow fever (Bashford 2006b).

However, these and other early examples of intergovernmental co-operation were not only concerned with the capacity of existing public health measures to contain epidemic diseases and protect states against unwanted external threats. For Mark Zacher and Tania Keefe (2008), they were 'rooted in the recognition that attempts to stem the spread of diseases at ports end… were unlikely to succeed. More likely to be influential were programs designed to curtail the incidence of diseases *within* state borders' (Zacher and Keefe 2008, p. 36. Emphasis added). This marks an important shift in the genealogy of global health. As Alison Bashford remarks, the international 'aspiration to promote health and prevent disease… resulted in pre-emptive activity *beyond* the border' (2006a, p. 2. Emphasis added). In order to grasp fully the implications of Bashford's statement we shall add further layers to our outline of international health during this period: the first relates to tropical medicine, which formed an important element of European and North American colonial administration, and the second to the health-related activities of transnational organisations such as the Rockefeller Foundation at the beginning of the twentieth century.

Tropical medicine

It might be argued that tropical medicine has its roots in environmentalist explanations of disease causation circulating throughout Europe and North America from around the eighteenth century (see Chapter 3); what Bashford refers to as 'the (medicalised) question of geography and place' (Bashford 2006a, p. 4). According to this understanding, diseases associated with tropical medicine, which had rendered tropical environments the proverbial 'white man's grave' (Anderson 2002), were attributed to the geographical features of a region – to the qualities of the atmosphere, climate, soil and so on (see Box 14.1). Although not mentioned in name until around the 1890s – and prior to its being formalised as a branch of western medicine in sites such as the London School of Hygiene and Tropical Medicine in Britain, the Pasteur Institutes in Paris, France, and the Johns Hopkins Medical School in Baltimore, USA – 'tropical medicine' was largely practised by agents of European and later North American colonialism, for example by military and naval medical officers as well as by colonial physicians. Indeed, Alison Bashford goes so far as to say that tropical medicine 'institutionally, politically and intellectually' supported European and US colonialism (2006a, p. 4; see also MacLeod and Lewis 1988).

Box 14.1   Key Themes: Tropical Medicine

For some scholars, tropical medicine is a sub-field of medicine that is generally regarded to have emerged in the late nineteenth century. Citing H.H. Scott's (1939) *The History of Tropical Medicine*, the historian David Arnold (1996) notes that prior to this point tropical medicine was regarded as a vague and largely unscientific enterprise that involved describing the relationship between climate, health and disease. In this view of the field, it was not until germ theory came to prominence that tropical medicine as we understand it today came into being, notably with the associated emergence of Patrick Manson, a pioneering British parasitologist and founder of the London School of Tropical Medicine in 1899, as a so-called 'father figure'.

  For many medical geographers it is this period prior to the establishing of tropical medicine as a distinct, scientific field that is of most interest. As Melinda Meade and Michael Emch (2010) note, the belief that cultural–environmental interactions (e.g. between people and climate) were important to disease aetiology and health links the disease ecology tradition of medical geography to variously named fields of study (e.g. geomedicine and medical topography) that drew their explanation and understanding from the Hippocratic tradition.

  Such constructions of sub-disciplinary genealogies have their place. However, tropical medicine (both in its pre- and post-germ theory formulations) is of much greater significance to us as critical geographers. Arnold is helpful here. As he notes, 'if we understand tropical medicine in a wider sense, as the specialist medicine of 'warm climates' and 'torrid zones' and 'as an integral part of the way in which Europeans perceived and sought to gain control over a large part of the globe' then we can recognise its role in helping to frame Western conceptions of the tropics and their inhabitants as 'Other' (1996, p. 3).

Beyond the support provided to such colonial administration, tropical medicine is important to our genealogy because it affords an example of the kinds of pre-emptive, cross-border, public health intervention mentioned by Zacher and Keefe (2008). In order to illustrate this significance we will focus on the example of tropical medicine as it was practised by US colonial authorities in the Philippines, which was occupied following US victory in the Spanish-American War in 1898 until independence in 1946. Public health interventions implemented during this period of US occupation came in three phases (Anderson 2006).

  The first mirrored colonial medicine as it was implemented in other parts of the world, as the emphasis was placed upon securing the health of military personnel and colonial officials who were regarded as being especially vulnerable to the rigours of the tropical climate. What this meant in reality was the attempted translation of domestic models of sanitary infrastructure and personal hygiene regimens into the colonial context, usually at sites of strategic importance for colonial administration and control such as the capital city of Manila.

  More significantly, US public health intervention in the Philippines was not only focused upon securing the health of Americans. Bringing modern hygienic practices and sanitary infrastructure to the country and its inhabitants was regarded as part of the civilising mission that the United States was embarked upon. As the first civil governor of the US-occupied Philippines, William H. Taft, remarked, 'the gradual teaching of the people the simple facts of hygiene, unpopular and difficult as the process of education has been [was] one of the great benefits given by the Americans to this people' (cited in Anderson 2006, p. 54). This civilising mission was informed by tropical medicine, which by the end of the nineteenth and beginning of the twentieth century was itself being re-shaped by the newly emerging discipline of bacteriology. As a result, during the second and third phases of US colonial administration attention shifted from the tropical environment to the bodies of Filipinos who were increasingly interpreted as 'reservoirs of disease organisms' and became the focus of extensive and intrusive public health campaigns to rid the country of 'unsanitary evils' (Anderson 1992, 1995).

A wealth of literature explores this element of sanitary reform and the tendency of resulting public health discourse to mark racial and social boundaries similar to that discussed in Chapter 2; the discourse in the Philippines was no different. As Anderson notes, racial and class stereotypes emerged in the colonial Philippines that contrasted a 'clean, ascetic American body with an open, polluting Filipino body' (2002, p. 687). This is a crucial point to consider when interpreting the discourse of tropical medicine and the kinds of public health interventions that were implemented in response to it. What scholars like Anderson record is a regimen that under the guidance of tropical medicine, and supported by large-scale disease surveys and especially laboratory investigations, traced the pathway of pathogenic organisms to the bodies of Filipinos or, more specifically, to their excreta. It was this kind of modern public health knowledge that legitimised the almost relentless scrutiny and regulation of the bodies of the Filipino poor and the spaces they inhabited. This not only involved traditional practices of isolation and quarantining during outbreaks of epidemic disease but also more invasive and socially intrusive practices. For example, during an outbreak of cholera in Manila, 1902, the belongings and homes of those individuals affected by the disease were burnt and public health officials forcibly bathed the victims in the disinfectant bichloride.

Transnational public health

Aspects of colonial administration such as those described previously were clearly problematic, not least because they were often overtly racist, as scholars such as Anderson have more than adequately demonstrated. Moreover, there are questions to be raised about the neglect of conditions that primarily affected colonial subjects (in this case Filipinos), for example tuberculosis, beri-beri and infant mortality, which at the turn of the century was approximately 400 per 1,000 births (McElhinny 2005). Beyond this, the significance of tropical medicine to our brief genealogy of global health is that it informed a strongly held belief in the power of western biomedicine to liberate the world's poorest and least developed populations from the health, and more broadly social, consequences of infectious diseases. As such, it was a principal feature of what Bashford refers to as pre-emptive global biopolitics. As Bashford notes (2006a), there is a particular spatiality to biopolitics, with governments in the nineteenth century initially problematising places and populations within their territories. The biopolitical concerns of colonial nations such as Britain, France and here the United States add a further dimension to this in their problematising and subsequently intervening in spaces that lay outside of their national borders.

Significantly, Bashford goes on to locate what she regards as the beginnings of a new global biopolitics in the transnational, rather than international or intergovernmental, activities of two further agencies: the Rockefeller Foundation's International Health Board

(IHB) and the League of Nations Health Organization (LNHO). We shall deal briefly with each in turn, as both played a crucial role in bringing the idea of global health into being. Established in 1914, the International Health Board, later Division, grew out of an earlier disease eradication programme targeted at hookworm in the southern states of America. Similarly to tropical medicine, this was a civilising mission whose key actors believed that education and disease eradication would liberate the population of the South from poverty and a lack of economic progress caused by a combination of ignorance and massive hookworm infection (Löwy and Zylbermann 2000). The success of the anti-hookworm campaign in the South encouraged the IHB to export its programme overseas, initially to the Caribbean and later to Asia and Latin America. As Ilana Löwy and Patrick Zylberman (2000) note, from an initial focus on hookworm the programme of work undertaken by the IHB grew rapidly and soon included campaigns to eradicate yellow fever, malaria and typhoid fever.

There are many ways to read the work of the IHB. While for some scholars it represented the velvet glove of US imperialism – promoting American values – for others this is too simplistic a reading and fails to account for the spatially and temporally specific contexts that shaped its work (Birn 2000). However we choose to read the intentions of the IHB, there is perhaps no doubting that it did signal, as Bashford suggests, the shift from international to world or global health as its activities transcended the direct concerns of the nation even though they remained closely tied to it. The IHB was not alone in helping to scale up fields of health concern and public health intervention that were previously only national or international in scope; Bashford also points to the part played by the *Office Internationale d'Hygiène Publique* in its capacity as a world epidemiological surveillance centre and the League of Nations Health Organization (LNHO), which was established in 1923. As she argues, similarly to the IHB, the LNHO began to manage health and hygiene in line with the aspirations of national and sometimes colonial governments. The examples that she gives to illustrate her argument are numerous. For instance, Bashford refers to the reorganising of the quarantine system in China, the surveying of nutrition in Chile and the concern with health and social rehabilitation in Liberia. This was, according to Bashford, 'technical work' that involved the transnational movement of expertise, knowledge and practice around the globe in a way that mirrored the activities of the IHB. Moreover, it was biopolitical because statistical and sanitary technologies were drawn upon to identify problematic spaces and populations and interventions designed that increasingly focused on the management of conduct, particularly around maternal health and infant welfare (Bashford 2006b, p. 77). It was out of this emerging assemblage of institutions concerned with transnational health that the World Health Organization emerged in 1948, and it is to this important institution of global health that we now turn.

Bureaucratising Global Health

Where the early periods have been referred to as the 'meeting and greeting' stage of international health, the subsequent years are considered the stages of its institution-building and bureaucratisation (Birn 2009). Although the origins of the World Health Organization (WHO) lie in the developments of these preceding years, its establishment in 1948 is closely tied to a decision by international delegates at the post-war United Nations Conference, held in San Francisco, February, 1946, to insert the word 'health' into the UN Charter. This decision, which resulted from the intervention of Brazilian and Chinese delegates at the conference, led to the recommendation to establish a permanent *international* health organisation (WHO 1948). Of particular interest here is why the shift from an international health organisation to a world one? The answer can be found in the activities of organisations such as the Rockefeller Foundation's IHB, the LNHO and other such institutions that signalled the emergence of health as a transnational question and one that was not only the international concern of nation-states. It was this transnationalism that influenced the naming of the WHO. As the proceedings of the resultant International Health Conference, held in New York, in June and July 1946, reveal, the term 'world' was preferred to international because it reflected the 'world-age' (WHO 1948). The establishment of the WHO following this conference signalled, then, the shift from an international to a world or 'global' perspective on health that Bashford describes (see also Brown et al. 2006).

It should be noted that this transition was not easy in practice (see Siddiqi 1995), and Bashford's (2006a) observation about the geopolitics at the heart of global health is a pertinent one. Setting these geopolitical tensions to one side for now, we turn our attention here to the health programmes that were first instituted by the WHO. Importantly, we should first acknowledge that the constitution of the WHO signalled a change to the concept of health and what national governments and international agencies such as the WHO should do to achieve it. As is now well known, the preamble to the constitution defines health 'not negatively or narrowly as the absence of disease or infirmity', but positively and broadly as 'a state of complete physical, mental and social wellbeing' (WHO 1948, p. 16). Out of this much broader definition emerged an equally broad expectation of what transnational cooperation on health should entail. As the report on the proceedings of the New York conference suggest:

> international collaboration in health matters was held to encompass the improvement of standards of national health in all countries, the dissemination of medical, psychological, and related knowledge throughout the world, and the development of an informed public opinion on health problems. (WHO 1948, p. 16)

As Birn (2009) notes, for the first time a single transnational institution was responsible for: standard-setting (e.g. the International Sanitary Regulations; renamed the International Health Regulations in 1969. See Fidler and Gostin 2006), data collection and epidemiological surveillance, training and research, emergency relief and many more things besides.

Although health was conceptualised more broadly, the public health programmes instituted by the WHO in its early years reflected a widespread belief that, in order for nations to develop and to progress economically, infectious diseases needed to be eradicated. These programmes, of which the malaria eradication programme was the first (Siddiqi 1995; see also Fenner et al. 1988 on the smallpox eradication campaign), were designed to wipe out single diseases. As Javed Siddiqi (1995) notes, they were remarkable both because they were the first of their type to be coordinated by a single transnational health organisation and for the fact that they helped to consolidate the WHO's position as the leading international authority in health-related matters. We will use the malaria eradication programme here to illustrate the scope and scale of the work, as well as to generate some critical questions of it and of these early interventions in global health more generally. The WHO's decision to target malaria came in response to the perceived success of national control programmes that had used the chemical agent and insecticide dichlorodiphenyl-trichloroethane (DDT) to control malaria by targeting the habitats of the *Anopheles* mosquitoes responsible for its spread.

As the proposal for the eradication programme, put before the World Health Assembly (WHA), the main decision-making body of the WHO, in 1955, stated:

> Nation-wide malaria control projects are well advanced in Argentina, Brazil, the British and French Guianas, Ecuador, Nicaragua, the United States and Venezuela; in Cyprus, Greece, Italy, Turkey and Yugoslavia; in Ceylon, India, Iran, Lebanon, the Philippines, Taiwan and Thailand; in Madagascar, Mauritius and the Union of South Africa. In a total world population of just over 2.5 billions, some 600 millions are exposed to malaria, but of these, some 230 millions either have been freed from malaria or are now being protected, chiefly by residual DDT spraying. (WHO 1955, p. 2)

Although residual spraying with DDT was found to be an effective measure in terms of its ability to interrupt the malarial cycle in a given area, the WHO, even at this time, was aware that mosquitoes might develop resistance to the effects of the insecticide and that in some areas where control programmes were in place they had adapted their behaviours to it. For example, the report notes that in Panama, where the US military had introduced a programme of malarial control using DDT in 1944, mosquitoes were observed to avoid treated surfaces and as such were not prone to the insecticide's toxic effects. The significance of this concern is that it was used to justify the establishment of a programme of malaria eradication rather than control, the argument being that eradication was economically and technically plausible at this juncture but that this would not be the case in the future owing to the potential emergence of resistant or behaviourally-adapted strains of mosquitoes. The declaration of the eradication programme in 1955 was followed by an immense global effort: by 1961, 65,000 tons of DDT and 5,000 tons of other insecticides were being sprayed by 130,000 sprayers in 60 different countries (Siddiqi 1995, p. 153). As Siddiqi suggests, the early results of the programme appeared to justify its vast scale and considerable costs, which were estimated to total $1,339 million during the period 1957–1967. According to figures produced by the WHO (see Table 14.1), after 10 years the number of people living in endemic malarious areas where eradication programmes had reached a 'maintenance' stage – that is, eradication had been achieved – was estimated to be nearly 650 million. A further 700 million people were living in malarious areas where eradication programmes were on-going. However, the picture across almost the whole of Africa was entirely different; the majority of the then 227 million population lived in areas where no eradication programme had even begun.

The mixed picture that emerged with regards to the malaria eradication programme was to an extent reflected in other similar single-disease programmes established by the WHO during this period. There were spectacular successes; for example the drive to eradicate smallpox culminated with the last naturally occurring case in Somalia in 1977 (Stern and Markel 2004). However, the overall picture was one that pointed to the limitations of relying too heavily on microbiological or pharmacological solutions. As Sara Davies (2010) notes, a second phase of the WHO's stated desire to improve world health centred on the humanitarian efforts of Halfdan Mahler, the organisation's Director-General between 1973 and 1988. It was during this period that representatives from all countries in the world gathered at the International Conference on Primary Health Care convened by the WHO and the United Nations Children's Fund (UNICEF) in Alma-Ata, Kazakhstan. As Mahler subsequently remarked, the Declaration of Alma-Ata, 1978, heralded a new era in global health because the kind of 'single victory' approach that saw smallpox eradicated would not 'have a lasting effect on the total health situation which is dependent on a vast host of factors

Table 14.1 Status of the WHO malaria eradication programme, September 1968.

Region	Population in thousands					
	Total	Where malaria not indigenous or disappeared without anti-malaria intervention	Of original malarious areas	Where malaria eradication claimed	Where malaria eradication programmes in progress	Where eradication programmes not started
Africa	227,194	17,331	209,863	3,907	3,160	202,796
America	492,889	316,659	176,230	102,679	73,551	—
South-East Asia	736,605	37,536	701,069	255,997	403,317	41,755
Europe	758,346	413,368	339,978	283,043	35,031	21,904
Eastern Mediterranean	255,574	45,375	210,199	7,509	152,918	49,772

(including socioeconomic ones) and on a system able to provide continuous promotive, preventive and curative health care to the total community' (Mahler 1988, pp. 144–5).

The Declaration is generally regarded as a landmark moment because it reaffirmed the WHO's definition of health and its commitment to it as a fundamental human right. However, its 10 core principles went much further than this. For example, the Declaration focused on the issue of health inequality between the so-called developed and developing worlds, not only declaring this to be 'politically, socially and economically unacceptable' but also linking health with social and economic development (WHO 1978, p. 2). The Declaration also asserted that the promotion of health was not only a government responsibility; individuals and communities had a right but also a duty to participate in the implementation of health care programmes. Most importantly, primary health care was at the heart of the desire to achieve health for all by the year 2000 (HFA2000):

> Governments have a responsibility for the health of their people which can be fulfilled only by the provision of adequate health and social measures. A main social target of governments, international organizations and the whole world community in the coming decades should be the attainment by all peoples of the world by the year 2000 of a level of health that will permit them to lead a socially and economically productive life. *Primary health care is the key to attaining this target as part of development in the spirit of social justice.* (WHO 1978, p. 3)

The conceptualisation of global health that emerged from Alma-Ata, and which was subsequently encapsulated in the WHO's HFA2000 global strategy (WHO 1981), was one that was built on attempts to implement comprehensive approaches to health care in countries outside of the advanced economies of the Global North. In the People's Republic of China (PRC), for example, a system of preventive health care was implemented soon after its founding by Mao Zedong in 1949. Recognising the need to move away from the fee-for-service system that provided health care to the country's largely rural population (at this time, approximately 85 per cent of China's 800 million population lived in rural areas), the PRC began to develop a co-operative medical system from the mid 1950s. The most well-known aspect of this new system is the 'barefoot doctors', rural peasants trained by qualified physicians as health workers. The duties of the barefoot doctors varied from commune to commune but generally included both preventive and primary care elements. The system was not without its difficulties; access to more technologically sophisticated medical care was biased towards urban areas, inequities in health care existed between the richer and poorer communes and the quality of the barefoot doctors and their levels of competence varied (Chen 2001). Nonetheless, there were significant improvements in population health after 1949, with epidemics of infectious diseases such as cholera, smallpox and venereal diseases less severe and overall life chances substantially increased (e.g. infant mortality rates declined from 250 per 1,000 live births in 1950 to less than 50 by 1981, and life expectancy increased from 35 to almost 70 in roughly the same period).

It was the international recognition of the role of health promotion and primary health care in the PRC that helped to shape the Declaration of Alma-Ata; however, the universal and humanitarian principles upon which it was based were both its strength and its weakness. As Mahler (1998) recalls, '[w]e had started with selective health-care programmes, [focussing on] single diseases such as malaria and tuberculosis in the 1950s and 1960s. Then we had this spiritual and intellectual awakening that came out of Alma-Ata, and suddenly some proponents of primary health care went back to the old selective approach again'. The reasons for this are many and complex and in part linked to the power and influence exerted by individual nations opposed to its plans for comprehensive health care; especially the United States (Davies 2010) as, importantly, the Declaration of Alma-Ata and the subsequent HFA2000 strategy coincided with the emergence of neoliberalism as a dominant economic and political orthodoxy. As Birn (2009) argues, the field of global health was from the mid 1980s increasingly influenced by financial institutions, such as the World Bank (the Bank) and the International Monetary Fund (IMF), that promoted private-sector, market-oriented solutions. A further consequence of this opening up of the policymaking arena to some of the main drivers of neoliberal ideology was that the WHO was 'no longer the hub of international health activity' (Birn 2009, p. 60; see also Lee 2009).

The Economisation of Global Health

In order to understand global health as we recognise it today, it is vital that we examine in a little more detail the nature of the ideological terrain in which it operates; to do so we shall turn to the growing influence of the World Bank. As Jennifer Ruger (2005) notes, as the Bank shifted its post-World War II focus from international reconstruction to economic growth it began to adopt a broader definition of development, one that encapsulated such concepts as 'human capital' and 'human development'. Under the stewardship of Robert S. McNamara, who became president of the Bank in 1968, poverty reduction, with its associated influence on health and economic growth, was placed centre stage. In the immediate years after McNamara's appointment, population control, family planning and nutrition were the areas targeted for intervention. However, in 1973 McNamara requested a broader health policy and the first formal statement on health from the Bank came with the publication of the *Health Sector Policy Paper*, 1975 (World Bank 1975).

The paper, which was heavily influenced by other UN agencies including the WHO, the Food and Agriculture Organization (FAO) and the United Nations Development Programme (UNDP) (Rowden 2009), emphasised the need for large-scale public sector investment in health and supported the idea of universal primary health care. What is, perhaps, most remarkable about this document is its perspective on the role of the state and the limited role of the market in the provision of health care. As the authors of the policy paper remark, the 'private market cannot be expected to allocate to health either the amount or composition of resources that is best from a social perspective' (World Bank 1975, p. 29). Moreover, the report argues that in relation to three distinct health-related situations, including the desire to control or eradicate specific diseases or promote the general health of the population, that 'a sizeable volume of government expenditure on health' can be justified as 'investment' and that the distortions of the market mechanism, especially in resource-poor economies, make the redistribution of welfare resources by governments, including health care, 'politically attractive' (1975, pp. 30–1).

That this was a vision shared by the Bank – one of the cornerstone institutions, along with the IMF and US Treasury, of the so-called 'Washington Consensus' (see Box 4.2) – might come as a surprise to some. But it did not last (Stein 2008). The fairly rapid departure from this position can be traced in reports emerging from the Population, Health and Nutrition Department (HNP) established by the Bank in 1979. As Ruger suggests, HNP has had a major influence on global health. For example, she points to the Bank's impressive and sustained work in the area of Safe Motherhood, which was initiated in 1987 following a co-sponsored conference – with the WHO and United Nations Population Fund – in Nairobi, Kenya. Between 1992 and 1999, US$385 million per annum was committed to projects that sought to reduce the burden of maternal mortality, representing 30 per cent of all HNP funding. This initiative continued under the auspices of the Inter-Agency Group (IAG) for Safe Motherhood and in September 2000 the reduction of maternal mortality by 75 per cent between 1990 and 2015 was identified as one of the Millennium Development Goals. While this figure has not been achieved, maternal mortality has been reduced by 45 per cent since 1990 and the number of maternal deaths per 100,000 births has reduced from 380 in 1990 to 210 in 2013 (United Nations 2015).

In addition to the Safe Motherhood Initiative, Ruger highlights the overall level of lending in this area by the Bank to exemplify its significant contribution – from a single HNP loan in 1970 to 154 active and 94 completed projects by 1997, worth a total of US$13.5 billion. More recently, David McCoy and colleagues reported that the annual HNP spending of the World Bank was US$0.8 billion in 2006, although this was less than the US$1.62 billion and US$4.19 billion spent on overseas aid for health by the United Kingdom and United States governments respectively (McCoy, Chand and Sridhar 2009). However, we need to return to early HNP reports and the influence of neoliberal ideology on them if we are fully to understand the consequences of World Bank intervention on global health. Rowden (2009) is quite clear on this point, arguing that HNP was influenced by neoliberal economics almost from its inception in 1979. He points in particular to the influential 1981 Berg Report (World Bank 1981), which reflected a growing consensus around the need for user fees to improve efficiencies in the health sector, and to the influence of the Princeton-trained economist, David de Ferranti, who had arrived at the Bank in 1981. De Ferranti, in particular, is regarded as playing a crucial role in shifting HNP policy away from the social democratic and humanitarian ideologies reflected in the support for universal primary health care towards a neoliberal one that was to shape global health over the next decade and beyond.

Howard Stein (2008) is especially critical of de Ferranti's influence on HNP, and while we do not have the scope to offer a full analysis of his critique, it is worth our drawing out some of the key points that he makes. As Stein argues, de Ferranti, in a series of 10 papers authored or co-authored by him in the period 1981–1985, set out a neoliberal policy agenda that actively undermined the Bank's position of only a few years earlier. The most straightforward illustration that Stein offers relates to the association of neoliberalism with market fundamentalism (Sparke 2009; Schrecker and Bambra 2015): where the Bank had previously argued that competitive markets were 'generally not desirable' in health care (see also World Bank 1980), in de Ferranti's view they were analogous with maximising efficiency. A central feature of de Ferranti's argument for market competition in health care involved the controversial introduction of 'user fees'. The argument here is recognised to be complex (see Gilson and McIntyre 2005). However, as Stein notes, de Ferranti overlooked some of the more controversial aspects of the debate, notably those relating to increased costs to already vulnerable people and associated inequalities in access to health care. Rather, he asserted that the economic principle of individual rational choice when applied to user fees would remove the 'free-ridership' that he associated with some preventive services and allow patients to make informed decisions about accessing services based upon the increased quantity and quality that greater market competition would bring.

The most important point to observe in relation to de Ferranti's application of neoliberal economic principles to health care decision-making is that we can see the traces of this logic in subsequent Bank policy. This was perhaps most apparent in the mid 1980s when the Bank, along with the IMF, introduced a policy of structural adjustment to support the economic recovery of the world's poorest and most indebted countries (see Box 14.2).

SAPs were a form of condition-based lending that demanded drastic cuts in consumption (e.g. food) and public spending (e.g. education, health, housing and social welfare services) in order to reduce inflation and debt. As Box 14.2 reveals, SAPs are argued to have had a significant and largely negative impact on population health, and institutions such as UNICEF were very quick to target them for critique (Cornia et al. 1987; see also Buckley and Baker 2009; Harman 2009). Putting their direct and indirect impact on health aside, SAPs have also been described as 'coherent with the neo-liberal policies dominant in the USA and Great Britain' (Maciocco and Stefanini 2007, p. 481) with the Bank reports *Financing Health Services in Developing Countries* (World Bank 1987) and the *World Development Report* (World Bank 1993) serving as good illustrations of how far neoliberal ideology was transferred into practice during this period. As Sophie Harman suggests, the latter of these documents makes a clear statement both of the 'Bank's role at the centre of global health, and its commitment to privatised forms of healthcare' (2009, p. 229).

Box 14.2   Key Concepts: Structural Adjustment Programmes and Global Health

Structural adjustment programmes (SAPs) emerged in the 1980s and 1990s as a central feature of international development policy in the world's poorest and most indebted countries. In the face of economic crisis, the IMF and the World Bank, the two Bretton Woods institutions that along with the US Treasury Department form the so-called 'Washington Consensus', adopted 'structural adjustment' as their main prescription to problems of poverty and debt. SAPs, as they are commonly referred to, are a form of conditional lending provided through the Bank and the IMF that required nations to implement policies that emphasised economic management, macroeconomic stability, privatisation, trade liberalisation and public sector contraction. Put simply, SAPs promoted policies that supported the economic and political principles of neoliberalism (Rowden 2009).

According to Jennifer Ruger (2005), critics of SAPs have highlighted that they resulted in the reduction of health care spending and have had deleterious health effects. For example, referring to the UNICEF 1989 report, *The State of the World's Children*, she notes that it was estimated that SAPs 'may have been linked with some 500 000 deaths of young children in a 12-month period, even though a 1998 study of the effect of structural adjustment operations on health expenditures and outcomes and the World Bank's own research found no negative impact' (2005, p. 67). While Ruger seeks to provide a balanced view on the negative health impact of SAPs, other scholars have been much more damning in their criticisms of them. Geographers such as Susan Craddock, Ezekiel Kalipeni and Joseph Oppong are among such critics. For example, Kalipeni (2000), commenting on stubbornly high levels of child mortality in countries such as Malawi, Zambia and Zimbabwe, notes that while the Bank appeared to blame poor governance it failed to account for the impact of its own policies. As he argued, 'adjustment programs have had dramatic negative effects on quality of care, health service utilization due to the imposition of user fees, search for alternative sources of health care, changes in mortality and morbidity and nutritional status' (2000, p. 978). Such a critical assessment of SAPs remains the dominant perspective upon them (Rowden 2009; Schrecker and Bambra 2015).

Critical Geographies of Global Health

If we move into the contemporary period, the on-going influence of neoliberalism on global health remains apparent. Indeed, it has been argued that global health is now dominated by notions of economic rationalism; for example, the disability adjusted life year (DALY), a measure that affords higher value to those individuals who are the most economically productive, is used to calculate the global burden of disease and as a mechanism for determining global health priorities (Buse and Walt 2000). Also, the Global Fund to Fight AIDS, Tuberculosis and Malaria created by the G8 countries in 2000 has faced criticism from civil society because of its prioritisation of certain population groups on the basis of their economic significance (Lee 2009). The examples cited here are the favouring of HIV/AIDS programmes that target economically productive adults rather than children and the focus on the so-called 'BRIC' (Brazil, Russia, India and China) nations, which are regarded as economically important to donor countries.

Geographers such as Matthew Sparke have also developed powerful critiques of the political and economic processes that underpin global health. The broader significance of his work is that it points to two further ways in which global health is mapped out and in so doing it opens up to geographers additional avenues of critical engagement. The first corresponds with the previously discussed notion of market fundamentalism and most especially its associated flattening of global space through the normalising of such ideas as the 'level playing field'. Sparke's argument is as straightforward as it is incisive. The advocates of market fundamentalism, he argues, have reconstituted and flattened the terrain of global health through the promotion of free trade legislation and especially the removal of tariff barriers to trade. Here, the Trade Related Aspects of Intellectual Property Rights (TRIPS) Agreement put in place by the World Trade Organization (WTO) stands out as an exemplar as it protected the intellectual property rights of for-profit pharmaceutical companies most commonly found in the countries of the Global North and at the same time created barriers to those nations wishing to produce free or cheap generic drugs, often in the Global South (see Chapter 12).

For geographers concerned with the contradictions of global capitalism and the inequities it produces, this aspect of global health has proven an important area of investigation both with regards to its regulatory aspects and most especially its impact on those countries least able to provide for the health needs of their citizens. For example, countries in the Global South most affected by HIV/AIDS have been a particular focus of concern (e.g. Craddock 2007). However, the flattening out of space associated with market fundamentalism has affected the terrain of global health in other equally contradictory and problematic ways, from the global trade in bodily commodities to the (re)emergence of medical tourism (see chapters in Parry et al. 2015; Connell 2006; Chapter 13). Geography's contribution has not only been to identify the main characteristics of such entrepreneurial (and sometimes illegal) endeavour but also to outline the important material consequences of it on the least powerful and most disconnected people and places.

The second additional way in which global health has been mapped out according to Sparke is through the discourse of market foster-care. Similarly to market fundamentalism this discourse is associated with the idea that the solutions to the problem of global health are closely aligned with the market economy and more broadly with capitalist growth. Simply put, proponents of this position, who include most significantly the economist and one-time chair of the WHO Commission on Macroeconomics and Health, Jeffrey Sachs, argue that disease and poor health are the root cause of poverty in the world's most impoverished regions and that this has important consequences for global security. According to this argument, and as Sparke notes it is a compelling one, international intervention to improve health would help such regions to rise above extreme poverty and 'enable them to become stable neighbours and trading partners instead of havens of terror, disease, unwanted mass migration, and drug trafficking' (Sachs 2004. Cited in Sparke 2009, p. 146). Sparke's analysis is again insightful as amongst other issues he points to the ways in which this particular discourse pathologises those places whose health it seeks to secure.

Again geographers have made notable contributions here and a central question has been to consider who is being protected and from what diseases in this discourse (Coker and Ingram 2006). The implication behind this question is that interventions in global health are as concerned with protecting the interests of the countries of the Global North as they are with promoting the health of those in the Global South. It is important not to overlook or undermine the considerable efforts of the many individuals and agencies involved in such work, and here we should not forget the very considerable but equally controversial impact of philanthropic organisations such as the Bill and Melinda Gates Foundation (Sparke 2009). However, as geographers like Alan Ingram (2009) have revealed, in his case through the extensive engagement with US foreign policy around HIV/AIDS in Africa, such interventions are often shaped by the exigencies of wider geo-political interests, and how the imaginative geographies of national and international institutions construct intersections between disease and immigration, national security and notions of refuge/asylum. Other dimensions of geographical work in this area have focused on the kinds of pathologising discourse expounded by people like Sachs and the fears that it raises in an increasingly inter-connected, hypermobile world, perhaps most obviously exemplified by severe acute respiratory syndrome (SARS) at the beginning of the twenty first century (see Chapter 11).

The geopolitical concerns of the Global North are those that are most often cited as key reasons why global health has been securitised. However, the *World Health Report 2007* (WHO 2007) highlights a much wider range of factors that it also regards as important in the securitising of global health; these include armed conflict, microbial evolution and antibiotic resistance, animal husbandry and food processing, weather-related events associated with global climate change, industrial accidents and sudden chemical and radioactive events. Each of these factors is worthy of further discussion; after all, each will have a considerable impact on global health. Taking the example of armed conflict, the *World Health Report 2007* draws upon a range of recent wars, primarily from the African continent, to illustrate their potential to impact upon population health within and beyond the borders of a single country. Thus, it reports on the deadliest epidemic of cholera to be recorded during the last hundred years in the Democratic Republic of Congo in 1994 (Siddique et al. 1995; see Chapter 11). The outbreak, which can be traced to refugees from the 1994 Rwandan crisis crossing into its territory in large numbers (upwards of 800,000) and settling in camps on the outskirts of the Congolese cities of Goma and Bukavu, resulted in around 70,000 cases and 12,000 deaths (Bompangue et al. 2009).

Given the geopolitical situation that the world finds itself in today, especially with the conflicts raging in the Middle East, the kinds of events described above are likely to continue well into the future; indeed, in Syria, where conflict has been on-going ever since the 'Arab Spring' of March 2011, some 6.5 million people have been displaced from their homes, and while fears of a cholera epidemic have yet to be realised, poliomyelitis has returned to an area once considered to be free of the disease (Sharara and Kanj 2014). However, while international agencies such as the WHO define global health security as an event that endangers the collective health of populations across international borders, this does not mean that we should focus our attention only on outbreaks of epidemic disease. As Stefan Elbe argues, there is a 'more subtle link between health and security' that has been 'postulated by public health officials in relation to a number of non-communicable diseases' (2010, p. 9; see also Brown 2011), namely those relating to the consumption, or arguably over-consumption, of alcohol, food and tobacco. The so-called 'lifestyle time bomb' (Elbe 2010, p. 132) is, then, another dimension of contemporary global health that demands health geographers' attention.

Conclusion

In summary, this chapter has traced the emergence of global health from nineteenth-century concerns with how to mitigate the effects of epidemic diseases, to its bureaucratisation in the mid twentieth century and to the influence of neoliberal economics on the wide-ranging issues captured by the field today. Our ambition in offering such a broad, but by no means conclusive, overview is to provide students with a range of possible entry points into this field. While geographers have not always been at the forefront of research in these areas, they have recently begun to make a considerable contribution to them. Most notably this contribution has involved unpicking the national and international response to the problems of global health and submitting them to critical scrutiny. Such work not only requires paying close attention to the differing ways in which global health is imagined (historically as well as in the contemporary period) but also considering the effects of such imaginings on the material, lived experiences of those most affected. It is hoped that this chapter will act as a starting point to further enquiry in this area.

Questions for Review

1. What are the main differences between international health and global health?
2. To what extent has neoliberalism shaped international responses to global health issues?
3. What would the key components of a critical geography of global health look like? What would you focus your attention on as a critical geographer?

Suggested Reading

Bashford, A (2006b) Global biopolitics and the history of world health. *History of the Human Sciences* 19, 67–88.
Brown, T, Craddock, S & Ingram, A (2012) Critical interventions in global health: governmentality, risk, and assemblage. *Annals of the Association of American Geographers* 102, 1182–89.
Herrick, C (2014) (Global) health geography and the post-2015 development agenda. *The Geographical Journal* 180, 185–90.
Sparke, M (2009) Unpacking economism and remapping the terrain of global health. In: Kay, A & Williams, O (Eds) *Global health governance: crisis, institutions and political economy (International Political Economy Series)*. Palgrave Macmillan, Basingstoke, 131–59.

References

Anderson, W (1992) 'Where every prospect pleases and only man is vile': laboratory medicine as colonial discourse. *Critical Inquiry* 18, 506–29.

Anderson, W (1995) Excremental colonialism: public health and the poetics of pollution. *Critical Inquiry* 21, 640–69.

Anderson, W (2002) Going through the motions: American public health and colonial 'mimicry'. *American Literary History* 14, 686–719.

Anderson, W (2006) *The cultivation of whiteness: science, health and racial destiny in Australia.* Melbourne University Press, Melbourne.

Arnold, D (1996) Introduction: tropical medicine before Manson. In: Arnold, D (Ed) *Warm climates and western medicine: the emergence of tropical medicine, 1500-1900.* Clio Medica 35. Rodopi, Amsterdam, 1–19.

Bashford, A (2006a) 'The age of universal contagion': history, disease and globalization. In: Bashford, A (Ed) *Medicine at the border: disease, globalization and security, 1850 to the present.* Palgrave Macmillan, Basingstoke, 1–17.

Bashford, A (2006b) Global biopolitics and the history of world health. *History of the Human Sciences* 19, 67–88.

Birn, A-E (2009) The stages of international (global) health: histories of success or successes of history? *Global Public Health* 4, 50–68.

Bompangue, D, Giraudoux, P, Piarroux, M, Mutombo, G, Shamavu, R et al. (2009) Cholera epidemics, war and disasters around Goma and Lake Kivu: an eight-year survey. *PLoS Neglected Tropical Disease* 3, e436.

Brown, T (2011) 'Vulnerability is universal': considering the place of 'security' and 'vulnerability' within contemporary global health discourse. *Social Science & Medicine* 72, 319–26.

Brown, T & Moon, G (2012) Commentary: geography and global health. *The Geographical Journal* 178, 13–7.

Brown, T, Craddock, S & Ingram, A (2012) Critical interventions in global health: governmentality, risk, and assemblage. *Annals of the Association of American Geographers* 102, 1182–9.

Brown, TM, Cueto, & Fee, E (2006) The World Health Organization and the transition from "international" to "global" public health. *American Journal of Public Health* 96, 62–72.

Buckley, RP & Baker, J (2009) IMF policies and health in Sub-Saharan Africa. In: Kay, A & Williams, O (Eds) *Global health governance: crisis, institutions and political economy (International Political Economy Series).* Palgrave Macmillan, Basingstoke, 209–26.

Budd, L, Bell, M & Brown, T (2009) Of plagues, planes and politics: controlling the global spread of infectious diseases by air. *Political Geography* 28, 426–35.

Buse, K & Walt, G (2000) Global public-private partnerships: part I – a new development in health. *Bulletin of the World Health Organization* 78, 549–61.

Chen, MS (2001) The great reversal: transformation of health care in the People's Republic of China. In: Cockerham, WC (Ed) *The Blackwell Companion to medical sociology.* Blackwell, Oxford, 456–82.

Cliff, A, Haggett, P & Smallman-Raynor, M (1998) *Deciphering global epidemics: analytical approaches to the disease records of world cities, 1888-1912.* Cambridge University Press, Cambridge.

Coker, R & Ingram, A (2006) Passports and pestilence: migration, security and contemporary border control of infectious diseases. In: Bashford, A (Ed) *Medicine at the border: disease, globalization and security, 1850 to the present.* Palgrave Macmillan, Basingstoke, 159–76.

Connell, J (2006) Medical tourism: Sea, sun, sand and … surgery. *Tourism Management* 27, 1093–100.

Cornia, GA, Jolly, R & Stewart, F (1987) *Adjustment with a human face: protecting the vulnerable and promoting growth. A report for UNICEF.* UNICEF, New York.

Craddock, S (2007) Market incentives, human lives, and AIDS vaccines. *Social Science & Medicine* 64, 1042–56.

Cueto, M (2007) *The value of health: a history of the Pan American Health Organization*. Pan American Health Organization. Washington, DC.

Curtis, SE & Oven, KJ (2012) Geographies of health and climate change. *Progress in Human Geography* 36, 654–66.

Davies, S (2010) *Global politics of health*. Polity, Bristol.

Day, P, Pearce, J & Dorling, D (2008) Twelve worlds: a geo-demographic comparison of global inequalities in mortality. *Journal of Epidemiology and Community Health* 62, 1002–10.

Elbe, S (2010) *Security and global health*. Polity Press, Cambridge.

Fee, E & Brown, TM (2002) 100 Years of the Pan American Health Organization. *American Journal of Public Health* 92, 1888.

Fenner, F, Henderson, D, Arita, I, Jezek, Z & Ladnyi, I (1988) *Smallpox and its eradication*. WHO, Geneva.

Fidler, DP & Gostin, LO (2006) The new International Health Regulations: an historic development for international law and public health. *The Journal of Law, Medicine & Ethics* 34, 85–94.

Gilson, L & McIntyre, D (2005) Removing user fees for primary care in Africa: the need for careful action. *BMJ* 331, 762–65.

Harman, S (2009) The World Bank and health. In: Kay, A & Williams, O (Eds) *Global health governance: crisis, institutions and political economy (International Political Economy Series)*. Palgrave Macmillan, Basingstoke, 227–44.

Herrick, C (2014) (Global) health geography and the post-2015 development agenda. *The Geographical Journal* 180, 185–90.

Howard-Jones, N (1950) Origins of international health work. *BMJ* 1(4661), 1032–7.

Howard-Jones, N (1975) The scientific background of the International Sanitary Conferences, 1851-1938. *WHO Chronicles* 28, 159–71.

Huber, V (2006) The unification of the globe by disease? The international sanitary conferences on cholera, 1851–1894. *The Historical Journal* 49, 453–76.

Ingram, A (2005) The new geopolitics of disease: between global health and global security. *Geopolitics* 10, 522–45.

Ingram, A (2008) Pandemic anxiety and global health security. In: Pain, R & Smith, SJ (Eds) *Fear: critical geopolitics and everyday life*. Routledge, London, 75–86.

Ingram, A (2009) Biosecurity and the international response to HIV/AIDS: governmentality, globalisation and security. *Area* 4, 293–301.

Kalipeni, E (2000) Health and disease in southern Africa: a comparative and vulnerability perspective. *Social Science & Medicine* 50, 965–83.

Koplan, JR, Bond, TC, Merson, MH, Reddy, KS, Rodriguez, MH et al. (2009) Towards a common definition of global health. *Lancet* 373, 1993–5.

Lee, K (2009) Understandings of global health governance: the contested landscape. In: Kay, A & Williams, O (Eds) *Global health governance: crisis, institutions and political economy (International Political Economy Series)*. Palgrave Macmillan, Basingstoke, 27–41.

Löwy, I & Zylberman, P (2000) Medicine as a social instrument: Rockefeller Foundation, 1913–45. *Studies in History and Philosophy of Science Part C: Studies in History and Philosophy of Biological and Biomedical Sciences* 31, 365–79.

Maciocco, G & Stefanini, A (2007) From Alma-Ata to the global fund: the history of international health policy. *Revista Brasileira de Saúde Materno Infantil* 7, 479–86.

MacLeod, RM & Lewis, MJ (Eds) (1988) *Disease, medicine, and empire: perspectives on western medicine and the experience of European expansion*. Routledge, London.

Mahler, H (1988) Editorial: the battle for health. *World Health Forum* 9, 143–6.

Markel, H (2014) Worldly approaches to global health: 1851 to the present. *Public Health* 128, 124–8.

McCoy, D, Chand, S & Sridhar, D (2009) Global health funding: how much, where it comes from and where it goes. *Health Policy and Planning* 24, 407–17.

McElhinny, B (2005) "Kissing a Baby Is Not at All Good for Him": Infant Mortality, Medicine, and Colonial Modernity in the U.S.-Occupied Philippines. *American Anthropologist* 107, 183–94.

Meade, M & Emch, M (2010) *Medical geography. Third Edition.* Guilford Press, New York.

Papworth, A, Maslin, M & Randalls, S (2015) Is climate change the greatest threat to global health? *The Geographical Journal* 181, 413–22.

Parry, B, Greenhough, B, Brown, T & Dyck, I (Eds) (2015) *Bodies across borders: the global circulation of body parts, medical tourists and professionals.* Ashgate, Farnham.

Pearce, J & Dorling, D (2009) Tackling global health inequalities: closing the health gap in a generation. *Environment and Planning A* 41, 1–6.

Peters, FE (1994) *The Hajj: the muslim pilgrimage to Mecca and the holy places.* Princeton University Press, Princeton, NJ.

Rowden, R (2009) *The deadly ideas of neoliberalism: how the IMF has undermined public health and the fight against AIDS.* Zed Books, London.

Ruger, JP (2005) The changing role of the World Bank in global health. *American Journal of Public Health* 95, 60–70.

Schrecker, T & Bambra, C (2015) *How politics makes us sick: neoliberal epidemics.* Palgrave Macmillan, Basingstoke.

Sharara S & Kanj SS (2014) War and infectious diseases: challenges of the Syrian civil war. *PLoS Pathogens* 10, e1004438.

Siddiqi, J (1995) *World health and world politics.* University of South Carolina Press, Columbus, SC.

Siddique, AK, Akram, K, Zaman, K, Laston, S, Salam, A, Majumdar, RN, Islam, MS and Fronczak, N (1995) Why treatment centres failed to prevent cholera deaths among Rwandan refugees in Goma, Zaire. *The Lancet* 345, 359–61.

Sparke, M (2009) Unpacking economism and remapping the terrain of global health In: Kay, A & Williams, O (Eds) *Global health governance: crisis, institutions and political economy (International Political Economy Series).* Palgrave Macmillan, Basingstoke, 131–59.

Stein, H (2008) *Beyond the World Bank agenda: an institutional approach to development.* University of Chicago Press, Chicago.

Stern, AM & Markel, H (2004) International efforts to control infectious diseases, 1851 to the present. *Journal of the American Medical Association* 292, 1474–9.

WHO (1948) *Constitution of the World Health Organization.* WHO, Geneva.

WHO (1955) *Malaria eradication: proposal by the Director-General. Eighth World Health Assembly A8/P&B/10.* WHO, Geneva.

WHO (1978) *Declaration of Alma-Ata.* WHO, Geneva.

WHO (1981) *Global strategy for health for all by the year 2000. 'Health for all' series, no. 3.* WHO, Geneva.

WHO (2007) *The world health report 2007: a safer future: global public health security in the 21st century.* WHO, Geneva.

World Bank (1975) *Health sector policy paper.* World Bank, Washington, DC.

World Bank (1980) *World development report.* World Bank, Washington, DC.

World Bank (1981) *Accelerated development in Sub-Saharan Africa.* World Bank, Washington, DC.

World Bank (1987) *Financing health services in developing countries: an agenda for reform.* World Bank, Washington, DC.

World Bank (1993) *World development report.* World Bank, Washington, DC.

United Nations (2015) *The millennium development goals report 2015.* United Nations, New York.

Zacher, M & Keefe, T (2008) *The politics of global health governance: united by contagion.* Palgrave Macmillan, New York.

Zylberman, P (2006) Civilising the state: borders, weak states and international health in modern Europe. In: Bashford, A (Ed) *Medicine at the border: disease, globalization and security, 1850 to the present.* Palgrave Macmillan, Basingstoke, 21–40.

Index

Page references to Boxes, Figures or Tables will be followed by the letters 'b', 'f' or 't' in italics as appropriate

---

Health Geographies: A Critical Introduction, First Edition. Tim Brown, Gavin J. Andrews, Steven Cummins, Beth Greenhough, Daniel Lewis, and Andrew Power.
© 2018 John Wiley & Sons Ltd. Published 2018 by John Wiley & Sons Ltd.